EVERYDAY LIFE IN
RUSSIA PAST AND PRESENT

INDIANA-MICHIGAN SERIES IN RUSSIAN AND EAST EUROPEAN STUDIES
Alexander Rabinowitch and William G. Rosenberg, editors

EVERYDAY LIFE *in* RUSSIA PAST *and* PRESENT

Edited by
**CHOI CHATTERJEE, DAVID L. RANSEL,
MARY CAVENDER,** and **KAREN PETRONE**

Afterword by
SHEILA FITZPATRICK

INDIANA UNIVERSITY PRESS
Bloomington & Indianapolis

This book is a publication of

Indiana University Press
Office of Scholarly Publishing
Herman B Wells Library 350
1320 East 10th Street
Bloomington, Indiana 47405 USA

iupress.indiana.edu

Telephone orders   800-842-6796
Fax orders   812-855-7931

⊚ The paper used in this publication
meets the minimum requirements of
the American National Standard for
Information Sciences—Permanence of
Paper for Printed Library Materials,
ANSI Z39.48–1992.

Manufactured in the United States of
America

Library of Congress Cataloging-in-
Publication Data

Everyday life in Russia past and present
/ edited by Choi Chatterjee, David L.
Ransel, Mary Cavender, and Karen
Petrone.
     pages cm. — (Indiana-Michigan
series in Russian and East European
studies)
     Papers from an interdisciplinary
workshop entitled "Everyday Life in Russia
and the Soviet Union," held in May 2010 on
Indiana University's Bloomington campus.
     Includes bibliographical references.
     ISBN 978-0-253-01245-6 (hardback :
alkaline paper) — ISBN 978-0-253-01254-8
(paperback : alkaline paper) — ISBN
978-0-253-01260-9 (ebook) 1. Russia—
Social life and customs—Congresses.
2. Soviet Union—Social life and customs—
Congresses. 3. Russia (Federation)—
Social life and customs—Congresses.
4. Russia—Social conditions—Congresses.
5. Soviet Union—Social conditions—
Congresses. 6. Russia (Federation)—
Social conditions—Congresses. 7.
Interpersonal relations—Russia—
History—Congresses. 8. Interpersonal
relations—Soviet Union—History—
Congresses. 9. Interpersonal relations—
Russia (Federation)—History—
Congresses. I. Chatterjee, Choi. II. Ransel,
David L. III. Cavender, Mary W., [date] IV.
Petrone, Karen.
     DK32.E776   2014
     947—dc23
                                    2014020094

1 2 3 4 5 20 19 18 17 16 15

CONTENTS

ACKNOWLEDGMENTS

WE WANT TO express our gratitude to the following four Indiana University grant programs or offices for their generous support of the workshop that launched this book: New Frontiers in the Arts and Humanities, College Arts and Humanities Institute, Office of the Vice President for International Affairs, and Multidisciplinary Ventures and Seminars Fund. Thanks also go to Professor Sarah Phillips of the Indiana University Department of Anthropology, who assisted us in obtaining this funding and participated in the discussions at the workshop. We also wish to express our appreciation to Aleksandr Kamenskii of the Moscow State Higher School of Economics, Rebecca Friedman of Florida International University, and Maria Bucur and Ben Eklof, both of Indiana University, for presenting papers and critical commentary at the workshop. Other prominent scholars who served as critics and commentators include Padraic Kenney, Alexander Rabinowitch, and Jeffrey Veidlinger, all of Indiana University.

We owe a special debt of gratitude to Janet Rabinowitch and Rebecca Tolen of the Indiana University Press. They took an enthusiastic interest in this project from its start. They attended sessions of the workshop, encouraged us to build a book out of its contributions, and gave useful tips and guidance along the way toward that goal. We also wish to acknowledge editor Nancy Lightfoot for her help with the last stages of the project; Jeremiah Nelson, a graduate assistant at the University of Kentucky who formatted the files submitted by the contributors; Mary M. Hill, who copyedited the entire volume; and Audra Yoder, who created the index.

Finally, our sincere appreciation goes to Mark Trotter, assistant director and outreach coordinator of the Indiana University Russian and East European Institute, and to his energetic staff for organizational and logistical support in connection with the workshop.

EVERYDAY LIFE IN
RUSSIA PAST AND PRESENT

Introduction

The Genesis and Themes of
Everyday Life in Russia Past and Present

This volume originated from a series of interlinked and parallel conversations among the editors. These discussions explored new possibilities for transnational collaboration and developments in critical theory on the nature of the quotidian. Our initial deliberations led to the convocation of an interdisciplinary workshop entitled "Everyday Life in Russia and the Soviet Union" in May 2010 that was generously funded by Indiana University and held on its Bloomington campus. Our aim from the outset was ambitious: we wanted to expand our intellectual horizons and cast our research net as broadly as possible. Rather than restrict ourselves to our own subfields of academic expertise, we organized the meeting as a working conference or seminar that would allow us to familiarize ourselves with new scholarship in the fields of history, anthropology, literature, art, and film studies. Over the course of three days, specialists in imperial, Soviet, and post-Soviet studies from Russia, the United Kingdom, and the United States considered developments in their particular fields of research and searched for linkages, continuities, and discontinuities across periods and disciplines. The chapters in this volume reflect the intellectual breadth of our workshop deliberations and our common desire to transcend boundaries imposed by disciplinary orientation and standard periodization.

The elusive and ill-defined nature of everyday life invites a reexamination of the analytical categories generated in the aftermath of the Bolshevik Revolution of 1917. Because the presumed otherness of Soviet life has lost its persuasiveness since 1991, we can now see the possibilities for escaping the interpretations of *Homo sovieticus* as a member of a species whose unique ecology demanded special modes of inquiry. Methodologies borrowed from postcolonial and transnational history allow us to pursue the reintegration of both the Russian past and present into the narrative of global history. Moreover, the fall of the Soviet Union opened opportunities for Russian and foreign scholars to conduct sustained fieldwork in anthropology and sociology free of overt political constraints and to collaborate in designing pioneering research projects that are based in part on multiple interpretations of a shared corpus of critical theory.[1] At about the same time, historians of Russia in the United States, Russia, and Europe became interested in questions of everyday life and of the domestic sphere. After decades of research on topics located in the public theaters of politics, class formation, and statecraft, researchers turned to an examination of the contact zones of daily life where grand historical events and ideological contests are personally experienced.[2] Our aim is to highlight and integrate current work in a variety of fields in which the analytical focus is on identities and subjectivities that were formed in the nexus of everyday life. We are excavating the cultural practices, power relations, and learned behavior that regulated everyday existence in the past and in the post-Soviet present.

Everyday life necessarily includes a range of activities such as repetitive domestic actions relating to the reproduction of physical life itself, participation in social networks, cultural performances in normative rites and rituals that both uphold and destabilize power relations, and self-reflexive acts conducted in a variety of contexts to delineate selfhood. Investigation of everyday life affords a new lens through which to view the formation and elaboration of categories such as gender, ethnicity, class, nationalism, and subjectivity. Indeed, we can narrate the history of Russian and Soviet modernity through the changes in the consumption and communication patterns of the population, the restructuring of familial and social relationships, the systems of cultural meanings that governed interactions with ideological authorities, and evolving practices at home, at the workplace, and at sites of leisure. The distinctive texture of modernity and its qualitative differences from preceding historical eras may well be best understood at this level of microanalysis of everyday life and practices.

Western discourse on Russia for over a century has been framed by the liberal paradigm of tension between a poorly developed civil society and an oppressive state, and on the opposition between the intimate private sphere of genuine self-expression and the public domain of surveillance, punishment, and state-enforced conformity. Recently, inspired by the Foucauldian criticism of Western modernity and liberalism, some scholars have cast doubt on the very existence of authentic subjectivity and have argued that Soviet citizens, inspired by a Hegelian reading of historical materialism, internalized the norms and conditions of Soviet modernity through an active process of self-creation as well as individuation.[3] These categories, drawn from structuralist and poststructuralist theories, have proven to be both productive and problematic in their application to Russian history. Customarily, Russians have distinguished between the routine, or *byt,* of everyday life and the more emotionally fulfilling *bytië,* which represents a spiritually elevated mode of existence where one can achieve self-realization. They have rarely used the opposition between the bourgeois public and private spheres of life to understand their own society. Moreover, according to Svetlana Boym, both Russian and Soviet intellectual elites sought to banish the realm of what they considered to be the ordinary and the banal from artistic, ideological, and scholarly consideration.[4]

In this volume authors have consciously abandoned the notion that there is an a priori everyday life, a subterranean and ordinary domestic existence that continues in profane or banal time, separate from and impervious to transformation by internal and external forces. Everyday life in modern times, whether in the West or in the socialist bloc, provided little refuge from the power of the state and that of well-intentioned experts and professionals. As Christina Kiaer and Eric Naiman's pioneering volume shows, daily life became a site of overt ideological intervention as Soviet citizens were exhorted to take the revolution into their homes, their kitchens, their bedrooms, and even their souls.[5] Yet this intervention could not fully control its objects or shape the outcomes of the cultural policies instituted from above. While people learned to speak Bolshevik, they also ingeniously fashioned displays of unconventional selfhood, nourished rich emotional communities, constructed ethical systems that were partly based on Marxist thought, and created avant-garde art forms that had global resonance.

Ideologues and politicians may project a mythologized or utopian future, but human beings inhabit the world in the units of quotidian time that serve as commentary on the process of historical change.[6] We may experience the present in different emotional registers, through moments of revolutionary élan, hoping for a radiant future, fearing loss and dispossession, suffering the pain of exile and homelessness, contending with boredom, or even enjoying moments of quiet contentment, but the narrative of life is written inexorably in the language of the everyday. It is later reproduced by the languages of art, literature, memory, and the social sciences.

In her chapter, Olga Shevchenko cautions us that, rather than interpret all responses to acts of power as resistance, we should use the term with more discrimination. We would like to supplement Shevchenko's timely theoretical intervention by adding that popular discourse and practice should not be considered as mere adaptation or accommodation to the dictates of the state and experts. In contrast to interpretations that are often predicated on these binary oppositions of private and public, sacred and profane chronologies, banal and extraordinary time, and resistance and accommodation, the contributors to this volume conceive of everyday life as a series of spatial, discursive, and experiential locations. They have analyzed the complications of becoming Soviet or even post-Soviet, uncovering the many authentic as well as pragmatic negotiations that this self-fashioning entails. Individual and collective subjectivities are simultaneously sustained and transformed by grids of articulation and representations, and many of the chapters analyze the functioning of normative cultural codes in different periods of history. Finally, some of the contributors probe the ambiguity of responses to the everyday Soviet experience by visiting travelers or by citizens returning from abroad.

Daily life cannot be captured only in evocative moments, potent memories, and clear snapshots that profess to represent an entire historical era. Everyday life is in endless flux, and the contributors to this volume have been sensitive to considerations of time, space, and historical change. A primary goal of the volume is to link the recent work on everyday life in the imperial, Soviet, and post-Soviet eras, as well as to demonstrate the utility of everyday life as an analytical category for integrating scholarship in anthropology, history, and literary and film studies. Because of the fine-grained nature of their analysis, scholars of everyday life tend to work on discrete units of historical time in order to create a sense of narrative cohesion as well as to tease out the exceptional characteristics of the period under study. With a few exceptions, such as David Ransel's survey of village mothering and Catriona Kelly's history of Russian childhood, scholars have avoided longitudinal studies that map changes in everyday life through an entire century.[7] We hope that the chronological time span of our volume will nevertheless enable readers to consider the developments that occurred in everyday life in the Russian empire beginning with the early part of the nineteenth century and ending in the post-Soviet present. In our opinion, considerations of change over time put into question preconceived notions of a persistent, banal, and secret everyday life that evades or resists power and yet is hidden from view and unavailable for analysis.

THEMATIC OVERVIEW

We have divided the chapters of this collection into five thematic parts. In the first, entitled "Approaches to Everyday Life," Mary Cavender and David Ransel analyze the contributions that Western and Russian scholars have made to establish the terrain of everyday life as an important field in the social sciences and the humanities, and Douglas Rogers and Olga Shevchenko introduce new approaches to the study of everyday life in post-Soviet times.

In the opening chapter, David Ransel traces the way that scholars from Western Europe, Russia, and the United States have used local and microhistory research to edit, amend, and revise metahistorical narratives. Ransel addresses the creative tension between the two historical discourses and explains that local histories, contrary to popular wisdom, do not merely flesh out and confirm the changes and policies that are enacted at the national level. Rather, a close analysis of microsites of power reveal that they contain internal dynamics that may force elites to reconsider policies instituted at the highest level. A radically reduced view of local life can cause us to rethink our conceptions of macrohistorical processes. In a companion piece, Mary Cavender demonstrates that a progressive segment of the nobility, concerned with improving the economy of the country and the health of its people in the nineteenth century, tried to popularize scientific practices in agriculture and medicine. After the Great Reforms, this pursuit became a primary goal of many Russian professionals who, through service in the zemstvos, local government schools, and medical clinics, sought to uplift and modernize the people. At the national level their leaders carried on this fight in their emerging professional societies and in the national political forums created after the Revolution of 1905.

In a nuanced study, Cavender explains that even if many of the provincial gentry were unable to institute scientific agronomic practice on their estates, the fact that they regarded themselves as modern and improving landlords is important in understanding the many ways that individuals ascribe meaning to their daily lives and actions. While Ransel considers how local practices and actions destabilize the intentions of elites and the state, Cavender shows that elite self-representation, even when it is detached from actual practice, can help us understand the complexities of a historical era.

Olga Shevchenko presents an ironical reading of the fetishization of the theme of popular resistance by academics and claims that in a desire to unearth the subjectivity and creativity of the ordinary historical subject, scholars have sometimes endowed them with inordinately subversive and antiauthoritarian characteristics. She argues that many Russians responded to the distress caused by the sudden shift to a market economy after 1991 by seeking to demonstrate their practical competence in these new conditions. In so doing, many of Shevchenko's interviewees, rather than resisting elite discourses that were playing havoc with their lives and livelihood, inadvertently reinforced neoliberal values and practices.

Douglas Rogers provides a useful illustration of how the concepts of byt and *povsednevnost'* might be juxtaposed to produce fresh understandings of post-Soviet life. Rogers draws initially on a set of articles published by the Russian ethnographer and historian Natalia Pushkareva in which she suggests that Soviet scholarly work on byt produced an abstract representation of folk practices without indicating how the folk actually experienced and reflected on these reified lifeways. Rogers studies the initiatives by the oil-producing giant Lukoil to fund folk artisans and local craft festivals in the Perm region as a means of buying off potential criticism from local intellectuals. This corporate intervention produces an aestheticized and reified byt as an abstract phenomenon that is then re-presented through cultural artifacts and spectacle. Rogers records the varied responses by the local inhabitants to the corporate program and finds that local residents are in general appreciative of Lukoil's attempts to sustain and revive folk practices and artifacts (byt), even as they worry that Lukoil is polluting the environment that nurtures "authentic" folk culture. They also criticize the new craft-based occupations for generating only meager incomes (povsednevnost').

The next part, entitled "Public Identities and Public Space," contains chapters by Natalia Pushkareva, Elizabeth Skomp, and David Ransel that explore how the public identities of mothers, professional academics, and disempowered and dispossessed citizens are shaped by the complex interplay of normative discourses as well as individual and group aspirations that play out in the arena of everyday life. In her contribution, Pushkareva examines the everyday lives of women academics, their motivations for choosing a life of scholarly research and teaching, and their interpretations of career obstacles. Common to their experience, almost universally, is intense mentoring by parents and other family members and, perhaps surprisingly, little articulated awareness of gender discrimination, even as the women recount events that make evident its effect on their lives.

Unlike the uncomplaining women academics, Soviet novelists in the post-Stalinist period produced powerful, if subtle, critiques of everyday life in the workplace and the conflict between obligations to one's profession and the needs of one's family. Literary scholar Elizabeth Skomp examines the themes of maternalism and motherhood in the work of writers Natal'ia Baranskaia and I. Grekova. Skomp points to the discrepancy between Soviet conduct literature about motherhood and narrative representations of the daily life of Russian women. According to her, Grekova and Baranskaia, without venturing into overt opposition or dissidence, raised uncomfortable questions about the double burden and the unrealistic state expectations placed on working mothers.

David Ransel examines a threat to working people in the post-Soviet era, when many of the resources for recreation and social support that they had assumed to be a birthright suddenly vanished or, in the case of woods and meadows, fell into the hands of private developers to be fenced off for the exclusive use of the newly wealthy. Because of these losses and continued threats to other properties, small islands of social advocacy have begun to appear and may signal the emergence of a more articulate civil society. The chapters in this part reveal that individuals understand their own lives and practices from multiple perspectives, and their actions may even contradict their self-professed belief systems. A careful researcher has an obligation to explain the complexity of the situation rather than reduce it to fashionable analytical categories.

The next thematic part is entitled "Living Space and Personal Choice." Deborah Field, Steven Harris, Susan Reid, and Ilya Utekhin analyze the ways in which emotional ties, social relationships, ideological visions, and the physical architecture of living space shape subjectivity. While some of the chapters consider the intervention of the state, professionals, and members of the intelligentsia in creating normative categories for everyday living, others explore the interpretations that Russians themselves gave to quotidian experiences. Many scholars have identified the post-Stalin period as a time of transformation in the state's relationship to everyday life. Alexei Yurchak has suggested that the post-Stalin period saw a transformation in the way that a new generation of Soviet officials understood the daily state rituals in which they participated. These young Communists collected new day-to-day meanings and practices under the umbrella of "official culture," and these deviant ideas and practices eroded the power of state discourse from within.[8]

Deborah Field shows that while citizens could define the private in new ways in the post-Stalinist period and were indeed encouraged to exercise autonomy in their personal lives, the reform of byt remained a central concern of the state in areas such as contraception, abortion, and communal housing. Field shows that Soviet citizens navigated the absence of physical privacy by innovative practices that included the manipulation of time and the reimagining of social and emotional relationships. The Khrushchev era was also known for the breakneck construction of new apartment houses, the notorious "Khrushchev slums" (*khrushchëby*). At the time, however, the new housing was much appreciated by people who escaped from communal apartments to the privacy of these single-family dwellings. Steven Harris devotes his chapter to an analysis of the many unexpected ways that Soviet citizens were able to create new communities in what we have traditionally considered depersonalized socialist spaces. While some citizen associations grew out of shared grievances with the deficiencies in apartment infrastructure, others took the extreme step of illegally occupying apartments or taking over empty plots to build their own homes. Still others appropriated official rhetoric to build a communist way of life in the new housing estates. Like Field, Harris notes the blurred lines of state intervention and private endeavors in creating communities and notes the repeated commingling of public and private values.

The chapter by Susan Reid is based on extensive oral interviews with residents of Khrushchev-era private apartments. She shows that although the state created homogeneous housing projects with the explicit aim of social engineering, the residents used aesthetic preferences and consumer practices to produce distinctive interiors that became sites for modern self-fashioning. But Reid is careful to collapse the imaginary distance between an interventionist Soviet state and the home as a sacred refuge conferring absolute privacy on the individual. Instead, Reid argues that, like the subjects in Field's chapter, the residents from this era used mass-produced consumer goods to create a sense of modern individuality.

Despite the campaign to replace communal apartments with single-family dwellings starting as far back as the Khrushchev era, the communal apartment has not entirely disappeared to this day. This is the subject of Ilya Utekhin's contribution to this volume. He points out that while the notion of "communal apartment" carries with it a fixed image of practices and social relations embedded in the Soviet era, communal apartments today are very different. Having been radically transformed by new technical devices such as microwave ovens and cell phones that allow for greater privacy and inhabited by labor migrants and other new types of lodgers, communal apartments cannot be compared to those we know from Soviet times. Utekhin also examines popular attitudes and representations of the communal apartment and discusses the reasons for the power of lingering misrepresentations.

In the part entitled "Myth, Memory, and the History of Everyday Life," Peter Pozefsky, Serguei Oushakine, and Benjamin Sutcliffe consider representations of daily life in the Soviet Union through the use of film, literature, and documentaries created in post-Soviet times. These authors analyze the gaps and narrative uncertainty in these more recent art forms and explain how they serve as troubling commentary on the Soviet past as the potency of the Soviet ideology begins to fade. As the period of rapid change from the late Soviet period through the first decade of the twenty-first century engendered new forms of historical memory, historical thinking, and public discussions about the search for a "usable past," film emerged as an important medium for the discussion of such representations.

Peter Pozefsky looks at late Soviet and post-Soviet films about the Stalinist era and finds that film directors used the everyday lives of "ordinary people" to project simultaneous revulsion and nostalgia for a time that had fostered utopian dreams and communal solidarity but was also characterized by brutal repressions and unnecessary sacrifices. Pozefsky argues that the nostalgic retelling of the Stalinist past was not intended to whitewash a difficult period of history but to mourn the loss of hope of utopian community in the post-Soviet present. In a different vein, Serguei Oushakine considers the work of recent documentary filmmakers. Oushakine points out that while they have embraced the everyday as a supposedly nonideological window on late Soviet life, filmmakers have not shaped the subject into a coherent story that destabilizes official versions. Instead, they have opted to construct nonnarrative visual catalogs, inventories, and dictionaries that reprise the emotional texture of late socialism without adequately explaining it or providing a definitive interpretation of the past. Oushakine traces the ideological arc of Stalinist era metanarratives dissolving in the factology of the post-Soviet present.

In his discussion of Liudmila Ulitskaia's novel *Medea and Her Children,* Benjamin Sutcliffe argues that the heroine's home and the everyday life of its inhabitants serve as a discursive refuge from the brutality of twentieth-century life in Russia. Sutcliffe shows that Ulitskaia uses the rituals of everyday life and the quotidian rhythms of Medea's home in the Crimean Peninsula as a bulwark against the false history of Stalinism. Medea's multiethnic and multigenerational family represents an ethical microcosm of a utopian global community.

The final thematic part, "Coming Home: Transnational Connections," brings something new to the study of Russian everyday life. In this section, Elizabeth McGuire, Choi Chatterjee, and Karen Petrone explore the transnational links that connected the Soviet Union with individuals and groups in both the East and the West. While Soviet utopia rarely lived up to the expectations of either foreign travelers or returning Soviet citizens, their uneven interpretations of daily life experiences in the Soviet Union had serious political repercussions in the domestic and the international arenas.

Foreign Communists came to Russia in great numbers for training in revolutionary action and socialist construction. But apart from a few famous figures, little has been written about the experiences of these expatriate protégés of the Soviet regime. This is especially true of the Chinese, the subject of Elizabeth McGuire's contribution. McGuire follows the everyday experience of Chinese students in military training in the Soviet Union of the 1920s and their outbursts of anger when they did not receive the support for their cause that they had anticipated. Although they formulated their discontent in terms of everyday material needs, they resented most of all the failure of the Soviet regime to accord them personal respect and practical support for the socialist cause in China. Choi Chatterjee analyzes the physical experiences of international visitors from the United States and finds that, regardless of political orientation, their responses to everyday material difficulties in the Soviet Union were fairly similar. All were wedded to an American consumerist model of material comfort, and the lack of consumer goods and services in the Soviet Union caused them to view it as an alien and unappealing form of modernity. Karen Petrone explores the complex figure of the Soviet Afghan veteran who, like his American counterpart, the Vietnam War veteran, struggled to return to "ordinary life" after his service abroad. Even as the veterans' dilemmas were publicized in striking new ways during the glasnost era, the veterans' homecoming from Afghanistan turned out to be very different from their initial expectations.

We hope that this volume will advance the study of everyday life in Russia and elsewhere and convince readers of the value of approaching the themes of everyday life from a variety of disciplinary perspectives, including those of anthropology (where everyday life is a natural object), history, literature, and film studies. Everyday life is a primary site for the examination of the tensions inherent in modern political projects that seek to control and shape the lives of citizens. It is also the proper site for investigating tensions in the relationships of citizens to one another. In this realm we can observe closely the conflict and cooperation that mark a community's response to the larger forces acting on it and gain new insight into the social, political, and economic life of a nation. As the contributions to this volume demonstrate, the fluid and variegated interactions of daily life produced sets of social relations, emotional bonds, and palpable material circumstances that conditioned, limited, and enabled the life choices of citizens as well as the influence of the state.

An afterword by Sheila Fitzpatrick, to whose pioneering analysis of everyday life in the 1930s we owe much of our scholarly inspiration, concludes the book.

NOTES

1. Ilya Utekhin, Alice Nakhimovsky, Slava Paperno, and Nancy Ries, *Communal Living in Russia: A Virtual Museum of Soviet Everyday Life,* http://kommunalka.colgate.edu/. See also renowned documentary filmmaker Marina Goldovskaya's approach to memory and everyday life in films such as *House on Arbat Street* (1994), *The Children of Ivan Kuzmich* (1997), and *The Prince Is Back* (1999).

2. We have borrowed the idea of the "contact zone" from Mary Louise Pratt's pathbreaking work *Imperial Eyes: Travel Writing and Transculturation* (London: Routledge, 1992). For particularly insightful analyses from the post-Soviet context that exemplify this approach, see Nancy Ries, *Russian Talk: Culture and Conversation after Perestroika* (Ithaca, N.Y.: Cornell University Press, 1997); Ilya Utekhin, *Ocherki Kommunal'nogo byta* (Moscow: OGI, 2001); Caroline Humphrey, *The Unmaking of Soviet Life: Everyday Economies after Socialism* (Ithaca, N.Y.: Cornell University Press, 2002); Douglas Rogers, *The Old Faith and the Russian Land: A Historical Ethnography of Ethics in the Urals* (Ithaca, N.Y.: Cornell University Press, 2009); and Olga Shevchenko, *Crises and the Everyday in Postsocialist Moscow* (Bloomington: Indiana University Press, 2009).

3. Choi Chatterjee and Karen Petrone, "Models of Self and Subjectivity: The Soviet Case in Historical Perspective," *Slavic Review,* no. 4 (Winter 2008): 967–86.

4. Svetlana Boym, *Common Places: Mythologies of Every Day Life in Russia* (Cambridge, Mass.: Harvard University Press, 1994).

5. Christina Kiaer and Eric Naiman, *Everyday Life in Early Soviet Russia: Taking the Revolution Inside* (Bloomington: Indiana University Press, 2006); Sheila Fitzpatrick, *Everyday Stalinism: Ordinary Lives in Extraordinary Times* (Oxford: Berg, 2002); Stephen Kotkin, *Magnetic Mountain: Stalinism as a Civilization* (Berkeley: University of California Press, 1995); Jochen Hellbeck, *Revolution on My Mind: Writing a Diary under Stalin* (Cambridge, Mass.: Harvard University Press, 2006); Igal Halfin, *From Darkness to Light: Class Consciousness and Salvation in Revolutionary Russia* (Pittsburgh: University of Pittsburgh Press, 2000); Halfin, *Terror in My Soul: Communist Autobiographies on Trial* (Cambridge, Mass.: Harvard University Press, 2003); David Crowley and Susan E. Reid, eds., *Socialist Spaces: Sites of Everyday Life in the Eastern Bloc* (Oxford: Oxford University Press, 2002); Nataliia Lebina, *Entsiklopediia banal'nostei: Sovetskaia povsednevnost', kontury, simvoly, znaki* (St. Petersburg: Dmitrii Bulanin, 2006).

6. See Katerina Clark's seminal analysis of what she calls the "Great Time" in her *The Soviet Novel: History as Ritual,* 3rd ed. (Bloomington: Indiana University Press, 2000).

7. David L. Ransel, *Village Mothers: Three Generations of Change in Russia and Tataria* (Bloomington: Indiana University Press, 2000); Catriona Kelly, *Children's World: Growing Up in Russia, 1890–1991* (New Haven, Conn.: Yale University Press, 2007).

8. Alexei Yurchak, *Everything Was Forever, Until It Was No More: The Last Soviet Generation* (Princeton, N.J.: Princeton University Press, 2006).

PART I.
APPROACHES TO EVERYDAY LIFE

The Scholarship of Everyday Life

DAVID L. RANSEL

Since the fall of the Soviet Union historians in Russia and in the West have enthusiastically taken up the study of everyday life in Russian history and related fields. This trend in the two scholarly communities is not so much a convergence, although that too is gradually occurring, as a case of both communities drawing on a powerful movement in European historical studies and adding to it on the basis of past Russian writing and new researches in archives and memoirs.[1]

In our own community, Svetlana Boym and Sheila Fitzpatrick offered early examples of this approach, and they have found many followers.[2] A collection of essays by historians and literary scholars of the early Soviet period appeared in 2006, showing the wide array of topics of everyday life that were then being researched.[3] The current volume brings to readers another group of practitioners of this art from a variety of fields, including history, anthropology, literature, and film studies. A number of monographs have also appeared in recent years, including Jeffrey Jones's study of daily life in Rostov-on-Don after the devastation of World War II, Catriona Kelly's detailed investigation of the daily life of children from the late tsarist era to the collapse of the Soviet Union, and Donald Raleigh's oral history of the Soviet "baby boomers" in Saratov and Moscow, to name just a few.[4] We could add to this list an extraordinarily well-conceived documentary film by Robin Hessman, *My Perestroika*, which records the impressions of middle-aged Russians as they looked back on their early lives and schooling in Soviet times.[5]

In Russia much of what is appearing under the rubric of everyday life history is aimed at a broad readership of ordinary citizens and constitutes a reworking of earlier ethnographic studies and literary productions. In a large number of cases the publications are simply standard historical accounts with the "everyday life" label tacked on to attract readers. A striking example of this fashion is the series published by Molodaia Gvardiia Press under the rubric *Zhivaia istoriia: Povsednevnaia zhizn' chelovechestva* (Living history: The everyday life of humankind), which includes eighty-five titles, all beginning *The Everyday Life of . . .* and featuring topics in history and recent public affairs throughout the world. A substantial number focus on Russia, for example, *Povsednevnaia zhizn' ballerin russkogo imperatorskogo teatra* (The everyday life of ballerinas of the Imperial Theater), by O. G. Kovalik; *Povsednevnaia zhizn' blagorodnogo sosloviia v zolotoi vek Ekateriny* (The everyday life of the nobility during the Golden Age of Catherine II), by O. I. Eliseeva; and *Povsednevnaia zhizn' Moskvy v XIX veke* (The everyday life of Moscow in the nineteenth century), by V. M. Bokova, to name just a few.[6] Although books in this series are done by both amateurs and professionals and vary in quality, solid works of historical scholarship based on thorough excavation of archival sources are appearing in this series and elsewhere. Among these are Ol'ga Kosheleva's microhistorical examination of one section of Petersburg as it became settled in the early eighteenth century and Aleksandr Kupriianov's study of the urban culture of provincial Russia in the era of the Enlightenment, which explores the formation of a Russian national culture in the institutions that connected the capital cities and provincial towns such as schools, libraries, theaters, noble assemblies, and clubs. He follows the emergence of urban identities in letters, petitions, clothing, and attitudes to events.[7] A close study of a provincial town that examines the interactions of the various social groups in fascinating detail can be found in Aleksandr Kamenskii's study of the city of Bezhetsk in the eighteenth century.[8] Another book set in the same era is Evgenii Akel'ev's portrayal of the criminal world of Moscow based on case records from the police archives.[9] Everyday life in the cities of the Volga during the entire tsarist era is explored by Andrei Zorin in what he calls a historical-ethnographic study.[10] The popularity of everyday life history reached a point a few years ago that it influenced university curriculum. Faculty at Moscow University published a two-volume primer composed of narrative and documentary readings. At Kazan University instructors produced a textbook on everyday life focused on the history of the city of Kazan.[11]

This upsurge of interest should not surprise us. The roots of everyday life studies run deep in Russia, and what we are seeing today is in some measure a revival of an art that flourished in imperial Russia. As far back as the late eighteenth century Russian scholars and writers, following the fashion of Europeans, began to explore their own past and define a national identity grounded in fanciful notions of popular culture.[12] Serious studies of daily life followed in the middle of the next century under the influence of Slavophile and populist thought. Every historian of Russia is familiar, for example, with the works first published 150 years ago by Ivan Zabelin on the "home life" of the tsars and tsaritsas of the sixteenth and seventeenth centuries. In the second of these studies Zabelin treated the position of women in Russian society more generally, for which he probably deserves the title of the first historian of Russian women.[13] Zabelin also sketched the domestic life of boyars and their landed estates and the daily life of the people more generally.[14] At about the same time, Nikolai (or Mikola in Ukrainian) Kostomarov produced a detailed study of the everyday life of Russians in the sixteenth and seventeenth centuries. Kostomarov surveyed town life and morals, housing, furniture and tools, clothing, food, health, customs, beliefs and rituals, entertainment, and drunkenness.[15] The Decembrist officer and historian Aleksandr Kornilovich wrote about daily life during Peter the Great's time.[16] Another revolutionary, this time from the period after the Great Reforms, Ivan Pryzhov, wrote a history of Russian taverns and produced a collection of materials on the history of beggars in Russia.[17]

The everyday in provincial life also found its writers. Best known is perhaps Nikolai Chechulin's broad survey of provincial life in the late eighteenth century, but large numbers of less well-known local historians and boosters, known as *kraevedy*, were actively researching the past of their provinces.[18] These early studies of the everyday, though set in the past, were not strictly chronological accounts but mingled history, folklore, and ethnography. More purely ethnographic works also appeared describing the everyday life of rural dwellers. These usually static representations provided later historians with insights into the daily life of villagers. They included the detailed descriptions of village life left by Aleksandr Tereshchenko, Aleksandra Efimenko, and Sergei Maksimov. Although works of this type make fascinating reading, they are not historical.[19] One partial exception may be the short, unfinished survey of Riazan village life in the late imperial period by Ol'ga Petrovna Semenova Tian-Shanskaia, who offered comments on the dynamic changes occurring in village life.[20]

Folkloric works that sought to serve as histories can also be found. Best known are perhaps the huge compendiums of material produced by the poet Apollon Korinfskii and by the collector of Slavic antiquities Mikhail Zabylin.[21] A rich source of everyday life observations in the Russian past can likewise be found in literary works and sketches of city life, such as Mikhail Pyliaev's *Staryi Peterburg,* Pavel Buryshkin's *Moskva kupecheskaia,* and the delightfully intimate portrayal of Moscow cultural life by Mikhail Gershenzon, *Griboedovskaia Moskva,* in which the author described the interests, manners, morals, and daily behavior of Moscow society on the basis of the Rimskii-Korsakov family's personal correspondence, plus memoirs and letters by others.[22]

The advent of Soviet power brought an end to this development. Historians and those in related disciplines had to abandon efforts to examine everyday life and turn to questions of economic development, class struggle, and other problems defined by Marx, Engels, and Lenin as keys to understanding the stages of history leading to the emergence of a socialist state. With a few exceptions, studies of everyday life in the past became the province of ethnographers, and, even then, major studies did not appear until after World War II. Some of these works were welcomed by historians, for example, Vera Kruprianskaia and N. S. Polishchuk's *Kul'tura i byt rabochikh gornozavodskogo urala: Konets XIX–nachalo XX v.* (1971) and Mikhail Rabinovich's *Ocherki etnografii russkogo feodal'nogo goroda* (1978). For their part, historians were able to publish only a handful of studies of this character, and the few who tried it wisely confined their writing to early periods that were slightly less sensitive to ideological dictates than was recent history. Among such works were Boris Romanov's *Liudi i nravy drevnei Rusi* (1947, reprinted in 1966) and Lidiia Semenova's *Ocherki istorii byta i kul'turnoi zhizni Rossii: Pervaia polovina XVIII v.* (1982). Though not ignored by historians, these works remained outside the mainstream.[23]

In a different sphere, studies of provincial life occasionally appeared from the pen of dedicated local patriots such as the Nizhnii Novgorod historian Dmitrii Smirnov.[24] The one place during the Soviet era that the study of daily life in history became an explicit focus of theoretical and descriptive analysis was in the work of Iurii Lotman and the Tartu school of semiotics.[25] The thanks Lotman got from Soviet authorities for his brilliant contributions in this field was a near total ban on his contacts with the West.[26] I will have more to say about Lotman's theories later in this chapter.

It is also worth noting here that the few studies of daily life that appeared in Soviet times treated urban, factory, or, in Lotman's work, upper-class life before the Soviet era. Studies of village life in Soviet times, in particular, were discouraged. Ethnographers and folklorists were severely constrained in their ability to report honestly about the living conditions of the communities they studied, as they would have had to report on the destruction of the countryside by the forced collectivization of agriculture and mass deportation of those who resisted. Even historical works by folklorists were gutted by Soviet censorship, as I learned in the 1970s from the Leningrad scholar Antonina Martynova, whose studies of lullabies could not include disapproved forms and whose anthology of works by S. V. Maksimov was stripped of any references to Jews, as if Jews had not lived in Russia and been studied by Maksimov.[27] Only toward the end of the Soviet period did Russian specialists begin cautiously to conduct studies of the countryside.

As for foreign researchers in cultural anthropology and sociology, they were unable to carry out long-term participant observation studies in Russia until after the collapse of Communist power.[28] Once the barriers came down, however, researchers quickly entered the field and began producing a wealth of new studies of Russian everyday life, including works by Bruce Grant on a fishing community in Sakhalin, Nancy Ries on the languages of perestroika, Margaret Paxton on village life in the north, Alexei Yurchak on the double life and language of late Soviet times, Tova Höjdestrand on homeless people in Petersburg, Olga Shevchenko on accommodation to the crisis of the 1990s, Douglas Rogers on the Old Believers of the Urals, and others.[29] Russians were, of course, making their own fresh contributions to the ethnographic study of daily life.[30]

For Western historians of Russia and increasingly for Russian specialists as well, the focus on quotidian life since the fall of the Soviet Union found its inspiration in Western works referred to under several different labels, including history from below, the Annales school, microhistory, *Alltagsgeschichte*, and everyday life history. While we can cite extraordinarily incisive and influential works appearing under these rubrics, questions remain about the general applicability of such a research orientation. Scholars have, for example, expressed doubts about the intellectual coherence of an everyday life approach to historical studies.[31] To mention the most obvious, it is difficult to know what could be excluded from the scope of daily life study, for it can embrace any subject of a repetitive character, including material culture, technology, social life, political life, emotional life, ritual and religious practice, domestic life, forms of social, economic, and political organization, and others. It can likewise occupy any temporal or geographic space. One might also ask why, if the study of daily life represents a coherent approach, it appears under so many methodological labels.

The general approach of history from below owes much to a few highly influential individual works that cannot be assigned to particular schools of historiography. These include the Dutch historian Johan Huizinga's *The Waning of the Middle Ages: A Study of Forms of Life, Thought, and Art in France and the Netherlands in the Dawn of the Renaissance,* which appeared in English as early as 1924, Norbert Elias's *The Civilizing Process,* published in German in 1939 in two volumes, and E. P. Thompson's *The Making of the English Working Class,* which came out in 1963.[32] Studies drawing inspiration from these now classic texts and also from the growing influence of the Annales school first emerged on a broad front in the 1970s under the rubric of social history. Soon after, we learned about the approach as microhistory, Alltagsgeschichte, and historically oriented cultural anthropology.[33] Russians used the label *byt i nravy* (roughly, "manners and morals") until adopting almost universally the more fashionable tag *povsednevnaia zhizn'* (literally, "everyday life"). Indeed, each major intellectual community in Europe seems to have spun off such an orientation. Do the different names represent distinctive approaches, or do they merely reflect a desire of particular communities to claim originality?

Some scholars believe that the turn to everyday life history started with the Annales school in France in the pre–World War II era, when Lucien Febvre and Marc Bloch advocated replacing the dominant mode of historical study centered on political and diplomatic events with research into long-term social, economic, and cultural structures that shaped the general mental outlook of a people. Others would contend that, on the contrary, the focus on detailed community studies first emerged in reaction to the work of historians of the Annales school and of their social history disciples elsewhere who sought to put together long series of data on large population groups to reveal enduring shifts in attitudes and behavior. For example, the Italian scholars who launched microhistory in the late 1970s and 1980s were reacting against not only the traditional grand narratives but also the "serial" methods associated with quantification and the Annales school.[34] It might be of interest to Russian specialists that the Italians took their inspiration from Tolstoy's theory of history in *War and Peace.* They saw grand narratives and serial methods as sharing the functionalist practice of taking a series of observations and imposing on them a constructed order or regularity. The Italians preferred Tolstoy's notion of the contingent character of historical actions. By experimenting with observations on a radically reduced scale, they discovered that the interpretations built on the macrohistorical or serial methods obscured or even remained blind to relationships that were essential to an understanding of the social order. As Giovanni Levi, one of the founders of microhistory, recently remarked, the point was "the recovery of complexity." Microhistorians did not seek so much to reject grand narratives as to examine them "closely with a view to correcting their simplifications and modifying their perspectives and assumptions."[35] To take one example from Levi's own research, in a close investigation of land transactions in northern Italy he discovered that what historians working on the macro-level thought to be a modern "depersonalized" market in land turned out on closer inspection to be a land exchange in which prices were set by social and kinship bonds.[36]

One of the key theoretical problems of microhistory is the degree of fit between macro- and micro-observations. The photography critic and historical theorist Siegfried Kracauer, using an analogy from film, adopted a highly pessimistic stance on this question, contending that no necessary correlation existed. What you see in a grainy aerial photo may not correspond in any essential way to what you see when you are on the ground.[37] Ideally, researchers would like to discover the relationship between tightly focused observations and a wide angle of vision in order to measure accurately the influence of large events on the local and, in turn, the ability of local communities to resist attempts to impose alien practices and to make choices contrary to the normative reality or hegemonic discourse of their time.

Microhistory and everyday life history seem to be similar in some respects and different in others. Microhistory is most concerned with the fit between the grand narrative and the essential social dynamics at the local level that fail to be captured in the larger picture. Note the example of Italian land markets mentioned earlier. Better known is Carlo Ginzburg's celebrated study of the miller Mennochio, whose testimony opened our eyes to a religious world tenaciously resistant to the domination of the Catholic Church.[38] Everyday life history, as practiced by the Alltagsgeschichte group and its followers, seems to have been an approving response to the Italian approach of microhistory and a reaction against the heavy structuralist emphasis of German social history. But while following the Italian practice of viewing subjects on a radically reduced scale, the historians of Alltagsgeschichte also sought to modify it based on the ideas of the French anthropologist Michel de Certeau. As can be detected in the etymology of the central concept of the German practitioners, *Eigensinn*,[39] it refers to something that moves inward toward one's way of thinking about things and therefore suggests the kind of individual behavior that de Certeau wrote about, namely, the "tactics" that people employ to evade the panoptic surveillance desired and designed by elites.[40]

Because social systems are continually evolving, they expose pathways and interstices not immediately subject to elite surveillance and control. Although de Certeau did not take his analysis beyond identifying the gaps that permit individuals scope for nonnormative behavior, it can be hypothesized that these actions could in time, if adopted by enough others, realign webs of social interaction and in turn evoke responses from the powerful that would shift and redefine the institutional and structural components of a society. This seems to be what the Alltagsgeschichte historians mean when they say that ordinary people are at once the objects and the subjects of history. Is it valid then to say that microhistory is primarily about what is observable at a particular range of inquiry, while Alltagsgeschichte seeks to understand how people locally understand their conditions and their ability to maneuver through or evade given social and legal strictures in ways that give them increased latitude for making their own choices? If so, perhaps the two approaches are not really very different. The variation may lie merely in the angle of vision of the researcher, whether it is from outside the action, observing behavior, or from inside the perceptions of the historical actors. In both cases, the object seems to be to explore the ability of ordinary people to act contrary to the normative reality and therefore to cause the established structures to bend or be reformulated in response.[41]

The most helpful theoretical approach to this problem may come not out of Western but out of Russian literary and historical studies, namely, the work of Iurii Lotman, especially his concept of the semiosphere. As Jonathan Bolton pointed out in a 2006 essay, Lotman crafted a more robust model than did either Michel Foucault or Michel de Certeau for understanding the interaction of the local or everyday and the dominant cultural discourse of societies.[42] Foucault's scheme does not allow for manipulation and modification by ordinary people of the classifications imposed on them in the dominant discourse. They remain passive participants in the descriptive categories constructed by the disciplining professions. De Certeau, in search of a corrective to Foucault, recognized that individuals could evade identities imposed in the dominant discourse if they occupied the unobserved and therefore unsupervised interstices of normative systems. In his model, subjects do not, however, rewrite in their own language the descriptions imposed on them in the dominant discourse, let alone explicitly resist them. Instead, they employ "tactics" of evasion in their everyday practice that open spaces for behavior contrary to the rules. Reminiscent of this approach in our field is Alexei Yurchak's analysis of the last Soviet generation, whose members performed the required political rituals while behaving contrary to their prescriptions in nonritualized settings.[43] The semiosphere concept of Lotman (who, tell-ingly, was not among the many theorists invoked by Yurchak) provides a more multifaceted and instructive model for understanding the interplay of the dominant discourse and the local sign systems, including the ability of local languages to rewrite the descriptions emanating from the center of the semiosphere and hence reshape the hegemonic discourse and limit its homogenizing effects. Unlike de Certeau's or Yurchak's subjects, who evade the strictures of "them" without positing an "us," Lotman's design includes an "us," which is expressed in everyday practices of the local lan-guage and system of signs.[44] The efforts of the center to rewrite the codes of peripheral cultures are always a matter of translation and therefore not easily reproducible. In Bolton's expressive metaphor, "Lotman's careful at-tention to meaning-generating mechanisms . . . suggests just how difficult it is to throw a net of power over any complex reality; nets of power are nets of meaning, and they will always settle onto the contours of the reality they are trying to contain, themselves becoming misshapen or tangled in the process."[45] Lotman provides an excellent model for the exploration of everyday practices undertaken by the authors in this book.

Ultimately, the most useful distinction to make may be one between these several new microhistory and everyday life approaches, taken as a group, and another still popular genre, local history. The writers of local history do not, as a rule, challenge established grand narratives but seek to fill in the details at the level of the region, town, village, community organization, or business firm. They wish to supplement the broad-brush histories with local color and to bring attention to the contributions of people whose actions are not thought of as History with a capital H. In contrast, what these variously labeled new approaches have in common is an aspiration to reveal dynamics that affect the behavior of actors and in-stitutions that figure in the grand narrative but that operate below or out-side (pick your metaphor) of the field of vision of historians who produce the grand narrative. In other words, the new approaches seek to illuminate dynamics at the local level that have one of two consequences. Either they demonstrate the incompatibility of macrohistorical views with behavior at the local level and, accordingly, their inability to provide an accurate account of the past, or they offer insight into the power of local actors to make choices that reshape social relations in ways that modify dynamics and developments at the macrolevel. In short, everyday life studies must be more than good local history. They have to show how local action modifies our understanding of macrohistorical processes.

A recent attempt to provide a model for how this can be done is Catherine Evtuhov's Braudelian study of Nizhnii Novgorod province. In explaining her approach, she remarks that while we have an increasing number of local studies, what we are still missing is "a coherent perspective on the Russian provinces—an approach and a methodology that would permit the deconstruction of nineteenth-century Russia into smaller provincial units, and a subsequent reconstruction that will provide us with a revised vision of the country as a whole." She quotes Susan Smith-Peter's observation that "the local is a window onto Russia. It provides the scholar with a much richer understanding of how the majority of Russians lived, many of them far away from the capitals. After extensive and intensive study of all of Russia's regions, scholars in both East and West will have a clearer vision of how events and social processes actually unfolded."[46]

Finally, let me offer a couple of examples from earlier research projects of mine as illustrations of how a close look at what is happening in localities can reveal social dynamics less visible when viewed from on high, that is, from the angle of vision provided in the standard narratives of Russian history.

The first example comes from my study on the abandonment and fosterage of Russian children in the imperial period. The study reveals the ability of local people to transform a government program on an impressive scale. The imperial foundling homes were receiving large numbers of unwanted children in the nineteenth century, as many as twenty-five thousand per year at the two largest homes, Moscow and Petersburg, counted together. The children were put out to be nursed and fostered by village women in the provinces surrounding the capital cities, where tens of thousands of them could be found at any one time. In many villages this work constituted the largest source of nonfarm income. The village women who cared for the children received along with each child a pay booklet, which they were to present at a central point monthly to collect their pay. The central authorities for more than a century touted the foundling homes as an example of tsarist benevolence and enlightenment, and they paraded distinguished Russians and foreign visitors through the institutions to show off the facilities and explain the workings of the fosterage system.

It eventually came to light, however, that villagers had steadily transformed this carefully designed system with its printed booklets and pay offices to serve their own needs. The government intended to achieve one purpose but learned that the peasants could adapt the mechanism to other ends. The government, perhaps with a dose of idealization of village people and with the intention of advertising its care for the unfortunate, recruited village women to nurture and bring to adulthood the unwanted children of the country, and it contracted with the peasants through the agency of a pay booklet. In creating this instrument, the government had unwittingly instituted what the villagers recognized as a property right that they could put to their own uses. Officials wanted to make the foundling children better off, but the peasants wanted to make themselves better off. They generated a set of roles and institutions to serve their needs, including peddlers to deliver nurslings to village women tied down at home, runners to facilitate the distribution of monthly stipends, and systems of brokerage that supplied credit and goods to the wet nurses and foster families. In other words, the peasants treated foundling care like any other trade and channeled this commerce through the same types of credit and delivery networks that operated in the case of other commodities. When disputes arose between brokers and wet nurses, they adjudicated them in the peasant courts just as villagers did other business transactions.[47]

Sadly, the commerce was conducted in infants and young children, most of whom died in a short time, a perishable commodity in an economic exchange between the cities and the countryside. Although officials eventually recognized the commercial character of the fosterage programs and lamented the self-interested behavior of the villagers, which was accompanied by soaring mortality rates and the uncontrolled transfer of infants and pay booklets between villagers, it was scarcely surprising that the peasants behaved as they did. Since the government had constructed the system on material, not moral, incentives, families worked out arrangements that allowed the fosterage programs to meet their needs most effectively. They took the government institution and reengineered it to fit into a village world based on strategies of small commercial operations that allowed them to eke out an existence. In doing so, they obliged the government to institute a number of modifications in an effort to regain control.[48]

To take another example, my examination of an eighteenth-century Russian provincial merchant began explicitly as a microhistory project. This close-up look revealed that the wealthiest commercial people in the provinces were living and behaving in ways quite different from what we were led to believe from wide-angle studies of Russian history. The principal subject of the study, although appearing to follow social dictates and even exceeding the norms for expected civic and charitable works, was pushing beyond the bounds of what was officially permitted to people of his station and opening space for others in his position to occupy an expanded range of tolerated behavior. His standard of living equaled that of most local nobles, he sent his son to be educated at a private school in Moscow that taught foreign languages, and he even owned serfs fifty years after the law had forbade anyone but a noble to own them. Because he was scarcely alone in this behavior, the government was constrained to respond in two ways: it brightened the lines between social estates, but it also conceded status markers to the aspirations of the merchants.[49] The tactics employed by ordinary people to evade rules that were intended to brand them as inferior caused a shift in the web of local relationships sufficient to compel readjustments in the hegemonic social model.

In summary, the scholarship of everyday life in Russia draws on a long tradition of study dating to at least the middle of the nineteenth century and encompassing researches on history, ethnography, folklore, and literary commentary. Though marginalized from the 1930s to the 1990s, works on daily life have returned to Russia and to Russian studies across a broad front since the fall of the Soviet Union. The subject is engaging talented researchers and writers and finding a large popular as well as professional readership. Some of the works in this new surge of publications merely repackage earlier findings, while others add new discoveries without fresh analyses. The best of the new work, however, is opening entirely new areas of inquiry such as early town life, the criminal underground, and the worlds of women, merchants, religious minorities, and more and is informed by the theoretical contributions of cultural anthropology, microhistory, Alltagsgeschichte, and pioneering Russian work in semiotics.

NOTES

I want to thank Aleksandr Kamenskii, Boris Mironov, and Elena Marasinova for bibliographic suggestions.

1. See my essay "A Single Research Community: Not Yet," *Slavic Review* 60, no. 3 (Autumn 2001): 550–57, on the responses of the two communities to a major Russian work on social history at the end of one decade of post-Soviet Russia. The differences I found then have since begun gradually to diminish.

2. Svetlana Boym, *Common Places: Mythologies of Everyday Life in Russia* (Cambridge, Mass.: Harvard University Press, 1994); Sheila Fitzpatrick, *Everyday Stalinism: Ordinary Life in Extraordinary Times* (Oxford: Berg, 2002).

3. Christina Kiaer and Eric Naiman, eds., *Everyday Life in Early Soviet Russia: Taking the Revolution Inside* (Bloomington: Indiana University Press, 2006). A volume of collected essays focused primarily on early Russian history appeared in 2010 under the rubric of everyday life, although a number of the contributions were standard historical accounts and not everyday life studies. See Gary Marker, Joan Neuberger, Marshall Poe, and Susan Rupp, eds., *Everyday Life in Russian History: Quotidian Studies in Honor of Daniel Kaiser* (Bloomington: Slavica Publishers, 2010).

4. Jeffrey W. Jones, *Everyday Life and the "Reconstruction" of Soviet Russia during and after the Great Patriotic War, 1943–1948* (Bloomington: Slavica Publishers, 2006); Catriona Kelly, *Children's World: Growing Up in Russia, 1890–1991* (New Haven, Conn.: Yale University Press, 2007); Donald J. Raleigh, *Soviet Baby Boomers: An Oral History of Russia's Cold War Generation* (Oxford: Oxford University Press, 2011).

5. The film premiered at the 2010 Sundance Film Festival.

6. See the entire lineup of books at the Molodaia Gvardiia website, http://gvardiya.ru /shop/books/povsednevnaya_zhizn_chelovechestva, accessed June 26, 2012.

7. O. E. Kosheleva, *Liudi Sankt-Peterburgskogo ostrova petrovskogo vremeni* (Moscow, 2004); Aleksandr Kupriianov, *Gorodskaia kul'tura russkoi provintsii: Konets XVIII–pervaia polovina XIX veka* (Moscow: Novyi Khronograf, 2007).

8. A. B. Kamenskii, *Povsednevnost' russkikh gorodskikh obyvatelei: Istoricheskie anekdoty iz provintsial'noi zhizni XVIII veka* (Moscow: Izd. RGGU, 2006).

9. E. V. Akel'ev, *Povsednevnaia zhizn' vorovskogo mira Moskvy vo vremena Van'ki Kaina* (Moscow: Molodaia gvardiia, 2012).

10. A. N. Zorin, *Goroda i posady dorevoliutsionnogo Povolzh'ia: Istoriko-etnograficheskoe issledovanie naseleniia i poselencheskoi struktury gorodov rossiiskoi provintsii vtoroi poloviny XVI–nachala XX v.* (Kazan: Kazan University Press, 2001).

11. *Rossiiskaia Povsednevnost': Ot istokov do serediny XIX veka. Uchebnoe posobie* (Moscow: KDU, 2006), and *Rossiiskaia Povsednevnost': Vtoraia polovina XIX–nachalo XXI veka* (Moscow: KDU, 2009), both done under the editorship of L. I. Semennikova. For Kazan, see E. A. Vishlenkova, S. Iu. Malysheva, and A. A. Sal'nikova, *Kul'tura povsednevnosti provintsial'nogo goroda: Kazan i kazantsy v XIX–XX vekakh* (Kazan: Kazan University Press, 2008).

12. Hans Rogger, *National Consciousness in Eighteenth-Century Russia* (Cambridge, Mass.: Harvard University Press, 1960), esp. chap. 4.

13. I. Zabelin, *Domashnii byt russkikh tsarei v XVI i XVII st.*, 2nd ed. (Moscow: Grachev, 1872), and Zabelin, *Domashnii byt russkikh tsarits v XVI i XVII st.*, 3rd ed. (Moscow, 1901). The introductory section of the study of tsaritsas, which is about the position of women more

generally, was published separately in 1905 as a popular work: *Zhenshchina v dopetrovskom obshchestve* (St. Petersburg: Suvorin, 1905).

14. *Bol'shoi boiarin v svoem votchinnom khoziaistve*, 1871; *Domashnii byt russkago naroda v XVI i XVII st.*, 2 vols. in 3 (Moscow: A. I. Mamontov, 1895–1915).

15. N. I. Kostomarov, *Domashniaia zhizn' i nravy velikorusskogo naroda v XVI i XVII stoletiiakh (ocherk)*, ed. S. A. Nikolaev (Moscow: Ekonomika, 1993). Kostomarov first published the study in the journal *Sovremennik* in 1860. An expanded edition appeared in 1887 and then in further editions thereafter.

16. Aleksandr Kornilovich, *Nravy russkikh pri Petre Velikom*. First published in journals of the mid-nineteenth century, this work later came out in a popular edition in the Deshevaia Biblioteka (St. Petersburg: Suvorin, 1901).

17. I. G. Pryzhov, *Istoriia kabakov v Rossii v sviazi s istoriei russkogo naroda* (St. Petersburg: Vol'f, 1868); Pryzhov, *Nishchie na sviatoi Rusi* (Moscow: Smirnova, 1862).

18. N. D. Chechulin, *Russkoe provintsial'noe obshchestvo vo vtoroi polovine XVIII veka* (St. Petersburg, 1889). For a bibliography and survey of the recent revival of local studies, see G. A. Mel'nichuk and N. V. Stepanova, "Dva desiatiletiia rossiiskogo kraevedeniia," *Bibliografiia*, no. 5 (2010): 43–50, http://www.kraeved74.ru/content/article110.html, accessed July 11, 2012.

19. A. V. Tereshchenko, *Byt russkogo naroda* (St. Petersburg, 1848). A 1997 republication is available online at http://az.lib.ru/t/tereshenko_a_w/text_0020.shtml; A. Ia. Efimenko, *Issledovaniia narodnoi zhizni* (Moscow: Kasperov, 1884); S. V. Maksimov, *Nechistaia, nevedomaia i krestnaia sila* (St. Petersburg: Golinke i Vil'borg, 1903).

20. O. P. Semenova-Tian-Shanskaia, *Zhizn' "Ivana": Ocherki iz byta krest'ian odnoi iz chernozemnykh gubernii*, Zapiski imperatorskogo russkogo geograficheskogo obshchestva po otdeleniiu etnografii, tom XXXIX (St. Petersburg, 1914); see my edition of the same work in English, which is revised and expanded with the addition of material from the field notes of the author held in the archives of the Geographic Society: *Village Life in Late Tsarist Russia* (Bloomington: Indiana University Press, 1993).

21. A. A. Korinfskii, *Narodnaia Rus': Kruglyi god skazanii, poverii, obychaev i poslovits russkogo naroda* (Moscow: Izdanie Kliukina, 1901); M. Zabylin, *Russkii narod, ego obychai, predaniia, obriady i sueveriia* (first published in 1880?; new ed., Moscow: EKSMO, 2002).

22. M. I. Piliaev, *Staryi Peterburg: Rasskazy iz byloi zhizni stolitsy* (St. Petersburg: Suvorin, 1887). Piliaev did a similar work later on life in Moscow; P. A. Buryshkin, *Moskva kupecheskaia* (New York, 1954). This work is now available in full online via Yandex. Gershenzon's work first appeared in the magazine *Golos minuvshego* in 1913. Reprinted as M. O. Gershenzon, *Griboedovskaia Moskva: Izbrannye trudy* (in 2 pts.), pt. 1 (Moscow, 2010), 29–112. For a fresh portrayal of life in Moscow in English, see a new work by Alexander Martin, *Enlightened Metropolis: Constructing Imperial Moscow, 1762–1855* (Oxford: Oxford University Press, 2013), in which Martin uses foreign, especially German, observations on life to good effect.

23. These and a few other similar works published in the Soviet period were discussed at the "Everyday Life in Russia and the Soviet Union" workshop in May 2010 by the Moscow historian Aleksandr Kamenskii in his paper "Recent Studies on the History of Daily Life in 18th Century Russia: Problems and Achievements."

24. See his *Ocherki zhizni i byta nizhegorodtsev XVII–XVIII vekov* (Volga-Viazatskoe izdatel'stvo, 1978). This work is combined with his *Kartinki nizhegorodskogo byta XIX veka* in a new edition of his writings: D. N. Smirnov, *Nizhegorodskaia starina*, ed. G. Shcheglov

(Nizhnii Novgorod: Nizhegorodskaia iarmarka, 1995). For more on the work of local historians and boosters in this province, see the new book by Catherine Evtuhov, *Portrait of a Russian Province: Economy, Society, and Civilization in Nineteenth-Century Nizhnii Novgorod* (Pittsburgh: University of Pittsburgh Press, 2011).

25. His best-known essays on this subject were translated in the 1980s as "The Poetics of Everyday Behavior in Eighteenth-Century Russian Culture" and "The Decembrist in Daily Life (Everyday Behavior as a Historical-Psychological Category)," in *The Semiotics of Russian Cultural History,* ed. Alexander D. Nakhimovsky and Alice Stone Nakhimovsky (Ithaca, N.Y.: Cornell University Press, 1985). They first appeared as "Poetika bytovogo povedeniia v russkoi kul'ture XVIII veka," in *Trudy po znakovym sistemam,* no. 8 (Tartu, 1977), 65–89, and "Dekabrist v povsednevnoi zhizni," in *Literaturnoe nasledie dekabristov* (Leningrad, 1975), 25–74.

26. In the early 1980s, when I was editor of the *Slavic Review,* I wrote to him a few times to ask him to contribute but did not receive a reply. When I met him in Tartu in May 1990, he told me that all his mail from the West was blocked in those years.

27. The mangled work in question was S. V. Maksimov, *Kul' khleba: Rasskazy i ocherki,* ed. and comp. A. N. Martynova (Leningrad: Lenizdat, 1987).

28. Caroline Humphrey was possibly the one exception of a Western scholar who did extended field research for her study of a collective farm in the far east: see her *Karl Marx Collective: Economy, Society and Religion in a Siberian Collective Farm* (Cambridge: Cambridge University Press, 1983). Marjorie Balzer was able briefly to join an expedition to the north in Soviet times. Her work on the project was finished and appeared only after the end of the Soviet regime. See Marjorie Balzer, *The Tenacity of Ethnicity: A Siberian Saga in Global Perspective* (Princeton, N.J.: Princeton University Press, 1999).

29. Bruce Grant, *In the Soviet House of Culture: A Century of Perestroikas* (Princeton, N.J.: Princeton University Press, 1995); Nancy Ries, *Russian Talk: Culture & Conversation during Perestroika* (Ithaca, N.Y.: Cornell University Press, 1997); Margaret Paxson, *Solovyovo: The Story of Memory in a Russian Village* (Bloomington: Indiana University Press, 2005); Alexei Yurchak, *Everything Was Forever, Until It Was No More: The Last Soviet Generation* (Princeton, N.J.: Princeton University Press, 2006); Tova Höjdestrand, *Needed by Nobody: Homelessness and Humanness in Post-Socialist Russia* (Ithaca, N.Y.: Cornell University Press, 2009); Olga Shevchenko, *Crisis and the Everyday in Postsocialist Moscow* (Bloomington: Indiana University Press, 2009); Douglas Rogers, *The Old Faith and the Russian Land: A Historical Ethnography of Ethics in the Urals* (Ithaca, N.Y.: Cornell University Press, 2009).

30. Best known perhaps is the work of a contributor to this volume, Il'ia Utekhin. See his *Ocherki kommunal'nogo byta* (Moscow: OGI, 2004). See the analysis and literature cited in articles by another contributor to this volume, Natalia Pushkareva, "'Istoriia povsednevnosti' i 'istoriia chastnoi zhizni': Soderzhanie i sootnoshenie poniatii," *Sotsial'naia istoriia,* no. 8 (2004): 93–112, and "Istoriia povsednevnosti: Predmet i metody," *Sotsial'naia istoriia,* no. 11 (2007): 9–54.

31. Catriona Kelly, "Ordinary Life in Extraordinary Times: Chronicles of the Quotidian in Russia and the Soviet Union," *Kritika: Explorations in Russian and Eurasian History* 3, no. 4 (Fall 2002): 638.

32. Johan Huizinga, *The Waning of the Middle Ages* (London: E. Arnold & Co., 1924); Norbert Elias, *Über den Prozess der Zivilisation,* 2 vols. (Basel: Haus zum Falken, 1939), English translation published by Basil Blackwell, Ltd.; E. P. Thompson, *The Making of the English Working Class* (New York: Vintage Books, 1963).

33. A general survey of developments in the various subgenres can be found in Sigurður Gylfi Magnússon, "Social History, Cultural History, Alltagsgeschichte, Microhistory: In-Between Methodologies and Conceptual Frameworks," *Journal of Microhistory* (2006), http://www.microhistory.org/pivot/entry.php?id=20.

34. A brief background to the development of this approach in Italy can be found in the introduction by Edward Muir, "Observing Trifles," in *Microhistory & the Lost Peoples of Europe,* ed. Edward Muir and Guido Ruggiero, trans. Eren Branch (Baltimore, Md.: Johns Hopkins University Press, 1991); the essays in the book are examples of the method.

35. Giovanni Levi, "Microhistory and the Recovery of Complexity," in *Historical Knowledge: In Quest of Theory, Method and Evidence,* ed. Susanna Fellman and Marjatta Rahikainen (Newcastle upon Tyne: Cambridge Scholars Publishing, 2012), 124, 129–30.

36. Giovanni Levi, *Inheriting Power: The Story of an Exorcist* (Italian original, 1985; Chicago: University of Chicago Press, 1988).

37. For Kracauer's view, see his posthumously published *History: The Last Things before the Last* (New York: Oxford University Press, 1969), esp. chap. 5. For a recent detailed explication of Kracauer's ideas about history, see Dagmar Barnouw, *Critical Realism: History, Photography, and the Work of Siegfried Kracauer* (Baltimore, Md.: Johns Hopkins University Press, 1994).

38. Carlo Ginzburg, *The Cheese and the Worms: The Cosmos of a Sixteenth-Century Miller,* trans. John and Anne Tedeschi (Italian original, 1976; Baltimore, Md.: Johns Hopkins University Press, 1980).

39. The term is translated variously as "willfulness," "eccentricity," "obstinacy," but these do not capture the full sense in which Alltagsgeschichte historians use it.

40. Michel de Certeau, *The Practice of Everyday Life,* trans. Steven Rendall (Berkeley: University of California Press, 1984).

41. Another distinction that has been noted is the emphasis of the Italian microhistorians, initially at least, on the early modern period. German researchers focused primarily on the modern period, where they sought explanations for the terrible events of the twentieth century. This distinction breaks down, however, if we include in the Italian group the pioneering corps of oral historians whose work is analogous to microhistory. Likewise, Hans Medick and some others affiliated with the Alltagsgeschichte scholars work on earlier periods and in Medick's case seem to have been inspired more by cultural anthropology than social history. We also know that the writings of the Alltagsgeschichte historians have evolved and branched out in a number of directions that complicate efforts to furnish a crisp definition either of their method or of their preferred era for study. If you read Norwegian, a good survey and explanation of the Alltagsgeschichte approaches can be found in Ingar Kaldal, *Alltagsgeschichte og mikrohistorie,* Skrifserie fra Historisk Institutt no. 2 (Trondheim, 1994).

42. Jonathan H. Bolton, "Writing in a Polluted Semiosphere: Everyday Life in Lotman, Foucault, and de Certeau," in *Lotman and Cultural Studies: Encounters and Extensions,* ed. Andreas Schönle (Madison: University of Wisconsin Press, 2006), 329. I want to thank Choi Chatterjee for pointing out Bolton's excellent study.

43. Yurchak, *Everything Was Forever.*

44. Yuri M. Lotman, *Universe of the Mind,* trans. Ann Shukman (Bloomington: Indiana University Press, 1990), pt. 2. One could say that Yurchak's subjects, young Communists who indulged in nonprescribed ideas and practices in nonritual settings, contributed to the erosion of the power of state discourse from within.

45. Bolton, "Writing in a Polluted Semiosphere," 329.

46. Evtuhov, *Portrait of a Russian Province*, 9. The quote is from Susan Smith-Peter, "How to Write a Region: Local and Regional Historiography," *Kritika: Explorations in Russian and Eurasian History* 5, no. 3 (Summer 2004): 541–42.

47. For a detailed explanation of the commerce, see David L. Ransel, *Mothers of Misery: Child Abandonment in Russia* (Princeton, N.J.: Princeton University Press, 1988), esp. chap. 10.

48. Finally, railways, improved communication, and a national press made the deadly conditions of the fosterage system and its commercial character visible to educated society and compelled reorganization of these care institutions on entirely new principles.

49. David L. Ransel, *A Russian Merchant's Tale* (Bloomington: Indiana University Press, 2009).

2

Provincial Nobles, Elite History, and the Imagination of Everyday Life

MARY CAVENDER

What was "everyday life" in the country for Russian nobles? In *Anna Karenina,* the wealthy landowner Levin finds himself annoyed by his brother Koznyshev's attitude:

> Sergius Ivanich Koznyshev, wishing to take a rest from mental work, went to stay with his brother in the country instead of going abroad as usual. According to his views country life was preferable to any other, and he had now come to his brother's house to enjoy it. . . . In spite of his affection and respect for Koznyshev, Constantine did not feel at ease with his stepbrother in the country. To Constantine the country was the place where one lived—that is to say, where one rejoiced, suffered, and laboured; but to Koznyshev the country was, on the one hand, a place of rest from work, and, on the other, a useful antidote to depravity, an antidote to which he resorted with pleasure and with a consciousness of its utility. To Constantine the country seemed a good place because it was the scene of unquestionably useful labour; to Koznyshev it seemed good because one could and should do nothing there.[1]

Here Tolstoy outlines two powerful and opposing experiences of rural life, each of which claimed partisans among the Russian gentry.[2] This dichotomy of views regarding the countryside entered analyses of the proper role for the nobility as early as the emancipation from service of 1762. Was the countryside a temporary retreat from the real work of state service to which one escaped for brief periods in the summer? Or was it possible that full-time residence on the estate might provide scope for meaningful work? Oblomovism, or provincial apathy and inactivity, named after the title character of Goncharov's novel, stalked members of the rural gentry even before the appearance of Goncharov's work—were only lazy or worthless nobles remaining on their estates? What was the true meaning of everyday life on the provincial estate?

If most scholars of everyday life have labored, at least in part, with the goal of exploring the lives of those less powerful, what utility could study of the everyday life of elites have? Might it only reify power structures already established in the minds of scholars? I don't think it must necessarily do this. This chapter explores some questions related to the everyday life of elites, particularly in provincial Russia, and gives one example of the ways in which the methods of everyday life scholars can help historians even in areas and periods (nineteenth-century provincial Tver', in this case) that provide a patchy source base. In contrast to more statistical types of social history, the exploration, in particular, of understandings and beliefs about the quotidian can prove extremely fruitful for the study of such societies.

Many historians of everyday life have envisioned the enterprise as an exploration of the ways in which those without power of various kinds coped with their situations. Thus, the investigation of "tactics" by Michel de Certeau shares, in spite of its focus on the "ordinary," much with the various inquiries into the Stalin period, with their focus on "ordinary life in extraordinary times."[3] Some scholars have investigated the ways in which day-to-day strategies ensured the survival of those in extremely difficult situations; others have investigated the political implications of actions of the disempowered. *Alltagsgeschichte* initially grew from interest in the complicity of many ordinary Germans with Nazism, and its practitioners had a goal of counteracting the narrative that blamed a small elite for the horrors of that regime while seeing most Germans simply as victims.[4] This has proven an extremely valuable avenue of research, opening up new ways of understanding a wide variety of societies. The history of everyday life can also help us to understand the exercise of power from above, in some ways an equally thorny problem for scholars. The history of great men, of course, can include the quotidian. Such histories probably would not fit even into a "big tent" conception of the history of everyday life. However, exercise of power involves groups of elites as well, whose everyday practices and belief systems in many cases revolve around both the sustaining of networks and practices of power, that is, preservation of power, and the deployment of that power in a variety of settings. Both of these aspects of everyday power relations provide important dynamics for the scholar, for the workings of power among those who wield and wish to retain it matter a great deal not only to elites but also to those coerced by such actions.

The study of the everyday life of elites, then, need not be an elitist history but can shed light on power relations more broadly in a society. How, for example, did the Russian Empire, relatively undergoverned in the nineteenth century, manage to mobilize resources over vast, relatively lightly populated areas? A fuller understanding of the provincial nobility helps to explain the power of the regime in the later imperial period, when, beset by the challenges of radical politics, industrialization, and nationalism, among others, it seemed unlikely to hang on. Local elites helped to maintain order in rural areas and to govern remote territories. A sense of privilege and of loyalty to the regime, a smugness about the gentry's natural leading role in smaller cities and rural areas, and a belief that nobles controlled, to some extent, the destiny of themselves and those around them provide a stark contrast to studies of those caught up in the whirlwind of Stalinist purges. Nonetheless, and however illusory such an understanding of noble power may in fact have been, the ways in which local elites imagined that they controlled events and people, and the ways in which they expressed a notion of their duties and of what ought to be done in the provinces, help to flesh out our understandings of the daily workings of provincial Russia. Much as the study of masculinity has deepened our study of femininity and the ways in which its deployment (in various guises) has shaped the lives of countless women (as well, obviously, as extending our study of men), the study of the everyday life of elites deepens our understandings of the everyday lives of those subject to their authority.

As far back as the nineteenth century, Russian writers have examined everyday life in the history of Russia.[5] Many large statistical and anthropological studies from nineteenth- and twentieth-century Russia provide social-historical studies of peasant structures, while more recent social histories, such as Stephen Hoch's study of a village in Tambov, provide a microhistorical look at individual estates.[6] Other scholars have investigated the wealthiest aristocracy's relationship with its provincial holdings, political engagement in the late imperial period, the provincial connections of important cultural figures such as Pushkin and Tolstoy, and the late imperial dacha, among other topics. In the 1990s an explosion of popular interest occurred, especially in the history of elites.[7] This was mirrored, to some extent, in scholarly circles by an expansion of research agendas away from a previous focus on revolutionary intellectual, labor, and peasant topics toward questions of empire and the frontier and, as far as our topic of everyday life is concerned, questions related to the nature of imperial society and politics on their own terms, rather than with reference to the coming revolution. For example, Aleksandr Kamenskii's wonderful book on eighteenth-century Bezhetsk, in Tver' province, examines in detail the everyday life of urban dwellers.[8] Other books have included examinations of civil society, voluntary organizations, and so on, and they have included works that look more carefully at the everyday life of previously little-studied groups such as the merchants and provincial nobles, to take the topics of two monographs I will examine in more detail, as well as of my own work. Two recent books, by David Ransel and John Randolph, respectively, address the importance of ideas in the everyday life of elite Russians.[9]

David Ransel's work, *A Russian Merchant's Tale: The Life and Adventures of Ivan Alekseevich Tolchënov, Based on His Diary,* uses the unusual diary kept by a wealthy trader to delve into the self-fashioning of a provincial merchant of the eighteenth century. Tolchënov, a sometime grain merchant of Dmitrov with links to St. Petersburg and Moscow, interacted with people from a wide variety of social stations, but it is primarily his personal engagement with new notions of the individual, of refinement, and of ideas and practices such as gardening, reading, and other markers of status that interests Ransel. He also emphasizes Tolchënov's continued religiosity and intense practice of pilgrimage, devotion to icons, and so on. Tracing the psychological and philosophical development of its author across the years of the diary and including later summaries of each year that Tolchënov appended when he recopied the diary, this microhistory outlines the ways in which an individual flexibly negotiated changes in circumstances, as well as his daily engagement with people and ideas.

Ransel uses Pierre Bourdieu's concept of habitus to describe the fixed parameters of his subject's life and aims to explore the ways in which he exerted agency within the relatively fixed context in which he operated. Thus, a history of everyday life in a quite literal sense, at least of every day recorded in the diary, leads Ransel not only to illumination of concrete historical information, such as the nature of the grain trade with St. Petersburg and the relative elasticity of the social order, but also to an examination of the influence of elite ideas emanating from the Enlightenment on people farther down the social scale.

John Randolph, in his *The House in the Garden: The Bakunin Family and the Romance of Russian Idealism*, is also interested in self-fashioning, this time of the men who understood themselves in monumental terms as progressive philosophers who would advance ideas and society in Russia. Randolph also brings the Bakunin women into the story and elucidates their role in the intellectual history of Russia more generally. He describes the Bakunin estate, Priamukhino, as the "stage" for the working out of philosophical concepts, as the young Bakunins and their circle sought to enact their intellectual development in the activities of daily life. The Bakunin estate, envisioned as the ideal domestic realm, nurturing the ideal family, propelled members of the family and their friends and colleagues into intellectual discussion, and, in their recounting of their personal development as exemplary men and, to a lesser degree, women, they created what Randolph terms the "romance of Russian Idealism." Much of the mythmaking centered on personal intellectual development and its relationship to the events of private life. Reading Hegel, for example, and pondering further elaborations and implications of Hegelian thought might lead to a new understanding of marriage and love in the abstract and of the personal meaning of particular marriages, with implications, for example, for decisions about whether to remain in a marriage or not. Randolph extends the focus on the personalities and philosophical development of the Bakunins to other important figures of their circle, such as Vissarion Belinsky. Even when the latter rejected the Bakunins' vision of Priamukhino as a domestic idyll, he continued to use the estate as a touchpoint for describing problems in modern Russian society. Thus, the domestic sphere of everyday interactions contained universal implications crucial to understanding the nature of Russian society in a broad sense. Randolph's mythmakers proved so effective that the legend of their exemplary behavior and influence on Russian intellectual history lives on in the general reliance on this small circle as instigators of new ideas in Russian thought. Thus, although *The House in the Garden* might more easily be labeled a work of intellectual history for its focus on leading thinkers and the development of their ideas, Randolph's concentration on the home and on the treatment of everyday conflict between generations, or between husband and wife, for example, offers a great deal for the historian of everyday life.

Obviously, in addition to the domestic lives of the landowners, everyday life on the estate involved exploitation and domination and the maintenance of a hierarchical system that provided the base of agricultural production and reproduction for the Russian Empire. Hoch's microhistory of a peasant community in Tambov suggests the importance of village structures in upholding hierarchy in the countryside, in their replication of authoritarian regimes at the village and household levels. In general, however, sources are problematic for approaching the history of everyday agriculture on the provincial estate. Peasants left very few records, and only the occasional, unusual cache of documents opens a window onto pre-emancipation peasant life. Even records left by the gentry are patchy, especially if one pursues the study of the gentry as a whole, in its great variety, rather than concentrating on the aristocrats who left copious records.[10] With relatively limited possibilities for certainty about everyday practice on the many smaller estates, what might the history of everyday production on the estate entail?

History of everyday life of members of the middle and petty gentry can be most revealing when scholars pursue the study of the ideas informing everyday life. This approach allows a fruitful investigation into areas that would be difficult to explore using more traditional techniques of social history. Underpinning arguments about the possibility of meaningful work on the provincial estate were various understandings of everyday life in the countryside. For many of those in state service, a life filled with useful work was impossible away from centers of government. Military service might put members of the elite in remote places, but the centrality of the military encampment and the high respect accorded military service ensured that distance from the capitals did not diminish its importance.

Educated Russians also saw civilian service in the capitals or at a high level in the provinces (e.g., as governor) as useful, but jobs held by clerks, policemen, and others were not regarded as respectable for the nobility. Beginning in the eighteenth century, a number of writers addressed the problem of meaningful life in the countryside by urging provincial nobles to take up agronomy in the interests of self, state, and society. In publications of the nineteenth century, my focus here, partisans of agronomy negotiated the question of everyday life for provincial nobles, attempting to define what was currently the everyday experience and what future possibilities might be. In so doing, some of them presented themselves as provincial nobles transforming their own estates. They presented themselves as acquainted with everyday life in the country and as competent to advocate for its reform.

In investigating beliefs about agronomic practice on provincial estates both in my book and in the research presented here, I am not primarily concerned with practice. In large part this is because of the lack of reliable sources on agricultural practices instituted by landowners, as I will discuss below.[11] Nonetheless, the beliefs of agronomists and nobles about the importance of science in everyday life on the estate played an important role in understandings of the larger role of the nobility in imperial Russia. Although we can have little confidence that widespread reform of farming was taking place, attitudes that celebrated new techniques were widespread. Michael Confino's study of activists of the St. Petersburg Free Economic Society in the eighteenth century convincingly demonstrates that this small group of nobles, at least, failed to understand basic economic principles and that this severely limited the possibilities for successful reform on their estates.[12] Reformers of the eighteenth and early nineteenth centuries, as described by Confino, attempted to institute the appearance of order and efficiency through numerous rules and a militaristic approach to management. Of course, the peasantry resisted such hyperregulation of their lives, which led to disillusionment and a loss of faith in the potential of rational reform. As I argue in my book on the provincial gentry, by the second quarter of the nineteenth century, proprietors, while still failing to grasp basic concepts of profitability, earnestly defended the adoption of rational and scientific principles connected specifically with production. Their commitment to these notions of science and rationalism on the estate, even in the face of limited practical reform, reflects beliefs about the everyday importance of the presence of the nobility on estates in the nineteenth century.

Agronomic writers of the first half of the nineteenth century addressed an audience of high state officials (and even Tsar Nicholas), on the one hand, as they made a career of influencing state agricultural policy, and an audience of literate provincial nobles, on the other. Many of them defended serfdom and Russian national character.[13] In addition, they refrained from attacking provincial gentry landholders as lazy or stupid—after all, these people formed a large part of their potential audience. What did agronomic writers believe the provincial gentry were doing on their estates? What, in their analyses, did such nobles care about? And finally, what unexplored possibilities might provincial landowners discover with some changes to their everyday practices on their estates? In articles both in the provincial newspapers and in independent publications, proponents of a meaningful life of work on the estate revealed their understandings of the everyday, at least for the elite, in the provinces. This provided a positive alternative to those who derided country life as idiotic and also resonated with local discourses that challenged literary and urban stereotypes of life in the country.

The Tver' provincial newspaper, the *Tverskie Gubernskie Vedomosti,* provides a wealth of information about provincial life in the second quarter of the nineteenth century. Founded in 1839 by the imperial government, the newspaper included an official section with information such as gentry arrivals and departures from Tver', as well as an unofficial section that often featured long articles on subjects such as local history and homeopathic medicine. The newspaper allows us to imagine some everyday concerns of the provincial gentry. These include prices of labor, reports of runaway serfs, lost documents, rates of ruble conversion (silver/assignats), new publications, the announcement of gentry elections, news of fires, and the previous week's weather. The paper also included agricultural information of many types, suggesting that provincial readers were indeed engaged with farming on an everyday basis. Information on navigating the state bureaucracy, such as rules for the use of stamped paper, suggests an audience not perfectly familiar with government procedures. Following a list of children admitted to government educational institutions, detailed instructions are given for students (when to arrive, what kinds of qualifications were required on arrival, etc.). In sum, the imagined audience appears to be those less familiar with the apparatus of empire— nobles primarily resident in the countryside. It is this representation of their everyday concerns that provides a context for the larger agronomic debates.[14]

Article authors at times exhort readers to take an interest in improving their incomes, suggesting that such attention would benefit Russian society as a whole. For example, in an article from Saturday, March 30, 1840, entitled "The Vocation of Those Zealous for the Public Good," Admiral Count Mordvinov, the president of the Free Economic Society (VEO), contrasted expensive charitable outlays for the building of hospitals and other institutions with the profitable investment of capital in the improvement of agricultural techniques. He concluded that the latter had more benefit for society, with advantages "for all levels of the people: for the nobleman, merchant, artisan and peasant." For the nobility, specifically, such investment would increase income. The author went on to encourage the foundation of provincial societies along the lines of the VEO and to suggest the possibility of improvements in gardens, farm machinery, animal husbandry, the draining of swamps, and banks, among other innovations. Couched as advice on how to make the most effective charitable contributions, Mordvinov's article appealed to the pecuniary motives of provincial landowners as well.[15]

On Saturday, September 21, 1840, in the Supplement to the Tver' paper, appeared an article by Grigorii Iatsenkov that analyzed the current state of land use in Russia. This article specifically addressed the three-field system, still widely used in Russia, and contrasted it with the development over the previous fifty years of new techniques in other parts of Europe. In particular, the author advocated for a four-field system, which was popular in Germany and, more recently, in the Baltic provinces and which a few "enlightened and solicitous landowners" had tried to implement in central Russia "with more or less success." In spite of some difficulties, always connected with new undertakings, the author contended, the system was continuing its spread. In arguing against the three-field system, the author described "our ancestors" as using the three-field system "time out of mind" and described Russian agriculture as in a state of "infancy." He also cited the loss of income, which he described as a creeping phenomenon affecting all landholders, as motivation for change.[16]

Other articles in the newspaper focused on the gentry household, discussing medicine or preserving. One article, from Saturday, March 16, 1840, discussed chronic, intermittent fever in the "common man." This article purported to explain the common people's understanding of the causes and cures of fever, comparing it with "our" understanding of methods of curing a cold. The article outlined accepted methods for curing intermittent fever without, however, condemning folk remedies, which appear to have been largely homeopathic.[17] Another article, reprinted on March 4, 1839, cited many doctors, including a number of foreigners, in communicating medical advice for combating toothache.[18] On June 3, 1839, the paper warned against using a particular cheese for food unless cooked, due to "fatal consequences."[19] These articles addressed the ignorant but interested reader, communicating scientific approaches to everyday problems on the estate and introducing new techniques for dealing with the perennial difficulties of illnesses and household maintenance.

In publishing such articles (and many others appear in the period under discussion), the newspaper assumes that readers are engaged with farming and household management sufficiently to read them but suggests that readers have little modern scientific training and need substantial instruction in order to improve their harvests or housekeeping. Authors appeal to readers' charitable and patriotic instincts as well as to their economic motivations. Scholarly literature suggests that provincial landlords in the second quarter of the nineteenth century were under increasing financial pressure as income from estates dwindled and expenses mounted.[20] In this period, success in government service and society required more investment in children, in particular through education.[21] The consumer economy of Europe more generally also provided more opportunity for expenditure, leading landowners to search for more liquid capital.[22] Certainly, authors of the time appear to imagine an audience resident on estates and looking for new ways to increase income. These readers were literate and capable of purchasing equipment and developing farm techniques but were deemed unfamiliar with scientific literature. For these writers, the role of "enlightened" landowners was to spread knowledge, whether through the publication of articles or, as authors frequently recommended, through the establishment of profitable farming along modern lines on their estates.

Advocates of reform of agricultural practices also published in agronomic and husbandry journals such as the popular *Agricultural Newspaper, Agricultural Journal, Notes on Estate/Household Management, Journal for Sheep-Breeders, Journal of Horse-Breeding and Hunting,* and so on.[23] Some also wrote stand-alone works containing detailed and elaborate programs for improving Russian agriculture, complete with international comparisons. Noted author and advisor to the imperial government D. P. Shelekhov wrote several works, among them *The People's Guidance in Agriculture, A Course in Empirical Russian Agriculture,* and *The Principal Bases of Agriculture.*[24] In these works he addressed readers in a style similar to those used by writers in the provincial newspaper. In *The People's Guidance,* Shelekhov argued for the adoption of a five-field system primarily in the interests of encouraging landowners to invest capital in improving their estates. Although he also raised questions of national importance, such as improving the security of the Russian people with improved yields, Shelekhov attempted to sell his method on the financial benefits accruing to progressive farmers. A defender of serfdom, Shelekhov at the same time advocated the improvement of peasant agricultural skills and even the independence of peasants along the lines of tenant farmers. (How this would differ from *obrok,* or "quitrent," is not clear.) Like other agronomic writers, Shelekhov addressed his works to an audience imagined as male, emphasizing both the Enlightenment ideal of the scientific man and the educated reader of serious national publications. Although women participated in both of these spheres, as well as managing their own property during this period, sometimes quite actively (thus appearing in court documents and even occasionally in agronomic literature), the language of the publications is gendered male and puts forth a masculinist model of the ideal cultivator.[25] Such a person, educated, active, decisive and hardworking, Shelekhov was sure, would receive quick results on putting the plan into action—within three years, according to one work.[26]

Agronomists seem to have been prone, however, to exaggerating the success of agronomic experiments. Shelekhov came under fire in the 1820s for claims that his estates, as well as those of two other local landowners, Ral' and Ladyzhenskii, operated under a new system of crop rotation. The

finance minister, Count Egor Kankrin, ordered investigation of these estates, with the response from local officials that Shelekhov's claims to have
reformed were fictional. However, these observations were performed in
the winter.[27] Claims about revolutionary agricultural innovations appear
to have less to do with the practice of everyday life than with beliefs about
the meaning of everyday life. Writers focused on the attitude and intentions of the proprietor rather than on practical success in implementing
change, with an emphasis on the enlightened outlook of the landowner.
Such an understanding of the proprietor's role helps to illuminate part
of the experience of everyday life for those nobles living full-time in the
country. Absent the self-evident national importance of service in the
imperial bureaucracy or military forces, local landowners might justify
their "small" lives in terms of the structural importance of their day-to-day
activities on the estate as well as their function in spreading enlightenment. Whether their engagement with farming or progressive projects had
any concrete effect, the availability of the agronomic discourse promoted
their sense of importance in an increasingly sophisticated national context
from which they might otherwise appear to deviate too dramatically.

Where do peasants appear in this story? Serf owners might accomplish practical recommendations only with the cooperation of their labor
force, one notorious for its resistance to innovation. Everyday farming
as depicted by proponents of rational agronomy frequently avoids mention of labor management or relations between serfs and owners. Yet the
newspaper regularly published reports of runaway serfs as well as prices
for hired labor for transport or farmwork. Most agronomic advice seems
to fit into a genre focused on science and rationality, appealing on behalf of
the empire to provincials and offering them the possibility of participation
in the sophisticated projects of advancing knowledge. It thus seems rather
removed from a more practical analysis of the everyday life of provincial
landowners. Agronomic writers appear to regard provincial nobles as perfectly capable of devoting hours to the study and then implementation of
new processes, in short, as relatively unoccupied under the current regime.
This would seem to conform with the city attitude of country-dwellers as
stagnant.

Court papers and the correspondence of the provincial marshal of the
gentry, however, reveal the extent of actual interaction with serfs to have

been considerable. In a period of growing interest in abolition, concerns about abuse of serfs generated interest even at the highest levels: Nicholas I, for example, banned the breakup of serf families through sale. Provincial serf owners, however, strongly defended a system they defined as reflecting the paternalistic care needed by the poor serfs.[28] One serf owner, defending himself from a government investigation into his management practices, alleged that laziness and violent insubordination on the part of his peasants forced him to take violent measures himself.[29] The provincial marshal of the gentry backed his claims.[30] Memoirs and belles lettres, such as the works of Tolstoy, Turgenev, Gogol, and Goncharov as well as lesser-known memoirs such as those by M. K. Arnol'd, Prince Meshcherskii, Aleksandra Ishimova, and "The Englishwoman in Russia," testify to the commonsense notion that interaction between serfs and landlords was ongoing and multifaceted.[31]

How can one reconcile the popularity of apparently theoretical agricultural writing with the divergent experience of everyday life on the estate? I think that this divergence was only marginally relevant to the way provincial nobles understood their rural lives. Even if not reflective of day-to-day farming practices, the availability of interpretations that allowed for important and meaningful work on the estate enabled many provincial gentry men and women to imagine their lives in the country as having a significance beyond the local district. A variety of sources can shed light on the web of explanatory meanings through which nobles negotiated their lives in the country. Among the available discourses lay the progressive outlook expounded by agronomic and scientific writers as well as the aristocratic focus on the picturesque and the refreshing, or, alternately, on the ignorant and the squalid. Provincials wanted to combat metropolitan attempts to lump them together as backwater failures. Positive and activist representations of everyday life in the country allowed landowners more scope to determine the deep meaning and importance of life on the provincial estate to the empire as a whole. A justification of useful private life on the estate helped nobles to make the case for the continued importance of their class to the empire and thus for their legal privileges and their continued power over peasants and others in the provinces. The nobles' traditional role in state service was extended, in this view, to encompass their private work on provincial estates.

The exercise of individual agency in action or interpretation remains controversial among scholars of culture, with some insisting on the all-powerful force of discourses or structures. Rather than make a case here for or against the possibility of individual freedom, I'll simply posit that the narrative or feeling of experience often includes this possibility, even among those with less power. Giovanni Levi's suggestion that people make independent choices, within limits, from among available discourses is particularly appealing.[32] Whether or not scholars, operating at a remove particularly evident to historians of the more distant past, accept the possibility of real action on the part of individuals, people's accounts often reflect a belief in such agency. Thus it behooves us to examine the possibility of meaningful choice, because daily life is often experienced in this way. The examination of the imagination of independent action in everyday life, even if the independence of the actors proved to be illusory, would still form an important part of our studies.

Focusing attention on understandings of ordinary life, even without significant evidence about practice, can lend great insight into understandings of everyday life in provincial Russia. Insofar as provincial Russians formed their self-understandings from everyday experience as well as education, reading habits, and so on, representations from reformers played an important role. By the middle of the nineteenth century, nobles believed the countryside could provide a site of progressive labor, rather than remaining simply a cesspool of laziness and parasitism, if they directed their attention to the management of household, land, and peasants. Serfdom, they believed, posed no obstacle to an improved regime in the countryside, provided that enlightened paternalism ruled the day. (Nobles believed that petty and vicious serf owners, not the system, posed the danger, as I have argued elsewhere.)[33] In this view, the work of the provincial gentry, even in the service of its private interests, furthered social and state interests as well, giving nobles reason to feel comfortable with their residence in the countryside.

Even in the 1870s of *Anna Karenina*, following the watershed of the emancipation of the serfs, this latter view found its partisans. Although most nobles living and working in Moscow and St. Petersburg, like Koznyshev, continued to regard the country as a sleepy idyll, many others, some of them, like Levin, quite wealthy, espoused the rural realm as an arena of useful work. Such nobles would engage more energetically in politics, too, as the century wore on.[34] Although the degree of actual agronomic change wrought on estates or in peasant-landowner relations is most certainly doubtful (and even in the postemancipation period the gentry experienced great difficulty investing in estates, generally preferring to sell off its land), these representations held great importance for everyday life, for it was within these understandings that rural nobles imagined the ongoing strategic importance of their everyday provincial existence.

NOTES

1. Leo Tolstoy, *Anna Karenina,* trans. Louise and Aylmer Maude (Oxford: Oxford University Press, 1995), 237.

2. Although the viewpoints mentioned here to some extent reflect the influence of self-representations drawn from the English gentry, on the one hand, and the French nobility, on the other, Russian nobles developed a unique understanding of their role in the countryside. Thomas Newlin, in *The Voice in the Garden: Andrei Bolotov and the Anxieties of Russian Pastoral, 1738–1833* (Evanston, Ill.: Northwestern University Press, 2001) discusses the ambivalence of the provincial writer and polymath Andrei Bolotov and others toward rural life. See also my *Nests of the Gentry* (Newark: University of Delaware Press, 2007).

3. Michel de Certeau, *The Practice of Everyday Life,* trans. Steven F. Rendall (Berkeley: University of California Press, 1984); Sheila Fitzpatrick, *Everyday Stalinism: Ordinary Life in Extraordinary Times* (Oxford: Berg, 2002).

4. Alf Lütdke, introduction to *The History of Everyday Life,* trans. William Templer (Princeton, N.J.: Princeton University Press, 1995).

5. See David Ransel's essay in this volume, "The Scholarship of Everyday Life," for an excellent overview.

6. Stephen Hoch, *Serfdom and Social Control in Russia* (Chicago: University of Chicago Press, 1986). Hoch discusses much of the Russian-language literature on the topic of peasant life in the imperial period.

7. See the last chapter of Andreas Schönle, *The Ruler in the Garden: Politics and Landscape Design in Imperial Russia* (Bern: Peter Lang, 2007).

8. A. B. Kamenskii, *Povsednevnost' russkikh gorodskikh obyvatelei: Istoricheskie anekdoty iz provintsial'noi zhizni XVIII veka* (Moscow: RGGU, 2006). Kamenskii also provides an in-depth discussion of Russian, American, and European historiography on the subject of everyday life, among other topics, in his introduction.

9. John Randolph, *The House in the Garden* (Ithaca, N.Y.: Cornell University Press, 2007); David L. Ransel, *A Russian Merchant's Tale: The Life and Adventures of Ivan Alekseevich Tolchënov, Based on His Diary* (Bloomington: Indiana University Press, 2009).

10. Such as those explored by Priscilla Roosevelt in *Life on the Russian Country Estate* (New Haven, Conn.: Yale University Press, 1995) and Douglas Smith in *The Pearl* (New Haven, Conn.: Yale University Press, 2008).

11. As David Ransel points out, Soviet scholars were able to determine that commercialization of estates was taking place in some regions of nineteenth-century Russia. This topic is beyond the scope of this chapter, but in Tver' province it appears that landlords were more likely to pursue manufacturing enterprises than to introduce new crops, rotation techniques, and so on, as I discuss in *Nests of the Gentry*.

12. Michael Confino, *Domaines et seigneurs en Russie vers la fin du XVIIIe siècle: Étude de structures agraires et de mentalités économiques* (Paris: Institut d'Études Slaves de l'Université de Paris, 1963).

13. For example, see D. P. Shelekhov, *Narodnoe rukovodstvo v sel'skom khoziastve* (St. Petersburg: Tip. A. Smirdina, 1838–39).

14. *Tverskie Gubernskie Vedomosti* (*TGV*), 1839–55. The newspaper consisted of two parts, the Official section and the Supplement.

15. *TGV*, Saturday, March 30, 1840, Official sec., 95–97.

16. *TGV*, Saturday, September 21, 1840, Supplement, 167–69.

17. *TGV*, Saturday, March 16, 1840, Supplement, 32–36.

18. *TGV*, Saturday, March 4, 1839, Supplement, 47.

19. *TGV*, Saturday, June 3, 1839, Official sec., 146.

20. Michael Confino, among others, discusses financial pressure on the nobility. See his *Société et mentalités collectives en Russie sous l'Ancien Régime* (Paris: Institut d'Études Slaves, 1991).

21. Shelekhov, *Narodnoe rukovodstvo*, 28–29.

22. Vasilii Preobrazhenskii, *Opisanie Tverskoi Gubernii v sel'sko-khoziaistvennom otnoshenii* (St. Petersburg: Tip. Ministerstva Gosudarstvennykh Imushchestv, 1854), 114, 277; Baron August von Haxthausen, *The Russian Empire: Its People, Institutions, and Resources*, trans. Robert Faire (London: Frank Cass & Co., 1968), 111, 118; Shelekhov, *Narodnoe rukovodstvo*, 26–29. Norbert Elias describes similar difficulties for the French nobility of an earlier period. See his *The Court Society*, trans. Edmund Jephcott (New York: Pantheon Books, 1983).

23. In Russian, *Zemledel'cheskaia gazeta*, *Zemledel'cheskii zhurnal*, *Khoziaistvennye zapiski*, *Zhurnal dlia ovtsevodov*, and *Zhurnal konnozavodstva i okhoty*, respectively.

24. *Narodnoe rukovodstvo v sel'skom khoziaistve*, *Kurs opytnogo russkogo sel'skogo khoziaistva*, and *Glavnye osnovaniia zemledeliia*.

25. Michelle Marrese discusses noblewomen's property management in her *A Woman's Kingdom: Noblewomen and the Control of Property in Russia, 1700–1861* (Ithaca, N.Y.: Cornell University Press, 2002).

26. Shelekhov, *Narodnoe rukovodstvo*.

27. Gosudarstvennyi Arkhiv Tverskoi Oblasti (State Archive of the Tver' Region, Tver') (GATO), fond 59, op. 1, d. 975, ll. 1–80b.

28. Cavender, *Nests of the Gentry*, chaps. 2, 3.

29. GATO, fond 103, op. 1, d. 2590, ll. 1–50.

30. GATO, fond 672, op. 1, d. 725, ll. 1–20.

31. The works of the well-known novelists are widely available; I provide here the references for the memoirs mentioned in the text. M. K. Arnol'd, "Vospominaniia M. K. Arnol'da (1819–1833)," *Golos Minuvshego*, no. 2 (1917); A Lady, *The Englishwoman in Russia* (New York: Arno Press and the New York Times, 1970); Prince A. V. Meshcherskii, *Iz moei stariny: Vospominaniia kniazia Aleksandra Vasil'evicha Meshcherskogo* (Moscow: Universitetskaia

tipografiia, 1901); Aleksandra Ishimova, *Kanikuly 1844 goda, ili poezdka v Moskvy* (St. Petersburg: Tip. Imp. AN, 1846).

32. Giovanni Levi, "On Microhistory," in *New Perspectives on Historical Writing,* ed. Peter Burke (University Park: Pennsylvania State University Press, 1991), 93–113.

33. I discuss this in more detail in chapters 2 and 3 of *Nests of the Gentry.*

34. Roberta Manning, *The Crisis of the Old Order in Russia: Gentry and Government* (Princeton, N.J.: Princeton University Press, 1982); I. A. Khristoforov, *"Aristokraticheskaia" oppozitsiia Velikim reformam. Konets 1850–seredina 1870-kh gg.* (Moscow: Russkoe Slovo, 2002).

Resisting Resistance

Everyday Life, Practical Competence, and Neoliberal Rhetoric in Postsocialist Russia

OLGA SHEVCHENKO

The notion of "everyday life" seems to hold an instantaneous, almost intuitive, appeal for ethnographically inclined observers whose interest in lived experience thrives in the investigation of quotidian details. I share this fascination with the "everyday," but I must start this chapter on a skeptical note: I am not entirely sure what "everyday life" means.[1]

My reservations arise from the difficulty of creating a working definition of everyday life that is simultaneously narrow and rigorous and that does not smuggle in a number of problematic assumptions.

Approaches to defining the everyday often begin at one of three interrelated points: a dubiously bounded range of subjects (usually "the powerless"), a particular way of looking (the everyday as the repository of resistance), or an arbitrarily predefined range of topics (such as leisure, consumption, morals and manners, or another interest of the author). None of these points is wholly satisfactory, yet we would be throwing the baby out with the bathwater if we tried to avoid the range of topics and questions usually lumped together under the rubric of "the everyday." It is better that we carve out a more precise working definition of the everyday while taking care not to load it with value-laden assumptions that burden the notion by default. I would like to outline and critique these problematic assumptions using my own work on everyday life in postsocialist Russia as an illustration.

Current work on everyday life owes much to the German tradition of history of the everyday (*Alltagsgeschichte*), which is most often taken to mean "history from below"—an investigation into the lives of "historical 'losers'" or into "nonestablishment views of the processes of change."[2] This interest in history from the ground up has yielded rich results, but as a definition of the everyday it appears deficient because it seems to treat everyday life as a class category. In other words, it implicitly presumes that historical "winners"—economic elites, intellectuals, or members of the political establishment—have no everyday life of their own.

Aside from sneaking assumptions about social class into a category that should not be limited in this manner, we also risk embracing a number of problematic dichotomies, such as the above-mentioned "losers" and "winners" (with seemingly little space needed for anything in-between) or—perhaps more insidiously—between domination and resistance.[3] While numerous Alltagsgeschichte studies avoid this danger (e.g., Alf Lüdtke offers the example of studies on everyday life under Nazism that unveiled how deeply "ordinary people" were implicated in the support of Nazi ideology), sociological inquiries into the everyday tend to take seriously Everett Hughes's dictum to "elevate the humble, humble the proud" and proceed in its spirit.[4]

As a result, sociological studies of the everyday often suffer from limitations imposed by what John Roberts called the "redemptive model" of the everyday.[5] In this model, everyday life as a focus of inquiry designates not so much a bounded range of subjects (the powerless) but a particular way of looking, one that tends to emphasize the spontaneous, subversive, and antiauthoritarian character of daily practices. Traditionally deemed marginal and unimportant, these daily practices are taken to represent acts of resistance to the dominant rhetoric and official codes of behavior.

In its American formulation, this "redemptive model" is best exemplified by the work of James Scott, whose approach to the everyday combines it with the class-based principle that I mentioned above.[6] Scott interprets everyday discursive forms (such as anecdotes, rumors, jokes, etc.) and rituals of subordinate groups as acts of their collective resistance to domination. Denied the "luxury of direct confrontation," Scott argues, these groups follow elaborate strategies in order to express themselves in disguised and indirect forms.[7] The multifaceted and polyvocal character of everyday life makes it particularly suited for diffusing resistance, channeling it through a multiplicity of alternative acts and even masquerading it as compliance.

As far as Scott identifies everyday life with the practices of resistance among subordinate classes and social groups, this notion of the everyday appears far too narrow. But it can also, paradoxically, turn out to be too broad, as happens when the everyday is taken to designate the transformative and creative potential of daily life, as is often assumed in the French tradition of the *sociologie de la vie quotidienne:* "The everyday is platitude (what lags and falls behind, the residual life with which our trash cans and cemeteries are filled: scrap and refuse); but this banality is also what is most important, if it brings us back to existence in its very spontaneity and as it is lived—in the moment, when, lived, it escapes every speculative formulation, perhaps all coherence, all regularity."[8]

Maurice Blanchot (as well as Guy Debord, Henri Lefebvre, and others) sees individuals' ability for creative action as part and parcel of the structure of everyday life, with the latter being viewed as a benign and utopian space capable of preserving the human potential of individuals against the cold embrace of modernity with its propensity to "turn the world into prose."[9]

The trouble with uncritically adopting this vision as a starting point for a study of everyday life is that it offers no guidance for what everyday life is, with the consequence that it can be practically anything in which a trace of spontaneity can be detected. There are numerous studies of consumption, popular culture and the media, habits, morals and manners, and so on in which "the creative powers of the consumer [are seen to] operate freely in the heartlands of mass culture."[10] But they typically don't offer compelling reasons for why these, as opposed to any other fields of practice, should be considered constitutive of "the everyday," leaving one to wonder whether "everyday life" excludes anything at all.

After traveling in these concentric circles, we then arrive at the paradoxical conclusion that "everyday life" seems simultaneously too narrow and too broad a term. All of this was very much on my mind when I was doing the fieldwork for what eventually became my book, in which I talked with Muscovites from various walks of life about their experience of the postsocialist transformation.[11] While I started telling both my subjects and myself that I was interested in the changing structures of everyday life, the breadth of that term, as well as the multiple assumptions with which it was laden, quickly became apparent and unsettling. At the same time, the term seemed to make immediate sense to my Russian interlocutors, for whom the sphere of the everyday—or *byt,* or *povsednevnost'*—referred to all those tasks of running the household and making ends meet that suddenly became so problematic after 1991. Perhaps more importantly (and flying in the face of visions of the everyday as a class category), conversations about post-Soviet byt appeared to cut across social and economic boundaries, providing the same currency of sociability as baseball in America and weather in Great Britain. In other words, while there was no doubt that the post-Soviet era affected everyone differently, my interlocutors seemed to assume a layer of shared meaning and discourse on what the changes entailed for everyday life and on what it took to stay afloat in their midst.

This assumption of a shared, commonsense understanding is exactly what Harold Garfinkel examines in his writing on the indexicality of social behavior when he observes that every social interaction is premised on a tacit agreement of the participants not to question the nature and properties of the surrounding context in which issues are embedded.[12] This observation might explain why I found it so hard to part with the notion of everyday life despite all of its problems, for it points out that some aspects of life, at any time and place, are marked as self-evident and are expected to be mastered by any member of a given social group. These are areas of what I came to call "practical competence," the social stock of knowledge that all reasonable people can be expected to understand and that is, of course, in fact all but self-evident.[13] Rather, it is an outcome of a complex process in which particular aspects of reality are highlighted, institutionalized, and marked as important and relevant while others are de-emphasized. This process is both cognitive and institutional and thus invites questions about the mechanisms through which a particular symbolic universe, and, with it, a particular definition of practical competence, comes to take precedence.

A question framed in terms of practical competence, then, shares some of the elements that I have mentioned in my cursory review of approaches to everyday life (e.g., an interest in the paradoxical coexistence of banality and spontaneity in daily practices), but it is more explicitly centered on the nexus between the cognitive and the institutional, on how particular structural conditions both inform and reflect taken-for-granted definitions of what constitutes a practically competent person. In their article on everyday life in Cameroon, Achille Mbembe and Janet Roitman articulate this connection between the cognitive and the institutional when they remark that any approach to a social crisis needs to pay attention to the "regime of subjectivity" that it forms through concentrating on "a shared ensemble of imaginary configurations of 'everyday life,' imaginaries which have a material basis; and systems of intelligibility to which people refer in order to construct a more or less clear idea of the causes of phenomena and their effects, to determine the domain of what is possible and feasible, as well as the logics of efficacious action."[14] Using their terms, I was after both the postsocialist "regime of subjectivity" and the material or, rather, social-structural basis that informed it.

One thing that the notion of practical competence does not presume is the intention of resistance through everyday life. Indeed, I will try to show that the post-Soviet definitions of practical competence turned out, albeit unintentionally, to be rather compatible, if not with the neoliberal market reforms that were introduced in the early 1990s, then with the forms of neoliberal political subjectivity that followed in their wake.[15] In a further ironic twist, the one notion that invited resistance in the postsocialist cultural context was the notion of resistance itself, that is, the assumption that the obligations of citizenship somehow entail a readiness to adopt and enact an oppositional stance. If anything, a competent postsocialist subject could be first and foremost recognized by his or her political disengagement and readiness to leave, as I frequently heard it formulated, "politics to politicians."

"THE STATE OWES ME NOTHING, AND I OWE NOTHING TO THE STATE"

Let us drink to our attachment to our country, . . . to the minimum of contacts with power, with medicine, with the police, with the press, with television, with wherever we may learn the things we'd rather not know.
— Mikhail Zhvanetskii[16]

Pierre Bourdieu summarized the neoliberal political project as "*a pro-gramme of the methodical destruction of collectives,*" which is achieved, among other things, by "the imposition everywhere, in the upper spheres of the economy and the state as at the heart of corporations, of that sort of moral Darwinism that, with the cult of the winner, schooled in higher mathe-matics and bungee jumping, institutes the struggle of all against all and *cynicism* as the norm of all action and behavior."[17]

The fieldwork for my book was done very far from the upper spheres of the economy and the state,[18] and I had little interest in or expectation to encounter the species of the Russian neoliberal that Alexei Yurchak has described in his work on the culture of business in the new Russia.[19] Indeed, while the popularity of bungee jumping might be on the rise in Russia, the most interesting way to deploy Bourdieu's definition in the context of postsocialist Russia might be not the descriptive but the pre-scriptive one. By this I mean to say that, although neoliberal economic axioms of free markets and free trade may remain controversial for many, and although Yurchak's "true careerists" may be few and far between, the prescriptive model of subjectivity that Bourdieu describes resonates in important ways with the model of post-Soviet practical competence that is shared far beyond the upper spheres of the economy and the state.

This was evidenced, for example, in the spontaneous reader reactions to a recent newspaper column in the popular daily *Moskovskii Komsomolets* written by the journalist Yulia Kalinina.[20] Responding to the suggestion offered by President Dmitri Medvedev to Russian millionaires on the eve of September 1, 2011, in which he invited them to visit Russian schools with a lesson on "how to achieve success in life," Kalinina attempted to specu-late on what such a lesson would look like. Her hypothetical millionaire arrives at the school in an armored Mercedes with bodyguards and, after a comprehensive search of the school staff for firearms and explosives, starts his lesson by offering the following recipe for success: "Rob and steal, and if someone objects, beat the hell out of him." The list of pointers goes on in the same spirit and ends with, "Remember, children, man is wolf to his fellow man."

The online comments the column received were overwhelmingly en-thusiastic: Kalinina's readers found the satire not only accurate but also fair, and one of the commentators extended the column's logic further by suggesting that "the only thing left to mention [was that] those who are unable to follow such 'recipes for success' are the so-called 'losers,' i.e. misfits."[21] While this reader did not miss the satirical tone of the column and was far from morally endorsing the offered "recipe for success," this response also indicated that she or he considered the fault lines between the "winners" and "losers" in postsocialism to be roughly equivalent to the line separating "wolves" from "men" and that, consequently, anyone interested in leading a successful life in Russia could not dismiss the millionaire's advice.

How does this admittedly extreme rhetorical position translate into Mbembe and Roitman's domain of everyday notions of "what is possible and feasible, as well as the logics of efficacious action," if it translates at all? To explore this question, let me dwell for a moment on the politics of the Russian playground. I spent much of 2007–8 in Russia, where I was doing fieldwork for a study of family photography and generational memories of socialism. My infant daughter and my husband relocated with me, and, due to Mila, I got to spend quite a few hours of my sabbatical outdoors, on the playground located in a park just across the street from where we lived. On one particular April morning, Mila was in an especially rambunctious mood, and before I had any chance to protest, I witnessed her rapidly expropriating sandbox equipment from one of her toddler playmates and throwing it as far out of the sandbox as her eighteen-month-old throwing skills allowed. The culture of the Russian playground is generally noninterventionist, with parents (mostly mothers and grandmothers) sitting on the benches and observing from a distance while their offspring sort things out amongst themselves. But the infringement seemed grave enough, and I leaped to the victim's defense while offering apologies for Mila's bossy ways to the little girl's mother. "Don't worry," the young woman generously reassured me with a casual gesture. "That's a good thing. That's how one should be these days." Grateful as I was for her giving me a way "out" of the situation, I protested that, while assertiveness was a good thing, aggressiveness was not. But the girl's mother simply shrugged her shoulders and reiterated, "I don't know, I would be happy if I were you. She will not let herself be bossed around."

In singling out a child's ability to stand up for herself as a particularly useful character trait, this young mother was not alone. Indeed, a national survey conducted in the same year by the polling agency Levada Center found that "the ability to stand up for one's own interests" and "the ability to achieve one's goals" were the two single most important qualities that respondents wanted to develop in their children (by contrast, "love of learning" ranked seventh, down two points from an identical survey conducted in 1998).[22] But while these aspirations might sound similar to the cult of the winner decried by Bourdieu, my contention is not that they are in some fundamental way inherently "neoliberal." Instead, I would like to suggest that post-Soviet standards of practical competence and political subjectivity have origins that are far from Bourdieu's "hearts of corporations": they can be traced both to the Soviet-era political imagination and in the more recent social and cultural dislocations. However, despite their local origin, these sensibilities do align surprisingly neatly with a number of values Bourdieu associates with a neoliberal outlook (aggressive emphasis on personal autonomy and self-sufficiency, the "cult of the winner" at all costs, a moral legitimation of inequality, and an aggressive pursuit of self-interest, to name a few). As a result, they may indeed be co-opted to facilitate the acceptance by the population of the ongoing neoliberal political and economic reforms on the national level.

My argument goes against the grain of the resilient master narrative, which describes postsocialist political subjects in terms of their supposedly entrenched paternalism. Barely reconstructed *Homo sovieticus*, so the criticism goes, was all too ready to trust the state with solutions to all major social problems, all the while having no aptitude or desire to take responsibility for his or her own life. Drawing on nearly ten years' worth of ethnographic fieldwork in several Russian cities and towns, I suggest that this criticism is inaccurate on several levels. First of all, even in the last decades of socialism, paternalistic rhetoric went hand in hand not only with frequent cases of de facto self-reliance but also with the tendency to view autonomy and self-interest as a measure of cultural and class distinction. Second, and more importantly, the cultural shifts that occurred after the fall of socialism further contributed to the legitimation of inequality and to the attractions of autonomy and personal independence as the new ideology of citizenship.

The ways in which the policies of the Soviet state underlay the current tendency to dismiss egalitarianism and concern with social justice as signs of residual Soviet mentality are well discussed by Michele Rivkin-Fish.[23]

Rivkin-Fish is concerned with the recent embrace of inequality in Russia, and she traces its roots to the late Soviet conflation between class
and moral caliber, which can be seen, among other places, in the popular
reception of the film *Heart of a Dog* (1988). Based on the satirical novel
by Mikhail Bulgakov (1925), the film tells the story of a well-intentioned
surgeon, Professor Preobrazhensky, who in the course of a medical experiment transforms a loveable mutt into a vulgar and aggressive human
being of unmistakably proletarian provenance. The story chronicles the
ease with which this crass "human" rises to prominence in the new Soviet society, eventually turning against his educated and well-intentioned
benefactor, whom he threatens to denounce as an "alien class element."

Rivkin-Fish points out that the film's main character, Professor Preobrazhensky, is taken by her contemporary informants to represent both the
historical fate of pre-Soviet Russian intelligentsia and the traits of character that were lost with the elevation of "uncultured," uneducated social
classes to positions of social prominence after 1917. Chief among these
features are a sense of earned privilege, disdain for state intervention,
and a fundamental insistence on one's personal autonomy that borders on
demonstrative disengagement. In one of the most loved and often-cited
episodes of the film, the professor disdainfully refuses to buy a magazine
to benefit German war orphans, a move that was often cited to me during my own fieldwork in support of a point that a precondition for a good
society is that "everyone should be minding their own business."[24]

There is, of course, a world of difference between the principles espoused by Professor Preobrazhensky and the more brutal models of social
and moral Darwinism one encounters in today's Russia, even if the latter
may (and often do) cite Bulgakov for support.[25] What happens here is not
by any means direct lineage but rather a borrowing in which the fierce
individualism that often comprised the oppositional stance of a Soviet-
era intellectual gets deployed as a moral justification for radical social
disengagement in a dramatically different, post-Soviet setting.

An additional line of borrowing concerns class subjectivities. In the
1980s, when the film came out and generated a cult following, the earned and
morally justified privileges of the essentialized and much-mythologized
intelligentsia were pitted in opposition to the undeserved privileges of
the "proletariat." This "unnaturalness" of the postrevolutionary situation
bemoaned by Professor Preobrazhensky is now seen as a justification of

the naturalness of the rampant inequality and social disengagement of today. And the fact that the more brutal elements of the post-Soviet business outlook are reminiscent of the Soviet-era caricatures of capitalism, with their emphasis on aggressive competition, exploitation, and the "war of all against all," only contributes to the further naturalization of the new order. "Everything they told us about socialism was a lie," went a particularly pessimistic postsocialist joke. "But everything that they told us about capitalism was true."[26]

This brings me to my second theme—the ways in which the social and cultural transformations of the 1990s may have contributed to the appeal of neoliberal-sounding rhetoric in Russia. I would particularly like to concentrate on the allure of self-sufficiency to which this section's heading alludes (the quotation comes from an interview with an entrepreneur who did not seem in the least burdened by his disconnection from the state—or aware of the multiple ways in which this independence was imagined rather than real) and connect it to the question of freedom, both economic and political, as it was experienced in the immediate aftermath of the Soviet Union's collapse.

An irony that was not lost on many Russians is that, while the 1990s marked the end of strict ideological controls and censorship, most of them felt not more but less free in their everyday life. This came through clearly in the conversation I had in 1999 with Victor, who worked as a lathe operator at the ZIL factory.[27] Victor said, "In the very beginning of perestroika, a bit more freedom appeared. If a person wants to do something, no one would forbid him. Maybe there was even a little illegality at times, they would look the other way if you are breaking some regulation, as long as you're working. Before that, there was no possibility for small business to exist, none at all." And yet, economic freedom notwithstanding, Victor considered himself at the time peculiarly unfree: "Our freedom exists only in words, and as for reality . . . The mass media, they all depend financially on those who pay them. So they are not free, we have no freedom of the press, or of information. And as long as they are financially dependent, they will not be free. Even me, I may stand at my lathe at work and feel free, but I'm not. Because financially, I depend on the boss."

Victor was not alone in his sense that, despite—or, in many ways, because of—the expansion of the market, the individual freedoms of rank-and-file citizens shrank instead of expanding. This includes not only those the political scientists call "losers of the transition" but also the individuals who fared relatively well. For example, around the same time, Mikhail, a well-placed state bureaucrat in the Ministry of Construction, confessed to me that "until fifteen years ago, I was doing the things I wanted to do, and afterward, the things I was forced to do by external circumstances."

If we were to take Victor's words for what they are, his claim is that genuine freedom is impossible in the conditions of the market economy when "financially you depend on your boss." This statement is as far from the neoliberal rhetoric as one can possibly get, far enough to make Marx very happy, because its logical conclusion is that no genuine freedom is possible unless the institution of private property is abolished. Victor's politics, however, were far from communist, first of all because his views left space for enjoyment of purely economic freedom, the freedom to compete and consume, and second because they coexisted with an intensely private outlook, an emphasis on personal responsibility in providing for his family, and an outright dismissal of any political solutions. A supporter of Putin, Victor voted for him in both elections solely for pragmatic reasons: he wanted to avoid the second round of elections, which were bound, he was convinced, to squander taxpayer money. "One needs to work," he repeated, as if paraphrasing Professor Preobrazhensky. "Work at one's own workplace and not waste time on politics."

The broad resonance of Victor's sensibility in the early 2000s was particularly apparent in the coverage and treatment of the tenth anniversary of the 1991 putsch, which at the time inspired massive anticommunist resistance and heralded the end of the USSR. This event, which, as Andrei Zorin points out, originally had the potential to become a "regeneration myth, the myth of the people finally realizing their right to freedom, overcoming totalitarian tyranny and joining the rest of the world," by the late 1990s to early 2000s was commemorated solely as a moment of gullibility, the day, as Zorin puts it, "when we were all deceived."[28] At stake here was not only the disappointment with particular politicians (although that was certainly the case) but a broader reevaluation of the meaning and value of resistance and collective action.[29] "People will be defending their financial interests now, and not the political ones," proclaimed a twenty-six-year-old Muscovite cited in an anniversary article published in the popular daily *Moskovskii Komsomolets* in August 2001 under the telling title "God, How Naive We Had Been!"[30] My contacts agreed:

When this euphoria was with the White House . . . when Yeltsin invited everyone to defend democracy, and people came out . . . my husband's colleague from the university went, and they only found him several months later, killed. Can you imagine? There was such euphoria, people went to defend the White House, Yeltsin, but when they saw everything that followed—that's it, no one will go anymore. People are tired. . . . But the important part is that people understood that they were defending Yeltsin . . . and so what? . . . Nothing changed because of the change in government. And now it's not millions who go to these demonstrations but handfuls, and it's all because people understand the worth of this activity. They understood that politics isn't worth anything. Everyone should take care of their own business. If you chose the politicians, fine, they should think about the people, but they don't do it, they only look after their own interests. And now people have understood that and don't even go to vote. Instead, everyone started taking care of their own lives. They understood that if they don't take care of their lives, no one will.[31]

To understand how one gets from A to B, from the loss of freedom many experienced in the immediate aftermath of 1991 to the pragmatic self-reliance and disengagement, it is worthwhile to consider both in the light of another of Bourdieu's notions, that of *habitus hysteresis*. While the concept has been frequently and fruitfully used by many scholars of postsocialism, what interests me here is specifically a new angle it gives us on the question of freedom (or lack thereof). In the most basic terms, habitus hysteresis refers to a lack of fit between the individual's internal dispositions (the habitus) and the social conditions in which he finds himself.[32] Such a mismatch can happen in a variety of circumstances, both societal—in the conditions of social change when the logic of the entire social field radically shifts—and personal—as happens in cases of rapid social mobility when a person with the habitus and outlooks of, say, a petit bourgeois finds herself in a university setting where the institutional logic and the structure of expectations are different from those to which she is socialized. This concept makes it easier to understand why, despite all exterior signs of success, Mikhail had felt "forced to do things" ever since the late 1980s: when the logic of the field comes in conflict with the dispositions of the habitus, the experience is not unlike that of wearing a badly tailored dress or wrong-sized shoes, when every move is associated with the experience of discomfort and constraint, regardless of whether our hypothetical fashion victim makes it to the destination.

So how does this bear on the question of the meaning of individual freedom? According to Bourdieu, of course, individuals are never truly free, because they exist in a field of powerful social forces. But they can feel free, provided they do not experience the constraints of the structures that surround them as something alien. This is only possible when a person's habitus—her internal dispositions—correspond to the social field that exists around her. As soon as a mismatch between them is introduced, the constraints of the structure become apparent, and they do not feel natural anymore. In other words, contexts of social change, where social structure, channels of mobility, and criteria for success rapidly shift, make any talk of personal freedom highly problematic. Or, to be more precise, they make the personal lived experience of constraint and, hence, unfreedom so immediate that it can belie whatever appreciation one may or may not have for the more abstract and remote ideals of civil liberties.

Here we come to a point where we can understand why the questions of personal competence, control, and safety in the 1990s were so often articulated through the metaphors of separation, boundary maintenance, and disengagement. Everyone who has been to Moscow is familiar with the physical manifestations of this drive for autonomy—fences carving personal spaces and boundaries out of formerly public yards and passageways, makeshift car shelters, iron doors in formerly open arches and in building entryways, and so on. What I want to propose here is that these walls and partitions are the physical manifestations of the practices of autonomy and disengagement that are also evident elsewhere in broader public life, from the affirmations of self-interest to the distrust of collective action.[33] We may think about these actions of withdrawal and self-protection as, among other things, efforts to reestablish a sense of personal freedom by keeping the environment in check so that in one's immediate surroundings the logic of the social field is predictable and does not pose immediate threats to the habitus.

I would like to emphasize two key points here. First, the intended function of these arrangements has been, and remains, self-protection, not resistance. In other words, these physical and mental demarcations of autonomy emerged as "fortresses," not "weapons," of the weak, and as fortresses, they are in many ways parallel to similar exclusions and partitions that are employed on a grander scale by the newly formed elites, who are in a much better position to implement their visions in durable architectural forms. At the moment, the entire fabric of postsocialist cities is being reshaped by the many building projects pursuing the same logic of exclusion, privatization, and boundary maintenance at the expense of openness and publicity, a move that Ekaterina Makarova compellingly connected to the Soviet (and, I would add, post-Soviet) elevation of privacy as the last domain of personal freedom.[34] That this transformation of space is possible or at least palatable to those whom it excludes is because they, too, have unquestioningly pursued the logic of autonomy in their daily lives.

Second, the processes that may have started as compensatory with time become institutionalized and naturalized. While the Muscovites I spoke with in the late 1990s framed their actions and choices as historically specific responses to a catastrophic social upheaval, the young mother I cited above seemed to take the "winner takes all" morality as a given. The same spirit pervades a comment by well-known Russian writer Viacheslav Pietsukh, who in an interview remarked that "the chief life's work of any cultured person, both today and before, is a complete self-isolation from Russian reality."[35] While the sense of frustration with the structure of political opportunities is palpable in this statement, it is difficult to imagine a stance less suited to challenge it. The political subjectivity that these comments signal is as disengaged and as centered on the freedom from (as opposed to the freedom for, to appropriate Isaiah Berlin's distinction) as the practical arrangements that I discussed earlier. And if Bourdieu is correct in identifying the neoliberal agenda with "a programme of the methodical destruction of collectives," it will not find much to undo here.

But the equation so many Russians drew between practical competence and psychological divestment from politics is not the only problem. Another, related one is that the project of creating practical autonomy from the Russian state was perhaps too successful in the sense that by the end of the first postsocialist decade Muscovites were quite convinced that, in the words of one respondent, "my only real concern is the health of my parents. Well, and the cat, and what else? The rest of it is entirely irrelevant. Because all of this petty movement and squabbling up above [among the elites] does not reflect on me whatsoever."

Whatever opinion one may hold about the accuracy of this conclusion, it is hard to miss the relevance of the famous W. I. Thomas dictum that "if men define situations as real, they are real in their consequences." In other words, regardless of how justified the individuals' sense of autonomy was, their firm belief that their lives were already virtually disconnected from politics ("the government is on its own, and people are on their own," as it were) was consequential because it allowed for the possibility of further retrenchment of state services and obligations. And in some ways it might have even given a semblance of legitimacy to the less palatable aspects of the postsocialist social and political order. Having partitioned and privatized the formerly public spaces of their own yards and building entryways, rank-and-file Muscovites might find it easier to accept a construction of an "elite condominium" in place of a formerly public neighborhood skating rink and to generally recognize as legitimate the gated communities, partitioned neighborhoods, and controlled access roads that are popping up all over Russia today, making the urban fabric of the country look increasingly like neoliberal city plans all around the world.

There is thus an elective affinity between the psychological and cognitive autonomy that many Russians embraced as a way to insulate their lives from the effects of the protracted instability and the political climate conducive to the creeping neoliberal reforms. That is more than a little ironic. As the people I spoke to would be quick to point out, it was the much-detested neoliberal reforms of the early 1990s that triggered massive inflation and social dislocations that they struggled to counteract. There is nothing they would have wanted less than to contribute to their own marginalization. Their goal was simply to retain a sense of personal competence and control in a world that was rapidly shifting all around them. And yet, the ways in which my decisively non-neoliberally inclined informants dealt with their own challenges made the privatization of all things public look subjectively more palatable than it should have. Any analysis of everyday life in Russia should pay attention to these unexpected, sometimes counterintuitive resonances.

Abandoning the vision of the everyday as the response of a resilient vital force against the pressures of an impersonal system does not mean that we should deny social actors their capacity for creative action or, for that matter, resistance. Indeed, the wave of protest activity that swept over Moscow and other large Russian cities in the winter of 2011–12 suggests that the same spirit of autonomy could be employed in another, more subversive spirit of collective action. Yet it is perhaps not coincidental that people who have emerged as the figureheads of oppositional activity are either explicitly apolitical,[36] or, like Alexey Navalny, they position themselves as independent crusaders against government corruption.[37] In this way, they, too, bear the hallmarks of the culture of autonomy and distrust of politics that I have described.[38]

Regardless of one's assessment of the prospects of civil resistance in Russia today, the point is more general: it would be prudent to avoid presumptions about (1) the ends to which everyday actions are directed and (2) the social significance these actions have in the larger social field, regardless of the intent of their authors. It is all too common for everyday life to play the role of a universal repository for resistance in the eyes of an educated observer. This is because, to quote Stephen Crook, "the everyday comes to bear . . . theoretical-political weight as radical intellectuals have lost faith in previously favored agents or bearers of resistance, from the proletariat to 'youth' to social movements."[39] We would do more justice to the richness of everyday life if we resisted the temptation to reduce it to resistance by default.

Here I have tried to argue that the taken-for-granted notions of practical competence in post-Soviet everyday life eased the acceptance of the neoliberal reforms for broad sectors of the Russian populace. If neoliberal rhetoric rang familiar to many Russians, this is to a large extent because some of its themes resonated with the virtues they ascribed to the independent-thinking and anticollectivist prerevolutionary intelligentsia, while others evoked the caricatured image of the unapologetically self-interested and aggressive capitalist familiar from Soviet critiques of capitalism. These resonances were further amplified in the 1990s by the post-Soviet embrace of autonomy and the tendency to equate practical competence and freedom with distance—almost autarky—from both the Russian state and any framework of collective action.[40] What the notion of resistance does push us to consider, however, is this resistance to the very idea of resistance itself and the role it may play for the kind of future that is being imagined both for and by Russian citizens today.

NOTES

I am grateful to the participants of the "Everyday Life in Russia and the Soviet Union" workshop at the University of Indiana and especially to the workshop organizers and editors of this volume for a lively and generative discussion and for the many helpful comments and suggestions. I would also like to thank my Williams colleague, Michael F. Brown, who generously asserted that "titles cannot be copyrighted" when I had discovered that the working draft of this chapter bears a title strikingly similar to the excellent essay he had published in *American Anthropologist* over a decade ago. See Michael F. Brown, "On Resisting Resistance," *American Anthropologist* 98, no. 4 (1996).

1. This is an embarrassing thing to admit after having just published a book with "everyday life" in its title. But luckily, I am not alone. Writers from Norbert Elias to Catriona Kelly, both of whom have examined various aspects of everyday life, especially manners, profess a similar ambivalence. See Norbert Elias, "On the Concept of Everyday Life," in *The Norbert Elias Reader: A Biographical Selection,* ed. Johan Goudsblom and Stephen Mennell (Oxford: Blackwell Publishers, 1998); and Catriona Kelly, "Ordinary Life in Extraordinary Times: Chronicles of the Quotidian in Russia and the Soviet Union," *Kritika* 3, no. 4 (2002): 631–51.

2. Geoff Eley, foreword to *The History of Everyday Life: Reconstructing Historical Experiences and Ways of Life,* ed. Alf Lüdtke (Princeton, N.J.: Princeton University Press, 1995), ix, quoting Hans Medick and David Sabean, introduction to *Interest and Emotion: Essays on the Study of Family and Kinship,* ed. Hans Medick and David Sabean (Cambridge: Cambridge University Press, 1984), 1.

3. For a theoretically sophisticated critique of the notion of resistance that remains relevant, see Timothy Mitchell, "Everyday Metaphors of Power," *Theory and Society* 19, no. 5 (1990).

4. Charles Bosk, *All God's Mistakes: Genetic Counseling in a Pediatric Hospital* (Chicago: University of Chicago Press, 1992), xiv.

5. John Roberts, *Philosophizing the Everyday: Revolutionary Praxis and the Fate of Cultural Theory* (London: Pluto Press, 2006).

6. James Scott, *Weapons of the Weak: Everyday Forms of Peasant Resistance* (New Haven, Conn.: Yale University Press, 1985); and Scott, *Domination and the Arts of Resistance: Hidden Transcripts* (New Haven, Conn.: Yale University Press, 1990).

7. Scott, *Domination,* 136.

8. Maurice Blanchot, "Everyday Speech," *Yale French Studies* 73 (1987): 13.

9. Henri Lefebvre, *Everyday Life in the Modern World* (New Brunswick, N.J.: Transaction, 1984), 30.

10. Roberts, *Philosophizing the Everyday,* 2.

11. Olga Shevchenko, *Crisis and the Everyday in Postsocialist Moscow* (Bloomington: Indiana University Press, 2009).

12. Harold Garfinkel, *Studies in Ethnomethodology* (Englewood Cliffs, N.J.: Prentice-Hall, 1967).

13. The term "practical competence" is inspired by Berger and Luckmann's notion of "pragmatic competence in routine performances." See Peter L. Berger and Thomas Luckmann, *The Social Construction of Reality: A Treatise in the Sociology of Knowledge* (New York: Doubleday, 1967), 42.

14. Achille Mbembe and Janet Roitman, "Figures of the Subject in Times of Crisis," *Public Culture* 7 (1995): 324, 325 (my italics).

15. For a discussion of the contours of this subjectivity as well as of some the mechanisms of its production, see Alexei Yurchak, "Russian Neoliberal: The Entrepreneurial Ethic and the Spirit of 'True Careerism,'" *Russian Review* 62 (January 2003): 72–90; and Tomas Matza, "Moscow's Echo: Technologies of the Self, Publics, and Politics on the Russian Talk Show," *Cultural Anthropology* 24, no. 3 (2009): 489–522.

16. Mikhail Zhvanetskii, *Dezhurnyi po Strane* (On duty for the nation), TV program, first shown on Russia One Channel on December 30, 2002, transcript available from http://www.jvanetsky.ru/data/text/vs/dejurnyi07/.

17. Pierre Bourdieu, "The Essence of Neoliberalism," *Le monde diplomatique*, December 1998, http://mondediplo.com/1998/12/08bourdieu (italics in the original).

18. The book was based on ethnographic observation and informal conversations in various urban sites in Moscow from 1998 to 2000, as well as over 110 more formal interviews with 33 Muscovites whom I recruited through a modified snowball sample. My respondents (16 men and 17 women) belonged predominantly to lower and middle-income brackets but came from a variety of educational and occupational backgrounds, which enabled me to trace the commonalities in which these divergently positioned individuals approached, both practically and rhetorically, the complexities of the postsocialist transformation. In assessing a respondent's income, I used the definition of VCIOM (now Levada Center), which identified as low-income individuals those whose per capita household income in 1997 was 200,000–400,000 rubles a month (about $40–$80) and as middle-income bracket those with 400,000–600,000 rubles a month ($80–$120) per capita. See Leonid Gordon, Anatolii Terekhin, and Elena Budilova, "Opyt Mnogomernogo Opisaniia Material'no-Ekonomicheskoi Differentsiatsii Naseleniya" (Multi-indicator description of economic differentiation of the population), *Monitoring Obschestvennogo Mneniia: Ekonomicheskie i Sotsial'nye Peremeny* (Public opinion monitoring: Economic and social changes), vol. 33 (1998).

19. See Yurchak, "Russian Neoliberal."

20. Yulia Kalinina, "Vy v Dole, Marivanna," *Moskovskii Komsomolets,* September 2, 2011, http://www.mk.ru/social/article/2011/09/01/619912-vyi-v-dole-marivanna.html.

21. Comment from "Spetsialist," available online at http://www.mk.ru/social/article/2011/09/01/619912-vyi-v-dole-marivanna.html?action=comments.

22. Olga Sveshnikova, "Rossiiskie Roditeli: Novoe v Povedenii i Mirovospriatii" (Russian parents: New trends in behavior and outlook), *Pro et Contra* 48, nos. 1–2 (January–April 2010): 61–77.

23. Michele Rivkin-Fish, "Tracing Landscapes of the Past in Class Subjectivity: Practices of Memory and Distinction in Marketizing Russia," *American Ethnologist* 36, no. 1 (2006): 79–95.

24. Compare this to the rather categorical statement made in an interview by the popular actress Elena Safonova: "Community work [*obschestvennaia rabota*] is when you have to do what was overlooked by others, those whose responsibility it was to do it in the first place. It is not my thing. And in general, it is my opinion that it is absurd, illogical, wrong to lead a public life. People are born not for that but for living a private life of their own in their families." See Natalia Zhuravleva, "Subbotniaia Vstrecha: Interview s Elenoi Safonovoi" (A Saturday get-together: An interview with Elena Safonova), *Moskovskii Komsomolets,* December 26, 1998.

25. For one, Preobrazhensky's individualism did not preclude active membership in professional (and, one might speculate, prerevolutionary civic) associations. His protest against the aid campaigns of the early Soviet era could also be read as a protest against the

authoritarian style in which they were conducted, against the substitution of distant causes for the causes that were in plain sight, or against the lack of accountability that characterized these efforts. None of these interpretations are evident in the readings of *Heart of a Dog* that Rivkin-Fish explores.

26. In a similar spirit, the Russian American sociologist Vladimir Shlapentokh notes the correspondence between the capitalist utopia of Ayn Rand and Marxist critiques of capitalism, writing that "one of Rand's chief goals was, it seems, to verify that the vulgar Marxist image of the capitalist, as described, for example, in [Maksim] Gorky's *The City of the Yellow Devil* or by [Samuil] Marshak in *Mister Twister,* is truly accurate. Rand's heroes profess the same [traits] that Marxists had deplored in capitalists—egoism, lack of interest in the common good, indifference to the suffering of others." In other words, Shlapentokh suggests that Rand and the Marxist writers are in complete agreement about the fundamental features of capitalism—except, of course, that they assign inverted values to them. See Vladimir Shlapentokh, "Dekonstruktsia Filosofii Ayn Rand: Ee Marksistskie i Bol'shevistskie Korni" (Deconstruction of Ayn Rand's philosophy: Its Marxist and Bolshevik roots), April 15, 2010, http://vladimirshlapentokhrussian.wordpress.com/2010/04/15/деконструкция-философии-айн-рэнд-ее-м-2.

27. All respondents' names have been changed.

28. See Andrei Zorin, "In Search of a New Identity: Visions of the Past and Present in Post-Communist Russia," in *Myth and Memory in the Construction of Community: Historical Patterns in Europe and Beyond,* ed. Bo Stråth (New York: Lang, 2000), 324, 325.

29. This reevaluation of the meaning of popular resistance may be one of the key factors behind what Balzer calls "one of the most politically debilitating myths about August 1991," "the claim that few people supported Yeltsin or opposed the coup." See Harvey Balzer, "Ordinary Russians? Rethinking August 1991," *Demokratizatsiya* 13, no. 2 (2005): 195. Indeed, those members of my sample who spent their days (and some, their nights) on the streets of Moscow in August 1991 tended to minimize their involvement with the events or downplay their emotional involvement with the resistance, often asserting that they had *already* been divested from politics when they went onto the streets.

30. Svetlana Liuboshits, "Bozhe, Kakimi My Byli Naivnymi!," *Moskovskii Komsomolets,* August 22, 2001.

31. Interview with Karina, a sixty-three-year-old retiree.

32. See the discussion of *habitus hysteresis* in Pierre Bourdieu, *Outline of a Theory of Practice,* trans. Richard Nice (Cambridge: Cambridge University Press, 1977).

33. I take up these manifestations of autonomy in much greater detail in *Crisis and the Everyday.*

34. Ekaterina Makarova, "The Changing Boundaries of Public and Private: The New Spaces of Consumption in Moscow," paper presented at the annual meeting of the American Sociological Association, New York, August 11, 2007.

35. From the interview with Pietsukh in Alex Alekhin, "Pisatel Protiv Chasovoi" (A writer against the clock), *Ekspert* 16 (2008).

36. Social movement scholar Oleg Yanitsky observes with some concern that the protesters gravitated toward the authority of writers such as Boris Akunin and scientists such as Mikhail Gelfand, "persons intelligent but not public and who have no political biography to speak of." See Oleg Yanitsky, "Mitingi Povsiudu: Reabilitatsia Grazhdanskogo Aktivizma v Rossii" (Meetings everywhere: The rehabilitation of civic activism in Russia), *Obschestvennye Nauki i Sovremennost'* (Social sciences and modernity), no. 3 (2012) (my translation).

Even Maxim Katz, one of the newly elected municipal deputies who organized the legal defense of those detained after the protests at Bolotnaya Square in Moscow in May 2012, has repeatedly refused the label of an oppositional politician, insisting that he is "a neutral figure and not an opposition." See http://echo.msk.ru/blog/maxkatz/890633-echo/. For details on Katz, see Michael Schwirtz, "Opposition, to Its Surprise, Wins a Bit of Power in Moscow," *New York Times,* March 8, 2012.

37. For more on Navalny, see Julia Ioffe, "Net Impact: One Man's Cyber-crusade against Russian Corruption," *New Yorker,* April 4, 2011.

38. There is too much diversity within the opposition movement to write about it in the singular. But it is worth noting that it is not in any way free of neoliberal strands. To give just one example, another one of Katz's frequently reiterated convictions is that governance requires competent individual managers rather than inclusion and public deliberation. See it stated on Katz's Twitter feed on May 19, 2012.

39. Stephen Crook, "Minotaurs and Other Monsters: 'Everyday Life' in Recent Sociological Theory," *Sociology* 32, no. 3 (1998): 536.

40. There are reasons to think that these changes are not confined to Russia; one distinguishes a similar legitimation of self-interest, for example, in the words of the Romanian journalist Cristian Stanescu. Stanescu explained the political clout of Ceausescu's son, which enabled the latter to successfully lay claim to much of his father's art collection, in terms directly reminiscent of the Russian rhetoric of self-interest: "Since the revolution the country is only about private enterprise. Romanians sympathize with Valentin because he worked the system to his advantage. Our idea of culture now is making money. We still have too many basic needs to worry about elevated ones like art and the state." See Michael Kimmelman, "Romania Shrugs Off Reminder of Its Past," *New York Times,* February 25, 2009.

4

The Oil Company and the Crafts Fair
From *Povsednevnost'* to *Byt* in Postsocialist Russia

DOUGLAS ROGERS

Protecting Traditions—Lukoil-Perm.
—Billboard outside the main offices of Lukoil-Perm, 2008

The 2009 "Obva: Soul of the Riverlands" festival, celebrated in recent years by four rural districts clustered around the Obva River in the Russian Perm Region, was coming to a close. By all accounts, it had been a success. The weather was glorious. Folklore ensembles had proudly presented the unique identity of each district in costume and song. There was heavy traffic at a bazaar where local artisans displayed and sold their wares. A day of friendly competition among districts in everything from volleyball to skits had gone off without a hitch. Andrei Nikolaevich, an elected official representing the Il'inskii District, stepped to the microphone to deliver one of a series of ceremonial closing speeches. After a few words of thanks and some playful sparring with the heads of other districts, he concluded by inviting the gathered masses to yet another festival, scheduled to take place a few weeks hence, that would mark the 430th anniversary of the town of Il'inskii. He stepped off the stage and, shaking his head and smiling, commented to a cluster of organizers and local politicians: "We just go from one feast day to the next these days, don't we?" Had they heard, he continued, the story about a visitor to one of Russia's remote monastic communities? The visitor had tracked down one of the hermits in the forest and asked him, "How do you live like this, out here by yourself day after day?" The answer: "As soon as one feast day ends, I start preparing for the next one." That's what life was starting to look like in the Perm Region, Andrei Nikolaevich concluded, and went off to shake more hands.

Participating in the 2009 "Obva: Soul of the Riverlands" festival and speaking with its organizers and attendees, I was again struck by how much had changed since the 1990s in the Perm Region, when everyday discussions were much more likely to concern things like how to feed one's family than friendly disputes about which district's folklore ensemble had performed better. It has, as Andrei Nikolaevich said, been hard to miss the omnipresence of festivals and cultural spectacles in the Perm Region in the past several years. The regional Ministry of Culture declared 2009 be a year of "The 59th Region's 59 Festivals," saturating the spring and summer months with jubilees, celebrations of local culture, and displays of folk handicrafts.[1] The program was deemed such a success that it was extended indefinitely—by 2011, the Perm Region had taken to calling itself "The Region of 59 Festivals." These festivals, in turn, became one plank in Governor Oleg Chirkunov's campaign to have Perm declared a cultural capital of Europe by 2016.

The ongoing evolution of the Perm Region's "festival movement," as it is sometimes called, is closely caught up in the recent history of the region's oil industry. Not only do taxes on Lukoil-Perm—the main oil company with a presence in the region—make up roughly a third of the regional budget, including that of the very active Ministry of Culture, but the company is a direct sponsor of many festivals, including both "Obva: Soul of the Riverlands" and Il'inskii's 430th jubilee. In the early 2000s it was midlevel managers at Lukoil-Perm who promoted the idea of spending some of the increasing flow of oil money on the preservation and celebration of traditional culture. Indeed, several years before the regional Ministry of Culture became involved, Lukoil-Perm was running its own festivals, seeking to revive folk arts and crafts, and building museums to showcase the distinctive characteristics and histories of the peoples of the Perm Region.

This chapter considers the intersection of new oil wealth and everyday life in the Perm Region after socialism and accounts for some of the transformations undergirding the widespread sense that life had gone from a series of crises and uncertainties in the 1990s to a series of festivals by 2009. My argument has two parts. First, at the conceptual level, I sug-

FIGURE 4.1.

"Protecting Traditions—Lukoil-Perm." Billboard outside the main offices of
Lukoil-Perm, 2008. Photo by the author.

gest that this shift is usefully framed as a movement between two aspects
of everyday life indicated by the Russian terms *povsednevnost'* and *byt*.
Second, I show that Lukoil-Perm's effort to legitimate its enormous and
increasing wealth in the eyes of the population through "corporate social
responsibility" projects was a prime mover behind this shift. Inasmuch as
Lukoil-Perm's projects have become closely interlaced with state projects
like the "59 Festivals" initiative, an analysis of changes in the experience
of everyday life in the Perm Region offers some new insights into the
anatomy of Russia as petrostate.[2]

POVSEDNEVNOST' AND BYT

In a series of recent and enlightening essays, Natalia Pushkareva has
carefully charted the ways in which the study of "everyday life" has (and
has not) entered Russian historiography.[3] Pushkareva explains that the

Russian term *povsednevnost'* most closely lines up with what Western an-thropologists and historians usually mean when they write about every-day life—a zone in which people experience, contemplate, and act on the world around them in the ordinary, habitual, unremarkable times of their lives. Povsednevnost' indicates a zone of practice, of muddling through, of quotidian decision making. At least in its current form, it is a fairly new topic of concern in Russian historiography, largely a child of the increased traffic between Western and Russian scholarly concepts in the 1990s.

Pushkareva contrasts povsednevnost' with several other historiographi-cal traditions, including the study of byt—one of the main objects of study of Russian, Soviet, and post-Soviet ethnography. In studying byt, ethnographers abstract from the domain of the everyday as lived practice. They seek to distill and present a generalized collection of elements— from material culture to beliefs and rituals—that characterize the dis-tinctive social and cultural elements of a particular group's life. Museum exhibits or festivals featuring the byt of peasants in the Perm Region, for instance, often include distinctive elements of dress, "traditional" farming implements, and perhaps elements of architecture, folklore, or religious/ spiritual life. Museums might compare and contrast these items for dif-ferent ethnic groups, such as Russians and Komi-Permiaks, while festi-vals like "Obva: Soul of the Riverlands" often staged a series of folklore performances, one from each participating district, each incorporating distinctive elements of byt.

Museums and festivals are the twin domains in which byt is displayed for public consumption and edification. Especially in museums and in the scholarly writings of ethnographers, byt is often presented as everyday life. It would not be at all uncommon, for instance, to hear a museum tour guide narrate an exhibit by explaining that it contains the main items that such-and-such people use in their households. A scholarly compilation of folk songs would likely present them as the songs a particular group sings in the fields or at weddings. But in both cases byt is, in fact, usually fairly far removed from the everyday described by povsednevnost'. As Pushkareva notes, an ethnographer studying byt is not interested in how people themselves relate to, think about, or experience those objects or songs.[4] The systematicity of a particular group's byt and the careful recon-struction and presentation of the ways in which its elements cohere into a distinctive and consistent worldview are artifacts of the research process rather than indications of how everyday lives are lived in a particular time and place. Byt indicates an abstracted, systematized representation of practice that emerges through indifference to, rather than appreciation of, the murkiness and indeterminacy of the everyday.

Pushkareva also shows that the groups whose byt is described in books or displayed in museums are almost always exotic, removed in space and/or time from the modern world inhabited by the viewer or reader. We might productively extend her argument by noting that the abstractions and generalizations of byt have also been closely caught up in techniques of state power in Russia and the Soviet Union. In an instructive study of the Russian Geographical Society in the mid-nineteenth century, for instance, Nathaniel Knight locates the emergence of byt as a central concern of ethnographers within a distinctively Russian imperial order, one quite different, he argues, from the overseas European colonial orders produced, in part, through early anthropologists' concepts of culture and civilization.[5] Francine Hirsch persuasively makes a similar argument for the Soviet case, showing how museums dedicated to byt were significant sites for the projection and consumption of Soviet imperial ideologies.[6] Ethnographers and ethnography, she shows, were some of the central players in transforming the old byt of far-flung peoples into the new byt of socialism.[7]

Pushkareva argues elegantly for the study of povsednevnost' as an improvement over the study of byt. Although many of my own sympathies lie here as well,[8] I also think that the moment in Russian historiography that she describes, one suspended between the byt long studied by ethnographers and the povsednevnost' more recently adapted from certain Western historians and anthropologists, can be instructive for the study of everyday life more broadly. I want to argue, in fact, that the tension between povsednevnost' and byt can be analytically useful. Both terms point to important aspects of the broader category of everyday life, a category that is never entirely practice and never entirely captured by the classificatory schemes of states or other powerful actors. Whereas povsednevnost' reminds us that there are always elements of underdetermined practice in everyday human existence, byt reminds us that this everyday existence is also tightly linked to the power of states and corporations—in their classifying, organizing, and abstracting modes—to see, control, and shape human lives.

In this chapter I approach everyday life in contemporary Russia as a field that includes elements usefully described by both povsednevnost' and byt. This approach has two main virtues. First, it mediates between some large issues in recent social, cultural, and historical theories at their broadest scales—structure and agency, power and knowledge—and categories that continue to be relevant in Russia. Especially in light of the developed and developing Russian scholarly literature on these topics, I would suggest that thinking about everyday life through local terms such as these is much preferable to simply imposing theoretical categories and definitions from outside. Second, and emerging from this focus on Russian terms, I show that keeping an eye on both povsednevnost' and byt opens a useful way to track changes in the nature of everyday life over time. Shifts in the mix and predominance of povsednevnost' and byt, that is, are useful diagnostics of the changing nature of state and corporate power.

My argument will be that byt gradually eclipsed povsednevnost' as the first decade of the twenty-first century wore on in the Perm Region: everyday life as underdetermined practice gave way to displays of everyday life as a means by which Russian state agencies and corporations like Lukoil-Perm categorized and classified people and projected their own emerging power. Worry about how one might feed one's family on a week-to-week basis in the 1990s (the zone of povsednevnost') became a never-ending series of festivals displaying items of local cultural distinctiveness (the zone of byt). I should underscore immediately that I do not mean by this that the domain of povsednevnost' has vanished or that a concern with presenting byt in the 1990s was entirely absent (or, for that matter, that people do not still struggle to feed their families). In the overall framing I outlined above, povsednevnost' and byt cling to each other; neither can simply vanish. I mean, rather, that the preponderance of activity in the overall arena of everyday life had shifted significantly from the zone of povsednevnost' in the 1990s and toward the zone of byt by the turn of the 2010s. Abstracted and generalized displays of byt as a technology of state and corporate power now fill the air, crowding out the practical dilemmas of povsednevnost' that were so salient in the 1990s. In the Perm Region, I suggest, the reasons for this shift are to be found in the rise of Lukoil-Perm and its collaborative relationship with the regional state apparatus. If byt is again central to the operation of power in Russia, as it was in the earlier periods of Russian history studied by Knight and Hirsch, it is significant that the forces behind its return in the post-Soviet period are as much corporate as state, as much oil company as Ministry of Culture.[9]

POSTSOCIALIST POVSEDNEVNOST', 1990s–2002

Scholars have devoted a lot of attention to everyday life after socialism, and rightly so; as Henri Lefebvre well understood, rapid and pervasive change pushes the everyday to the forefront.[10] In 1990s Russia, with structures crumbling all around and with every sort of relationship undergoing fundamental change, quotidian decisions were far more structurally and institutionally determinative in human life than they often are.[11] The 1990s was, that is, a time when the dilemmas and practices central to the zone of povsednevnost' were particularly salient and especially consequential. For most residents of the Perm Region, these dilemmas and practices gathered around household production and petty trade, the most common ways to support oneself in the wake of near collapse in both agricultural and industrial sectors. These postsocialist practices are well documented.[12] For my purposes here, it is important to note that the experience of the everyday for workers in the oil industry diverged considerably from that of most residents of the Perm Region.

The oil industry was a bright spot in the regional economy even before the massive boom of the early 2000s. When Lukoil was born out of the structures of the former Soviet Ministry of Oil and Gas in the early 1990s, its holdings did not extend to the wells, pipelines, and major refinery in the Perm Region. In a process that lasted into the late 1990s, the company gradually gained control over the Perm Region's local oil companies and their associated infrastructure, from exploration and drilling through the sale of gasoline and motor oil. By 2010 Lukoil, through local subsidiaries like Lukoil-Perm, had extensive production and refining operations in around half of the forty-eight municipalities (i.e., districts and cities) of the Perm Region. Taxes on its massive profits had made it a "budget-making" (biudzhetobrazuiushchyi) enterprise for the entire region.

At the level of everyday life, the story of early postsocialist oil is interesting for what it does not feature: tales of deprivation, rationing, and demonetization. One former Lukoil-Perm employee I knew summed up his evaluation of the period from the late 1990s to around 2002—the time of Lukoil's ascendance in the Perm Region—as follows:

> [In the Soviet period] it was all simpler and easier to understand. There was no Lukoil, there was a state oil system, and it didn't bother anybody. Oil was pumped for the people, and the profits went to the people. Everything was fine.... [But in the post-Soviet period] a sharp divide began to arise between oil workers and other people living in those areas in income and in the ability to obtain things—televisions, VCRs, refrigerators. Oil workers aren't the majority of the population in any district [i.e., this new wealth was spread unevenly]. And then these oil magnates appeared at the top.... [Ordinary] people's evaluation [of the oil industry] was about as negative as it could be.

Some of the postsocialist era's largest and most evident inequalities in wealth in the Perm Region began to emerge most visibly in precisely those districts where Lukoil-Perm operated production facilities, as workers in those areas began receiving modest cash bonuses at the time that workers in nearly all other sectors of the economy were experiencing salary delays, receiving in-kind compensation, or not working at all. Lukoil-Perm, that is, began its rise to prominence in the Perm Region at precisely the moment when everyday dilemmas of "getting by" were debated and discussed everywhere, from kitchens to newspapers, from villages to urban centers.[13] Numerous scholars have shown that at the level of everyday experience and conversations—the level of povsednevnost'—these postsocialist inequalities were often measured precisely at the point of consumption.[14] In the case of Lukoil-Perm, we have a comparatively rare case in which a minority of workers, mostly in oil-producing districts, suddenly could obtain refrigerators and VCRs, those iconic everyday objects of desire in the early postsocialist years, while their much more numerous neighbors could not.

From the perspective of Lukoil-Perm, the divergence of everyday experiences between oil workers and most of the rest of the Perm Region created a potential problem, for this was, as the quotation above indicates, also a time of tremendous popular dissatisfaction with "New Russians," oligarchs, and postsocialist inequalities in general. The question of how to mitigate this discontent and ensure smooth operations fell to Lukoil-

Perm's newly minted Connections with Society Division (Otdel Sviazi s Obshchestvennostiu). One former member of the division framed the question with which she and her colleagues wrestled in those days as, "How are you going to relate to [the non-Lukoil residents in oil-producing districts]?" The answer they arrived at over the course of 2000–2002, she told me, was, "You have to meet them where they are"—a framing that acknowledges the already wide gulf between the oil company and the rest of the region. The company's solution, although not articulated or planned precisely as such at the outset, was gradually to transform the dilemmas, inequalities, and uncertainties of 1990s povsednevnost' into the fixities, displays, and traditional festivals of byt.

THE ROAD TO BYT

During my visits to the Perm Region in 2009–11, I inquired frequently about the origins of the festival movement. Although the regional Department of Culture was active to some extent in the 1990s, its budget was small, and its focus was on attempting to modernize a worn infrastructure of clubs, libraries, museums, and performance venues. The real impetus and financing for the large-scale revival of interest in byt—from museum exhibits to folklore festivals—came from Lukoil-Perm. Executives at Lukoil-Perm were, in the early 2000s, centrally concerned with a pair of issues, one at home, one much more global. At home, as I have already noted, they were eager to improve the reputation of the industry and ensure that the increasing difference in standards of living in the Perm Region did not negatively impact their business. On a more global scale, they were looking to model their company on successful Western oil companies. Indeed, Vagit Alekperov, president of Lukoil, made no secret of the fact that his dream was to fashion a private Russian oil company that would compete with the likes of BP and ExxonMobil.

Out of the confluence of these two issues arose Lukoil-Perm's effort to aggressively and publicly support the districts in which it pumped oil by adopting—and adapting—the practice and language of corporate social responsibility (CSR). CSR is a set of practices that grew up among global corporations based in the West in large part as a result of critiques of environmental destruction and unfair labor practices.[15] CSR operations usually assume that corporations, rather than states, are the best regulators of firms' relationships to the communities in which they have a presence. In terms of mission and personnel, CSR projects often blend with more traditional state-led "development" initiatives. Although they include the post-Soviet specificities and nuances described below, these global tendencies in CSR are visible in Lukoil-Perm's efforts to head off critiques of its massive new wealth.

In 2002 the Connections with Society Division at Lukoil-Perm began offering grants for a wide range of "social and cultural projects" in the districts where the company had operations. The funds were distributed on a competitive basis: interested organizations could submit proposals in a variety of categories to be judged by a panel of experts, some of them Lukoil-Perm employees, some of them acknowledged experts in their fields in the Perm Region. One of the most popular categories, and the one that Lukoil-Perm focused its primary energy on in the early days of its CSR efforts, was folk handicrafts. In 2002, after a judging process that included ethnographers and museum experts, the company gave grants to a number of carefully selected artisans with the goal of enabling them to begin their own businesses producing and selling folk handicrafts.

I asked a former Lukoil employee why Lukoil-Perm's initial focus was specifically on artisanal handicrafts.

> That [decision] was linked to the high level of unemployment in those districts. In the north of the Perm Region, in the Cherdyn', Usol'e, and other districts, there was never any agriculture that could feed people. What was there to do? And so the idea of self-employment [samozaniatost'] was born [in the Lukoil Connections with Society Division]. . . . Sit home, . . . sew, make pottery, do something else, and maybe you can get some sort of income. Miserly income, but at least you have something to do. In the beginning, there was, perhaps, an illusion [at Lukoil-Perm] that you could actually develop folk crafts, and develop whole towns on the basis of folk crafts, but then it became clear that [for this] you needed a strong local tradition, more than one generation. And there was the problem of materials—where to get them, where to sell them. . . . There were no great successes, but there was a lot of noise. The press was interested.

Some of the classic dilemmas of the first postsocialist decades are here. How to create employment and income in districts that were struggling to survive without socialist-era subsidies? How to acquire materials and to sell them on the market? How, in general, to manage the turn to household production and petty trade across rural areas? What is interesting is that these challenges were taken on by Lukoil-Perm in a domain that had nothing to do with oil, at least in a direct sense. Through CSR, the company understood itself—and certainly advertised itself—to be working hard to close the gap between oil workers and nearly everyone else in the experience of everyday life.

In the first weeks and months of this new program, company representatives made frequent trips from Perm to the northern districts—three to four hours by car each way—to bring their new craft specialists raw materials with which to work. They would return to Perm with finished products for sale. Very quickly, though, these specialists realized that this was not, by itself, a sustainable business model. It would not be possible to erase the deeply felt differences in wealth between oil workers and the remainder of the population simply by giving seed grants to artisans and watching revenues pour in. If this seems unsurprising, it is only so in retrospect. The vast majority of Western advisors and consultants blanketing Russia at the time shared Lukoil-Perm's faith in the magic of markets and entrepreneurship. Indeed, they were an important source of it.

In a key moment for the transformations I am tracing, specialists at Lukoil-Perm decided that, in order to make the company's grants-for-handicrafts program successful, the tourism industry as a whole would need to be developed so that residents of Perm and other cities would make their own ways to remote northern districts and boost local economies. A new Lukoil-Perm program that was launched not long after the first grants were distributed to folk artisans sponsored small festivals and other events in areas that the company identified as "Historical Cities and Population Centers of the Kama River Basin." These festivals—all of them in oil-producing districts—were intended to offer contexts for Lukoil-Perm's chosen craftspeople to sell their wares and for specialists to gather and plan further festivals, exhibits, and ways to market crafts across the region. These early festivals sought to commercialize involution, to make some profit out of the turn to household production across those rural areas that were home to oil operations.[16] They were also an important step on the way from a focus on the dilemmas of everyday life associated with povsednevnost' to one featuring the more abstracted displays and categorizations associated with byt.

In addition to the mobile "Historical Cities" festival, Lukoil-Perm adopted other strategies to draw tourists to its production districts to spend money in ways that would help local economies. For instance, at the company's initiative, the annual "Garden, Field, Farm" trade show held at the Permskaia Iarmarka (a combination exposition center and trade show facility) each year included a new element beginning in 2002: a show and sale of local crafts featuring everyday gardening items. Under a banner reading "Yes to Social Partnership!" and featuring Lukoil's red logo, artisans sponsored by Lukoil-Perm from eight northern districts sold handmade baskets, belts, tools, and other items. Oil company specialists helped them adjust their prices to the urban market and, on the sidelines of the exhibition, ran seminars designed to offer instruction in how to further develop a business without Lukoil-Perm's support.

Lukoil-Perm's interest in folk crafts quickly grew from the region's northern districts—sites of largely new exploration for the company—to include the districts exploiting established oil fields in the south. In 2004, for instance, the first regional festival of children's folk crafts was held in the Orda District. *Zvezda*, the Perm regional newspaper, carried the thoughts of the head of the district administration on the festival:

> 2004 has been full of happy events for us. . . . But the happiest of them, as for the whole region, has been the seventy-fifth anniversary of Perm oil. And we are delighted that the oil industry organized the first such wonderful festival in the region in honor of that date. It's not a coincidence that the festival was held in our district. More than four hundred thousand tons of oil are pumped from our territory every year, and our traditional folk crafts are recognized not only in Russia but in many foreign countries as well.[17]

A smaller-scale project took place in 2004 in the southern district of Barda, one of Lukoil's major production centers in the Perm Region, as announced in the local paper:

> The regional nonprofit fund for the support of the population (based in the city of Chaikovskii) decided to unite the old and the modern in practice. Modernity is when people, having studied old folk crafts, can earn some money for themselves. This is how the project "The Folk Artisan," which was chosen in Lukoil-Perm's Third Annual Social and Cultural Projects Competition, was born. It's well known that the oil industry, beginning with the very first competition, is reviving historical traditions

in those territories where they work, making good on the slogan, "Lukoil: For the Good of the Perm Region." The goal of the project is to teach folk crafts to the poor and unemployed residents of Barda.[18]

As these media descriptions of Lukoil-Perm's projects in Orda and Barda suggest, grants to support the folk handicraft industry that were initially designed mostly to provide work and some income for populations struggling to get by became more and more identified with celebrations of local identity and cultural distinctiveness. The zone of the everyday so salient in the 1990s, captured under the rubric of povsednevnost', was becoming more directly associated with the kind of abstracted identity claims and spectacles showcasing traditional culture—the domain of byt.

This shift is also apparent in the reflections of most of the participants in this process as they looked back on nearly a decade of CSR focused on arts and crafts. The majority of intellectuals and political figures I spoke with in the Perm Region in 2009 and 2010—at both the regional and district levels—judged Lukoil-Perm's handicraft projects to have been influential and largely successful. However, the criteria by which success was measured had shifted from the project's earliest goals. Academic specialists in folk culture and handicrafts, although initially wildly enthusiastic about Lukoil-Perm's interest, by 2010 frequently mourned the fact that what they saw as authentic traditions had mostly fallen by the wayside, replaced by a mix of what, in their view, was often kitsch, cheap imitation, or invented rather than linked to the history of the districts in which it was produced. These specialists put more attention into museums and academic publications, where they had more control over what counted as "tradition." In another departure from initial expectations, a career in folk handicraft production had not become lucrative for anyone, much less an entire district (as the original planners had hoped). Lukoil-Perm was, though, widely perceived to be a moving force in reviving cultural traditions in the Perm Region. This reputation—rather than any appreciable dent that folk crafts put in agricultural involution or the dilemmas of unemployment—went at least some way toward undercutting the previously widespread perception that the company was merely interested in pumping out oil and raking in money.

Here is the same former employee I quoted at length above, reflecting on eight years of the company's interest in folk crafts and other cultural initiatives:

[Since the late 1990s] Lukoil has done something enormous. It has, step by step, changed the way people relate to it. The most interesting thing is that, among much of the population, the evaluation of Lukoil is still negative.... "If they're rich, that means they are stealing, they're taking our subsoil resources," and so on.... All of these [social and cultural] projects gave the possibility to the population to feel that they can, precisely with the help of Lukoil, do something themselves. And so the payoff for Lukoil was high.... This all gives Lukoil the ability to work calmly in oil-producing areas.

Lukoil-Perm's initiatives, as this comment indicates, enabled the company to burnish its reputation through cultural projects even though those projects did not significantly reduce inequality between oil workers and others in its production districts or, for that matter, entirely eliminate the critique of Lukoil as profiting at the expense of the population and its subsoil resources. They worked, rather, through giving the population a "feeling" that they were partners with Lukoil in the transformation of the Perm Region. At least according to this observer, CSR did not so much eliminate everyday problems as it shifted the way in which the everyday was experienced and felt.

I am arguing, then, that the problems of the 1990s, so often experienced and discussed as everyday dilemmas and uncertainties about how to get by in difficult times, have not entirely disappeared. But they are increasingly accompanied by, and often overwritten by, an omnipresent cultural production. Concrete questions about how one might go about making a living in a rural district after socialism have been transformed into abstracted displays and festivals celebrating, and not infrequently inventing, the distinctive lives of people in those same rural districts. This process has unfolded in large part as a result of Lukoil-Perm's efforts to respond to critiques of its new wealth.

BYT EVERYWHERE: ARTS, CRAFTS, AND FESTIVALS, 2010–2011

In early March 2010 I attended the fourth annual folk handicrafts exhibition and sale at the Perm Exhibition Hall. The exhibition had grown from its origins on the margins of the 2002 "Garden, Field, Farm" exposition into its own large event beginning in 2007. This development is a nice illustration of the extraction of byt from the domain of practice

FIGURE 4.2.

Lukoil-Perm's sponsorship of artisans from its production districts was
evident throughout the exhibition hall. Photo by the author.

indicated by povsednevnost'. No longer, that is, were the display and sale
of folk handicrafts part of a larger turn to domestic economies, one way
for impoverished rural districts to reorient their economic circumstances
in concert with new farming technologies featured in the "Garden, Field,
Farm" trade show. The display and sale of handicrafts had become an event
in and of itself, more closely tied to the displays and classifications that
attend byt than to the practical dilemmas of povsednevnost'.

By 2009 the exhibition was drawing scores of artisans from all over
the Perm Region and over fifteen thousand visitors over the five days it
was open. Signs of Lukoil-Perm's influence were everywhere, beginning
with advertisements for the exhibition scattered throughout the city. The
company not only funded many of the exhibitors through its ongoing
grant competitions dedicated to craft production but also acted as a "general partner," providing a significant portion of the funds necessary to
stage the exhibition each year. The organizers arranged exhibitors by dis-

FIGURE 4.3.

An aisle at the 2011 Folk Crafts Exhibition. A folklore ensemble performs
onstage in the background. Photo by the author.

trict of origin within the Perm Region, often with more than one artisan
from each district occupying a booth. The display stands of oil-producing
districts of the Perm Region were grouped together in the center of the
exhibition space under banners featuring Lukoil-Perm's distinctive logo
(see figures 4.2 and 4.3). In 2009 the exhibition even opened a day early
to accommodate the travel schedule of a very important guest: Vagit
Alekperov, president of Lukoil, who was visiting from Moscow to sign
the company's yearly agreement on cooperation with the Perm regional
government.

I had hoped that attending the exhibition would allow me time to speak
at some length with artisans from all over the Perm Region, both those
who were sponsored and funded by Lukoil-Perm and those who were not.
This turned out to be harder than I expected. The exhibition hall was simply mobbed for five straight days, making conversations far more fleeting
than I had hoped. Nevertheless, some of the broader characteristics and

events of the exhibition offer some insight into the configuration of oil and everyday life in the Perm Region at the time, a configuration in which Lukoil-Perm's handicraft projects effectively merged with the regional state administration's "59 Festivals" initiative into a giant display and sale of the byt of the peoples of the Perm Region.

At the opening of the exhibition in 2010, officials from the Perm regional administration and Lukoil-Perm welcomed the exhibitors, linking handicraft items to both local cultural distinctiveness and the larger political and economic shape of the Perm Region. A representative of the Perm regional government began: "We often ask ourselves how to preserve our identities, how to preserve our ethnic-national values. We ask questions. But there are artisans in the Kama River Basin who, with their own hands and souls, assert our ethnic-national uniqueness, who show how we are very different from other regions in the richness of our diversity." A representative of Lukoil in the Perm Region then greeted the participants "on behalf of all the oil workers" in the region. He continued: "Probably more than half of the participants here are from . . . districts where our company extracts oil. This isn't a coincidence. In collaboration with the heads of districts, the company has actively supported the revival of traditions for many years, including folk crafts, in the districts where it works. The words 'Lukoil—Protecting Tradition' are not just a slogan. Brands such as Elokhov fish and Uinsk honey have become known far outside of our region. This is all the result of our work with you."

At least in the staging of the event for the public, the 2010 exhibition was a collaborative company-state project dedicated to showcasing, and selling, the byt of the different districts of the Perm Region. When I returned again in 2011, this company-state relationship had deepened still further, and the exhibition had begun to overlap with that other classic domain for the display of byt: festivals. The state office charged with administering the "59 Festivals" program had a prominent booth of its own featuring a large map of the Perm Region with dots showing the location of many festivals and a long list of the rest; a large-screen television played clips from a year's worth of television coverage of festivals on a continuous loop. An entire program of folk songs had been added to each day of the exhibition, arranged so that representatives of many of the fifty-nine festivals would appear briefly, showcase their traditional attire, sing a song or stage a skit, and then invite those present to visit their upcoming festival.

In 2010 and again in 2011 I wandered among the stands, buying little gift items and chatting with exhibitors about Lukoil-Perm's interest in crafts. I was particularly curious about what the gathered artisans had to say about the domain of povsednevnost' and issues of "getting by" in difficult post-Soviet conditions—the issues with which Lukoil-Perm was so concerned when it began supporting artisans in 2002. Responses varied. At several booths I was told that grants from Lukoil-Perm had, indeed, given a welcome boost to already-growing craft businesses and that Lukoil-Perm's interest had certainly helped to create a market by stimulating the tourist industry. "Who else is going help us except Lukoil?" said another exhibitor. "Oil is the only thing we have in our district!" A larger number of exhibitors were more skeptical, explaining, as one put it, "It's not possible to survive on handicrafts" (Remeslom ne vyzhit'). Representatives from one district that had received grants to open a folk crafts store in 2005 told me that, as far as they could tell, "Lukoil has already forgotten about us." They were left to eke out a living on their own, they said.

Only a few exhibitors were willing, at least in this heavily overdetermined context, to offer any detail on how handicrafts production had or had not had an impact on the povsednevnost' side of everyday life in their districts. One exhibitor sold me a simple birch-bark necklace that, she said, was the result of her attempts to give youth at the local school something to do other than stand around and smoke. There was almost no work to be had in the district, she went on, and Lukoil was not helping in the slightest. Lukoil-Perm staffed its own operations with specialists who worked in weeklong shifts, arriving and departing on a bus and staying in a self-sufficient dormitory. Villagers were left with little but a salty taste in their drinking water supply (the result of pumping saltwater into old wells to increase output). She would go back to the teenager who had made this necklace with my 150 rubles, she told me, and try to show him that he could perhaps make a living with folk crafts, that there was someone who would buy what he made with his own hands. She didn't sound particularly convinced herself. In this case, even a critique of Lukoil-Perm was accompanied not by an alternative but by a restatement, however unconvinced, of the bargain offered by Lukoil-Perm at the level of everyday life: we'll pump the oil out from under you; meanwhile, perhaps we can help you try your luck at folk handicrafts.

OIL BOOM BYT

CSR comprises an important and understudied dimension of the ways in which oil and gas are transforming Russian society, state, and culture in the 2000s.[19] Most studies of the relationship between oil companies and the Russian state focus on battles among oligarchs and the Kremlin, on the restructuring of laws and tax codes to shunt oil revenues into the federal budget (or into private hands), or on Russia as "energy superpower" in the international arena. Although many of these approaches are instructive, they are not adequate to the ways in which Russian citizens have actually come to encounter the new role of natural resource wealth in their lives.

The progression from a focus on the everyday dilemmas of povsed-nevnost' to the display of byt over the course of roughly a decade was likely more evident in the Perm Region than elsewhere in Russia. There are multiple reasons for this. For one, Lukoil-Perm was an early inno-vator in applying the language and techniques of global-style CSR to a Russian context. For another, the company received a big boost from the regional state administration's own efforts to place cultural production in the center of public consciousness as part of Governor Oleg Chirkunov's campaign to make Perm a cultural capital of Europe. But the Perm Region was hardly unique. In 2002, with its eyes on global markets, the board of directors of "big Lukoil"—the Moscow-based holding company—issued a "Social Codex," a detailed statement of the company's responsibilities to its workers and the regions and districts in which it worked. Lukoil-Perm, with its folk handicraft initiatives already under way, became an early model of how to fulfill these obligations. Indeed, the practice of holding open grant competitions to fund social and cultural projects—and then assuring that Lukoil's name was closely associated in district and regional media with each carefully selected project—spread quickly from Lukoil-Perm to other subsidiary oil companies under the Lukoil umbrella. CSR projects are now an almost universal element of Lukoil's operations in

Russia, and many other companies, large and small, strive to imitate them. To the extent that the reemergence of byt in the post-Soviet period recalls the role of cultural display, museums, and spectacles of state power in the imperial and Soviet periods, it is significant to note that, this time around, a private oil company has led the way, followed only later by Russian state agencies.

To be sure, not everyone in the Perm Region—nor even everyone in its oil-producing districts—bought into Lukoil-Perm's presentation of itself as responsible corporate partner and sponsor. Nevertheless, as I have shown, its CSR initiatives set some powerful conditions for the ways in which residents of the entire region encountered and participated in everyday life in the first decade of the twenty-first century. One outcome of the movement from povsednevnost' to byt that I have traced was that, in the midst of all the noise, display, and constant parade of festivals, the debates and dilemmas about everyday life that were so prevalent in the 1990s had all but vanished from public view. Given that those early post-socialist debates and dilemmas were a common forum for critical reflections on the nature, morality, and equity of capitalism, we might surmise that, whatever their initial intentions, members of Russia's new elite have only welcomed oil boom byt.

NOTES

The fieldwork on which this chapter is based was funded by the National Science Foundation Cultural Anthropology Program (BCS-0924178), the National Council on East European and Eurasian Research (with funds provided by the Title VIII Program), and the MacMillan Center for International and Area Studies at Yale University. I am grateful to Ian Convey and David Willey for research assistance. Except for public figures speaking or already quoted in public contexts, all names in this chapter are pseudonyms.

1. The Perm Region is Russia's fifty-ninth, according to the official federal numbering system, most often visible on license plates.

2. On the convergence of state-sponsored spectacle and oil booms in other times and places, see Andrew Apter, *The Pan-African Nation: Oil and the Spectacle of Culture in Nigeria* (Chicago: University of Chicago Press, 2005); Fernando Coronil, *The Magical State: Nature, Money, and Modernity in Venezuela* (Chicago: University of Chicago Press, 1997); and RETORT, *Afflicted Powers: Capital and Spectacle in a New Age of War* (London: Verso, 2005). State-sponsored festivals in post-Soviet Uzbekistan are comprehensively covered in Laura Adams, *The Spectacular State: Culture and National Identity in Uzbekistan* (Durham, N.C.: Duke University Press, 2010).

3. Natalia Pushkareva, "'Istoriia povsednevnosti' i 'Istoriia Chastnoi Zhizni': Soder-zhanie i Sotnoshenie Poniatii," *Sotsial'naia Istoriia* 8 (2004): 93–111; and Pushkareva, "Istoriia povsednevnosti: Predmet i metody," *Sotsial'naia Istoriia* 11 (2007): 9–54.

4. Pushkareva, "Istoriia povsednevnosti: Predmet i metody," 34.

5. Nathaniel Knight, "Science, Empire, and Nationality: Ethnography in the Russian Geographical Society, 1845–1855," in *Imperial Russia: New Histories for the Empire,* ed. Jane Burbank and David L. Ransel (Bloomington: Indiana University Press, 1998), 108–42.

6. Francine Hirsch, *Empire of Nations: Ethnographic Knowledge and the Making of the Soviet Union* (Ithaca, N.Y.: Cornell University Press, 2005).

7. Studies of the history of Western anthropology and other forms of knowledge in the European colonial encounter have demonstrated that the abstracted cataloging and presentation of a another group's lifeways is an archetypical technique of modern state power; see, among many others, Benedict Anderson, *Imagined Communities: Reflections on the Origin and Spread of Nationalism* (London: Verso, 1986); and George Stocking, ed., *Objects and Others: Essays on Museums and Material Culture* (Madison: University of Wisconsin Press, 1998).

8. See Douglas Rogers, *The Old Faith and the Russian Land: A Historical Ethnography of Ethics in the Urals* (Ithaca, N.Y.: Cornell University Press, 2009).

9. As other chapters in this volume indicate, the display and representation of byt stretched across many aesthetic genres in the imperial and Soviet periods. My focus is intentionally on the ethnographic display of byt, for it is the domain in which Lukoil-Perm, with its extractive operations based largely in rural areas that might be cast as home to "folk traditions," was most interested. As the concern with cultural production spread from Lukoil-Perm's Connections with Society Division into the Perm Region's state agencies over the 2000s, it also spread to other genres of cultural production, including art, literature, and film. Indeed, these state-sponsored initiatives often employed a language of broad-based "cultural revolution" that recalled the early Soviet period.

10. Henri Lefebvre, *The Critique of Everyday Life,* vol. 1, *Introduction* (1947; London: Verso, 1991) and vol. 2, *Foundations for a Sociology of the Everyday* (1961; London: Verso, 2002).

11. See, for example, Michael Burawoy and Katherine Verdery, introduction to *Uncertain Transition: Ethnographies of Change in the Postsocialist World,* ed. Michael Burawoy and Katherine Verdery (Lanham, Md.: Rowman and Littlefield, 1999), 1–2; and Caroline Humphrey, *The Unmaking of Soviet Life: Everyday Economies after Socialism* (Ithaca, N.Y.: Cornell University Press, 2002).

12. See Rogers, *The Old Faith;* and Frederico Varese, *The Russian Mafia: Private Protection in a New Market Economy* (Oxford: Oxford University Press, 2001) for examples from the Perm Region, and most of the anthropological literature on postsocialisms for various takes on the salience of everyday dilemmas in the 1990s.

13. See also Tullio Buccellato and Tomasz Mickiewicz, "Oil and Gas: A Blessing for the Few. Hydrocarbons and Inequality within Regions in Russia," *Europe-Asia Studies* 61, no. 3 (2002): 385–407.

14. See, e.g., Humphrey, *The Unmaking of Soviet Life;* Jennifer Patico, *Consumption and Social Change in a Post-Soviet Middle Class* (Washington, D.C.: Woodrow Wilson Center Press and Stanford University Press, 2008); and Olga Shevchenko, *Crisis and the Everyday in Postsocialist Moscow* (Bloomington: Indiana University Press, 2009).

15. See, for example, Marina Welker, "'Corporate Security Begins in the Community': Mining, the Corporate Social Responsibility Industry, and Environmental Advocacy in Indonesia," *Cultural Anthropology* 24, no. 1 (2009): 142–79.

16. On post-Soviet involution, see, for instance, Michael Burawoy, Pavel Krotov, and Tatyana Lytkina, "Involution and Destitution in Capitalist Russia," *Ethnography* 1, no. 1 (2000): 43–65.

17. "75 let Permskoi nefti," *Zvezda* (g. Perm), July 29, 2004.

18. "Narodnyi umelets," *Rassvet* (s. Barda), July 28, 2004.

19. See also Douglas Rogers, "The Materiality of the Corporation: Oil, Gas, and Corporate Social Technologies in the Remaking of a Russian Region," *American Ethnologist* 39, no. 2 (2012): 284–96.

PART II.
PUBLIC IDENTITIES AND PUBLIC SPACE

"We Don't Talk about Ourselves"

Women Academics Recall Their Path to Success

NATALIA PUSHKAREVA

The study of professionals, including academics, is a new branch of cultural anthropology. It lies at the intersection of ethnology and qualitative sociology, with its in-depth interviews, participant observation, and case studies. Although the application of the term "ethnology" to professional academics may seem odd,[1] their traditions can be analyzed in the same manner that one analyzes other subcultures that are defined by their signs, symbols, attributes, folklore, social and behavioral norms, forms of communication, and stereotypes. In this essay I explore the environment of women scholars, the official standards and the unofficial codes of behavior, lifestyles, attributes, and practices.[2]

Because of its focus on gender my research project examines power relations in the academic environment. By emphasizing power, my project draws upon feminist theory for methodological approaches. Specifically, my analysis relies upon the opposition between *traditional* and *feminist* research as enunciated by the American cultural anthropologist Renato Rosaldo. Traditional science is marked by *objectivism*—the claims of scientific objectivity and political and emotional neutrality; *imperialism*—the objectivization of the subject, in which the researcher "looks down" upon the observed phenomenon in the imperialist manner (the same manner in which the "white traveler" observed barbaric aborigines); and *monumentalism*—the assumption that such phenomena as the structural parameters of social equilibrium and ethnoculture are unchanging. Feminist anthropology adopts a different methodological stance. The claims of objectivity are replaced by empathy and involvement, recognizing that the ethnographic and social-psychological information of respondents has its own worth, as do the personal experiences of analysts, even though traditional scholarship tried to marginalize them. Feminist anthropology eschews imperialism and the denigration of the culture under study in favor of a thorough analysis of the superstitions and prejudices that analysts bring from their own culture.[3]

Investigation of the everyday life of women academics provides fertile soil for validation of the methods adopted in feminist anthropology. Responding to the appeal of German historians researching "everyday life," to dig in the soil on which you stand ("Grabe, wo Du stehst!"),[4] Belarusian and Russian researchers have developed a project focusing on the routine realities of women scholars in the socialist and postsocialist periods. The project focuses on women employees of the Russian Academy of Sciences who have enjoyed professional success.[5]

A proper understanding of the everyday life of contemporary women scholars in Russia requires a few introductory clarifications. First, since the eighteenth century knowledge production in Russia has been divided between scholarly research organizations (in the institutes of the Russian Academy of Sciences) and the universities. People who work in research institutions are not required to perform teaching duties, although many do nevertheless work half-time in institutions of higher education. People who work in the institutions of higher education have fewer research demands than do scholars in the Academy of Sciences and, indeed, may have none at all once they reach a particular rank. The focus group for my study consisted primarily of women scholars in the humanities and natural and mathematical sciences who were employed in institutes of the Academy of Sciences in Moscow, Petersburg, and Novosibirsk. These cities are the most important research centers in the country. More than half of the scholars in the Academy of Sciences work in these cities.

I conducted extensive life interviews with these women scholars. A portion of the material for my study was also gleaned from another source, namely, "personal stories" published in the popular press by women researchers at institutions of higher education. For comparative purposes I also drew on a handful of life interviews with male scholars that likewise appeared in the popular press.

Second, it is important to point out that the recruitment of women into academic life in Russia occurred in three phases. The first phase came in the 1920s, when the Soviet leaders sought to eliminate gender asymmetry in science. The second took place in the 1960s, when additional employment opportunities in academic institutions were created. The third was a feature of the postperestroika period and was connected with the outflow of men into more lucrative activities and to positions abroad. At present, women make up 33.7 percent of academic employees, although this overall figure includes the overrepresentation of women in humanities institutions, where they exceed 50 percent.[6]

This project seeks to gain insight into the mechanisms of change, utilization of time, and modes of the replication of gender asymmetry. For that purpose, I have compiled both typical and atypical cases and address the following questions: How are the routine realities of women scholars constructed? What meanings are assigned to the activities of women scholars in specific social interactions? How does the academic community treat women's labor and scholarly success? How do other women treat such women? This approach permits a focus on details of everyday life and the opinions of women scholars about their life experiences.

The primary respondents were women of the educated urban elite. The project was based on several dozen oral interviews, which were taped and later transcribed. The questions presented to the respondents did not take the form of a tightly structured questionnaire, and the time allotted to the interviews was not limited. Respondents who provided the most complete answers about their life experiences were selected for follow-up interviews in which they could recount in greater detail the stories about themselves. Although these parameters may have limited opportunities for generalizing from the results, the advantages outweighed the possible drawbacks.

Interviewers prompted respondents only to "talk about yourself, about your life experience," and respondents divided these two options into primary and secondary categories on their own. The researchers helped to establish the progression of events, their cause-and-effect connections, suggesting that the interviewees think about the means of physical or social survival in the situations they recounted and their emotions and perceptions about what had happened. A particular group of questions concerned the actual life of the respondent: her familial situation, her relationship with her chosen profession, her satisfaction with it, and her expectations for the future. Through an analysis of the conditions of life and the direct answers of respondents, I strove to clarify the following:

1. What psychological factors and types of interactions help women to construct individual life strategies and gain confidence that they will be successful?
2. What values and life circumstances, arising from the family and the culture, turned out to be useful or detrimental to them?
3. What family resources were transmitted from grandparents to parents and then to children?
4. What emotional or psychological price did the women pay for their success in life?

Because I did not want to lose an integrated portrait of the cause-and-effect connections in women's life histories, I decided not to disaggregate the written interviews at first; the separate sequences seemed too simplistically schematized. Thus the complete transcripts of the extensive interviews came to have a value of their own. They were literarily complete, ready-made biographies. They contained coherent, relatively complete, and comprehensive histories of the lives of my respondents.

We did not have a control group; the major comparisons were drawn from within the ranks of those who were questioned. Their answers were based on their own memories, impressions, knowledge, and experiences relating to the events of their own lives and the lives of persons close to them.

Work on this project revealed how important a gendered symmetry between respondents and researchers was for maintaining contact and mutual understanding and for recognizing the similarity of experiences on both sides. The respondents and researchers conversed on an egalitarian basis, and for both sides, the recitations about life experiences and reflections on them played a therapeutic role. Here is a segment of the conversation between a respondent and a researcher:

> Respondent: My grandmother knew a lot of poems, and many different stories about them. She was of great value to the village—she was tactful and educated. And obviously, she knew a lot.

Researcher: You could be talking about my own grandmother—she was just like that. Even without any special education, she knew a lot of poetry. She read Pushkin. . . . I took that as a given.

The shared experience in roles could serve as a basis for understanding because the respondent and the researcher were of the same sex and the same generation, and they were similarly affected by the political and social changes the country was experiencing.

I compiled a cross section of the life of a generational cohort of women scholars who are now about age forty to forty-five. As I reviewed the stories of their lives, it became evident that they abounded in equivalent phrases, similar judgments about cause and effect, the same reading in youth and maturity. In keeping with that approach, rather than seeking a typical representative of the cohort or insisting upon a large sample (as in quantitative sociology), I was interested in uncovering the typological characteristics of life practices surrounding significant events, as well as models or patterns of interpretive activity. I thus set the goal of reconstructing history through the eyes of female representatives of a specific referential group, clarifying the specifics of their recollections and the unforeseen connections between the societal experiences of the informants.

The utility of oral testimony about everyday life lies in the fact that other sources often fail to record information about quotidian experience, regarding it as inconsequential. Although a superficial view might cause someone to ask what personal difficulties such a fortunate social group as academic women could have encountered, oral accounts of their subjective experience reveal that their achievements were not easily won.

The majority of autobiographical accounts exhibit the usual characteristics of oral historical testimonies, namely, that the accounts were not infrequently adjusted in keeping with what an account of one's life is supposed to be. The thematic of daily life appears in all accounts, even though tales of the difficulties of everyday living did not stand at the center of the narrative. The details of an ordinary life for academics are like the thread between the beads of important transformational events such as graduation from an institution of higher education, enrollment in graduate study, defense of one's candidate dissertation, and the publication of one's first monograph. They create a narrative base and allow the listeners (the women researchers) to assimilate the events the respondent is relating and to sense the empathy between the respondent and the person to whom the account is told.

It was the ordinary that evoked in listeners the emotions that allowed them to become alter egos of the narrators, empathizing with or disregarding their stories of their lives and careers. After absorbing the interview material thoroughly, I identified the central theme of the project and labeled it "most of the time, we keep quiet about ourselves."

It is not coincidental that many of our respondents compared their own life course and daily experience with that of their parents. What they had learned from their parents, or, more broadly, from the older generation, demanded confirmation and substantiation. The theoretical work of European psychologists (Murray Bowen and Virginia Satir) proved particularly valuable to the researchers in understanding this multigenerational process and its antithesis, a disjuncture. Although a comfortable balance between autonomy and contact between generations in some families and disjuncture in others did not show a direct cause-and-effect correlation in relation to satisfaction with one's life, there was a strong association between these factors.

A basic finding of this study is that women who strove to reject physically and emotionally the lifestyles of their parents and forgot about them proved to be less successful than those who relied upon the symbolic capital of emotional ties with older relatives, learning from them how to overcome difficulties (especially when the relatives were themselves scholars). In other words, the preservation and transmission across generations of a feeling of connection and belonging, of family identity and family values, can sustain individuals even under the stressful conditions of life in the Soviet Union and in postperestroika Russia. This hypothesis is confirmed by the life stories. Despite having highly varied personal experiences, the women who recounted their life histories shared one feature: all of them at some stage of their lives secured social advancement, success, or influence. What internal factors conditioned respondents' need for internal growth?

I found that the most important factor was the respondent's relationship with her father, her desire to fulfill his will, his choice, to justify his vision of his daughter's future, as illustrated in the following six comments by respondents:

He tried to develop my capabilities, because he had dreamed of having a son, but instead he had a daughter. And so he tried to develop in me male sorts of habits, so that being with me would be interesting to him. (mathematician, age sixty)

My dad was a scholar. And although there was no attempt to push me to follow the family path, that was how things worked out. (historian, age thirty-four)

My dad's self-esteem played a role. I think that's what he wanted, that his Marusia would be better than all the others. (biochemist, age forty-one)

Because my dad had a strong inclination toward the humanities—he wrote poetry and created crossword puzzles—he and I agreed that I would study at Moscow University in the Journalism Faculty. (physicist, age fifty-four)

In childhood I was a humanist, but my dad was a mathematician. Therefore, he drove me forcefully into mathematics school, and pushed me to take the entrance examinations with the admonition, "Well, do you really not want to test your own strength?" (astronomer, age forty-eight)

When my dad became a physician, he did not go to Moscow to study. Maybe, he said, I could realize his old dream? (philologist, age forty-one)

Obviously, the influence of fathers on the respondents was significant, although most of the women had mothers who had achieved professional success. The mothers also pressured their daughters to become self-sufficient professionals. The striving for independence, the sense of self-respect, the ability to achieve set goals and defend their positions—all this developed from childhood and from the relationship with fathers and mothers.

"Argue with me! Learn to defend yourself!" my mom demanded, and if I felt hurt or cried, she teased me as a crybaby. (historian, age forty-nine)

The regimen in our family was this: "After each failure, you need to have success; otherwise, you won't have any successes." My mom always said this to me, and my father added, "Hang on by your fingernails!" When I was a child, my favorite fairy tale, which was always told to me, was about two frogs who fell into a pitcher of milk—an optimist and a pessimist. You know it, right? The pessimist gave up and drowned. But the optimist kept churning, made butter and managed to get out. She saved herself. I was raised on that story. Everything is in our hands, and it's most important not to let things fall through. (ophthalmologist, age thirty-nine)

Even so, it was more often fathers than mothers who played the key role in stimulating ambition in daughters. They explained to their daughters that education was the fundamental means toward social mobility and professional accomplishment. These parents did not talk about possible marriage partners with their daughters but instead instilled in them dreams of scholarly achievement and recognition. The lifestyle of their families was exceptionally important for daughters. Most often, they came from academic families, or at least one of their relatives had some connection to the scholarly world. It was also important that parents and close relatives expressed pride in their daughters' abilities in childhood and believed in their strengths:

> I had an aunt who had a doctoral degree—a biochemist. I watched what she did, and how, and I really liked it. My parents didn't add anything serious to it [my enthusiasm], but they encouraged me. (anthropologist, age forty-nine)
>
> My parents treated me as though I were something exceptionally valuable, and they talked a lot with me, explained things, and did a lot with me. At home, all sorts of creative . . . games were common. (biologist, age forty-nine)

Even when future women scholars were not raised in academic families, they often came from families of the urban or rural intelligentsia, where books and reading, including reading aloud at home, played a large role.

> Tons of books were purchased; there were a lot of books. And all of them were read constantly, in dim light. A whole cupboard of books were read—I remember that exactly. . . .
> There were a lot of fairy tales, and a lot of books. Truly, that developed some sort of youthful imagination in me. In any case, it was clear. (astronomer, age forty-nine)

Parents typically perceived their daughters to be like sons, openly expressing disappointment that they were not born as boys. Many of the girls tried to prove that they were "no worse" than sons:

Mom told me, ironically, "Learn to iron shirts—it will serve you well in life!" And all my sentient life, it was testimony to the fact that I was not worse than if I had been a boy. (philologist, age fifty-one)

He tried to develop my abilities, because he dreamed of having a son, but instead a daughter was born, and so he tried to inculcate masculine habits in me. (biochemist, age fifty-one)

Other guiding personalities—most notably teachers—appear in auto-biographical accounts much more rarely than fathers, mothers, or close relatives. However, among respondents who came from rural families (in contrast to urban ones), it was nonrelatives who were most important in guiding respondents not only in the choice of profession but also in lifestyle:

For high school, we already went to a neighboring village. There we had a woman teacher, and I understood that that was my ideal. It seems to me that to this very day I imitate her in my dress, in everything. (anthropologist, age forty-nine)

The primary characteristic that distinguishes these girls, "born in place of boys," from typical sons was their exceptional orientation toward results, conscientiousness, and understanding of how to overcome difficulties:

When I complained about something at home, that I couldn't do any more, that nothing was going to turn out for me, Mom asked sternly, "After 'I can't,' what next?" (historian, age forty-nine)

Because I was accustomed to studying, and I had a sense of how study was indispensable, I studied and I studied and I studied. I thought every-thing over, reflected on everything, and analyzed everything. . . . There were horrible problems in pharmacology, and I couldn't cram it into my head, but then I learned it all. (pharmacologist, age forty-four)

Within the focus group of this study—those women who quickly and successfully established scholarly careers, defending their doctoral disser-tations (i.e., second-stage dissertations following candidate dissertations in the Soviet and the Russian system) before the age of forty—there were almost no girls who were slackers. Literally every one of the respondents recalled that she studied very hard:

Lessons, study. . . . The first order of business was study. From the very beginning, I was focused on how I had to graduate with the gold medal [with
honors]. And that's what I did! (endocrinologist, age forty-one)

I was the first person in my school in twenty years who received the
medal. My essay was recognized as the best in the district. (physicist, age
forty-two)

It is curious that among the respondents only one woman defended
her doctoral dissertation before the age of forty and was also selected as
a corresponding member of the Russian Academy of Sciences before the
age of fifty. Yet she reported that she had not demonstrated a passion for
knowledge from her youngest years and had not excelled in school; in
general, she had not distinguished herself as a "model student." Even so,
she was the one who was most professionally advanced at the time of the
interview. Could it be that the orientation toward achieving the highest
record in study and in scholarly activities deprived respondents of the
skills needed to establish relationships with friends and classmates and
therefore hurt their chances to develop administrative talent? Communication also involves work, and they may not have had time for it.

In accounts of Russian women scholars, unlike their peers in the West,
we do not encounter references to obstacles to a professional career coming during their youth from their parents or other close relatives.[7] Among
Russian women scholars we do not find feelings of abandonment, of deser-
tion, of loneliness, of a lack of support from the moment they chose a life of
scholarship. On the contrary, respondents were often the only children in
their families. Their parents believed in them and supported their choices:

In childhood, I won competitions at various levels—district-wide, city-
wide. As a result, everyone thought that I would study literature. (philologist, age fifty)

My father excited my interest in life. He was, truly, my first teacher; he
believed in me! (geographer, age forty-three)

Again, one should not forget that a mother, too, often played an important supporting role. Her strictness, her belief in the necessity of overcoming difficulties provided a solid personal foundation for many respondents. The mothers of all respondents were persons of the Soviet period
(members of the respondent cohort were all born between the 1940s and

the 1970s). The transmission of ambition from mother to daughter can be found in some of the biographical accounts:

> You know, I truly reached the goal that my mom did not achieve but very much wanted to. My mother had a different start to life: the early death of her mother, and then the departure of her father from the family to another woman, leaving her alone from the age of fourteen. Mom left the provincial city, became a Muscovite, defended two dissertations. My life path repeats that of my mother, only without the complications. Mom always demanded from me more and more. Well, if she didn't demand it, then she just expected it. (historian, age forty-nine)

The women who reached the doctoral degree at a young age achieved success in the face of difficulties. Every one of these early achievers claimed to have lacked the understanding and support of her senior colleagues. They recalled this happily because their accomplishments (such as the defense of two dissertations and their scholarly recognition) were all the more brilliant and salient because they had overcome difficulties. For the majority of narrators, the account of the obstacles they had surmounted was the basis for their assessment of their career success.

Respondents more rarely took note of another type of complications—complications that still obtain in current academic life and everyday life. Among these difficulties respondents named the envy of their colleagues:

> In school, I always had problems with classmates. . . . The class was really oppositional . . . and for something like . . . half a year . . . they bullied me. At first, I became a nervous wreck, but then I learned not to allow offenses, and to say always what I think, and not care about others' opinions. (astronomer, age forty-six)

> In school, little by little I was badgered . . . as the star pupil. In the sixth grade, some sort of negative gossip went on. . . . It was said, she has all As, and there's something not right about it. (historian, age thirty-seven)

Russians tend to view themselves as victims. This is especially true of women. However much they may have been knocked around by fate or employers or husbands, they nevertheless sometimes believe that they have suffered way beyond their just deserts. In addition, their successful husbands are often likely to remind them that their accomplishments are "undeserved." Here is such a case reported in a life interview with a woman professor of economics:

I always had the feeling that in life I was getting more [opposition] than I deserved. I never had any desire to enter into a competitive battle. But my husband, . . . he . . . so to speak . . . increased this tendency. He always reminded me where I came from, what my social roots were. . . . Now I know that he did this because he himself felt extremely insecure. The most amazing thing is that instead of supporting each other, he . . . in fact . . . tried to distance himself from me. (economist, age fifty-two)

We may conclude that difficult circumstances in a person's studies and early professional experience often stimulate energetic efforts to surmount them.

If I didn't succeed at something or I failed in some subject, for example, mathematics, I would reconsider the whole puzzle. (physicist, age forty-seven)

In my third year, I had a crisis about the meaning of life. . . . I very distinctly remembered that I chose my specialization because surgery is the most nonfeminine area of medicine. (surgeon ophthalmologist, age forty-four)

Everyone went to enter the university in the closest city—but I went to another country. (biophysicist, age fifty-three)

The understanding of success, reconstructed from the accounts of the informants, consists in an ability to pass through the stages required to reach the heights of scholarly recognition. When they experienced delays in getting hired, when their successes were overlooked by their supervisors, these incidents were noted as unjust. They considered the need to search for rewards for themselves—a new way of organizing work time, a departure from their own scholarly work in order to teach, supplemental work because a promotion at their primary job did not occur—as a reflection of the past and as an offensive strategy.

One of the most common themes to appear in the biographical narratives of women scholars is a collapse or complication in one's personal life. The divergence between societal expectations of well-being in family life and the reality was especially noticeable. Although in open-ended life interviews men could also have talked about complications in their personal lives, they did not, whereas women returned to these issues continually.

For women, the cost of a successful scholarly career—divorce and difficulty in maintaining friendships—was one of the most prominent themes.

The disinclination to praise professional success, the absence of a culture of recognition or a culture of praise, is characteristic of the scholarly world, yet this type of recognition is something for which women feel a strong need. The exception that proves the rule rings out in the account of one informant:

> My mom, along with several of her friends, created (at her initiative) a "Society of Mutual Adoration." That was how they called their accord—it was arranged that whatever was said about one or another of them about whatever or whenever, they would say only the best things. . . . Wouldn't that be nice, if my mom or I myself worked not in a "terrarium of the like-minded" (do you know that expression?) but rather in a situation of good will. . . . Really, we need to come to such an agreement and all of us found such a society. (historian, age forty-nine)

Women did not want to talk about their failures if they had not risen above them. The respondents avoided topics concerning their personal lives. Most of them had suffered complications:

> God! Oh, well, I don't talk about that to anyone. It's not necessary to tell about it. (sociologist, age thirty-nine)

In post-Soviet Russia, many businessmen have wives who are scholars. However, these men treat their wives' achievements as their own property, to be flaunted whenever the opportunity occurs. When both spouses are scholars in the same field, though, the men do not brag about their wives' scholarly accomplishments.[8] One woman lamented:

> My scholarly achievements did not help me to become happy. . . . We had been married for seventeen years when I defended my second dissertation. My husband was in a dismal mood at the party, and the next day he said to me that he had decided to divorce me because he "didn't want to be the husband of a Margaret Thatcher." I burst into tears. But what could be done in such a situation? That was how he showed which of us was the master. (historian, age forty-seven)[9]

In a clear majority of interviews with women who achieved success in the scholarly world, men appeared as rivals, envious of their wives' success, sometimes openly, as in the case just cited, but more often hidden under a guise of indifference. This picture is typical in the narratives of women scholars from other countries.[10] One of the German respondents in an analogous project called her path (in which her husband shared her success and helped her) "completely atypical."[11] As an exception, one of our respondents recounted a situation not in her own life but in that of a friend and colleague:

> My ex, well, he envied me in everything and always. It seems that this is typical in families where both the husband and the wife are scholars, even in the same field. I myself know of only one exception—they were colleagues of mine from Ukraine, philosophers by training. Here it was, in that family the husband helped the wife organize everything. He let her defend her doctoral dissertation first and become a leader in her field of expertise. How rare that is! I don't know any others like them. (philosopher, age forty-eight)

Women who have attained the highest academic degrees do not envy their female colleagues who gave up academic work and pursuit of the doctorate during perestroika and turned into so-called consumption managers—housewives to "New Russians." These wives of businessmen supervise the building of huge country mansions and discourage their daughters and granddaughters from intellectual pursuits.[12] In contrast, women academics are committed to the preservation of child-rearing techniques that were widespread from the end of the 1950s until the beginning of the 1970s and that fostered a girl's scholarly interests. In the twenty-first century they still adhere to the intellectual values their parents taught them. They maintain with conviction that they don't suffer from deprivation and discrimination; instead, they laugh together with their colleagues when hearing disparaging anecdotes about women scholars and deny that they are "oppressed." They contend that the flexibility in time scheduling, the fulfillment of intellectual work, the opportunities of personal advancement and self-realization, and the friendly relationships with other intellectuals offset their meager salaries.

It is characteristic of academic women to attribute their scholarly achievements such as the doctoral degree, professorial rank, department head, and membership in international organizations to a favorable conjunction of circumstances and the help of "other important factors." None of the women respondents admitted that she had been pressing for official recognition of her achievements. Quite the contrary, all of them realized that "they had been placed under artificial constraints, but they did not resist them, waiting for a day in the future when somebody would come and offer them a better opportunity."

The biographical narratives of women scholars revealed their fears of losing reliable defenders, of being left by husbands, of being unable to cope with uncertainty. They did not boast of personal achievements, even in the academic sphere. This discourse reflects the impact of the Soviet-era concept of the "working mother," who was valued not for her success in the professional arena but rather primarily as a wife who reared her children and earned extra money. A sizable majority (75 percent) of respondents who had gained prominence in the academic sphere were not married at the time of our interview. Thus, they had no obvious motive to adopt a deferential attitude toward marital obligations. But married women scholars tended to value family preservation; sometimes they placed it ahead of their professional achievements.

Another statistic shows that one of the casualties for women of an ambitious scholarly career is family life itself. It is probably not coincidental that 48 percent of male scholars have two children and 10 percent even three; conversely, 29 percent of women scholars and academics have no children (another 29 percent have two children, and only 2 percent have three). A "child-centered" family can be only a dream for many women scholars.[13]

Could it be that the reluctance of women academics to fight against constraints might explain why the "glass ceiling" continues to obstruct their progress? Even though officially it does not exist, an impenetrable barrier remains. At present, women scholars trying to gain official recognition in their academic communities encounter practically the same obstacles as their mothers did thirty years ago. In the registers of doctoral degree holders in Russia, women made up 20 percent in 2000 (compared with 14 percent in 1980), associate members of the Russian Academy of Sciences 15 percent, and the highest rank (*akademik*) 1.3 percent.[14] The Presidium of the Supreme Certification Commission, which approves resolutions by academic councils, is comprised of twenty-six men and one woman. Only one woman sits on the Council of the Russian Foundation for Humanities, which manages the financing of new scholarly projects. In the institutes of the Russian Academy of Sciences, only one-fifth of the laboratory headships are held by women, 4 percent of deputy directors are women, and 2 percent of directors are women.[15] However, few women seem likely to protest the existing practices: 67 percent of women scholars interviewed believe that management, including in the academic sphere, will remain men's prerogative.[16]

Why don't women scholars object to the inequitable relationship but instead take it for granted? Despite the low salaries, the women interviewed (from laboratory assistants to institute directors) emphasized that they are satisfied with their work (about 90 percent of respondents). This high rate of satisfaction implies that women are more interested in pursuing their scholarly work than in earning better salaries, higher positions, or even recognition for their academic achievements. As a professor of musicology said, "An attractive, honored profession is worth much in itself."[17]

The interviews reflect the existence of a complicated array of relationships between men and women in the academic setting. For example, while recounting their everyday lives as scholars, Russian women underlined the fact that the heads of their administrative units replicated familial relationships in their departments, preserving multigenerational structures and a complicated hierarchy under the leadership of an all-knowing head of family.[18] The posts of department heads in postgraduate and doctoral programs in our research institutes are almost without exception held by women acting as institute "mother hens." Just as in the traditional Russian patriarchal family and in the Soviet-era governmental structures, paternalistic relationships have continued to pervade our society, and academic life is no different. No matter who heads a unit, either a woman or a man, the unit's relationships take a typically patriarchal hierarchical form. The department head never performs the set-up for tea-drinking rituals or washes the cups of colleagues at the end of a working day. Relationships are governed by a strict hierarchy: those people holding higher posts are addressed with the polite form of "you" (except for members of the same research group, persons of the same age, and those people who are accustomed to socializing informally during research expeditions).

Women's value to their institutes would seem to rest more on their diligence than on their knowledge or talent. The statistics bear out this view:

52 percent of women employees of academic institutions and 57 percent of junior research assistants in scientific research institutes do not have an academic degree.[19] Women are abundant in the lower stratum of scholarly research, where their roles mimic those of housewives and of physical and emotional nurturers. It is in service professions—cleaner, cook, teacher, physician, psychotherapist—that women play the major role. From the home to the workplace, the notion that women belong in supporting roles prevails, even within the academic community.

The most important component of a scholar's everyday life is still preparation for and participation in meetings of scholarly congresses and other types of academic conferences. Respondents recalled vividly the severe reduction of such meetings that took place ten to fifteen years ago due to lack of financing. According to their accounts, in that period women scholars attempted to establish networks based on institutional "family" ties and began to hold meetings for "insiders."[20] Through their "secret," "quiet" leadership, women tried to retain a position for themselves in post-Soviet scholarly life. Their efforts could be seen as the real story of the period, although these efforts could not be recognized, unlike the open and theoretically legitimate and legal governance of men.

The second important component of everyday life for academics over the past twenty years has been the struggle to obtain grants. In accordance with official procedure, project principal investigators had to file all applications and prepare all reports. But often higher-ranking academics were named as the principal investigators in order to facilitate the acceptance of the grant applications, while women, who generally enjoyed lower status, were relegated to "project manager" positions and routine work. Thus, this aspect of everyday life in academic communities was marked by salient gender differences. This situation continues today.

Few male scholars started their careers as secretaries in a research sector where they had to type other scholars' articles or answer the telephone.[21] But for most women respondents, this was a typical rung on their career ladder. After a period of time, they proceeded to the second stage, that of writing a dissertation. Most women scholars described the third stage, preparation for the doctoral defense, as the most difficult. They faced great difficulties when they took the posts of professor, leading scientific officer, and especially principal scientific officer. Most respondents who decided to write the second or doctoral dissertation did so in secret and defended it at an institution far away from the one where they worked. Only a few had the courage to undertake the unequal struggle with their administration for promotion, with its concomitant stress and moral and psychological pressure.

When asked the direct question "At what stages of your career did you experience sex discrimination?," most women respondents pointed to the period before defense of the second dissertation and afterward, when the administration tried to ignore the defense and made no change in salary or position in light of it. Nearly half of the women interviewed emphasized that their contributions to scholarship were not appropriately valued and that their rights to their intellectual property were violated in the course of publication of their work.

> A chapter of a monograph was based on my manuscripts; however, I was not included in the list of authors since I was only an assistant to the chair at that time and then a candidate of medical science. I walked out and went to another scientific and research institute. (ophthalmologist, age forty-two)[22]

I encountered numerous examples of this type in interviews gathered in past years. In writing my report on this project, I wanted to include the most typical examples of social practices that devalued women at the highest levels of academic hierarchies. It is interesting to observe how pervasive discrimination can be. Women who hold doctoral degrees suffer practically the same indignities and obstacles as women who are junior research assistants and senior researchers. But, strange as it may seem, most of the respondents did not want to focus on discrimination and preferred to explain their situations as unrelated to gender:

> I would not term it gender discrimination; it is most likely just a matter of personal social capabilities, what might be called social competence, and the ability to build relations with the right people. It is a problem of a talent for survival in academia, rather than gender imbalance. Talented people always face difficulties, and in this situation it is talent that suffers such restrictions (and not being a woman). Forget your *gender*. (anthropologist, age forty-nine)[23]

Women tend to give their accounts an air of gender neutrality, including a reluctance to recall, unless they are pushed, incidents of discrimination and injustice on the basis of sex. This is yet another manifestation of women deploying verbal expression in accordance with societal expectations.

In many interviews one can observe an undervaluation of the achievements of the women. One respondent, an employee of a major academic institute, holder of a doctorate, and a professor, thoughtfully said in response to a request for an interview and a description of her own career in scholarship:

> Well, what kind of successful woman am I? Surely, I wouldn't do for [your project on successful women]. (biologist, age fifty-one)

The surprising conclusion of this analysis of life interviews of often highly successful academic women is that patriarchal stereotypes continue to permeate the scholarly community and are unlikely to be eradicated any time soon. When I raised the question of gender discrimination during the interviews, the overwhelming majority of respondents rejected the notion outright. A small number remarked that prior to our interview the idea of such discrimination had never even crossed their minds. It is hard to imagine that these intelligent and sensitive women do not feel injured in some way, and yet this would seem to be the case.

Women scholars appear to be happy for the opportunity to be included in a sphere traditionally reserved for men, the sphere of scholarly research and theorizing. Even if they understand that discrimination is a factor in their work relationships, they regard it as *normal* and make no effort to change the situation.

Despite their impressive accomplishments, most respondents presented their life stories as something unspectacular and merely a steady, gradual progression without crises or breaks. All of the women's accounts are histories of adaptation to circumstances. In their accounts, women narrators do not recognize their delusions or their deviations from their previous trajectory in life but rather see in their ability to adapt to changing conditions a great accomplishment and not in any way a concession.

However, this way of framing the question disguises a more positive reading of the evidence. Women who attained professional positions rarely complained about the lack of mutual understanding in the family, including in relationships with their children, whether their husbands left their professionally successful rival wives or remained with them to preserve the family and provide their wives emotional support. They set their goals and adjusted other aspects of their lives so that they could continue the scholarly work that gave them personal satisfaction and a desired identity. That is the core value. For the rest, "We don't talk about ourselves."

NOTES

1. H. Varenne, "About Pierre Bourdieu: 'Homo Academicus,'" *Teachers College Record* 91 (1988): 263–65; L. J. D. Wacquant, "For a Socio-analysis of Intellectuals: On 'Homo Academicus,'" interview with Pierre Bourdieu, *Berkeley Journal of Sociology: A Critical Review* 34 (1989): 4.

2. T. B. Shchepanskaia, "Antropologiia professii" (Anthropology of professions), *Zhurnal sotsiologii i sotsial'noi antropologii* 6, no. 1 (2003): 139–61.

3. R. Rosaldo, *Culture and Truth: The Remaking of Social Analysis* (Boston: Beacon Press, 1989), 33; M. Rosaldo, "The Use and Abuse of Anthropology: Reflections on Feminism and Cross-Cultural Understanding," *Signs* 5 (1980): 400.

4. S. Lindquist, "Grabe, wo du stehst: Geschichte von unten," in *Fragestellungen, Methoden und Projekte einer Geschichte des Alltags*, ed. H. Ehalt (Vienna: H. Bolau, 1984), 295–305.

5. I. R. Chikalova (Belarus) and N. L. Pushkareva (Russia), *Women Scientists in Belarus and Russia in the Post-Soviet Period: A Comparative Study of Social Identity, 1991–2001* (Moscow: Russian Foundation for the Humanities, 2004–5; Minsk, 2006).

6. E. Z. Mirskaia and E. A. Martynova, "Zhenshchiny-ucheny: Problemy i perspektivy," *Sotsial'naia dinamika sovremennoi nauki* (Moscow) (1995): 67.

7. Compare Angelika Wetterer, "Die soziale Konstruktion von Geschlecht in Professionalisierungsprozessen," in *Die soziale Konstruktion von Geschlecht in Professionalisierungsprozessen*, ed. Angelika Wetterer (Frankfurt am Main: Verlag Campus, 1995), 7–25; Brigitte Hasenjürgen, *Soziale Macht im Wissenschaftsspiel: SozialwissenschaftlerInnen und Frauenforschung an der Hochschule* (Münster: Westf. Dampfboot, 1996); Sabine Lang and Birgst Sauer, *Wissenschaft als Arbeit: Arbeit als Wissenschaftlerin* (Frankfurt am Main, 1997); Doris Indisch and Brigitte Lichtenberger-Fenz, *Hinter den Fassaden des Wissens: Frauen, Feminismus und Wissenschaft—eine aktuelle Debatte* (Vienna, 1999).

8. Compare V. J. Tichenor, "Status and Income as Gendered Resources: The Case of Marital Power," *Journal of Marriage and the Family* 61, no. 3 (1999): 212–21.

9. Recorded on September 14, 2008, in Moscow (from the personal archive of the author).

10. G. Dresse and N. Langreiter, "Nie Zeit, nie frei: Arbeit und Freizeit von WissenschaftlerInnen," in *Bewegte Zeiten: Arbeit und Freizeit nach der Moderne*, ed. S. Gruber, K. Löffler, and K. Thien (Munich, 2002), 121–38.

11. M. Kohlt, "Wissenschaftsgeschichte aus Lebensgeschichte," in *Geschichte und Soziologie: Studien zur kognitiven, sozialen und historischen Identität einer Disziplin*, ed. W. Lepenies (Frankfurt am Main, 1981), 1:428–65, see 463.

12. N. Ris, "'Profil' burzhuaznosti: Novaia elita o sebe," in *O muzhe(N)stvennosti*, ed. S. A. Ushakin (Moscow: Novoe literaturnoe obozrenie, 2002), 410.

13. N. A. Vinokurov, "Zhenshchiny i muzhchiny v nauke," *Sotsiologicheskie issledovaniia* 4 (1999): 82–86.

14. V. Troian, "Zhenshchina i nauka: Podrugi ili sopernitsy?," *Zerkalo nedeli,* January 5, 2002, 376.

15. *Nauka v Rossii 1994* (Moscow: Tsentr issledovanii statistiki nauki, 1995), 91.

16. L. S. Egorova, "Gendernye stereotipy v upravlenii," *Zhenshchina v rossiiskom obshchestve* 3–4 (2001): 16.

17. V. Elena Markova Gyzeeva, "Zhenshchina v nauke: Eto slozhno," *Slovo* 1 (2000): 371–72.

18. Verdery, *What Was Socialism,* 9.

19. *Vestnik statistiki* 1 (1987): 54–56; G. F. Beliaeva and I. D. Gorshkova, "Professionalnye problemy zhenskikh nauchno-pedagogicheskikh kadrov MGU // Tsentr sotsiologicheskikh issledovanii MGU im. M. V. Lomonosova," December 13, 1998, http://www.owl.ru/win/research/msu.htm.

20. A. Vasileva, Zhenshchiny v nauke i obrazovanii (beseda s matematikom G. Iu. Iaroshevskoi), http://www.owl.ru/win/womplus/1999/science.htm.

21. E. Iu. Meshcherkina, "Bytie muzhskogo soznaniia: Opyt rekonstruktsii maskulinnoi identichnosti srednego i rabochego klassa," in Ushakin, *O muzhe(N)stvennosti,* 281.

22. N. S. Agamova and A. G. Allakhverdian, "Rossiiskie zhenshchiny v nauke i vysshei shkole: Istoriko-nauchnye i naukovedcheskie aspekty," *Vopr. istorii estestvoznaniia i tekhniki* 1 (2000): 141–53.

23. Recorded on September 20, 2009, in Moscow (from the personal archive of the author).

6

The Literature of Everyday Life and Popular Representations of Motherhood in Brezhnev's Time

ELIZABETH SKOMP

In the mid-1960s Russian women writers began to articulate the contemporary experience of motherhood and thus to aspire to "that frequently stated goal of feminist study: seeing maternal points of view more fully, hearing maternal voices more clearly and variously, understanding maternal subjectivity more deeply and complexly."[1] Though they would have resisted the feminist label, Natal'ia Baranskaia and I. Grekova (the pseudonym of Elena Sergeevna Venttsel'), two of the first and most prominent women writers of the literature of everyday life, began to interrogate and challenge the expectations placed on the mother. In order to understand the context to which those literary maternal voices responded, I will examine some dominant themes of motherhood during Leonid Brezhnev's rule (1964–82) as they appeared in brochures and manuals on motherhood intended for popular consumption and in *Rabotnitsa*, the most widely circulated women's magazine of the Soviet period.[2]

Prose fiction and advice literature intersect and diverge in several significant areas.[3] As my analysis will show, both belletristic and didactic texts essentialized motherhood and utilized the inherited trope of maternal status as a natural inevitability for women. In moving from an examination of biological motherhood to practical motherhood, advice literature addressed the twofold enterprise (and persistent Soviet concern) of *vospitanie*, including the upbringing of children and the education of mothers themselves; the corresponding literary treatment of the subject revealed maternal anxiety about these mandates. The tension between the ideal and the real emerged more clearly in textual treatments of the double burden of responsibilities in work and domestic spheres; while Baran-skaia's 1969 novella *Nedelia kak nedelia* (A week like any other) exposed an existing problem by committing it to paper, advice literature would use the reality of the double burden to shape a new version of maternal identity. Similarly, the reality of the incomplete or "maternal" family is a topic that Baranskaia and Grekova repeatedly addressed, while its treat-ment in advice literature was relatively late and infrequent. The relation-ship between these two types of texts may also be understood in another way: writers of the literature of everyday life reformulated the concerns of advice literature and reconstituted those concerns in their texts from a female or maternal perspective, not the perspective of the state. Thus fiction complicated and at times undermined the exhortations present in didactic texts.

Everyday life is the point of convergence for the two types of texts examined in this chapter; they inhabited two different parts of a shared rhetorical space as they focused on the dual and interrelated areas of ma-ternal preparation and maternal practice.[4] In his study of everyday life literature, Benjamin Sutcliffe notes the persistent linking of *byt* and the feminine.[5] Such literature positioned and presented itself as document-ing the everyday, while the propaganda materials sought to bring about certain conditions in everyday life.

Jonathan Bolton's reading of Yuri Lotman's concept of the semiosphere (delineated in *Universe of the Mind* and defined there as "the semiotic space necessary for the existence and functioning of languages") helps to clarify how maternal identity may be "translated" from official discourse by fic-tion, a process in which "the original message is altered and augmented."[6] Bolton argues that Lotman's semiosphere may be useful "in exploring the complicated negotiations that constitute everyday life as a set of activi-ties mediating between our sense of who we are and our embeddedness in larger codes that seem external, yet not entirely irrelevant, to our own identities."[7] He also characterizes it as a sphere that encompasses both ideology and practice, center and periphery.[8] In other words, the literature of everyday life exposed the tension between officially constructed and individually experienced motherhood, even if the latter was not formulated as a reflection of "true" everyday life. Baranskaia's and Grekova's texts expressed an ambivalence about these larger cultural codes. While their characters are willing to accept motherhood as a natural and even a lofty achievement, they are uncertain of their ability to conform to societal prescriptions and expectations.

The anxiety inherent in these literary texts responded to elevated and mundane notions of maternal identity. Magazines provided an ideal illustration of this dual concern, as Catriona Kelly has argued; the formulaic layout of *Rabotnitsa,* for instance, included placement of nationally, globally, and ideologically significant topics near the front of the magazine, with pieces relating to quotidian life near the end.[9] The connection between text and practice was also laid bare in brochures that made explicit the attempt of propaganda to shape everyday life through "hero identification," as Oleg Kharkhordin has shown in his discussion of Ruvinskii's *Psikhologiia samovospitaniia* (The psychology of self-vospitanie, 1982). There the process of observing a "pedagogical image" eventually yielded to conscious imitation of it as a "personal ideal."[10]

In contrast, everyday life literature typically has focused on material existence rather than spiritual and philosophical issues. Sutcliffe notes that the documentary style employed by Baranskaia and Grekova "conditioned readers to see literature as an allegedly truthful commentary on everyday life and, by extension, the gendered problems inseparable from it," but he also warns against the misguided impulse to view these literary texts as a direct reproduction of reality.[11] The female purveyors of byt literature recorded and responded to the quotidian, while the brochures and magazine articles were advisory in their mildest form and, at their most extreme, explicitly prescriptive; these didactic materials aimed to shape everyday life. Taken together, these various literary and non-literary modes of speaking about maternity formed a composite—if not complete—picture of motherhood by addressing central maternal concerns on individual and societal levels.

Motherhood acquired a growing prominence in print during the Khrushchev years, and the need for the propagandization of motherhood grew during the Brezhnev period as the demographic crisis gained intensity.[12] Mary Buckley has described the reopening of the woman question in the 1960s as an effort in part to determine how women "could combine production with reproduction without neglecting either role."[13] In this sphere, literature did reflect an issue of contemporary concern: Baranskaia's *Nedelia kak nedelia* aptly illustrated the challenges women faced in coordinating their two spheres of responsibility and also underscored the growing attention to the demographic crisis. Previous advice literature and fictional texts by Baranskaia and Grekova had created a context that, along with everyday life experience, formed a backdrop for the novella; though the text received plenty of attention for the "newness" and freshness of the subject it treated, the topic was in fact far from new, as Kelly has noted, and resonated with many readers.[14] Baranskaia's novella also touched a nerve as it probed female anxieties. When the women in *Nedelia kak nedelia* must complete a questionnaire that requests information about how they spend a typical week, one of the characters offers a succinct assessment of the study's real purpose: it is intended to discover "why women don't want to give birth."[15] The literary exploration of the topic seems almost timid in comparison to the tone of a manual on marital life published in 1978, almost a decade after Baranskaia's text; its author attributed dire consequences to the demographic crisis when he suggested a direct correlation between increasing societal instability (*neustoichivost'*) and the decreasing number of children in families and thus alluded to the fear that ethnic Russians would become a minority in the Soviet Union.[16]

In texts responding to the demographic crisis, single-child families were the persistent target of criticism, and blame often rested squarely on the ethnically Russian women who were expected to mother multiple offspring. As part of a 1968 *Rabotnitsa* discussion that arose between mothers and young women as a result of the latter's anxieties about eventual motherhood, school director Kisinovskaia averred that only children often were egoists who adapted to the collective with difficulty. In contrast, those Russians from a multichild family were described as born collectivists.[17] In 1979 sociologist Igor' Bestuzhev-Lada concurred that vospitanie of only children presented special challenges and added, "Not without reason did [pedagogue] A. S. Makarenko call the one-child family . . . something unnaturally truncated."[18] Asia Umanskaia in Grekova's novel *Kafedra* (The faculty, 1978) is a notable if ambivalent example: though her unspoiled character and academic talent seem to refute the warnings against single-child families, she suffers from obesity ostensibly caused by her mother's age, and her mother feels "immeasurably guilty" for "having ruined her daughter's life."[19] Here maternal blame arises not as a result of incorrect vospitanie but due to maternal behavior, namely, the decision to become a mother after the age of forty and against doctors' orders.

Brochures and articles devoted to maternal themes often included elevated declamations about motherhood and women's natural suitability for maternity. Some texts framed essentialized motherhood with laudatory descriptions of the Soviet measures that protected mothers and children. One such text was Persianinov's 1969 *Zdorov'e zhenshchiny i materinstvo* (Woman's health and motherhood); in addition to defining pregnancy as a biological imperative, it simultaneously praised the Soviet mother and the institutions enabling her success: "Motherhood is the greatest joy of life, happiness, the pride of a woman. At all stages of the building of the Soviet government special attention has been given to questions of the protection of the health of women—future mothers, the protection of motherhood, and childhood."[20] Some of Grekova's characters voice similar views. When student Liuda in *Kafedra* announces that she is pregnant, her friend and roommate, Asia, spontaneously repeats the official rhetoric of motherhood by responding that "to have a child is a great happiness!"[21] In the same way, though Ada in *Vdovii parokhod* (Ship of widows) remarks on the "sanctity of motherhood," she herself has no children due to a life of admittedly selfish pursuits.[22] In Grekova's texts, the characters who utter such statements are not mothers, although some eventually will assume a mother role. They unhesitatingly echo meaningless platitudes about motherhood, Grekova implied, because they have not (or not yet) experienced motherhood in a practical sense. But Baranskaia and Grekova also suggested the inevitability of motherhood for any woman, as they equated femininity with maternity. Even those female characters who have no children are concerned with motherhood: they either become surrogate mothers (such as Vera in Grekova's *Khoziaika gostinitsy* [The hotel manager, 1976] and Asia in *Kafedra*) or are obsessed with the children they never had (Ada in *Vdovii parokhod*). Thus Baranskaia and Grekova reaffirmed the typical (and unambiguous) biological formulation of motherhood that one 1974 brochure offered: "The desire to have a child is inherent in every woman and is given by nature itself. Every woman, having married, should be ready to become a mother."[23]

Although biological motherhood was the central focus of the brochures and articles studied in this chapter, the motif of the adoptive mother also appeared in some texts. Issues such as infertility and adoption sometimes were discussed in surprising ways; though Anan'ev advocated adoption in his 1974 brochure *Devochka, devushka, zhenshchina* (Girl, young woman, woman) for instance, he none too subtly prefaced his discussion of the topic by mentioning the shunning and banishment of childless women in ancient times.[24] In fact, it is striking that adoption is not mentioned with greater frequency, given the many reconstituted and reassembled Soviet families in the postwar period.[25] The relatively infrequent portrayal of adoption, along with the evident reluctance of prescriptive literature to reflect real conditions and acknowledge the existence of the "maternal" family, suggests a link to the potentially contradictory dichotomy of "is" and "ought to be" that Katerina Clark has located as central to the socialist realist novel.[26] When adoptive mothers did appear in didactic literature, the exceptional nature of their accomplishments was stressed, and their achievements were often recounted in terms of service to the state.

One adoptive maternal exemplar was Natal'ia, a young widow and factory worker who became the guardian of six orphaned children and was the subject of a *Rabotnitsa* profile in 1964.[27] Upon learning of the death of the children's parents, the city council (*gorsovet*) decided that the factory would serve as father, but a mother would have to be found. When Natal'ia agreed to assume that role, she knew nothing of Makarenko but nonetheless "instinctively" followed his pedagogical teachings by forming a collective with the children and consulting with them. This example of female instinct shaped and tamed by male rationality continues the long Russian tradition of the binary model that couples female with nature and male with culture and reiterates the previously discussed assumption that all women possessed an innate maternal instinct.[28]

Other narratives indicated that an institution or the state could also serve as father even when a biological mother was present. Because railway junction worker M. G. Aristova, profiled in 1968, considered the father of her children unworthy, she chose not to accept child support payments from him; rather, Soviet power acted as a worthy surrogate father and helped her with the difficult task of raising her children.[29] As Sarah Ashwin has discussed, the state served as "father and provider, becoming, in effect, a universal patriarch to which both men and women were sub-ject."[30] In this context, a paternalistic state could serve as a general societal authority and protector and also fill an existing gap within the nuclear family.

Because biological limitations were not a factor, adoptive mothers could serve as hyperbolic examples of the hero-mother, as noted in a 1974 profile of Aleksandra Derevskaia, who adopted and raised forty-eight children of various nationalities.[31] Despite the diverse ethnic origins of the family's members, they asserted their shared identity by identifying their collec-tive nationality as Soviet. The Derevskiis presented a familial example of the oft-lauded friendship of peoples and an ideal manifestation of the reconstituted postwar family in which potentially divisive ethnic differ-ences have been erased. The impetus for the creation and augmentation of this inclusive family was Derevskaia's "maternal heart" (*materinskoe serdtse*).[32]

Despite the persistent praise of motherhood and frequent emphasis of its natural aspects, some authors exhibited a suspicion of maternal in-clinations. Though mothers were entrusted with the vospitanie of their offspring, the advice literature indicated that girls—and women them-selves—required training for their role as mothers.[33] One 1966 text re-jected the idea that simply becoming a mother would ensure the adequate vospitanie of children.[34] A 1972 brochure asserted that "in itself maternal instinct can be blind and reckless. How often it . . . complicates the choice of a correct decision . . . is at odds with reason and, more importantly, brings great harm in the rearing of our children."[35] Even if a woman was, as the literature suggested, biologically predisposed to motherhood, nature had to be shaped and refined, and many specialists considered existing educational programs inadequate. In her 1977 brochure *Sem'ia segodnia* (The family today), T. M. Afanas'eva lamented the lack of specialized vospitanie for "future mothers and wives": "If in home economics classes they are taught culinary basics, cutting and sewing, then no one ever ex-plains to them the laws of creation of the spiritual and moral 'food' that lies ahead [in order] for them to nourish the members of their family."[36] A program of upbringing and training for mothers was intended to negate the possibility of incorrect vospitanie, which would have an impact not only on the individual family but on the entire society. If mistakes were made, the mother was to blame.[37]

Just as texts urged adult women to engage in an ongoing process of self-education, they also underscored the importance of special vospitanie for daughters. A 1963 article by Liudmila Zaiats reminded mothers of their primary task: "making sure our daughters are not only physiologically but ethically and morally prepared for age-related changes and for future motherhood."[38] In pursuit of a parallel goal, pedagogue Vasilii Sukhomlinskii's technique of vospitanie aimed to elicit self-identification among each of his female pupils as "tomorrow's mother" with the "lofty mission given by nature and society" to bear children and to serve as the repository of morality as well as the educator (*vospitatel'*) of the "youth, man, [and] future father."[39] Exhibiting a similar focus on the future, the 1978 article "Rastet devochka" (A little girl grows) advocated special care of the "future wife and mother" and warned that mistakes in vospitanie and "deviations from the rules in care and feeding" could lead to suffering and misfortune later in her "subsequent female life"; namely, she could be "deprived of the happiness of motherhood."[40]

One 1966 article elaborated what was at stake in the process of vospitanie and warned parents that "even an accidentally dropped phrase or a thoughtless action can immediately overturn parental authority [and] reduce to nothing all the good that [parents] have managed to instill in their children."[41] This precarious balance also hinged on maternal demeanor; a 1965 brochure advised that "in child care, the mother should constantly be calm, tender, and affable."[42] The "terrible perfection" that Barbara Heldt has theorized as simultaneously elevating and entrapping Russian literary heroines evidently had its counterpart in advice literature.[43] But the oft-quoted words of eminent Soviet pedagogue Anton Makarenko were perhaps the clearest statement of what was at stake: "Child rearing is the most important area of our lives. Our children are future fathers and mothers. . . . Correct vospitanie is our happy old age. Bad vospitanie is our guilt before other children [and] before the whole country."[44]

While the importance of vospitanie was not in doubt, the question of whether its primary locus should be in maternal or societal hands provoked much more ambivalence during the Brezhnev period. The early

Khrushchev years had ushered in a renewed faith in collective vospitanie orchestrated by society, rationalized because the enterprise of upbringing was, as Gail Lapidus has stated, "far too important to the future Communist society to be left in the hands of untrained and overprotective mothers."[45] A letter submitted to *Rabotnitsa* in 1965 revealed conflicting ideas about the respective merits of communal and familial vospitanie.[46] A young woman, Valia, wrote to the magazine for advice in her relationship with a certain Viktor; upon learning that she worked as an assistant in a day care center, he told her they could no longer see each other if she did not abandon her "dirty work." In response to her protests that she loved her job and loved children, he suggested that they marry and that Valia could leave her job in order to bear and care for her own child, "to whom she could give all her love." Readers' subsequent responses to Viktor accused him of being an egoist, a petty bourgeois, and behind the times. It is significant that these negative reactions to Viktor likely stem from his suggestion that Valia exit the workforce and devote herself solely to child rearing. In the mid-1960s the importance of vospitanie in the home was emphasized even as pedagogues and specialists stressed that it should be conducted in concert with work (for the parents) and additional vospitanie (for the children) outside the home.

The prevailing view in the Brezhnev era apparently reaffirmed this idea: one 1966 text described mothering as a "great art" that a mother could master with the help of doctors.[47] In an article debating whether correct vospitanie could take place if confined to the family alone, a professor responded by enumerating the resources and research that had led to a special curriculum with a complete system of health-improving (*ozdorovitel'nyi*) and educational measures and also cited a survey in which two thousand parents responded to various questions about child rearing and answered very few of them correctly.[48] A 1973 article succinctly stated the relationship between social vospitanie and its familial counterpart: the former supplemented and sometimes corrected the latter.[49] Such an assertion explicitly articulated the relationship between institutional and individual motherhood and also recalled the power—both real and symbolic—of the myth of the Great Family that emerged under Stalin.[50]

If didactic literature viewed vospitanie as crucial, fictional writing exhibited a suspicion of its unquestioned applicability. A clear division between maternal preparation and maternal practice is evident in the criticism of vospitanie that emerges in Grekova's *Vdovii parokhod*. When the orphanage where Ol'ga Flerova is employed hires a new director who is also a pedagogue, Flerova disparages her as "unintelligent" and pedagogy as a "terrible science" because "it talks about the most alive things with the most dead words."[51] Flerova also advocates a natural rather than a learned approach to mothering, remarking on the abundance of "pointless" pedagogical materials: "All that mattered was the child: love him and play with him—and he'll love you back."[52]

The official pedagogical rhetoric of motherhood conjoined state-approved maternal preparation and maternal practice, a relationship that emerged from the basic Soviet equation of public and private. Deborah Field has noted that the Communist morality based on the Moral Code of the Builder of Communism "required the coordination of public and private life and denied any possible conflict between individual interests and public goals," and it specifically called for "mutual respect in the family [and] concern for the upbringing of children."[53] When Ol'ga, the protagonist of *Nedelia kak nedelia,* makes light of this expectation, her joke that she "had two children purely for state considerations" (rodila dvoikh detei iskliuchitel'no po gosudarstvennym soobrazheniiam) incites a major argument in which her colleagues variously mention the trumping of reason by animal instinct; the selfishness of childless women; and that one only becomes a real woman after having a child ("tol'ko ta zhenshchina nastoiashchaia, kotoraia mozhet rozhat'").[54] This hodgepodge of opinions about female and maternal roles is revealing not least because it demonstrates a lack of consensus on the part of the very women expected to participate in the state's grand plan for ensuring the reproduction of the population, and the unattributed speech creates ambiguity about whether the women are voicing their own opinions or responding to others'.

Baranskaia used the questionnaire as an organizing device for exploring the thorny questions of Brezhnev-era motherhood. If the central concern of her text emerged as an attempt to discover why women chose not to have children, another pressing inquiry centered on defining the maternal ideal. While plenty of hero-mothers and other exemplary maternal models populated the pages of *Rabotnitsa* and the many brochures concerning motherhood, an ideal mother on a more modest, quotidian scale was one who both worked outside the home and raised children: one who bore the double burden of work and family. Though the vast majority of Soviet mothers shouldered these responsibilities, which were presumed to be compatible, tending adequately to duties in both spheres was often problematic; the successful combination of personal and professional was contingent upon hospitable work conditions and adequate family support. When in *Nedelia kak nedelia* a colleague jokes that Ol'ga must feel like a "vestige of prerevolutionary Russia" (dorevoliutsionnyi perezhitok) as part of a nuclear family with a husband and two children, another coworker tells her, "You should be proud that you're a good mother and a good worker. You're a real Soviet woman!" Ol'ga, however, is not so sure. She questions her performance in the spheres of vospitanie and production—and wonders what really makes a "real Soviet woman."[55] Indeed, the coworker who praises Ol'ga embodies a now defunct feminine ideal of privileging ideas and ideals above practicality; it is for this reason that Ol'ga claims that "ordinary life was simply unknown to her."[56]

Despite the evident difficulties of balancing the double burden in the Brezhnev years, social stigma dogged those women who chose—or were forced—to bear only one of its halves. Despite the risk of social denigration, Grekova's working mothers regularly find that their professional responsibilities are easier to handle than their personal ones. In "Damskii master" (The ladies' hairdresser, 1963), Mariia Vladimirovna, the single mother of two rambunctious adult sons, claims that nothing, "neither love, nor motherhood," is so satisfying as solving a mathematical problem.[57] Similarly, the narrator of "Pod fonarem" (Under the streetlamp, 1967) describes the protagonist's unconditional love of her work in terms more typically used to express a mother's love for a child and describes the laboratory where the protagonist works as her "baby" (*detishche*).[58] As we will see, these mothers' security in the rational domain of scientific and mathematical work contrasts sharply with the uncertainty and anxiety that the upbringing of children provokes.

The 1977 brochure *Sem'ia segodnia* acknowledged the problems of the double burden and admitted that the "ideal" could be damaging to women, but its author also noted that women who chose to be "only" mothers and wives were the victims of condescension and disdain.[59] It is significant that Baranskaia's text already had engaged with this issue more insistently and directly by reframing the question in personal rather than societal terms, thus reflecting a female reluctance to operate solely in the domestic sphere: when Ol'ga's husband suggests that she stay home with the children, she responds in desperation that she would go mad without the opportunity to put her training to use.[60] By contrast, advice literature cast women who focused only on their careers as misguided.[61] Authors who objected to a female focus on vocation rather than family often legitimized parenting by describing motherhood as a profession in itself, as in one 1979 text whose author lamented the tendency of young women to romanticize their future careers but give little or no thought to their future familial roles.[62] The brochure framed parenting in professional terms presumably to augment its appeal for career-minded young women.

If women were to achieve a successful balance of duties at work and at home, the question of the domestic division of labor would have to be revisited, as one 1981 article noted. Proper vospitanie, the author suggested, would bring about domestic parity: "The entire structure [ves' stroi] of our life rears the young girl and the young woman in the spirit of equality of the sexes." Though the author claimed that the Soviet Union was on a path toward this equality, he also admitted that the desired state of affairs had not yet been reached.[63] As Buckley and Lapidus have pointed out, Brezhnev's invocation of "developed" or "mature" socialism in lieu of Communism and the nascent, though limited, acknowledgment of "shortcomings" and "contradictions" in system and society suggested that there still could be room for improvement in the position of women.[64] In short, the landscape of motherhood in late Stagnation revealed a gap between "is" and "ought to be."

The most forceful response to this issue in the literature of everyday life was absent from the original published version of Nedelia kak nedelia. The text had appeared in 1969 in abridged form; the missing passages were included only after twenty years had passed, together with the publication of Baranskaia's novel Den' pominoveniia (Memorial day, 1989).[65] One reinstated passage of particular note concerns the political seminar that Ol'ga attends. There, participation in a discussion about "'contradictions' in a classless society" results in her emotional outburst about the double burden and inadequate support: "Emancipation, a deserted hearth, spoiled children, broken families, what's that?—nothing to do with contradiction? Children left alone, without brothers or sisters. The mother with a full-time job, an overload."[66] Even with a twenty-year delay, the problem of the lack of "time to perform everyday duties at home" had not been solved, as Mikhail Gorbachev acknowledged during perestroika.[67]

While emphasizing the demands of motherhood, Brezhnev-era advice literature educating mothers on the role they should play also cautioned them not to abandon themselves fully to their maternal responsibilities. While selflessness remained an attribute often ascribed to the mother figure, advice texts repeatedly disparaged the self-abnegating mother deeply entrenched within Russian culture and literature; instead, they sought to refine readers' understanding of "appropriate" concessions to be made for their offspring. One 1965 article, in line with the advice of Makarenko, eschewed self-sacrifice in favor of self-vospitanie.[68] Though many authors emphasized the difficulty of proper vospitanie and the necessity of certain privations, a 1978 text warned that "false and harmful 'self-sacrifice' on the part of the mother, when she is the slave of her child, cripples the child no less than [does] a lack of love."[69]

Everyday life literature apparently concurred that such extreme sacrifice was negative. In Grekova's *Vdovii parokhod*, Anfisa emblematizes the overly selfless mother; her feeding of the newborn Vadim, who is described as "her master," foreshadows the relationship the two will have.[70] The subsequent years spent as a "victim and slave of maternal love" hasten Anfisa's physical deterioration, and Vadim's subsequent selfish behavior indicates the grave consequences of Anfisa's exclusive focus on her son.[71] But after his mother suffers a stroke, Vadim emulates her previous behavior; his care for her involves complete devotion to the task and disregard for everyone and everything else, eventually sapping him of common sense and humanity.[72] It is only after Anfisa's death that Vadim dreams of his sins against his mother, repents, and begins a "new life."

If *Vdovii parokhod* reinforced the oft-repeated admonition of advice literature against self-sacrifice, it, along with several of Grekova's other texts, presented the plight of single mothers and their anxieties about vospitanie, a topic little discussed in the didactic materials of this period. Just as Stalin-era child-care manuals had tended to ignore the fact that no father was present in many families and thus failed to advise women on negotiating single motherhood in a "maternal" (*materinskaia*) family, a

similar mindset held sway in the Brezhnev years as brochures and magazine articles showed a general reluctance to reflect actual family composition.[73] A 1967 *Rabotnitsa* article presented a typical argument that true
happiness was unattainable without a family and that a woman could
not "experience the fullness of her human essence without a firm and
strong connection with a man, without whom she wouldn't be a wife or
mother."[74] Infrequently, texts did address the death or absence of the father; "Sozdavaia novuiu sem'iu" (Creating a new family) offered advice
on how mothers might cope with rearing children alone and reminded
them to pursue their own lives in addition to devoting themselves to their
offspring, quoting Makarenko for added emphasis.[75] The 1980 publication of N. M. Erilovoi's *Vospitanie detei v nepolnoi sem'e* (The raising of
children in an incomplete family, translated from Czech), belatedly and
indirectly acknowledged the growing number of divorces and the absence
of fathers, though the "incomplete" family would become the norm in the
late Soviet years.[76] Advice literature did not fully acknowledge this growing problem until perestroika; later, scandalous texts such as Liudmila
Petrushevskaia's *Vremia noch'* (The time: Night, 1992) and the 1990 film
Rebro Adama (Adam's rib) provided literary and cinematic reflections of
the phenomenon.

   In contrast to the sparse portrayal of fatherless families in propaganda
materials, single mothers figure prominently in everyday life literature,
and these characters make no attempt to conceal their anxiety about vospitanie. In Grekova's novel *Kafedra,* Nina struggles to balance her professional academic responsibilities with raising three sons on her own. Even
so, she arouses the envy of at least one of her colleagues, who remarks that
Nina "is as good as childless," since her oldest child, Sasha, handles all the
shopping and cooking.[77] In fact, Sasha also takes charge of the vospitanie
of his two younger brothers, adheres to basic pedagogical rules, and in
many ways seems to be a more responsible parent than Nina herself.[78]
His success in the domestic areas typically designated as female thus
destabilizes the notions of maternal authority and responsibility within
the home.

   Like Nina Astashova, the protagonist of Grekova's "Pod fonarem" is
a scientist and the single mother of three children. Tat'iana Vasil'evna
"work[s] like a man and battle[s] everyday life [byt] like a woman"; the

narrator speculates that the latter is the more difficult task.[79] The neatly arranged furniture in Tat'iana Vasil'evna's apartment creates an orderliness that she finds soothing and that reminds her of "well-brought-up children."[80] Material possessions, easily arranged and controlled, contrast the domestic chaos she typically experiences. Despite her anxiety about vospitanie and her laissez-faire approach to parenting and household chores, her children have turned out well. Though a third Grekova protagonist, Mariia Vladimirovna of "Damskii master," is confident about her professional achievements, she is less certain of her success in raising her sons. Her inconsistent application of vospitanie and assumption of a motherly role are evident when she intervenes in a tasteless game at a young people's party; her condescending treatment of the assembled crowd is, as she eventually acknowledges, an example of inappropriately invoked maternal authority.[81]

In addition to probing the vicissitudes of single motherhood, Grekova responded to the question of the "incomplete family" by portraying family units with multiple mothers in positive, yet not idealized, terms. Husbands and fathers typically are of secondary importance in her works. Whether removed by war, illness, or sheer irresponsibility, they are replaced by women who may serve as mothers or fathers depending on context. Grekova privileged this alternative, reconstituted family but also acknowledged its pitfalls. From early in *Vdovii parokhod* the inhabitants of the communal apartment function as a collective female family; Flerova describes the neighbors as having a "peculiar kinship" that is "by no means loving, sooner contentious" (svoeobraznaia rodstvennost', otniud' ne liubovnaia, skoree svarlivaia), and though they often have disputes, "they're a family all the same."[82]

In *Khoziaika gostinitsy* Vera, Masha, and her nine-year-old son, Vladimir, form a new, makeshift family during the war. In the absence of Vera's controlling husband, Larichev, the family is configured in sororal terms: "Masha and Vera lived like the closest kin, like sisters, and they shared everything: bed, salary, rations, son, and [his grand]mother."[83] But this family arrangement also involves the assumption of new and flexible parental roles; when Masha's daughter, Viktoriia, is born, Vera meets mother and baby at the *roddom* (maternity home) as a father typically would. In the family she forms with Masha, Vera handles the daily and nightly tasks of motherhood despite her inexperience with newborns. Eventually, Vera argues to Masha that one of them must act as a father and breadwinner while the other is a mother and housekeeper; Vera adopts the latter role.[84] When Viktoriia comes to live with Vera many years later, Vera's actress lodger misreads the interaction between surrogate mother and recently returned daughter as a "stone Niobe weeping for her children."[85] But Vera has not committed Niobe's crime of hubris; instead, she has dared to bestow love and affection on children who are not biologically hers. The narrator primes the reader to accept Viktoriia's return as natural by cataloging Vera's maternal activities since Viktoriia's birth. Vera seemingly cannot evade motherhood, though it twice slips from her grasp as the result of a forced abortion and a fleeting opportunity to mother a stepson before his father swiftly sends him to boarding school. Though Vera does not give birth to Viktoriia, the act of mothering and the memory of it are described in physical terms that suggest a bodily link between the two women.[86]

In *Kafedra* Grekova reveals that the maternal family is not merely the result of wartime exigencies. When she learns she is pregnant, student Liuda wants to have an abortion but fears delays and pressure to have the baby if she goes to a clinic. When her friend and roommate, Asia, suggests that they bring up the baby together, Liuda is easily dissuaded from her plan for a termination; their professor Nina Astashova is an obvious role model for raising children without a father figure. Like Vera in *Khoziaika gostinitsy*, Asia assumes the role of primary caregiver in the shared mothering of Liuda's son, Matvei, and even names him.[87] Matvei is just as much Asia's son as Liuda's, the narrator suggests, because without Asia, "he never would have appeared in the world."[88] A certain ambivalence suffuses this dual mothering, however; even after Matvei learns to talk, he refuses to utter the word "mama."[89] When, at the novel's end, Liuda prepares to form a more traditional family with the man she loves, she hesitates to finalize the plans for her new life in part out of respect for Asia and the maternal family they comprise together. The strength of such female bonds is not confined to the walls of the home, as demonstrated by the female collective that appears in *Nedelia kak nedelia,* when mothers' task sharing helps to ease the double burden. Beth Holmgren has interpreted the image of Ol'ga striding down the street with her fellow mother-colleagues as a display of maternal strength within a "literal support group [that] shores up her function and magnifies her identity."[90]

In their study *Everyday Life in Early Soviet Russia*, Christina Kiaer and Eric Naiman assert that "the combination of the desire to become a Soviet subject, and the knowledge that that desire will always fall short in the face of one's own massive inadequacy, defines Soviet subjectivity."[91] Despite their inability to measure up to the official maternal ideal, the heroines of female-authored everyday life literature do not exhibit a tone of resignation or despair; instead, Baranskaia and Grekova argued for a more flexible definition of the maternal Soviet subject. Their characters display a determination that outweighs frustration, and their works of prose fiction may be read as a response to official discourse about motherhood. Both authors suggested that the solution to the problems posed by motherhood lay in female community and not within the nuclear family, as the state would have preferred and as the propaganda materials explicitly suggested. If, as Marianne Liljeström has argued, the biological determinism in sex roles that figured prominently during the Brezhnev years is itself an element that helps to create ideology, here "representations of gender [constitute] a site upon which ideological systems [are] simultaneously constructed and contested."[92] Indeed, it is in differentiating the portrayal of the mother in didactic texts and prose fiction that the beginnings of a shift in thinking about mothers and motherhood are evident. The maternal attitudes portrayed in everyday life literature, however, do not yet fully evince the shift from "duty" to "pleasure" that Olga Issoupova locates in the 1920s and 1930s and in the post-Soviet years, respectively.[93]

While both Baranskaia and Grekova accepted the dominant rhetoric of motherhood in some respects (conflation of femininity and maternity), they also distanced themselves from its prescriptions in significant ways (pedagogy). Their works exhibited greater ambiguity and ambivalence—and a greater range of voices—than did nonfiction advice texts of the same period. These works anticipated later advice literature in their less restrictive discussion of the problems of motherhood and in their characters' tendency to question pedagogical dicta. And their vision of maternity—not an ideal or idealized one but instead one born of necessity and pragmatism—linked to the documentary aim of everyday life literature; the texts of Baranskaia and Grekova were largely devoid of the lofty rhetoric of motherhood that was nearly omnipresent in brochures and frequently figured in the pages of *Rabotnitsa*. By depicting more honestly the challenges and anxieties of the working mother, portraying single motherhood as a widespread and nuanced phenomenon, and inserting maternal voices into the narration of motherhood (as formulated in the quotation by Elaine Tuttle Hansen that begins this essay), Baranskaia and Grekova initiated an effort to redefine female roles in Russian literature. They "translated," in Lotman's formulation, the official rhetoric of motherhood and amended it to permit the inclusion of maternal polyvocality. As Sutcliffe has demonstrated, these authors brought women's issues to the forefront and legitimized the literary depiction of everyday life.[94] While Baranskaia and Grekova may not have contested forcefully and consistently the state's construction of maternity, they certainly questioned it at several turns as they argued for a wider range of legitimate scenarios of everyday motherhood.[95]

NOTES

The author wishes to thank Benjamin Sutcliffe and the members of the Sewanee Women's Studies Writing Group for their comments on an earlier draft of this chapter and the participants in the May 2010 "Everyday Life in Russia and the Soviet Union" workshop at Indiana University, especially the editors of this volume, for their thoughtful feedback. Special thanks also are owed to the John B. Stephenson Fellowship of the Appalachian College Association for funding research that contributed to the writing of this essay.

1. Elaine Tuttle Hansen, *Mother without Child: Contemporary Fiction and the Crisis of Motherhood* (Berkeley: University of California Press, 1997), 20.

2. My analysis extends the research of scholars such as Lynne Attwood and Catriona Kelly. See Attwood, *Creating the New Soviet Woman: Women's Magazines as Engineers of Female Identity, 1922–1953* (New York: St. Martin's Press, 1999); Kelly, *Refining Russia: Advice Literature, Polite Culture, and Gender from Catherine to Yeltsin* (Oxford: Oxford University Press, 2001); and Kelly, *Children's World: Growing Up in Russia, 1890–1991* (New Haven, Conn.: Yale University Press, 2007).

3. My approach does not presume or claim comprehensiveness; many factors beyond the scope of this study influence maternal identity, particularly if we consider not only representation but lived reality.

4. As Catriona Kelly does in her study of advice literature, I utilize brochures and magazine articles as "contributions to ideology, rather than contributions to practical life" (*Refining Russia*, xxv).

5. Benjamin Sutcliffe, *The Prose of Life: Russian Women Writers from Khrushchev to Putin* (Madison: University of Wisconsin Press, 2009).

6. Yuri Lotman, *Universe of the Mind: A Semiotic Theory of Culture*, trans. Ann Shukman (Bloomington: Indiana University Press, 1990), 123; Jonathan H. Bolton, "Writing in a

Polluted Semiosphere: Everyday Life in Lotman, Foucault, and de Certeau," in *Lotman and Cultural Studies: Encounters and Extensions*, ed. Andreas Schönle (Madison: University of Wisconsin Press, 2006), 324.

7. Bolton, "Writing in a Polluted Semiosphere," 333.

8. Ibid., 326.

9. Kelly, *Refining Russia*, 283.

10. Oleg Kharkhordin, *The Individual and the Collective: A Study of Practices* (Berkeley: University of California Press, 1999), 248.

11. Sutcliffe, *The Prose of Life*, 23.

12. See Deborah Field, *Private Life and Communist Morality in Khrushchev's Russia* (New York: Peter Lang, 2007); and Lynne Attwood, *The New Soviet Man and Woman: Sex Role Socialization in the USSR* (Bloomington: Indiana University Press, 1990), 158. For an overview of the demographic crisis in the 1960s, see Mark G. Field, "The Health and Demographic Crisis in Post-Soviet Russia: A Two-Phase Development," in *Russia's Torn Safety Nets: Health and Social Welfare during the Transition*, ed. Mark G. Field and Judyth L. Twigg (New York: St. Martin's Press, 2000), 11–42.

13. Mary Buckley, "Soviet Interpretations of the Woman Question," in *Soviet Sisterhood: British Feminists on Women in the USSR*, ed. Barbara Holland (Bloomington: Indiana University Press, 1985), 39, 26.

14. Catriona Kelly, *A History of Russian Women's Writing, 1820–1992* (Oxford: Clarendon Press, 1994), 363.

15. Natal'ia Baranskaia, *Nedelia kak nedelia*, in *Den' pominoveniia: Roman, povest'* (Moscow: Sovetskii pisatel', 1989), 270. The questionnaire that vexes Ol'ga and her colleagues has a basis in fact, as Buckley notes ("Soviet Interpretations," 26).

16. Veniamin Zatsepin, *O zhizni supruzheskoi* (Moscow: Molodaia gvardiia, 1978), 19.

17. "Chetvertoe zasedanie—o materinskom schist'e," *Rabotnitsa*, July 1968, 1–3.

18. Igor' V. Bestuzhev-Lada, *Sem'ia vchera, segodnia, zavtra* (Moscow: Znanie, 1979), 25.

19. I. Grekova, *Kafedra, Novyi mir*, no. 9 (1978): 10–168, quotes at 69.

20. Leonid Persianinov, *Zdorov'e zhenshchiny i materinstvo* (Moscow: Znanie, 1969), 51, 3.

21. Grekova, *Kafedra*, 76.

22. I. Grekova, *Vdovii parokhod: Povest'* (Paris: Institut d'études slaves, 1983), 29.

23. Iakov Anan'ev, *Devochka, devushka, zhenshchina* (Volgograd: Nizhne-Volzhskoe kn. izd., 1974), 33.

24. Ibid., 108.

25. For a discussion of Soviet family laws pertaining to adoption, see Laurie Bernstein, "The Evolution of Soviet Adoption Law," *Journal of Family History* 22, no. 2 (April 1997): 204–26; and Bernstein, "Communist Custodial Contests: Adoption Rulings in the USSR after the Second World War," *Journal of Social History* 34, no. 4 (Summer 2001): 843–61.

26. Katerina Clark, *The Soviet Novel: History as Ritual*, 3rd ed. (Bloomington: Indiana University Press, 2000).

27. "'Chuzhoi' chelovek," *Rabotnitsa*, August 1964, 26–27.

28. For a survey of that tradition, see Helena Goscilo and Andrea Lanoux, "Introduction: Lost in the Myths," in *Gender and National Identity in Twentieth-Century Russian Culture*, ed. Helena Goscilo and Andrea Lanoux (DeKalb: Northern Illinois University Press, 2006), 3–29.

29. "Chetvertoe zasedanie," 2.

30. Sarah Ashwin, introduction to *Gender, State, and Society in Soviet and Post-Soviet Russia*, ed. Sarah Ashwin (London: Routledge, 2000), 1. Ashwin traces to Aleksandra Kollontai the notion of the socialist state as father.

31. Aleksandr Kosiak, "Materinskii podvig," *Rabotnitsa,* December 1974, 6–7.

32. Ibid., 6.

33. R. Bamm et al., *Semeinoe vospitanie: Slovar' dlia roditelei* (Moscow: Prosveshchenie, 1967). Because vospitanie is a rather capacious term that may in various contexts denote upbringing, child-rearing, parenting, education, nurturing, training, or the inculcation of morality, I have chosen to transliterate but not translate it. Vospitanie was to be conducted in several spheres; in addition to Communist and patriotic vospitanie, labor, aesthetic, emotional, moral, and antireligious education numbered among the values that were to be instilled in children.

34. E. B. Chernova, *Nravtsvennye osnovy otnoshenii iunoshi i devushki* (Leningrad: Znanie, 1966).

35. Antonina Bardian, *Vospitanie detei v sem'e: Psikhologo-pedagogicheskie ocherki* (Moscow: Pedagogika, 1972), 108.

36. T. M. Afanas'eva, *Sem'ia segodnia* (Moscow: Znanie, 1977), 33.

37. Vospitanie, blame, and parental responsibility had been yoked together for some time: "The underlying assumption of official pedagogy was that the Soviet government had fulfilled its promise to provide education, culture, decent housing, and sufficient leisure to all of its citizens and that those parents experiencing difficulties were themselves at fault" (Field, *Private Life,* 89).

38. Liudmila Zaiats, "Gigiena devochki," *Rabotnitsa,* February 1963, 30–31.

39. Vasilii Aleksandrovich Sukhomlinskii, *Rozhdenie grazhdanina* (Moscow: Molodaia gvardiia, 1971), 82–83.

40. S. Polchanova, "Rastet devochka," *Rabotnitsa,* May 1978, 22.

41. I. Blinkov, "Liubopytnie chelovechki," *Rabotnitsa,* January 1966, 24–25.

42. M. L. Farfel', *Vospitanie rebenka v sem'e* (Moscow: Meditsina, 1965), 29.

43. Barbara Heldt, *Terrible Perfection: Women and Russian Literature* (Bloomington: Indiana University Press, 1987).

44. Farfel', *Vospitanie rebenka v sem'e,* 40.

45. Gail Warshofsky Lapidus, *Women in Soviet Society: Equality, Development, and Social Change* (Berkeley: University of California Press, 1978), 240–41.

46. "Stydno li rabotat' nianei?," *Rabotnitsa,* April 1965, 16–17.

47. "V mir prishel chelovek," *Rabotnitsa,* February 1966, 16–17.

48. N. M. Askarina, "I sem'ia i iasli," *Rabotnitsa,* May 1969, 24.

49. M. Starodub et al., "Sto primet materinskoi zaboty," *Rabotnitsa,* June 1973, 12–13.

50. See Clark, *The Soviet Novel,* 114–35.

51. Grekova, *Vdovii parokhod,* 35.

52. Ibid., 36.

53. Field, *Private Life,* 1, 9.

54. Baranskaia, *Nedelia kak nedelia,* 282.

55. Ibid., 274.

56. The "exceptional" (*iskliuchitel'naia*) life of the seasoned "idealist" (*idealistka*) Mar'ia Matveevna, or "M.M.," has included participation in a "production commune" (*proizvodstvennaia kommuna*) at the beginning of the 1930s and work at the front in the "political sec-

tion" (*politotdel*) in the 1940s. Her life's interests are production and party work, and she has embraced her political responsibilities so fully that her daughters grew up in an orphanage (*detdom*) (Baranskaia, *Nedelia kak nedelia*, 274).

57. I. Grekova, "Damskii master," in *Pod fonarem* (Moscow: Sovetskaia Rossiia, 1966), 85.

58. I. Grekova, "Pod fonarem," in *Pod fonarem* (Moscow: Sovetskaia Rossiia, 1966), 43.

59. Afanas'eva, *Sem'ia segodnia*, 24.

60. Baranskaia, *Nedelia kak nedelia*, 314.

61. See L. N. Zakharova, *Rastut v sem'e mama i papa* (Moscow: Moskovskii rabochii, 1978), 153.

62. L. E. Kovaleva, *Mikroklimat sem'i* (Moscow: Znanie, 1979), 22–23, 43.

63. V. Perevedentsev, "Tebe polovina—i mne polovina," *Rabotnitsa*, March 1981, 19.

64. Buckley, "Soviet Interpretations," 41; Lapidus, *Women, Work, and Family*, xi.

65. See Thomas Lahusen, "'Leaving Paradise' and Perestroika: *A Week Like Any Other* and *Memorial Day*," in *Fruits of Her Plume: Essays on Contemporary Russian Woman's Culture*, ed. Helena Goscilo (Armonk, N.Y.: M. E. Sharpe, 1993), 205–24.

66. Ibid., 209.

67. M. S. Gorbachev, *Perestroika* (London: Collins, 1987), 117, quoted in Attwood, *The New Soviet Man and Woman*, 12.

68. L. Ivanova, "Materinskoe pole," *Rabotnitsa*, April 1965, 19.

69. A. N. Timoshchenko, *V sem'e rastet doch'* (Moscow: Znanie, 1978), 39.

70. Grekova, *Vdovii parokhod*, 29.

71. Ibid., 68.

72. Ibid., 80.

73. Kelly, *Children's World*, 127.

74. S. Gansovskii, "Sem'ia," *Rabotnitsa*, September 1967, 18.

75. I. Skliar, "Sozdavaia novuiu sem'iu," *Rabotnitsa*, February 1972, 25.

76. N. M. Erilovoi, ed., *Vospitanie detei v nepolnoi sem'e* (Moscow: Progress, 1980).

77. Grekova, *Kafedra*, 18.

78. Ibid., 25.

79. Grekova, "Pod fonarem," 43.

80. Ibid., 44.

81. Grekova, "Damskii master," 102.

82. Grekova, *Vdovii parokhod*, 14.

83. I. Grekova, *Khoziaika gostinitsy*, in *Kafedra: Povesti* (Moscow: Sovetskii pisatel', 1980), 276.

84. Ibid., 281.

85. Ibid., 264.

86. Ibid., 358.

87. Grekova, *Kafedra*, 120.

88. Ibid., 125.

89. Ibid., 155.

90. Beth Holmgren, "Writing the Female Body Politic (1945–1985)," in *A History of Women's Writing in Russia*, ed. Adele Marie Barker and Jehanne Gheith (Cambridge: Cambridge University Press, 2002), 234–35.

91. Christina Kiaer and Eric Naiman, introduction to *Everyday Life in Early Soviet Russia: Taking the Revolution Inside*, ed. Christina Kiaer and Eric Naiman (Bloomington: Indiana University Press, 2006), 12–13.

92. Marianne Liljeström, "The Soviet Gender System: The Ideological Construction of Femininity and Masculinity in the 1970s," in *Gender Restructuring in Russian Studies,* ed. Marianne Liljeström, Eila Mäntysaari, and Arja Rosenholm, Slavica Tamperensia 2 (Tampere, Finland: University of Tampere, 1993), 173.

93. Olga Issoupova, "From Duty to Pleasure? Motherhood in Soviet and Post-Soviet Russia," in *Gender, State, and Society in Soviet and Post-Soviet Russia,* ed. Sarah Ashwin (London: Routledge, 2000), 30–54.

94. Sutcliffe, *The Prose of Life,* 57.

95. See ibid., 28–29, for a discussion of the limitations of Baranskaia's and Grekova's depictions of everyday life.

7

"They Are Taking That Air from Us"
Sale of Commonly Enjoyed Properties to Private Developers

DAVID L. RANSEL

I would hope that my readers feel a sense of awe at the quality of human endurance, at the endurance of love in the face of a variety of difficulties; that the quotidian life is not always easy, and is something worthy of respect.

—Elizabeth Strout, *Olive Kitteridge*

The concepts of public and private were not well developed in Soviet times because ownership of property belonged in principle to the people and was managed on their behalf by the state administration. Marx and Engels wrote in *The Communist Manifesto* that the theory of Communism could be summed up in a single phrase: "abolition of private property." In Communist states private property was to be transformed into socialist property. When Communist rule collapsed, first in Eastern Europe and then in the Soviet Union, the process of transforming socialist property into private property was difficult and confusing, and, not surprisingly, it was accompanied by much unfairness. Some persons profited greatly, while many others suffered losses. The losses were not so much of private real estate, which hardly existed outside the farm sector.[1] The losses were properties and recreational opportunities that in practice were thought of as community assets to be shared and enjoyed by all at little or no personal expense. They included parks, woods, meadows, ponds, sites of historical interest, and other areas of common use that lent spiritual enrichment to the everyday life of Russians. In some cases, these sites offered material advantages as well, for example, opportunities to fish or to gather berries, mushrooms, firewood, and other provisions. These common properties and their accompanying benefits began to disappear as privatization took hold, yet among the many studies of privatization in Russia almost nothing has been written about this loss.

The lack of attention to this question may have stemmed from the absence of an organized community response in the early years of perestroika and post-Soviet Russia. Russians were enjoying at long last the right to express their opinions without fear, to practice their religion openly, and, if so inclined, to engage in private enterprise. The public seemed at first to applaud the opportunity that suddenly opened for some people to obtain land for a summer cottage. The costs of privatization were not yet apparent, as commonly used property was only gradually being alienated, and enterprises had not yet shed all of their subsidized recreational and social service facilities. When the losses finally became noticeable, the ordinary working people most affected did not have civic or political organizations to defend their interests. To the limited extent that these had existed in Soviet times in the form of Communist Party and workplace agencies, they had lost the ability to act, and citizens did not have the experience or means to form such bodies themselves. Only recently have a few islands of civic action arisen to protest the appropriation of properties by private developers.

Despite the radical realignment of economic policy and even the adoption by many people of the neoliberal rhetoric of self-reliance to affirm their competence in the altered conditions, most workers clung to their habitual understandings of what was fair and what belonged to them either as an implicit birthright or as a reward for their hard work and loyalty.[2] They lamented the loss of commonly available and apparently cost-free community properties and services whose steady alienation constituted an affront to their work and voluntary contributions to society and became a sign of the unjust appropriation of national goods by insiders.

Before looking into the responses of citizens, it would be useful to understand the process by which privatization took place.

In the Soviet Union, property was in theory owned by the people, but in practice the personnel of particular institutions exercised the rights of ownership. Reduced to its simplest terms, the property regime operated on the basis of split ownership. Managers of properties exercised control rights, and the people (in the form of the state and party administrations) exercised cash-flow rights. Managers made control decisions in response to the demands placed on them by state planners, and the proceeds generated by the properties, again in theory, flowed to the government. According to an analysis by Maxim Boycko, Andrei Shleifer, and Robert Vishny, the lack of alignment between cash flow and control invited inefficiencies, because managers concentrated their efforts on productive outputs and not costs. Plan fulfillment rather than cost effectiveness brought them rewards.[3] Accordingly, the planners wanted to transfer ownership of state enterprises to private hands in order to create a direct connection between control rights and cash-flow rights. But privatization would only bring the desired efficiencies if prices corresponded to relative scarcities. Therefore, the first objective of reformers of the post-Soviet era had to be an end to price controls on most goods and services. The government of Egor Gaidar in the early 1990s did this in a single sweeping move known as "shock therapy." The next step was to find a method for bringing control rights over property and cash-flow rights into greater alignment. This was the key objective in the privatization programs introduced soon after by Anatolii Chubais and his team of economists.

The reformers were determined to privatize a large share of the country's property in a very short time. Despite passionate discussions at the time about whether the process should be rapid or gradual, the reformers actually had little choice. In the chaotic political conditions and authority vacuum of the early 1990s, privatization was occurring spontaneously. Enterprise managers set up private firms in parallel with their current state-owned operations and sold products from the state enterprises at nominal prices to their private firms to be resold at much higher prices—or they simply "stripped" the enterprises of their assets and sold them. In short, "what is not privatized will be stolen," as the saying went at the time.[4]

The special powers that President Boris Yeltsin had acquired from the Congress of People's Deputies in November 1991 gave the reformers extraordinary leverage for realizing their program. But like any directed change involving massive assets, political approval by itself was not sufficient. Powerful interests had to be brought into the process and allowed to profit from it if their opposition was to be averted. The reform team led by

Chubais wanted above all to shut the central ministry bureaucracies out of the process. In the judgment of the reformers, the central ministries were the source of the inefficiencies of the Russian economy, its overregulation and separation of control and cash-flow rights. In their effort to exclude the ministries, the reformers were willing to cut deals with nearly everyone else who had a stake in the system. Their principal focus was on the enterprise managers, as they had control of the means of production and were already appropriating them. Moreover, the managers had technical knowledge and were, in the view of the reformers, the most able people initially to exercise ownership. But other allies were needed to thwart interference by the powerful central ministries.

The voucher privatization scheme was, for example, a device to garner broad public support for the changes and thus outmaneuver efforts by the central ministries to interfere. The scheme, at least according to the apologists for it, was to give every citizen a chance to own a small piece of a productive asset or, more commonly, a number of assets bundled in a mutual fund.[5] Another constituency that was well positioned to create problems for the reform was made up of the local authorities and managers of retail outlets and other small enterprises. Because the reformers were most interested in controlling the transformation of the large enterprises that dominated the economy and eager to avoid opposition from local officials, they decided to turn most retail outlets and some small firms over to the municipalities and to allocate to small institutions the properties they currently managed.[6] This decision had important implications for the use of what had long been considered areas of free public access, the kind of commons that truly actualized the communist promise of mutual use of the people's assets and enhanced the quality of everyday life for ordinary citizens.[7] Along with this acquisition of local property rights came the elimination of a variety of community services and welfare provision and a loss of commonly enjoyed parks, woods, lakes, rivers, and ponds.[8]

The principal threat arose from the desire of newly wealthy persons to acquire elite suburban housing (known in Russian as *villy* or *kottedzhi*) and second homes (*dachi*) in the most attractive settings surrounding the large cities, Moscow in particular. Developers of this type of housing were searching for desirable properties and working with local officials and institutions to acquire the rights to build on them. As early as December 1992 the Russian legislature amended the constitution to allow a free market in land that was to be used for "dacha construction, orchards, and private gardening, although not for full-scale farming." As a consequence, failing collective or state farms near large cities sold off plots of land to developers of housing projects.[9]

I first ran into the threat to attractive suburban natural sites and in this case also an archaeological site of importance while on an expedition to conduct oral interviews with village women in northeastern Moscow province in the summer of 1993. During a meal break, my truck driver and an assistant took me to a nearby complex of fifty ancient Slavic burial mounds (*kurgany*) that were dotted across a high bank of the Voria River (a tributary of the Kliazma River that passes through Moscow) adjoining the village of Kablukovo. The mounds, which dated from the twelfth and early thirteenth centuries, were discovered by archaeologists in the 1960s and partially investigated. Among the findings were a wide range of grave goods, including ceramics and other household items, coin necklaces, bracelets, metallic hair ornaments, decorative beads in glass, various sorts of metal, and much more. Especially interesting were apparent cases of violent death of both pagans and Christians, which lent support to the view that the Christianization of northern Russia was carried out violently and met violent resistance.[10]

To the misfortune of Russian heritage preservation, the picturesque setting attracted the attention of the wealthy fashion designer Viacheslav Zaitsev. Despite laws protecting such sites, Slava Zaitsev was able to purchase the land occupied by the burial mounds and made plans to build a large dacha right next to the mounds in a way that was certain to do irreparable damage to the site. A well-known historian and archaeologist, Sergei Chernov of the Russian Academy of Sciences, along with a representative of the local Shchëlkovo architect's office, rushed to the area, examined the conditions, and proposed that Zaitsev build his dacha on another piece of land two hundred meters to the south that was separated from the burial mounds by a ravine. The proposed site, moreover, gave a lovely view over the river. Despite hopes that the chief architect of the region would convince Zaitsev to use the alternate site, scholars learned in 1996 that the dacha was under construction at the original site on the north side of the ravine and that at least one burial mound had already been bulldozed. Official letters were sent to Zaitsev and to the chief architect of the Shchëlkovo region, asking them to immediately cease building on the site. In reply, Zaitsev explained that in 1994 he had invited another archaeological agency to render an opinion.[11] He was told that the construction would not damage the mounds and that he could proceed with his building project. On this advice, Zaitsev went ahead with his work of destruction.[12]

The seizure of what not long before were regarded as public lands by private interests affected not merely those who had a professional or personal interest in historic preservation. The loss of scenic properties to dacha settlements and suburban housing projects was occurring across the regions surrounding Russia's large cities. As already mentioned, the developments were designed to attract wealthy first- and second-home buyers from the central city, not to add to the housing stock available to the local working people of modest means. Indeed, the impact on local working people could be sudden and negative. The takeover violated what they had not unreasonably understood as an element of their citizenship, and it accordingly diminished their sense of community and civic rights.

The sources for my observations about ordinary working people and their feelings of loss are modified life interviews recorded from two generations of workers in the industrial suburbs of Moscow. The interviews, which were conducted over an approximately ten-year period from 1994 to 2003, explore the attachment of workers to social institutions such as family, community, workplace, union, church, party, and state. The first interviews were recorded in the summer of 1994 in the factory town of Khot'kovo northeast of Moscow.[13] The following remarks will be limited to that set of interviews.

Since the Middle Ages Khot'kovo had been a small settlement associated with a nearby monastery. Its modern growth began during the industrial drive of the 1930s when it acquired factories. In 1949 the settlement received the designation of "city." Khot'kovo's principal manufacturing enterprises produced electrical and other types of insulation, construction materials, and, more recently, textiles and polypropylene pipes. During the industrial collapse of the 1990s, local factories cut employment sharply. At the same time, inflation eroded the value of the pensions of retired people in the community. It was against this background of economic distress that the interviews took place.

Most members of the older generation had begun their lives in villages and had been driven from the countryside either by the collectivization of agriculture and ensuing famine or by the war. A variety of routes took them eventually to Khot'kovo for work in the newly established factories just before or after the war. The younger generation, those who had entered the workforce since about 1980, were the children and grandchildren of the migrants from the villages. Until the recent changes in the property regime, the citizens of Khot'kovo had enjoyed strolling in a nearby large woodland park that contained a pond where they could relax, bathe, and picnic. But much of this woodland had recently been taken over and developed as a dacha community. Oksana, a nineteen-year-old Khot'kovo resident and day-care center worker, explained the situation from the point of view of the local citizens.

> It is sad that they are cutting down the woods. And it is restricting the space we have available to ourselves. That is, we can no longer go there comfortably. . . . There used to be a pond, and we could freely walk to it. Essentially, it belonged to us. And now they put in those dachas, and they fenced in the pond. That is to say, now we have to go through all those dachas. . . .
>
> That is, the people there now look at us . . . well . . . look at us not in the way that we used to be able [to think of ourselves]. We felt as if we were the owners of the place.
>
> Now that is over. They have fenced in the area. We are forced to enter the grounds of the dacha settlement [to reach the pond], and the people there now look at us askance. We have to go through other people's fences. And that's not all. It was also apparent that the people there took their dogs to the pond and bathed them there. And, well, if you said something to them [about it], it would be useless. . . .
>
> It is really bad what they have done. . . . On the other hand, for them it is good. They come here to relax, so to speak, to breathe fresh air. But for us, quite the opposite, they are taking that air from us. That is, they are chopping down our woods and taking over our space.[14]

The sting of this loss of common property for strolls in the woods and picnics by the pond was undoubtedly intensified by the dearth of other recreational outlets in Khot'kovo at this time. Oksana complained about this situation—and not just Oksana. Nearly every young and middle-aged interviewee in Khot'kovo decried the lack of places to relax and socialize such as parks, playgrounds, sports centers, discos, clubs with social circles for discussing problems or engaging in crafts—in short, outlets and programs for healthy off-work activities.[15] Although older people did not mention the need for sports centers or discos, they also valued access to the surrounding woods and ponds.[16] Indeed, for one older man the nearby woods had been a resource of a special kind. He boasted of taking logs from the local woods to build a house when he first came to Khot'kovo in 1940.[17]

Concerns of this kind have more recently emerged in other communities in Moscow province. One case concerns the Dmitrovskii meadow adjoining Stepanovskoe village in the Krasnogorsk region west of Moscow. The villagers discovered to their dismay that this beautiful meadow along the banks of the Istra River that they had long thought of and used as a community property now belonged to a private company, OOO Sport-Modern, and was scheduled for development. The property had previously belonged to the "Lenin's Ray of Light" state farm and had been allocated to the Moscow Province Ministry of Property. The ministry, without notification or consultation with the villagers, sold the land to private interests. The villagers learned about the matter by chance when it was brought to their attention by persons waging a battle to protect a nearby eighteenth-century estate property from destruction by developers. A public hearing on the matter was called at which village residents were given a mere three minutes to state their case, a decision that enraged the audience. They nevertheless stated their concerns and sense of loss with great emotion and conviction. One woman explained the spiritual loss that she felt at being deprived of a space that had given her children a healthy upbringing: "I raised my two sons on that meadow. They did not become criminals or drug addicts but grew up to be respectable people because they had viewed such beauty!"[18] When the audience presented an area planning map approved by the government of Moscow province and showing that the land in question was one of the few remaining protected ecological sites in the province, the company representative who had come to respond to the protesters stated decisively: "We will solve that problem!"

How did it happen that the common spaces where people had for decades freely strolled, fished, picnicked, and dog walked suddenly became
appropriated for a private housing development? The simple answer is that
privatization radically altered the context in which Russian businesses
and farms operated and in the process caused an equally radical revalua-
tion of an institution's assets. We know this story from a broad macrohistorical point of view. As mentioned earlier, the reformers needed allies in
their effort to beat back opposition to their privatization program from
the powerful central ministries, especially those for industrial sectors.
They were relying on support from managers of large enterprises, who
had much to gain from the process, and from the broad public, who would
receive a stake in newly privatized companies by investing in them with
vouchers. Other potential opponents to reform were municipal authorities
and managers of retail outlets and other small businesses. The reformers
decided to forestall challenges from these people by allocating ownership
rights to them immediately.

Besides the politics of this decision, immediate "small privatization"
made sense administratively, for the government did not have the capacity
to separately sell tens of thousands of small operations and unprofitable
farms. Moreover, it was difficult to place a value on them. In a large number of cases, the assets of farms, small enterprises, and retail outlets were
essentially worthless. The outward appearance of most operations was
unattractive. Equipment was outdated and of little value in establishing
a competitive business. The inventory, in the context of the goods shortages under socialism, may have consisted solely of things that no one had
wanted to buy to begin with. To put such places up for auction would be
to ask a potential new owner to purchase something of negative value. In
many cases, the only element of such a property that had value was the
actual premises or real estate.[19]

Important in determining the fate of these newly privatized or leased
properties were the obligations of ownership. As Katherine Verdery discovered in connection with her study of privatization in postsocialist
Transylvania, people usually think first of the positive aspects of private
property. The "public discourse about property is saturated by talk of
rights," she remarked. In a "celebrated list of the eleven basic incidents
of a private property relation only two concern duties or liabilities rather

than rights."[20] But as soon as a property is transferred from state control into private hands, the obligations and risks of ownership become evident. In the land privatizations that Verdery was studying in Romania, just as in the leasing or privatizing of suburban lands, retail outlets, small manufacturing enterprises, and service facilities in the Russian case, the new owners had to operate in circumstances very different from those they had previously known. Socialist systems operated on soft budget constraints, and enterprises were routinely subsidized and, if unprofitable, bailed out. What is more, they often did business in noncompetitive markets and at prices fixed by the state. Now suddenly they were forced to operate in markets open to national and even international competitors and on the basis of hard budget constraints. They also had to come up with money to pay taxes and fees plus bring buildings and grounds up to standard. In Russia, moreover, municipal authorities imposed sometimes crippling limits on what owners or, more often, lessees could do with their properties. They did this to meet goals such as maintaining excess workers, continuing benefits, and providing the same products or services. These restrictions constrained innovation and continued the need for state assistance. Ultimately, competition from new entries into the marketplace doomed the older operations to liquidation and cleared a path for their sale to owners with fewer restrictions on what could be done with the properties. While this development produced greater economic efficiency, it likewise meant that lands and premises of local recreational or service value fell into the hands of developers to be turned into elite, gated residential communities or high-priced recreational and service facilities.

This gives the big picture. But it is worthwhile also to see how the changes played out at the local level and from the point of view of the people directly affected in their everyday lives. One of our interviewees, the supervisor of the electric shop at a Khot'kovo factory, explained how the reforms transformed the value of many of the assets in his industrial town, assets in which local firms had made substantial investments in Soviet times. He turned to the subject as he was relating a story about how excavations for a new installation broke sewer pipes that served a factory housing complex, and it turned out that no one was available to fix the sewer pipes. The personnel for that type of work had been let go. The supervisor continued:

The factory also built the club here. Now we see a paradox. Before, for example, it was considered prestigious to, let's say, have a day care center at the firm. You know, you would have a club, a cafeteria. You would build housing in order to have a supply of apartments. This would all be done with the goal of attracting workers to your enterprise. But now the upkeep on these very same structures is so difficult, so problem-filled that it is insupportable. It eats up practically the entire income of the enterprise. Well, now, here, thanks to the efforts of our director, the housing was turned over to the municipality. The day care center also went to the municipality. Only the club and cafeteria remain. And so there you are. As a result, of course, in connection with this democratization of production our living . . . or social arrangements, perhaps, again in connection with the market economy, our children are no longer cared for. They're neglected.[21]

He went on to say how the club used to sponsor all manner of social groups for adults that taught crafts, hobbies, and other classes on subjects of community interest. It also provided sports activities for the youngsters and instilled good values in them. But now to the extent any of these things continued, they had to be paid for by the people themselves, and few people could afford the extra expense.[22]

In other words, given the new property regime and hard budget constraints, enterprises could no longer afford to maintain and pay taxes and other fees for facilities that did not directly contribute to the manufacture of products or performance of services that earned income. When possible, enterprises transferred ownership to municipalities, as in the case of the housing at the Khot'kovo factory. Even when an enterprise retained control of a property—for example, the cafeteria and club of the Khot'kovo factory—it sought to make them turn a profit or at least pay for themselves. These changes deprived people of facilities and opportunities that they had long understood as an element of either their benefits package at work or their rights as citizens. And the loss was felt all the more keenly because it came at a time when people were suffering job losses, long delays in receiving pay, and runaway inflation.

This story raises a number of questions about what is private and what is public. In the command economy of Soviet times, many goods and services were allocated politically. In the case of suburban residences and recreational retreats, the supply was limited, and the most attractive sites and dachas were occupied by party officials and to a lesser degree creative artists and writers. Once the market economy began to operate, goods and services were more commonly allocated on the basis of money. The demand for suburban homes intensified. Under the new system entrepreneurs or professional specialists who were earning high salaries or acquiring wealth claimed the right to invest the fruits of their labors in attractive residences. Developers asserted the right to purchase properties and construct residences to satisfy the market. Conversely, local residents believed that they in some measure held ownership in areas of unusual natural beauty, ecological importance, and biodiversity to which they had enjoyed unimpeded access in Soviet times. The same was true of sites of historical and archaeological significance, places that told the story of the people and nourished the soul of the nation. Where should the line be drawn between those who see every natural or national heritage site in the Moscow region as worth preserving and those who wish to invest the fruits of their enterprise in attractive residential settings close to the capital city? Who should make the decision and on what basis?

Normally, these questions would be settled through a legal, political, or economic process—or some combination of the three. In Russia the rapid and arbitrary allocation of properties to small businesses and municipalities and the similarly swift authorization of the sale of collective farm acreage for dacha construction and small-scale enterprise created a dynamic market in land without adequate protection for the public interest. Where laws existed for consideration of community, environmental, or heritage claims they were sufficiently vague that people with money were able to circumvent them by paying experts of their choice to grant authorization. This is obviously what happened in the case of the collective farm property that was allocated to the fashion designer Slava Zaitsev. When obstructed by specialists at one institute of the Academy of Sciences, Zaitsev engaged a local archaeological board to approve his plans to build over an important cultural site. The developers of the Dmitrovskii meadow property, when compelled by a community outcry to hold a perfunctory public hearing, made it clear that they were going to find experts to override any objections to their exploitation of this attractive riverside property.

In the case of Khot'kovo and other communities whose previously accessible recreational properties were being alienated, one question would be what laws, if any, governed its protection for environmental or heritage purposes and accordingly placed limits on its disposal. In Russia, as we have glimpsed, laws and limits of this kind exist but seem to be rather vague and difficult to enforce, especially if powerful moneyed interests are determined to override them. Ownership is also a key question. If a municipality held ownership, the protection of the rights of ordinary citizens would belong in the political process. They could in theory pressure their representatives to reject the sale. Or if the municipality needed the funds promised in the sale, the citizens could impose taxes on themselves to offset the income that would come from the sale. Another solution would be a purely economic one. The people who had used the property for recreational and other purposes could outbid the dacha developers for possession of it. If the property had in some sense been "community owned," then negotiations would be conducted with a community body. If community members preferred to hold the property for recreational and other purposes, they would pay the required taxes, upkeep, and other expenses associated with ownership.

The trouble with these courses of action was the absence of responsive political mechanisms and civil society institutions that could coordinate a community response to the takeover of sites by private interests. To the degree that such organizations had existed in Soviet times, they were party bodies. The ones that workers most commonly turned to when they had needs and requests were the trade union and the party administrator in their place of employment. Unfortunately for the workers, these offices were losing political and financial support in postcommunist Russia. Although trade unions were an arm of the party and had acted primarily as providers of services such as subsidized vacations, they had on occasion intervened to mediate disputes with management or to save a worker's job. They were accessible local organizations. But workers now understood that even the modest assistance the unions may have given in the past was not to be expected in the new economy. This view was expressed best by a foreman at the maintenance department of the insulation plant, who stated that although the union had been the most important institution in his life and that it might have been able to intervene three or four years ago, "it was useless to talk about such things now. . . . If you go there now, they just throw up their hands."[23]

When asked who defended the interests of the workers, our interviewees could not think of any institution that played such a role. A few mentioned a particular boss who had fought to keep a factory or other enterprise alive, but most said that they had only themselves to rely on. In their view, it was the political elite who had created the crisis, and these national leaders had a responsibility to make things right. The workers could not conceive of organizations other than the state that might offer support. A couple of the interviewees had turned to the Orthodox church in their community for spiritual comfort, but they had not anticipated and had not received material assistance there.[24] Given the altered political context and contested elections, it might be expected that the interviewees would speak of voting for local representatives who would defend their interests. But they did not express this view. On the contrary, the workers saw the local office holders as mere extensions of the national leadership. Viktor, a forty-one-year-old businessman, argued that it was senseless to expect independence on the part of local officials. They just take orders from above. "Today they are told to be democrats, to play at democracy, and they do it. If tomorrow they are told to march the people to work at gunpoint, they will do that too. Seriously, I'm 100 percent sure they would."[25]

In an altogether singular and therefore surprising response, one woman, a bookkeeper at the insulation plant, expressed the need for something like civil society organizations that could help people find their way through the present crisis and beyond. We need institutions, she argued, that would shape a wholesome way of life such as organized classes for healthy activities and community meetings where people could get together to solve problems.[26] This self-help approach, in which a community organizes to solve problems and defend its interests, was not mentioned by other interviewees and, apart from the mutual assistance provided by family and friendship groups, was not rooted in Russian experience. Civil society organizations that had formed in tsarist Russia had in Soviet times been either abolished or colonized by the party and made into loyal arms of the regime. The neo-Tocquevillian political theory associated with the work of Robert Putnam considers civil society as the foundation of modern democracy, and the failure of civil society organizations to emerge and thrive after the fall of communism has, according to some scholars, undermined the development of Russian democracy.[27] Two recent well-publicized protests in Russia may, however, signal a change. First, a large number of fishermen demonstrated against the introduction of fees for angling on rivers and lakes that had been leased to private interests. The fishermen demanded continued open access to waterways and have persuaded the government at least to limit the leases.[28] Second, protests in St. Petersburg may have influenced the government to halt construction of a giant business center and tower that would have transformed the city skyline. The giant energy corporation Gazprom planned to build a 403-meter-high tower over an archaeological site in Okhta just behind the picturesque Smolnyi Convent complex. A campaign led by a few dozen intellectuals and artists in Petersburg mobilized popular opinion in the city and may have convinced powerful leaders in Moscow, including President Medvedev, to ask that the tower be built elsewhere. It is currently planned for Lakhta, a northwestern suburb of Petersburg.[29]

In the absence of a responsive political order and civil society or party organizations that could advocate for preservation of the recreational areas and social support facilities that were being lost to this working-class community, the people were left with only their anger and bewilderment.

One couple in Khot'kovo expressed these feelings powerfully. Both were age seventy-five at the time of the interview. The husband had been a victim of the famine of the early 1930s. When he was thirteen years old, his parents sent him and his brother away from their starving village in Saratov province to find distant relatives. His brother died along the way. The wife in the couple, too, claimed to have suffered from the famine and said that she and her sister survived by eating grass, chaff, and crayfish. Both members of this couple were uneducated, and they had worked at hard physical labor most of their lives. They spoke of having finally enjoyed a few years of security before perestroika. Now again, they lamented, life promised only renewed hardship and fears that they would not even have enough money to afford a proper burial. They were quite outspoken about perestroika. "Again, they have brought us capitalism. Again, it's time to dekulakavize . . . these millionaires . . . dekulakavize them. . . . These capitalists, they just rob people, don't earn money by their own efforts. They are speculators. As a result, the Mafia is spreading everywhere."[30] "And they murder people, they kill innocent people." As for Gorbachev, whom they blamed for starting the process, the wife offered a Russian adage: "If you can't drive, don't get in the sleigh!"[31]

Two male workers, age sixty-one and fifty-three, interviewed together, were quite aware that the assets of the local factories were being stripped and sold off by the managers. They railed against the mayor for failing to report this and other sins of the local elite to higher-ups. And they saw right through the voucher privatization program. Instead of vouchers, they said, each person should be given an antitank grenade so that they could use that—against the new capitalists, it was implied. One complaint about the voucher system was its failure to recognize the contributions of the people who had sweated their whole lives, since everyone, old and young, received a voucher. "I've lived for sixty years," the older worker said, "and get one voucher. Someone just born also gets a voucher. How fair is that?" But this unfairness was not really the point for them. These workers had an accurate understanding of the voucher privatization, at least as it ended up after changes the parliament had made to favor the managerial elite. "This is a rip-off of the whole state, you could say, of the entire population. It is actually legalized theft. The release of vouchers and their purchase. That is legalized theft on the part of the administration and leadership of the state." Interviewer: "Maybe so." Worker: "Not maybe. Definitely. Legalized theft. There, write that down!" He continued, "We need another Stalin, Stalin the Second. . . . Go over there and ask, there at the factory next door. It is idle. All the machines are idle. . . . People are not working. For six months no one has received wages."[32]

Here we see reflected the feelings of abandonment by the state. A measure of the depth of this attitude can be found in interviews our study recorded in the late 1990s and early 2000s in other industrial suburbs when the very mention of the state disappears in responses. In these early interviews the state is still included, but as a fast-receding sign of betrayal of all that had been promised and worked for by the generation that had recently retired or were coming up on retirement age.

Pëtr, a sixty-nine-year-old self-taught construction carpenter, expressed these feelings of dismay and loss that many of this generation felt at the time. After serving in World War II and toiling for three decades, he and his family finally began in the late 1970s to enjoy a few returns on their labor in the form of consumer goods, clothes, TV, and affordable foodstuffs. Pëtr even reached a point, like other workers of his generation, where he dreamed of buying a car. He saved up for years, even built a garage. "Then bang! The dream vanished," he exclaimed.[33] The hyperinflation that had accompanied the lifting of price controls (the policy known as "Shock Therapy") erased his savings almost overnight.

Variations of this story were common in the early 1990s. A truck driver, Feliks, who drove me to villages for interviews on another project likewise grumbled about how he had saved up and stood in line for years to purchase a Niva (a Soviet jeep/SUV) and then had his savings wiped out by inflation. Although the details of such stories would be hard to confirm, they were not really the point. The stories functioned as a means for people to affirm that they had played by the rules and then been cruelly betrayed by national leaders. "I should have acted sooner," Pëtr groaned. "I let the chance slip. . . . But who knew that one man could change life completely, could impoverish the nation? . . . If I could, I would have dumped that Gorbachev and put myself in his place. And now this Yeltsin, though he said he wouldn't, is continuing the same system." This disillusionment and anger was powerful enough that it could overturn the loyalty that these people had earlier felt to their country. My driver Feliks, for example, lovingly cared for the one expensive object that he had acquired before the price inflation, a video camera. He planned to cash it in for a ticket to leave the country (which his marriage to the widow of a deceased Jew permitted), and indeed he did emigrate. But for the workers of Khot'kovo the stories of betrayal and misery were not a prelude to emigration so much as the kind of "Russian talk" that the anthropologist Nancy Ries wrote about, namely, the construction of Russia as a realm of absurdity and injustice and a plea for sympathy and understanding. Talk of suffering and injustice was, according to Ries, a means of acquiring social capital that might compensate for material and spiritual losses.[34]

In sum, although much has been written about the benefits of privatization, little attention has been given to the losses of woods, ponds, meadows, and other formerly accessible recreational properties and social facilities that ordinary Russians used in their leisure time for rest and relaxation, not to mention for provisions such as fish, mushrooms, and berries. The loss of recreational sites and social services that had long been part of the everyday life of workers was keenly felt, especially at a time when workers were suffering financial and job losses. Working-class Russians who could not afford to purchase second homes or dachas in attractive natural settings considered the alienation of these once accessible recreational areas a diminution of their citizenship and an assault on the personal and collective rights that they earned through their work and voluntary contributions to their community. The privatization of these properties and community services likewise stood as a palpable, visible sign of the general withdrawal of public goods and of the protection of state and party organizations. Perestroika and the fall of communism had brought many changes, but this loss of local access to properties and social facilities long considered part of ordinary people's common birthright was especially dismaying because the formerly cost-free recreational opportunities of the natural surroundings increased in value as the expense of other leisure-time activities such as films, theater, travel, and the purchase of a car became prohibitive. To make matters worse, people had neither political nor civic organizations to combat the purchase and appropriation of these lands and facilities. Conversely, the everyday life of the well-to-do families who were acquiring these resources was enhanced. The young day care worker Oksana defined the dilemma well: "For them it is good. They come here to relax, so to speak, to breathe fresh air. But for us, quite the opposite, they are taking that air from us. That is, they are chopping down our woods and taking over our space."

NOTES

I want to thank the officers of the Slavic Research Center at Hokkaido University for providing support during my research on this essay and also Mie Nakachi and David Wolff of the same center for helpful comments. Michael Alexeev of Indiana University offered valuable criticism and advice. Sergei Zaremovich Chernov of the Russian Academy of Sciences provided indispensable source materials and critical comments.

1. While land in the countryside belonged to the state, residential structures had long been largely private. It is also true that Russians owned personal property, and impoverished people sold personal items in order to survive the grim immediate postsocialist years. Most urban citizens nevertheless also gained a resource when early in the privatization process they acquired ownership rights in their apartments, a nonliquid but in some cases highly valuable asset.

2. On the adoption of neoliberal rhetoric, see Olga Shevchenko's chapter in this volume and her book *Crisis and the Everyday in Postsocialist Moscow* (Bloomington: Indiana University Press, 2009).

3. See Maxim Boycko, Andrei Shleifer, and Robert Vishny, *Privatizing Russia* (Cambridge, Mass.: MIT Press, 1995). This very simplified explanation also contains a strong note of self-justification, as the authors were closely involved in designing and guiding the reform.

Another way to think about the process may be more helpful, since inefficiencies are in some degree defined by context. In a centrally planned economy, efficiencies have much to do with balancing allocations of resources. Planners value gross outputs that serve as inputs to other enterprises. From the planners' point of view, behavior that may be cost effective for a particular enterprise will not be efficient for the economy as a whole if it limits (unbalances) the allocation of resources needed by other enterprises. Similarly, it would not have made sense for Soviet enterprise managers to concern themselves unduly with net indicators such as profit and value added so long as prices did not reflect relative scarcities. I want to thank my colleague at Indiana University, Michael Alexeev, for pointing out how sensitive definitions of efficiency and balance were to context. On the question of balance in a command economy, see the classic essay by Gregory Grossman, "Notes for a Theory of the Command Economy," *Soviet Studies* 15, no. 2 (October 1963): 101–23, esp. 113–18. See also Richard E. Ericson, "The Classical Soviet-Type Economy: Nature of the System and Implications for Reform," *Journal of Economic Perspectives* 5, no. 4 (Autumn 1991): 11–27, esp. 15–17, 21–23.

4. Anders Åslund, *How Capitalism Was Built: The Transformation of Central and Eastern Europe, Russia, and Central Asia* (Cambridge: Cambridge University Press, 2007), 152–53.

5. The reformers made exaggerated claims for the benefits of voucher privatization, which turned out to be largely illusory. Only about 20 percent of the value of companies was transferred through vouchers, whereas over 50 percent went to insiders, managers, and employees at nominal cost. In fairness to the reformers, it should be recalled that this "second option," which favored insiders, was not part of the original program but was added by the state legislature. Here again the reformers had to bow to reality. The managers used their political muscle to outmaneuver them. Åslund, one of the apologists for the reform, wrote that the funds created by the vouchers gradually "faded away" (ibid., 160–61). In fact, many "voucher investment funds" were Ponzi schemes that stole the investments of ordinary people, the effect being to enrich the criminal managers of the funds while exerting little impact on property distribution. See Andrew Barnes, *Owning Russia: The Struggle over Factories, Farms, and Power* (Ithaca, N.Y.: Cornell University Press, 2006), 77–79.

6. Boycko, Shleifer, and Vishny, *Privatizing Russia*, 73. The allocation was, however, done in a variety of ways, some of which placed restrictions on what could be done with the property and consequently often rendered it unprofitable.

7. For a recent review of the extensive rights of ownership that were conceded to local bodies plus a discussion of the subsequent legal development of the delineation of local and federal rights over property, see I. A. Ikonitskaia, ed., *Pravo sobstvennosti na zemliu v Rossii i ES: Pravovye problemy. Sbornik statei* (Moscow: Wolters Kluwer, 2009), esp. 45–57.

8. The topic of community services and welfare provision will only be touched on briefly in this chapter, as it deserves separate study. The threat has proved serious as well for important national heritage sites, a question that I plan to cover in a separate study.

9. The amendment can be found in *Sobranie aktov prezidenta i pravitel'stva Rossiiskoi Federatsii* 2 (1993): 92–101, cited in Barnes, *Owning Russia*, 89, see also 149.

10. *Arkheologicheskaia karta Rossii,* ed. Iu. A. Krasnov, *Moskovskaia oblast',* pt. 1 (Moscow: Rossiiskaia akademiia nauk, institut arkheologii, 1994), 237.

11. This was the Podmoskovnaia ekspeditsiia Instituta arkheologii, led by A. V. Engovatova.

12. Personal communication from Sergei Chernov, Institute of Archaeology, Russian Academy of Sciences, January 3, 2011.

13. The Khot'kovo interviews were conducted in June 1994 by Ol'ga Glazunova.

14. Oksana L., age nineteen, Khot'kovo, June 12, 1994. Other Khot'kovo workers complained more generally about the sale of forests and other resources for virtually nothing. See, for example, Vladimir Ch., age thirty-six, Khot'kovo, June 8, 1994.

15. Besides the interview with Oksana L., see interviews with Viktor P., age thirty-one, June 8, 1994, and Nadezhda B., age forty-two, Khot'kovo, June 11, 1994.

16. In contrast to the lives of their younger neighbors, the lives of the older generation had left them with little time for recreation. What socializing they did occurred with close family and friends, and much of their outdoor activity was devoted to their garden plots.

17. Nikolai P., age eighty-five, and wife, Aleksandra, age seventy-two, Khot'kovo, June 13, 1994.

18. A news report and audio clip of a portion of the protest can be found at http://www.kr-uz.ru/ku0029.htm, accessed February 19, 2011.

19. See the preface to John Earle et al., *Small Privatization: The Transformation of Retail Trade and Consumer Services in the Czech Republic, Hungary and Poland* (Budapest: Central European University Press, 1994). Reformers hoped that the buildings and grounds of such establishments could be sufficiently freed of restrictions on their use that enterprising people would be able to turn them into competitive businesses, but sometimes politically dictated constraints on changing personnel, product mix, and the like limited these prospects. See below.

20. Katherine Verdery, "The Obligations of Ownership: Restoring Rights to Land in Postsocialist Transylvania," in *Property in Question: Value Transformation in the Global Economy,* ed. Katherine Verdery and Caroline Humphrey (Oxford: Berg, 2004), 139, where she cites A. M. Honoré, "Ownership," *Oxford Essays in Jurisprudence,* 1st series, ed. A. G. Guest (Oxford: Oxford University Press, 1961), 107–47.

21. Nikolai N., age fifty-three, Khot'kovo, June 15, 1994.

22. Similar examples of the rapid divestment of social facilities and their local impact can be found in Serguei Oushakine, *Patriotism of Despair: Nation, War, and Loss in Russia* (Ithaca, N.Y.: Cornell University Press, 2009) and an essay on Kazakhstan by Catherine Alexander, "Value, Relations, and Changing Bodies: Privatization and Property Rights in Kazakhstan," in Verdery and Humphrey, *Property in Question,* 251–73.

23. Vladimir Ch., age thirty-six, Khot'kovo, June 8, 1994.

24. Aleksei P., age seventy-five, Khot'kovo, June 12, 1994; Oksana L., age nineteen, Khot'kovo, June 12, 1994; Nadezhda P., age thirty-nine, Khot'kovo, June 11, 1994. This last woman also sought solace and counsel in popular culture by viewing lectures by Valentina Moskalenko on alcoholism and family.

25. Viktor P., age forty-one, Khot'kovo, June 13, 1994.

26. Nadezhda B., age forty-two, Khot'kovo, June 11, 1994.

27. See on the general theory Robert D. Putnam (with Robert Leonardi and Raffael Y. Nanetti), *Making Democracy Work: Civic Traditions in Modern Italy* (Princeton, N.J.: Princeton University Press, 1994); and on Russia, Stephen E. Hanson and Jeffrey S. Kopstein, "The Weimar/Russia Comparison," *Post-Soviet Affairs* 13 (1997): 252–83. By the same token, according to other analyses, this failure may also have prevented the growth of neo-

fascism, inasmuch as the rise of Italian fascism and of German Nazism owed much to their mobilization of a wide range of civic organizations in those countries. See Steffen Kailitz and Andreas Umland, "Why the Fascists Won't Take Over the Kremlin (For Now): A Comparison of Democracy's Breakdown and Fascism's Rise in Weimar Germany and Post-Soviet Russia" (Moscow, 2010), Gosudarstvennyi Universitet Vysshaia Shkola Ekonomiki, Series WP14 Politicheskaia teoriia i politicheskii analiz, 3–43.

28. "Proverka prava na besplatnuiu rybalku," *Interfaks*, April 7, 2011, http://www.interfax .ru/print.asp?sec=1446&id=184670, accessed July 6, 2011.

29. See the chronicle attached to "Arkheologicheskii skandal razoraetsia vokrug 'Okhta tsentra,'" Neva24, http://bashne.net/?p=2380, accessed April 26, 2011, and the article itself: "Arkheologicheskii skandal razoraetsia vokrug 'Okhta tsentra,'" Neva24, http://bashne .net/?p=2380, accessed April 26, 2011. Some observers believe that the decision to move the structure from Okhta to suburban Lakhta had more to do with political infighting in Moscow than with civic actions in Petersburg (personal communication from Boris Mironov, St. Petersburg, May 6, 2011). On the decision to move the tower to Lakhta, see http://piter .tv/event/Novuyu_bashnyu_Gazproma_v/, accessed September 26, 2011, and http://www .maindoor.ru/geo/%D0%A0%D0%BE%D1%81%D1%81%D0%B8%D1%8F/news/10524.html, accessed July 5, 2011.

30. "Dekulakavize" is a reference to the campaign of dispossession, arrest, and exile of propertied villagers in the 1930s, the "kulaks." Though framed in the propaganda as a class conflict, any peasants, whether prosperous or not, who resisted collectivization of farming were branded kulaks and deported.

31. Aleksei and Mar'ia P., both age seventy-five, Khot'kovo, June 12, 1994.

32. Ivan, age sixty-one, and Iurii, age fifty-three, Khot'kovo, June 15, 1994.

33. Pëtr, age sixty-nine, Khot'kovo, June 8, 1994.

34. Nancy Ries, *Russian Talk: Culture and Conversation during Perestroika* (Ithaca, N.Y.: Cornell University Press, 1997).

Part III.
Living Space and Personal Choice

Everyday Life and the Problem of Conceptualizing Public and Private during the Khrushchev Era

DEBORAH A. FIELD

Scholars often use spatial metaphors to explain public and private. We describe these aspects of life as spheres or realms or, in Habermas's classic work, as linked rectangles.[1] However, such spatial images can collapse when we apply them to everyday life under Khrushchev; examining everyday life reveals the instability of public and private and indicates the difficulties in conceptualizing these categories.

There are two Russian words for everyday life, so it is essential to start with a definition of this key term. In this essay, I am referring not to *povsednevnost'*, which denotes a daily occurrence, but rather to *byt,* a term with a more complicated set of definitions. In prerevolutionary times, byt was mostly used to denote the "way of life" of ethnographic subjects, but in the revolutionary era it acquired different meanings. Byt referred to lifestyle but also took on connotations of banality, routine, backwardness; it was what had to be transformed in order to create Soviet citizens. The new socialist byt would emancipate women and eliminate ignorance, passivity, and *meshchanstvo* (an amalgam of pettiness, selfishness, materialism, and bad taste).[2] By the Khrushchev period the term *byt* included domesticity, lifestyle, and personal relations and continued to be the object of official and professional attempts at reform. According to the author of a text on Marxist ethics, "it is precisely in everyday life [*byt*] where the vestiges of old morals in relation to women, family, and the destruction of rules of common living . . . persist especially stubbornly."[3] The term *byt* was often paired with family. For example, in 1954 the catalog of all books published in the USSR contained a new subject heading called "Sem'ia i byt" (Family and everyday life), which encompassed works on an array of topics: housework and home decoration, love and romance, manners and etiquette, child rearing, family relations, the dangers of alcoholism.[4]

Byt would seem to belong firmly in the realm of private life. But a consideration of such everyday (bytovye) topics as child rearing, marriage, abortion, and relations among neighbors results in categorical confusion, as definitions of public and private seem to shift and change under examination. The difficulty in conceptualizing public and private stems in part from the contradictory policies of the Soviet state, which simultaneously enacted some policies aimed at merging public and private life and others that allowed for some separation between the two. A perhaps more fundamental problem arises because the meanings of public and private were both intangible and variable during this period.

ABORTION AND THE AMBIGUITY OF POLICY

During the Khrushchev period, state policy toward private life was inconsistent, and this has resulted in a certain amount of scholarly controversy. Sparked in part by Oleg Kharkhordin's widely cited and provocative assertion that Soviet citizens experienced less individual freedom and more social control than they had under Stalin, recently scholars have emphasized the coercive aspects of the Khrushchevian state and its incursions into private life.[5] Kharkhordin relies mainly on official documents such as party policy statements and Khrushchev's speeches, so his formulation captures some of the aspirations of the state but not the variable implementation of and popular response to government policy. Scholars employing a wider variety of sources have reached more nuanced conclusions; for example, in a recent article Edward Cohn characterizes the Khrushchev-era Communist Party's relationship to its membership as "less repressive, but more intrusive."[6]

However, even in the realm of state policy, Khrushchev's government displayed a paradoxical attitude toward private life. On the one hand, there were new attempts to monitor and regulate everyday life (byt) and personal behavior as a result of the government's emphasis on instilling communist morality. Communist morality, a much propagandized code of morality and behavior, was supposed to replace coercion as a means of ensuring political and social stability and economic growth. It required political loyalty, hard work, and the proper conduct of private life. Professionals and moralists in a variety of fields determined what attitudes and behaviors constituted a correct communist private life, putting forth specific instructions about sex, love, marriage, and child rearing. Trade union, party, Komsomol, and voluntary organizations were supposed to help enforce these standards.[7] The title of one didactic book exemplifies these principles: *Byt—ne chastnoe delo* (Everyday life is not a private matter).[8] Yet at the same time, the government initiated other reforms that allowed people more control over their personal lives; for example, divorce became progressively easier to obtain, and a new housing program was launched with the goal of providing families with individual apartments.[9] In literature and film, heroes were allowed to demonstrate their concern for intimate relationships as well as production.[10] The government's contradictory tendencies were usually embodied in different sets of policies. But the 1955 law re-legalizing abortion provided for both greater individual freedom and increased intervention in private life, all in one short decree, so it provides an especially clear example of the Khrushchev government's duality.

The 1955 law marked the third major policy shift of the Soviet era (abortion was first legalized in 1920 and then was prohibited again under Stalin in 1936). According to the decree announcing the 1955 decision, the purpose of the law was to prevent the threat to women's health posed by abortions performed outside of medical facilities but also to give women "the opportunity to decide the question of maternity themselves."[11] This characterization of reproduction as an individual's choice represents a radical innovation, as Soviet officials and experts had long characterized maternity as a social obligation, even during the relatively libertarian 1920s.[12]

At least some officials took seriously the radical promise that women should control their reproduction. At a meeting at the USSR Public Health Ministry, the prominent gynecologist Olga Nikonchik emphasized just this aspect of the legislation: "This decree is not intended so that at present many abortions will occur—no—but so that now in all areas of industries, in all branches of industry, woman will take one of the leading places, and [because] we have come to the moment *to give woman more rights to decide her personal life. . . .* Up until now she was restricted in her personal life" (my italics). Then, perhaps fearing she had gone too far in acknowledging government intrusion, she added what seems like a contradiction of her previous statement: "Our government has never encouraged abortion, but we have never infringed on the personal life of men and women."[13]

Nikonchik's ambiguous comments sprang from her uncertainty about what was publicly admissible, but they also echo the contradictory nature of the new law. The 1955 decree concluded with a resolve to prevent abortions through increased support of mothers and measures of an "educational and elucidating character."[14] In the same act, the government legalized abortion and initiated an effort to discourage it, thus granting women the right to choose abortion or reproduction but making it clear that there was only one correct choice.

The educational measures cited in the 1955 decree did not refer to sex education in the schools, which was not implemented until 1983.[15] Instead, physicians delivered public lectures and wrote a variety of pamphlets, books, and articles in women's magazines in which they warned women against abortion and in some cases provided information about contraception. These materials, like the legislation that spawned them, focused on both individual choice and the importance of heeding the experts. These seemingly incompatible themes of female autonomy and professional intervention were combined by means of a recurring trope of advice. Most of these texts included formulaic and melodramatic stories about women ignoring their physicians' counsel and then regretting abortions. For example, a gynecologist described the case history of Galina K. as a cautionary tale. Galina K. came to him for an abortion, although she was educated and married, because she said she did not want to start a family yet, she wanted to "enjoy herself a little." The gynecologist refused to perform the abortion, but Galina K. found someone else to do it. Six months later she returned to the gynecologist. There had been complications, she was in constant pain, and her husband was threatening to divorce her if she turned out to be infertile. The gynecologist had to tell her that it was too late, there was nothing he could do, and she cried and cried.[16]

In most of these stories, women who did not seek out or heed their doctors' advice were punished by inevitable complications and the agony of infertility.[17] Women who listened to their doctors were, in contrast, suitably grateful.[18] The women in these stories were never poor or unmarried, so that their reasons for having abortions were usually presented as petty or selfish: the desire to have free time or to pursue a career.[19] Nor was the difficulty of obtaining contraceptives acknowledged, although gynecologists discussed this problem repeatedly and fervently among themselves at professional conferences.[20] The infertility that always followed women's foolish choices was depicted as a complete catastrophe because of women's fundamentally maternal essence. In the pamphlet she produced, Nikonchik of the Ministry of Public Health declared, "Every woman strives to become a mother. Maternal feelings are awake in her since childhood." To illustrate this fact, the facing page featured a drawing of a young, chubby-cheeked girl cuddling her doll.[21]

Physician–sex educators portrayed abortion as primarily a self-destructive act, a betrayal of women's own true nature, but they only rarely described it as an offense against society as a whole.[22] This is surprising for a number of reasons. First, the social importance of motherhood had long been, and continued to be, an important theme in editorials published on International Women's Day, child-rearing manuals, and other forms of official discourse. More broadly, the social and political importance of private life was a major theme in communist morality, the tenets of which were ubiquitous in the prescriptive literature of this period. Finally, discussions of other aspects of sexuality during this period did stress the link between sexual activity and social responsibility. So, for example, sex educators condemned adultery specifically because it destroyed families and so imperiled proper upbringing of the next generation of communists.[23] Physicians and pedagogues depicted masturbation as dangerous because it resulted in enervated, solitary, self-absorbed individuals who deviated from the Soviet ideal of cheerful, energetic collectivism.[24]

Why did the physicians writing antiabortion materials neglect to remind women of the demographic cost of abortion and their duty to produce children? Why was physicians' rhetoric so focused on the emotional rather than the social consequences of abortion? It is likely that physicians believed that women's maternal instincts were stronger than their collectivism. Sincerely devoted to reducing abortions, physicians might have thought that scaring women by invoking the possibility of infertility would be more effective than appealing to their sense of social responsibility. Furthermore, antiabortion materials followed the logic of the 1955 law legalizing abortion. The law promised women the right to make their own reproductive decisions, a promise that was reflected in the depiction of abortion as a woman's individual choice with primarily personal consequences. Thus, an examination of abortion during the Khrushchev period reveals the inconsistent nature of Soviet policy toward private life, which promoted an uneasy combination of individual autonomy and expert intervention into all aspects of byt.

THE INTANGIBLE BASES OF PRIVATE LIFE

The inconsistency of state policy creates a certain amount of confusion, but a more fundamental problem with understanding public and private has to do with the fluctuating and intangible bases of these categories, which is especially apparent in the Soviet context during this period.

Scholarly definitions of private life usually contain two distinct but related components. Jeff Weintraub argues that these are what is "hidden or withdrawn versus what is open, revealed or accessible" and also "what is individual, or pertains only to an individual, versus what is collective, or affects the interest of a collectivity of individuals."[25] In the modern era, however, emotion, family, friendship, and sex are strongly associated with the private, perhaps because these aspects of life are, or were until recently, usually "hidden or withdrawn." These two aspects of private life roughly correspond to the two different Russian terms *lichnaia zhizn'* and *chastnaia zhizn'*. In Kharkhordin's perceptive analysis, these two terms together designate the English "private life," meaning "life within a family or with friends, and more generally life outside the realm of public duties and public organizations." Lichnaia zhizn', best translated as "personal life" because it comes from the word for "person" (*lichnost'*), coincides with the first part of Kharkhordin's English definition; chastnaia zhizn' corresponds to the second. The adjective *chastnyi* is derived from the word for a part of something (*chast'*), and it referred to private property (*chastnaia sobstvennost'*) in prerevolutionary Russia. Kharkhordin argues that a specific, communist kind of personal life (lichnaia zhizn') was promoted by the Soviet government at the same time that it sought to wipe out private life (chastnaia zhizn'), "the way of life ... based on private property," that is, life away from official institutions and in pursuit of particularistic goals. Although Kharkhordin describes the word *chastnyi* disappearing from Soviet dictionaries, despite what he calls a discursive assassination, both chastnaia and lichnaia zhizn', both intimate ties and individual interests, persisted, albeit in forms different from those in the West.[26]

In descriptions of bourgeois society, private interests (chastnaia zhizn') are based on property, created through the market and defended against the state through such organizations as newspapers and political parties. In the Soviet Union, in the absence of legal market mechanisms and substantial private property, people defined and protected their individual interests in a variety of other ways. Scholars, particularly those focusing on the Brezhnev era, have described some of the mechanisms: black market transactions and the use of personal connections to obtain scarce goods, jobs for relatives, and other privileges.[27] Another method that I have discussed at length elsewhere involved individuals appropriating official ideology and the institutions that were supposed to support it for their own purposes. This was evident in a variety of contexts but perhaps most clearly in divorce cases. Officially, divorce was discouraged; communist morality demanded that married people suppress their selfish passions in order to preserve the stable family life so important for their children and, by extension, the country's future. Party groups and social organizations, such as comrades' courts and house committees, were supposed to intervene to help troubled families stay together. However, in some cases hostile spouses took the initiative by seeking party interference in their troubled marriages, or they appropriated official language by accusing one another of such offenses as "disregarding the high principles of communist morality" during divorce proceedings. These actions were not necessarily aimed at ensuring the good of the collective but rather at achieving specific, particularistic, individual goals: reclaiming wayward spouses, subduing officious in-laws, gaining custody of children, retaining property such as tea sets, radios, and dachas.[28]

Soviet people defended private interests not through specific institutions such as newspapers, legislatures, and courthouses but rather through the manipulation of discourse and the management of relationships. A similar process comes into play in the other part of private life, intimate ties and personal life (lichnaia zhizn'). In modern Western societies, at least until the advent of reality television and the Internet, such relationships were carried out in private spaces; people required privacy for private life. Living conditions in the Soviet Union made this impossible. The rich scholarship on communal apartments indicates, however, that people strove to create privacy through a wide array of mental and emotional exertions. For example, a woman I interviewed in Moscow described avoiding an objectionable neighbor: "I knew her work schedule better than she did, so I planned to do laundry or clean if she was working in the evening."[29] In other words, she couldn't manipulate space, so she worked with the dimension of time. In Lynne Attwood's description of apartment life, she remarks that people refused to "live communally in a communal apartment" and did not share meals, utensils, or even lightbulbs in some extreme cases.[30] Katerina Gerasimova describes a similar attitudinal tactic, "depersonalization," in which people treated their neighbors as if they were "mere 'elements' of the setting"; she quotes an informant comparing her own attitude to that of aristocrats who paid no attention to the servants in whose presence they undressed or defecated.[31] Svetlana Boym argues that the many knickknacks and postcards so common in Soviet apartments represented an internal search for privacy because treasuring these objects was a way to recall, and find refuge in, personal, individual feelings and experiences.[32] All of these examples suggest an attempt to establish privacy through intangibles: imagination, memory, attitudes, habits. In a poem that dates from this period, Robert Rozhdestvensky suggested, in a similar vein, that it is the free expression of emotion that creates privacy. In "Uninhabited Islands" he plays with a metaphor that links true love with private property, describing lush, secret, deserted islands that belong exclusively to people who are in love. The lovers of this poem dream these islands into existence; their desire and imagination provide them with their own uninhabited island, and their love entitles them to this little piece of real estate because, as the poet writes, love "has asserted / its rights."[33]

Thus, during the Khrushchev period, private interests were defended through relationships, influence, appropriation of official discourse; privacy was created through emotion, attitude, imagination. Private life was based upon a versatile and changeable set of practices rather than physical privacy or specific institutions.

MULTIPLE AND VARIABLE PUBLICS

One of the difficulties in discussing the public is that its meaning shifts according to the analytic framework being deployed and the topic under study: it can refer to the state, in opposition to a "private" market; it can indicate the arena of active citizenship, or civil society, or the urban spaces where strangers interact.[34] Soviet studies specialists write about public opinion but often find the notion of a Soviet public sphere more problematic. Vladimir Shlapentokh has emphasized the lack of any kind of authentic public sphere in Soviet society, pointing to the absence of institutions that in a bourgeois society are supposed to mediate between state and society: churches, businesses, independent political parties, a free press.[35] Others argue that, for similar reasons, the notion of the social is more appropriate to the Soviet context than that of the public. For example, Marc Garcelon provides a tripartite model of society that consists of a domestic realm of intimacy and trust, an official realm of state and party power, and a social realm of workplaces, official associations, and organized leisure activities such as sports. This social sphere is the site of two different kinds of interactions: official, rule-based communication and "bargaining, reciprocal favors, mutual dependencies, networks of connections, dissimulation, circumvention of regulations and procedures." Garcelon groups these two types of interactions together under the rubric of "social" because they occur in "intermediate" spaces between the state and informal friendship networks; they also occur in the same locations (offices, stadiums).[36] In the discussion of communal apartments below, I want to consider these types of interactions separately and argue that at least in the context of apartment buildings, they constituted two related but distinct types of social worlds, one supervised by government and party and embodied in various committees and organizations, the other constituted by the chaotic and unpredictable relationships among communal apartment neighbors.

During the Khrushchev era, officials revived the idea that apartment buildings, like workplaces, should be a site for collective, organized activism, the transmission of official values, and the inculcation of a modern, socialist mode of everyday life (byt).[37] A confusing array of administrations actually managed Soviet apartment buildings, and, in addition, local party organizations and various volunteer groups were supposed to inspire residents with a sense of responsibility for the physical upkeep of the building and for the well-being and enlightenment of their fellow tenants. Parent committees, the party organizations associated with housing management bureaucracies, and house committees (*domkomy*) took on a wide variety of tasks: they organized leisure activities for children and young people, oversaw repairs, created playgrounds.[38] Comrades' courts were intended to supervise byt and bring it into adherence with Soviet values. They shamed, reprimanded, and fined those guilty of child neglect, disrespect toward women and parents, property damage, and insults. The courts were also supposed to help resolve everyday disputes among neighbors about the division of living space and the payment of utility bills.[39]

The effectiveness of these groups seems to have varied greatly. Some house committees reported a great deal of activity: construction of sandboxes and basketball courts, planting of trees and gardens, cleaning and maintenance of public areas, and entertainment and enlightenment of children and adults.[40] Similarly, some comrades' courts claimed efficacy; according to its own report, over the course of 1963, one Moscow comrades' court held forty-five discussions with troubled families and children and brought legal cases against nine drunken parents.[41] Legal journals recorded other successful cases in which neighbors ignored false, bourgeois notions of privacy in order to bring drunken, abusive spouses or inconsiderate tenants before the comrades' courts. In these accounts the community disapproval expressed during the hearings proved powerful, inspiring the violators' eventual reform.[42] But at the same time, those same journals also contained periodic complaints about the disorganization and ineffectiveness of comrades' courts, and local governments periodically found fault with them.[43] There is also evidence that some people resented social activism and that byt was resistant to transformation. At a meeting in 1960, an organizer scolded the other tenants of a Moscow apartment complex for their passivity. A tenant replied, expressing despair and a distinct lack of the enthusiasm and energy that were supposed to define Soviet citizens: "What does the everyday life [byt] of people depend upon? When are things good? In a well-equipped house things are good! The question of equipment, of planting greenery, of areas for children are raised, but when plaster flakes off on your head, when everything around is rotten and you await an accident, it could drive you to drink."[44]

The rule-based, purposeful social sphere constituted by official organizations did not exist at all times or in all buildings. And even where it did, the most competent and energetic comrades' courts and house committees could not change the fundamental fact that most people lived in crowded conditions. Alongside the committees and reports was another, inescapable social world, one that was made up of unavoidable encounters with neighbors.

Communal apartments have been the focus of much recent scholarly interest.[45] My brief description here draws on this work, as well as on oral history interviews and records from courts and the commissions on minors that were established in each Moscow city district in the late fifties and early sixties. Neighborly interactions varied greatly; here I am dividing them into three categories: conflict, surveillance, and help.

Everyday life inside communal apartments could be turbulent. The petty, retrograde, essentially selfish byt disdained by revolutionaries and criticized by Khrushchev-era officials was still very much in evidence. With so many families sharing kitchens, corridors, and bathrooms, it is not surprising that neighbors bickered over dividing utility bills and cleaning common areas.[46] Other disputes arose when neighbors accused one another of rudeness, insults, and literally taking up too much space; for example, one woman told me about a particularly troublesome neighbor who would get drunk and fall over: "Since he fell down in front of the door, on the floor, we had to lift him up and drag him to his bed, so he wouldn't get in our way."[47] In such close quarters, trivial incidents could escalate into battles, and neighborly rancor could turn violent. For example, in one 1960 case, a neighbor testified that the accused "rudely called me names. I asked her not to behave like a hooligan [khuliganit'], then she hit me on the head with a dirty birch switch, which she had in her hands at that moment, and then, going into a rage, grabbed my hair and began to drag me by the hair to the exit."[48]

Svetlana Boym has referred to communal apartment discord as "class warfare" because notions of culture, modernity, and urbanity and standards of hygiene and decorum became the basis for difference and sometimes conflict between neighbors.[49] Nationality was another potential source of contention. For example, in 1958, during an investigation of parental neglect, a neighbor testified that the alcoholic mother in question had taught her children to be anti-Semitic. The children frequently shouted under his door, "Beat the Jews, save Russia."[50]

Such conflict was not inevitable, however; many people I spoke to expressed pride at their ability to get along with neighbors despite their differences. But while some neighbors were able to secure a peaceful coexistence, privacy was a more elusive achievement, for crowded conditions inside communal apartments facilitated surveillance among neighbors. People not only heard and saw what their neighbors were doing, which was unavoidable, but sometimes kept track of behavior and tried to interfere. In Stalinist times, this intervention could take the form of denunciations to the secret police.[51] In the Khrushchev period, while this danger persisted, a less sinister version of surveillance prevailed that involved testifying in family court and to child welfare officials about the personal habits, family relations, and sexual behavior of neighbors. So, for example, in an acrimonious custody case initiated in 1954, one neighbor who lived adjacent to the family in question told a custody inspector that "earlier the child cried a lot at night, and the father, grandmother, or maid calmed him. She never heard the mother calm the child at night."[52]

Communal apartment dwellers not only were aware of their neighbors' routines but claimed knowledge of their emotional lives. In a 1960 custody case, a mother sought to regain custody of her children, who were living with their father. Her neighbors wrote a testimonial to the court affirming their thorough knowledge of the mother's character and of her relationship to the older child: "We have eleven rooms on the floor, and we live well and peacefully. We know each other's life, joys, and sorrows.... [The mother] lives under our eyes. We know everything, that she works at a difficult job.... After work we see her at home at six o'clock every day. She never goes anywhere.... Marinochka, her daughter, often visits. She loves her mother, and [her mother] loves her."[53]

As this case makes clear, people occasionally took the initiative in providing information about their neighbors. In a similar example concerning a 1957 divorce case, six of the couple's neighbors signed a letter addressed to the court affirming that they had witnessed the husband drunk, causing trouble, and beating his wife in the presence of the children.[54] In a 1958 suit to deprive a woman of her parental rights, one neighbor actually produced a tape recording that she had made of the older daughter reproaching her mother for spending all their money on alcohol and neglecting to buy milk for the younger child.[55]

That these neighbors volunteered information suggests the dual nature of *kommunalka* life. On the one hand, the information reveals the tremendous obstacles to privacy and the ubiquity and intimacy of neighborly surveillance. On the other hand, neighborly intervention, at its most benevolent, sprang from a sense of responsibility for other people; it demonstrates that neighbors cared about the fate of a battered wife or a neglected child enough to try to do something about it. The beneficial side of neighborly interference is especially evident in cases in which neighbors looked after abused and neglected children.[56] For example, in one such case a woman reported to a custody investigator that when her neighbor had locked his child in a room for several days and disappeared, she managed to pass the child food and water through the window.[57]

Even in less extreme cases, neighbors helped one another with the burdens of everyday life, which were always considerable in the Soviet context, despite plans for the modernization of byt. A woman gratefully described to me how her neighbors helped her after the birth of her son: "All the neighbors divided up the chores between them: someone went to buy groceries, someone cleaned, someone washed the child's diapers."[58] Many of the people with whom I spoke in the early 1990s expressed some degree of nostalgia about communal life, for example, describing how they used to celebrate holidays with their communal apartment neighbors or mentioning that they had remained friends with their former neighbors even after they had all moved on to individual apartments in the late sixties and seventies; this attitude is also evident in the interviews that are part of a virtual museum devoted to the subject.[59] The reason for people's perhaps retrospectively fond memories of communal life has much to do with post-Soviet developments. While the kommunalkas' forced communality was oppressive, it also provided an ultimate guarantee of human contact and protection against isolation, and it was precisely this sense of community that elderly people were conscious of losing in the post-Soviet era. "Now everyone is thrown to the tyranny of fate," an informant told me.[60]

Apartment dwellers participated in two different kinds of social or public life. The first was organized through committees, and its goal was to help citizens behave morally and live together cooperatively according to Soviet norms. The second was not organized at all but consisted of the diverse, changeable, and sometimes tumultuous relations among neighbors. The contrast between the structured, purposeful, official social world and the chaotic unofficial one is not surprising, given the perennial disjunction in Soviet society between the leaders' visions and everyday life. What is perhaps more interesting are the commonalities and connections between these publics. They were both variable: just as relations among neighbors differed and changed, so did the scope and effectiveness of official public organizations. Furthermore, although I've drawn a distinction between official and unofficial social worlds, they did not exist in isolation from one another. They often came into contact as people took their complaints about neighbors to the committees that made up the state-supervised social sphere. In the context of Soviet apartment buildings, then, no permanent institutionalized public predominated; instead, over time different kinds of social realms took shape, overlapped, and receded.

Our most commonly used metaphors for public and private (spheres, worlds, realms) do not always fit comfortably with descriptions of Soviet byt. Scholars end up describing overlapping spheres and shifting boundaries or devising new formulations. Gerasimova, for example, coined the phrases "public privacy" and "private publicity" to describe phenomena that do not fit into either category, such as the kind of neighborly surveillance I have described above or the use of public goods for private needs.[61]

Susan Gal argues for a semiotic approach. She defines public and private not as places, spheres, institutions, or practices but as cultural categories. She characterizes them as "indexicals," a linguistic term for expressions that change meaning according to altered contexts (such as "I"), and describes them as "fractals," that is, geometric shapes that can be divided into parts that are smaller versions of the whole. Thus public and private distinctions are constantly being reformulated, subdivided, and nested into one another. Gal provides concrete examples of this process: we distinguish between a private house and a public street, but within the private house there is a further subdivision as we set off the private space of the bedroom from the public living room. Similarly, in Hungary and elsewhere in Eastern Europe during the last years of socialism, private domestic life was further divided into family and intimate relations and "public-inside-the-private" activities such as small-scale home production of various goods for the marketplace.[62]

I have argued here that part of the difficulty for scholars in delineating public and private during the Khrushchev period results from the ambiguity of government policy. More important is the intangible and inconsistent way in which these categories were constituted. Private life was not based on spaces or institutions but rather created through practices and actions: the use of discourse, the management of relationships, acts of imagination and emotion. At the same time, people encountered multiple and ephemeral publics. My depiction of the messiness and variability of Khrushchev-era byt, with its officious physicians, accidental pregnancies, crowded apartments, unreliable house committees, and eavesdropping neighbors, shares with Gal's elegant theorizing a recognition of the inadequacy of our conceptions of public and private and of the necessity of formulating new metaphors that can encompass the crucial dimension of time. In this way the Soviet everyday poses conceptual problems similar to those of our own contemporary context. Habermas's separate rectangles represent a model based on the eighteenth century. Twentieth-century phenomena, such as the welfare state, have disrupted these separations by, for example, bringing private family matters into the public spaces of state bureaucracies. Twenty-first-century media have further destabilized the distinctions so that the variety of what we think of as public and private activities taking place in cyberspace ("friending" people, viewing pornography, organizing political movements) suggests the ever-changing constitution of those categories.

NOTES

I am grateful to the editors and workshop participants for their questions and suggestions. I thank the publisher for permission to reprint some of the material in this essay that appears in my book, *Private Life and Communist Morality in Khrushchev's Russia* (New York: Peter Lang, 2007).

1. Jürgen Habermas, *The Structural Transformation of the Public Sphere* (Cambridge, Mass.: MIT Press, 1991), 30.

2. Svetlana Boym, *Common Places: Mythologies of Everyday Life in Russia* (Cambridge, Mass.: Harvard University Press, 1994), 30–34; Victor Buchli, *An Archeology of Socialism*

(Oxford: Berg, 1999), 23–34; Vera Dunham, *In Stalin's Time* (Durham, N.C.: Duke University Press, 1990), 19–20.

3. A. F. Shishkin, "Stroitel'stvo kommunizma i nekotorye problemy Marksistkoi etiki," in *Voprosy Marksistko-Leninskoi etiki* (Moscow: Politizdat, 1960), 55–56.

4. *Ezhegodnik Knigi SSSR 1954* (Moscow: Izd. Vsesoiuznoi palaty, 1955), 1:249.

5. Oleg Kharkhordin, *The Collective and the Individual in Russia: A Study of Practices* (Berkeley: University of California Press, 1999), 279–80, 302–3.

6. Edward D. Cohn, "Sex and the Married Communist: Family Troubles, Marital Infidelity, and Party Discipline in the Postwar USSR, 1945–1964," *Russian Review* 68 (July 2009): 430.

7. For scholarly treatment of communist morality, see Richard T. De George, *Soviet Ethics and Morality* (Ann Arbor: University of Michigan Press, 1969); Deborah A. Field, *Private Life and Communist Morality in Khrushchev's Russia* (New York: Peter Lang, 2007); and Peter Juviler, "Communist Morality and Soviet Youth," *Problems of Communism* 10, no. 3 (1961): 16–24. For contemporary works, see, for example, Akademia Nauk SSSR, *Nvravstvennye printsipy stroitelia kommunizma* (Moscow, 1965); S. M. Kosolapov and O. N. Krutova, *Voprosy vospitaniia trudiashcheikhsia v dukhe kommunistichekoi nravstvennosti* (Moscow, 1961); A. F. Shishkin, *Osnovy kommunisticheskoi morali* (Moscow, 1955).

8. O. Kuprin, *Byt—ne chastnoe delo* (Moscow: Politizdat, 1959).

9. On housing, see Alfred John Di Maio, Jr., *Soviet Urban Housing* (New York: Praeger, 1974); Timothy Sosnovy, "Housing in the Workers State," *Problems of Communism* 5, no. 6 (November–December 1956): 31–39. On divorce, see Peter H. Juviler, "Cell Mutation in Soviet Society," in *Soviet Society and Culture: Essays in Honor of Vera S. Dunham,* ed. Terry L. Thompson and Richard Sheldon (Boulder, Colo.: Westview Press, 1988); and Juviler, "Marriage and Divorce," *Survey* 48 (1963): 104–17.

10. This observation has been made by many scholars. See, for example, Katerina Clark, *The Soviet Novel:History as Ritual* (Chicago: University of Chicago Press, 1981), 216; Julian Graffy, "'But Where Is Your Happiness, Alevtina Ivanova?': New Debates about Happiness in the Soviet Films of 1956," in *Petrified Utopia: Happiness Soviet Style,* ed. Marina Balina and Evgeny Dobrenko (London: Anthem Press, 2009), 237; George Gibian, *Interval of Freedom* (Minneapolis: University of Minnesota Press, 1960), 76; Elena Zubkova, *Russia after the War: Hopes, Illusions, and Disappointments, 1945–1957* (Armonk, N.Y.: M. E. Sharpe, 1998), 172.

11. "Ob otmene zapreshcheniia abortov, ukaz ot 23 noiabria 1955 g.," *Sbornik Zakonov SSSR* (Moscow: Izd. izvestiia sovetov deputatov trudiashchikhsia SSSR, 1975), 3:306.

12. Wendy Goldman, *Women, the State and Revolution: Soviet Family Policy and Social Life, 1917–1936* (Cambridge: Cambridge University Press, 1993), 25.

13. Olga Nikonchik, USSR Public Health Ministry, Gosudarstvennyi Arkhiv Rossiiskoi Federatsii (GARF), fond 8009, op. 2, d. 2176, ll. 38, 39.

14. "Ob otmene zapreshcheniia abortov," 3:306.

15. Lev Shcheglov, "Medical Sexology," in Kon and Riordan, *Sex and Russian Society,* 154–58.

16. L. S. Persianinov, *Abort i ego posledstvie* (Minsk: Znanie, 1958), 4–5.

17. In fact, abortions were made particularly dangerous by unhygienic conditions and shortages of doctors in women's clinics. Christopher Williams, "Abortion and Women's Health in Russia and the Soviet Successor States," in *Women in Russia and Ukraine,* ed. Rosalind Marsh (Cambridge: Cambridge University Press, 1996), 142. Furthermore, abortions were an intensely painful experience, since they were performed without anesthetic.

18. See, for example, B. A. Arkhangel'skii, *Mat' i ditia* (Moscow: Medgiz, 1954), 43; I. M. Kosoi, *Abort ne prokhodit bessledno (v pomoshch' lektoru)* (Moscow: Institut Sanitarnogo Prosveshcheniia, 1956), 25.

19. N. E. Granat, *Abort* (Moscow: Institut sanitarnogo prosveshcheniia, 1957), 25; Kosoi, *Abort ne prokhodit bessledno,* 10; M. S. Malinovskii, "Da, abort—eto zlo," *Sovetskaia zhenshchina,* no. 9 (1956): 45.

20. For discussions at local and national conferences, see, for example, Tsentral'nyi Munitsipal'nyi Arkhiv Moskvy (TsMAM), fond 552, op. 3, d. 698, l. 50; GARF, fond A528, op. 1, d. 8, ll. 75, 85.

21. O. K. Nikonchik, *Abort i ego posledstviia* (Moscow: Medgiz, 1956), 9.

22. For one example of this social rhetoric, see Malinovskii, "Da, abort—eto zlo," 46.

23. See, for example, A. A. Gabelov and E. B. Derankova, *Gigiena braka* (Moscow: Meditsina, 1964), 3.

24. Ivanov, "O polovoi gigiene podrostkov i detei," *Sem'ia i shkola,* no. 6 (1955): 19; L. V. Pisareva, *Nekotorye voprosy vospitaniia detei dlia roditelei* (Moscow: Uchepegiz, 1960), 46.

25. Jeff Weintraub, "The Theory and Politics of the Public/Private Distinction," in *Public and Private in Thought and Practice,* ed. Jeff Weintraub and Krishan Kumar (Chicago: University of Chicago Press, 1997), 5.

26. Oleg Kharkhordin, "Reveal and Dissimulate: A Genealogy of Private Life in Soviet Russia," in Weintraub and Kumar, *Public and Private,* 343–45, 359.

27. See, for example, Marc Garcelon, "The Shadow of the Leviathan: Public and Private in Communist and Post-Communist Society," in Weintraub and Kumar, *Public and Private,* 324–25; James R. Millar, "The Little Deal: Brezhnev's Contribution to Acquisitive Socialism," *Slavic Review* 44, no. 4 (Winter 1985): 694–706.

28. See, for example, TsMAM, fond 819, op. 3, d. 1062, ll. 49, 69. For a more in-depth discussion of this phenomenon, see Deborah A. Field, "Irreconcilable Differences: Divorce and Conceptions of Private Life in the Khrushchev Era," *Russian Review* 57 (October 1998): 599–613.

29. Elena Ia. interview by the author, tape recording, Moscow, December 6, 1993.

30. Lynne Attwood, "Housing in the Khrushchev Era," in *Women in the Khrushchev Era,* ed. Melanie Ilic, Susan E. Reid, and Lynne Attwood (Basingstoke: Palgrave Press, 2004), 180–81.

31. Katerina Gerasimova, "Privacy in the Soviet Communal Apartment," in *Socialist Spaces: Sites of Everyday Life in the Eastern Bloc,* ed. David Crowely and Susan E. Reid (Oxford: Berg Publishers, 2003), 224.

32. Boym, *Common Places,* 149.

33. Robert Rozhdestvensy, "Uninhabited Islands," in *The New Russian Poets, 1953–1966: An Anthology,* trans. and ed. George Reavey (New York: October House, 1966), 59–63.

34. Weintraub, "The Theory and Politics," 23.

35. Vladimir Shlapentokh, *The Public and Private Life of the Soviet People* (New York: Oxford University Press, 1989), 9.

36. Garcelon, "The Shadow of the Leviathan," 317.

37. For an in-depth discussion of this topic, see Christine Varga-Harris, "Constructing the Soviet Hearth: Home, Citizenship and Socialism in Russia, 1956–1964," unpublished manuscript.

38. H. G. Dmitriev, *V pomoshch' domovym komitetam* (Moscow: Izd. Ministerstve kommun. khoziastva RSFSR, 1963), 12–23; N. Dmitiriev and S. Rosantsev, *Spravochnik po zhilishchnym voprosam* (Moscow: Moskovskii rabochii, 1963), 70–71.

39. "Polozhenie o tovarishcheskikh sudakh," *Sovetskaia iiustitsiia*, no. 14 (1961): 26–28.

40. See, for example, reports from house committees: TsMAM, fond 310, op. 1, d. 382, l. 4; TsMAM, fond 197, op. 1, d. 1383, l. 3; TsMAM, fond 310, op. 1, d. 484, l. 46.

41. TsMAM, fond 328, op. 1, d. 773, l. 1.

42. A. Balashov, "Obviniaiut tovarishchi," *Sovetskaia iustitsiia*, no. 3 (1964): 24–25; see also letters from comrades' court officials published in *Sotsialisticheskaia zakonnost'*, no. 4 (1960): 49–50; no. 7 (1960): 52; no. 10 (1961): 72.

43. On comrades' courts, see K. Velinkin, "Povysit' uroven' rukovodstva tovarishches-kimi sudami," *Sovetskaia iustitsiia*, no. 12 (1963): 15–16; G. Apeeva and M. Gel'fer, "Nekotorye voprosy raboty tovarishcheskikh sudov," *Sotsialisticheskaia zakonnost'*, no. 3 (1964): 32. For local government criticisms of comrades' courts and house committees, see Tsentral'nyi Gosudarstvennyi Arkhiv Moskovskoi Oblasti (TsGAMO), fond 7335, op. 4, d. 52, ll. 180–81; Tsentral'nyi Arkhiv Obshchestvennykh Dvizhenii Moskvy (TsAODM), fond 298, op. 1, d. 3, l. 60. See also TsMAM, fond 273, op. 4, d. 1092, l. 31.

44. TsMAM, fond 399, op. 1, d. 567a, ll. 58–59.

45. For a critical review of this work, see Steven E. Harris, "In Search of 'Ordinary' Russia: Everyday Life in the NEP, the Thaw, and the Communal Apartment," *Kritika* 6, no. 3 (Summer 2005): 582–614.

46. For comrades' court officials' accounts of such quarrels, see, for example, TsMAM, fond 328, op. 1, d. 773, l. 87; *Sotsialisticheskaia zakonost'*, no. 11 (1960): 55; *Sovetskaia iustitsia*, no. 10 (1957): 39.

47. Ia. interview.

48. TsMAM, fond 901, op. 2, d. 2345, ll. 2–3.

49. Boym, *Common Places*, 144.

50. TsMAM, fond 257, op. 1, d. 510, l. 9.

51. Stephen Kotkin, *Magnetic Mountain: Stalinism as a Civilization* (Berkeley: University of California Press, 1997), 196.

52. TsMAM, fond 819, op. 3, d. 285, l. 114.

53. TsMAM, fond 901, op. 2, d. 1351, l. 17.

54. TsMAM, fond 819, op. 3, d. 1042, l. 21.

55. TsMAM, fond 819, op. 3, d. 1302, l. 132.

56. See, for example, TsMAM, fond 273, op. 4, d. 1113, l. 24; TsMAM, fond 901, op. 2, d. 1330, l. 4.

57. TsMAM, fond 901, op. 2, d. 732, l. 5.

58. Nina T., interview by the author, tape recording, Moscow, June 2, 1994.

59. Elena K. and Zoia M., interview by the author, tape recording, Moscow, May 27, 1994; Galina L., interview by the author, tape recording, Moscow, February 14, 1994; Ilya Utekhin, Alice Nakhimovsky, Slava Paerno, and Nancy Ries, *Communal Living in Russia: A Virtual Museum of Soviet Everyday Life*, http://kommunalka.colgate.edu/index.cfm.

60. Antonina L., interview by the author, tape recording, Liubertsy, May 1, 1994.

61. Gerasimova, "Privacy," 210.

62. Susan Gal, "A Semiotics of the Public/Private Distinctions," *differences: A Journal of Feminist Cultural Studies* 13, no. 1 (March 2002): 77–95, doi: 10.1215/10407391-13-1-77. Thanks to Olga Shevchenko for bringing this article to my attention.

9

Soviet Mass Housing and the Communist Way of Life

STEVEN E. HARRIS

In the 1950s and 1960s Nikita Khrushchev initiated a mass housing program that allowed millions of Soviet citizens to move from the overcrowded communal apartments, barracks, and dormitories of the Stalin era to single-family, separate apartments. Mass housing became Khrushchev's signature reform for taking Soviet society out of its Stalinist past, completing its postwar recovery, and making the final transition to communism. State and society alike viewed the separate apartment (*otdel'naia kvartira*) as a significant improvement over its defective other, the communal apartment (*kommunal'naia kvartira*), in which families occupied their own rooms but shared the kitchen and other common spaces with neighbors. The separate apartment allowed ordinary urban dwellers more privacy in a domestic space that the regime represented as the cutting edge of modern city life and a harmonious social order. It was built with modern industrial methods according to standardized designs and outfitted with the most technologically advanced equipment. In designing mass housing, Soviet architects drew from both domestic and international sources, such as 1920s Soviet constructivism and contemporary mass housing programs in other countries. But unlike the unrealized experiments of the past or mass housing programs in the West, Khrushchev's version would at last fulfill the goals of the Russian Revolution of 1917 and bring about a completely new everyday existence known as the "communist way of life" (*kommunisticheskii byt*).

In this essay, I focus on creating community as one aspect of everyday life that outside observers (and not a few inhabitants) have deemed difficult to achieve in the sterile concrete environments of mass housing.[1] Scholars who have examined mass housing in other contexts have demonstrated how communities came into being despite its standardized designs and inhospitable concrete landscapes.[2] A closer examination of Soviet mass housing reveals a similarly complex picture. I start by exploring the prescriptive discourse on the "communist way of life" that Khrushchev's regime hoped would materialize in mass housing estates and people's everyday lives. I then focus upon the strategies of creating community that Soviet residents deployed in urban spaces that suffered from poor designs and half-built neighborhoods with little infrastructure. While some residents explicitly invoked the term "communist way of life," others more often referenced its underlining values through their words and actions as they confronted the deficiencies of mass housing. Rather than undermine the mass housing campaign and discredit the Soviet regime, I argue, the shortcomings of this grand experiment in urban planning and social engineering opened a space for ordinary people to create community in ways that either presaged or adhered to the discourse on the communist way of life whereby citizens would take over the functions of the state and live with their neighbors in a harmonious social order.

As with the other essays in this volume, my broader aim is to demonstrate the importance of studying everyday life as a window onto Russian and Soviet history. Scholars of the Stalinist and Nazi regimes have turned to the everyday to explore how citizens experienced life and exercised their agency in totalitarian systems that appeared to leave little room for them to shape either.[3] The Khrushchev era created a radically different context for the everyday lives of Soviet citizens in ways that historians are only beginning to delineate. Khrushchev and his reformers curtailed the worst excesses of Stalin's terror state, opened flows of information and exchanges to the West, revived the communist project and cleansed its ideology of past deviations, and invested heavily in raising ordinary people's standard of living. Moreover, Khrushchev's regime did not neglect everyday life but focused on it with a renewed urgency as a critical sphere of Soviet life. In short, it was the Soviet state under Khrushchev— not scholars grappling for a new window onto social and cultural life—

that put everyday life on the map for understanding the lives of its citizens in a time of often bewildering changes. For Stalin's successors, the everyday was the chief site where they would discover whether or not the communist experiment had worked and whether their society's sacrifices under Stalin and in World War II had been worth it all along.

Among the reforms of the Khrushchev era, the mass housing campaign has proven to be especially fertile ground for scholars who wish to better understand how ordinary citizens experienced and shaped the period of intense and unpredictable change following Stalin's death.[4] What a study of the everyday demonstrates further are the concrete and sometimes unintended ways that officially sanctioned discourses became part of ordinary residents' daily interactions with a newly built urban environment, as well as the communal forms of housing they left behind. While the Soviet state defined the broad contours of the "communist way of life," the manner in which ordinary people used its wider meanings was largely in their hands as they attempted to forge local communities in mass housing estates beset with structural and design deficiencies. The study of everyday life thus helps to identify the agency ordinary Soviet citizens exercised in a time of reform while still recognizing the incredible power the Soviet state wielded in delimiting what its citizens could say and do. What emerges is a richer and more complicated account of how this state and its society interacted and sometimes overlapped on a daily basis through the built environment and the words each used to describe it.

THE COMMUNIST WAY OF LIFE

On April 12, 1961, Yuri Gagarin took his historic trip into the cosmos, becoming the first person to venture beyond the Earth's atmosphere. The mass press detailed this Soviet first with articles describing the flight and photographs of a clean-cut, smiling Gagarin.[5] Alongside images of futuristic space travel for the masses were stories of the ongoing mass housing campaign, which buttressed the promises of a technologically modern way of life that Soviet man's space travel represented.[6] The journal *Arkhitektura SSSR* (Architecture of the USSR) idealized well-designed neighborhoods known as microdistricts (*mikroraiony*) with their commercial and cultural services as modern satellites orbiting around older urban centers. They were clean and full of movement, with rapid public transport and automobiles providing residents with easy access to the entire city or beyond.[7] Khrushchev's regime worked assiduously to represent space exploration and mass housing as Soviet successes paving the way to communism. In 1959 Khrushchev foresaw the "communist way of life" as the eventual outcome of not only giving Soviet citizens their own apartments but showing them how to "properly use public goods, live properly, and observe the rules of the socialist community."[8] The separate apartment would play a critical role in balancing the private and public lives of its citizens that would characterize the future communist society.

Newspapers and other mass media further defined the communist way of life that lay beyond the next street corner.[9] One chronicler of the future, Mikhail Lifanov, began his 1961 essay, *O byte pri kommunizme* (On everyday life under Communism), by melding together images of space-age technology and urban life. "Imagine, reader, that we're walking with you along the streets of the city of the future. Wide thoroughfares filled with light nowhere intersect themselves on one level, and rushing cars, whose form reminds one of rockets, pass by us at great speed." The city of the future, Lifanov explained, would replace the "old city" of the nineteenth century, its dirty courtyards and tiny streets. Fresh air and sunlight would permeate the city, which "freely and deeply breathes with every particle of its great lungs." In announcing the arrival of the "new way of life," Lifanov explained, "there's no need to make a trip to the far-off future, because already today, we now see developed communist construction, which profoundly changes our entire way of life."[10]

Such pronouncements echoed earlier calls in Soviet history to discard the rot of prerevolutionary urban existence in the built environment and everyday social relations.[11] The concept of the microdistrict as a residential area outfitted to meet all commercial and social needs grew out of similar ideas in the 1920s and early 1930s for the socialization of everyday life in the *dom-kommuna* (house commune).[12] As the newspaper *Trud* declared in a 1963 article, "Dom zavtrashnego dnia" (The house of tomorrow), mass housing designs represented the latest "sprouts of the communist way of life." The newspaper invoked the dom-kommuna as a precedent for contemporary projects that inculcated proper collectivist values over selfish ones. But there were limits to what should be borrowed from the past. The champions of the dom-kommuna had taken the "socialization of a person's personal life" too far, and "instead of apartments, they designed so-called 'sleeping cabins.'"[13] The new mass housing of the Khrushchev period, predicated on the separate apartment, would not risk such excesses. Families would live in their own apartments with modern amenities and share the communal spaces and facilities of their building and neighborhood with other residents.

Trud clarified the meaning of the communist way of life in ways that suggested additional, subtle revisions to the dom-kommuna and its ideology of erasing the division between public and private life. The new housing of the Khrushchev period would ensure that people "lived in one friendly collective according to the principle that a person is a friend, comrade, and brother to another, and not according to the principle—my house is my castle." But the newspaper indicated that bringing this about no longer required the asceticism and collective regulation of everyday life of house communes from the past. All that was needed were well-designed apartment complexes with commercial services, gyms, cafeterias, and cafés so that people enjoyed "the maximum in conveniences and comfort."[14] In this formulation, the communist way of life meant a community whose members got along because the good fences of separate apartments made good neighbors, and everyone enjoyed all the comforts and consumer items of modern urban life. Far from encouraging residents to retreat from public life into their private castles, the separate apartment would engender healthy family relations that expanded outward into harmonious neighborly relations and a collectively shared desire to properly care for housing as Khrushchev himself had advised.

In the book Dom budushchego (House of the future, 1962), the Soviet architect Aleksandr Peremyslov similarly explored the emerging communist way of life by taking Soviet readers on a futuristic journey to a couple's separate apartment in a newly built microdistrict sometime in the very near but still indeterminate future, or, as he put it, in "Moscow, the year 196. . . ." The microdistrict Peremyslov visited along with a philosophy professor was a harbinger of the communist way of life where public spaces took pride of place in socializing the new Soviet person. Upon entering the neighborhood, Peremyslov and the philosopher encountered a multitude of vibrant public facilities, including a stadium, a club, a swimming pool, an open-air theater, and greenhouses. The privileging of public over private spaces followed the two men as they entered the building of the couple whose apartment they had come to visit. A café, the building's maintenance office, a drop-off for laundry, and various vending machines greeted them on the first floor. A quick elevator ride brought them to the eighth floor, where each wing featured a common area bedecked with wild grapes. Peremyslov and the philosopher found the couple, Gennadii and Galina, with one of their two children, Lidochka, in the single-family apartment they had "received" (read: obtained as a public good, not privately owned property) from the Soviet state. Their modest two-room apartment featured space-saving and multiuse furniture that contributed to their home's "good taste and great culture." Even though it was a separate apartment, the family's home remained an organic part of the greater, public whole. "Our apartment," Gennadii explained, "isn't just two rooms, an entrance, and a bathroom, but also Lidochka's place at child care, a regular table in the dining hall of the cafeteria, and so on." As Galina explained, their home comprised their building and the entire microdistrict where their son, Andriushka, lived in a boarding school. In this expansive definition of home, the private and the public were harmoniously intertwined along a continuum of well-designed and complementary spaces. Their microdistrict was even situated next to a virgin forest, thereby signaling that the war the Bolsheviks had launched in the wake of the Russian Revolution between town and country and between nature and the built environment was finally over.[15]

In the transition to mass housing estates and separate apartments, the communal apartments of older parts of town proved to be an ambiguous legacy for writers like Peremyslov seeking to define the communist way of life. Leaving behind communal apartments and their endless squabbles was the order of the day in an era when millions of residents were happily moving into their own private apartments. But according to some media reports, the communal apartment could equally be read as nostalgia for a way of life that was disappearing and as a warning against effusive praise for the separate apartment's privacy and its potential to isolate residents from the socialist whole. As scholars have shown, the privacy and autonomy promised by the separate apartment were checked by the regime's insistence that these features not detract from but rather complement the creation of a socialist community of good citizens and responsible consumers.[16] The communal apartment was the perfect setting familiar to all urban residents where such a lesson could be taught.[17]

In 1961, for example, *Leningradskaia pravda* chronicled the transformation of communal apartments into paragons of the communist way of life. Neighbors had learned to get along: "Noble feelings of comradeship, mutual assistance, and friendship have strengthened; work with children has sharply improved; apartment squabbles have disappeared." The newspaper sang the praises of collectivism and foresaw the erasure of the petty individualism that evoked dysfunctional communal apartments. "Extra mailboxes and doorbells, and 'individual' electric lamps in common spaces are disappearing." Reformed communal apartment neighbors "forgo their personal telephones, add their own personal books to the house libraries, and exhibit for common viewing the collections of rare coins and stamps that they have collected over years and decades."[18]

In the same year, according to the journal *Zhilishchno-kommunal'noe khoziaistvo* (Housing and municipal affairs), a local "competition" in which communal apartment residents engaged in the "struggle for the communist way of life" further illustrated this collectivist spirit and a subtle critique of excessively private lifestyles in separate apartments: "Brigades, construction sites, and entire cities keep the path to communism. *Only everyday life hides as before from public opinion behind a solidly closed door.* And then the idea was born—to draft residents into competing for a new, communist way of life" (my emphasis). Such a claim echoed the heady days of the dom-kommuna, with its ominous threats to tear down the public-private divide allegedly impeding the path to communism. The successful competitors were those who shed the outward signs of a dysfunctional communal apartment and transformed themselves into collectives that thrived on the values of communal identity, equality, and sharing. "Under the doorbell, instead of a long list, hangs a small list: *'For all residents ring once.'* A small table has appeared in the hallway on which there is a new telephone. Previously it had belonged to one person" (emphasis in the original). Even their kitchen had undergone a significant make-over: "All the tables are covered with the same oilcloths. Matches, salt, soda, household soap, and a small broom have been turned over for common use."[19]

Whereas newspapers invoked the communist way of life to prescribe proper behaviors and warn against excessive privacy, residents drew upon this malleable discourse to serve their own ends when dealing with local housing officials. In 1961, for example, a family living on Tipanova Street in Leningrad's Moscow district seemed only capable of angering neighbors and local housing officials because of water leaking out of their apartment. The Versov family, as they were called, consisted of an elderly couple, their daughter, and their two grandsons. They had moved into their new apartment the year before and had constantly run afoul of the local housing office's chief engineer, Volodarets, and the technician-constructor, Sergeeva. According to an acquaintance, a certain G. Aron, who wrote to the head of the Moscow district soviet (the local municipal government) on the family's behalf, these two officials generally blamed residents for everything: "These workers got it into their heads that things don't break down in new houses; if something happens, it means the residents themselves are guilty, who only go on stubbornly in order to break [things] and maliciously take equipment away from a construction site. For them [Volodarets and Sergeeva] residents are an undifferentiated mass of malefactors and people who break the rules."[20] Aron was not interested in these lower-level officials' point of view and relished the opportunity to represent them as insensitive and incapable of meeting the everyday needs of upstanding citizens. In contrast, the Versov household was full of good people, "neither hooligans, nor drunks–debauched types." Aron himself had been a party member since 1927 and was senior editor in the sciences at the city's branch office of the Academy of Sciences' publishing house. He sanctimoniously informed his readers, "My heart of an old communist is filled with anger, and I raise my voice in defense of an honest Soviet family."[21]

Whoever was to blame, the Versovs' apartment suffered especially from plumbing problems, such as moisture that leaked from their kitchen to the apartment below. The leak required only minor repairs, but Volodarets had evidently been unhelpful. Aron conceded that the bathroom floor became soaked whenever the grandfather tried to bathe in the inconveniently small bathtub, but Volodarets accused the Versovs of doing this deliberately, and their downstairs neighbor had launched his own abuse on the family. "The Versov family is literally terrorized," Aron lamented. "Recently the household head from apt. 24, V. P. Koliado, a young, healthy man, stormed into their apartment and threatened the Versovs that he would come with a crowbar and destroy the entire bathroom. Now the Versovs are afraid to use their bathroom."[22] To further emphasize this injustice, Aron insisted that the Versovs adhered to the tenets of the communist way of life, whereas the housing officials did not.[23]

In his defense of the Versovs, Aron emphasized that they were part of their house's "competition for the title of house of the communist way of life" and that, "having signed this contract, they indeed live and work in a communist way." This distinguished the Versov family from the mean-spirited local housing authorities: "Instead of assisting in every way with the introduction of the communist way of life, these gravediggers deprive people of the elementary comforts of life: plumbing, light, water, a bathroom." Aron was using the communist way of life in much the same way that Khrushchev and the mass media employed the term. The Versovs were good people who wanted to enjoy their new separate apartment, keep it in good repair, and enjoy amicable but separate neighborly relations, and they were willing to participate in community affairs. The communist way of life in Aron's letter presupposed "an honest Soviet family" that battled disreputable local officials whose behavior threatened the larger social order. Aron concluded, "An especial keenness and even particular, sincere qualities are required of workers of housing offices, because if they are going to treat people the way Volodarets and Sergeeva do, people's lives will be spoiled."[24]

Residents like the Versovs moved into new neighborhoods that were more a work-in-progress than the product of careful design, as depicted in Peremyslov's house of the future. Next to such glowing reports on what life would be like,[25] Soviet newspapers chronicled the shortcomings residents faced in mass housing.[26] Buildings appeared in areas with little infrastructure and transportation. Open spaces between apartment houses became empty voids, and unlit streets aggravated residents struggling to find their homes among identical buildings. The gap between design and reality made residents' lives difficult and exposed shortcomings in the mass housing campaign. It also provided residents with the necessary space to shape their communities in ways unforeseen by urban planners but not necessarily at odds with ideal visions of the communist way of life. In the new neighborhoods of the Khrushchev era, "state" and "society" overlapped to constitute the mass housing community in ways that saw residents try to make the architecture, rhetoric, and institutions of the regime function as intended.

CREATING COMMUNITY

To deal with such problems as neighborhood upkeep and drunken behavior, Khrushchev's regime called on citizens to join neighborhood "social organizations" ranging from parents' committees to the more ominous neighborhood foot patrols (*druzhiny*).[27] As both residents of new housing and office-holders in social organizations, urban dwellers operated at the very intersection of "state" and "society" in their local communities. Under Khrushchev, engaged residents wanted the state to be part of their everyday lives. For example, those who complained of noise pollution turned to the state for help and supported a "war on noise" campaign.[28] Others joined druzhiny and comrades' courts to police the neighborhood for public drunkenness, violent behavior, and "antisocial" conduct.[29] While social organizations constrained the behavior of some residents, they provided others with a platform for voicing their complaints and spurring neighbors to action within the bounds of the discourse on the communist way of life.

The archived minutes of Soviet residential meetings provide us with a unique window onto social organizations and residents' strategies for creating community. For example, at a meeting of fifty-two residents from a mass housing estate in Leningrad's Moscow district in the late 1950s, a resident and head of the area's local soviet housing office explained how the community combated hooligans, drunkards, and even simple loafers through parents' committees, house committees, and comrades' courts. In reference to the state's support for such community involvement, a certain Metskevich stressed the "new edicts about responsibility for minor hooliganism and beefing up the struggle against those who shy away

from socially useful work and carry on an antisocial and parasitical way
of life, drunkards, and so on." In response, he called on his community to
create a druzhina. Metskevich stressed that only "honest and exemplary
comrades" from the neighborhood would serve on its patrols.[30] Social
organizations thus enabled residents not only to create community but to
identify internal divisions between the self-proclaimed best citizens and
those they sought to marginalize. Like the discourse on the communist
way of life, social organizations afforded urban residents a powerful tool
in making these distinctions. As we saw in his letter defending the Versovs,
Aron invoked the communist way of life in a similar way to differentiate
between "an honest Soviet family" and the "gravediggers" from the local
housing office.

A meeting in 1957 of sixty-three residents from 182 Moskovskii prospekt
in Leningrad shed light on other ways that residents, courtesy of their social assistance commission, created community. Television, normally an
atomizing force, united these residents primarily because they appeared
to have only one in a building where most people lived in communal
apartments. The resident reporting on the commission's work explained
that "the viewing of television programs has been set up for residents and
children, and someone is put on duty for this every day." For the past two
years, the commission had set up an ice-skating rink and provided for a
children's playground. It teamed up with the parents' committee to organize a "contest on the ice," as well as a "performance of figure skaters." It
put together three tours around the city for residents and one out-of-town
trip for children. A sewing circle had been set up for interested residents,
and the parents' committee had established a group called Capable Hands,
made up of children referred to as Timurovites (*deti-timurovtsy*), which
suggested that its purpose was to lend assistance to elderly residents and
war invalids.[31] At 182 Moskovskii prospekt, social organizations existed on
a continuum of community organization (not unlike Peremyslov's vision
of a microdistrict) that began in these residents' communal apartments
and extended outward to their building and the neighborhood.[32]

The harmonious community life of 182 Moskovskii prospekt contrasts
sharply with our typical notions of the communal apartment. Residents
were eager to exchange its daily squabbles and cramped conditions for the
private bliss of a separate apartment. Yet the new mass housing neighbor-

hoods they entered had their own problems, including unfinished apartment buildings, insufficient public transportation, and too few buildings for commercial and cultural uses. Residents' letters of complaint exposed these structural deficiencies but also revealed how such problems drew them together as a community. For example, four residents living on Grazhdanskii prospekt in Leningrad's Vyborg district demonstrated a collective consciousness centered on neighborhood life and its everyday problems in a letter to *Izvestiia* in 1964: "Grazhdanskii prospekt, seven o'clock in the morning. Lights turn on in the windows of houses. Residents of the new quarter get ready for work, and each one, exactly each one, has one thought: Will he succeed today to sit on the bus, leave on time, take the baby to day care or to school, and not be late for work[?]" A single bus route provided this area with access to the Lenin Square metro station. Residents were forced to wait for several full buses to pass before they caught one. "The working day begins with the storming of bus doors, throngs [of people], arguments, a spoilt mood."[33] The residents also complained that only the light coming from people's apartments illuminated the broad expanses separating houses of this microdistrict, which became dark once people turned in for the evening. "It would seem that especially now," the residents continued, "when all around everything isn't set up, construction goes on, foundation plots and trenches have been dug up, asphalted paths begin and break off at the most unexpected places, [that now] good lighting is needed. But no. We get by with the moon."[34]

While such deficiencies brought some residents together, other problems risked dividing the mass housing community along new social lines. Residents who owned automobiles were a particular source of tension. Similar to the separate apartment and its new line of modern furniture and household appliances, automobiles became items of mass consumption in the Khrushchev period and especially under Brezhnev.[35] Those who wanted to park their cars near their apartment buildings faced off against neighbors who found that automobiles unfairly occupied and ruined a neighborhood's public spaces. In a letter to the All-Union Meeting of Constructors in December 1954—a critical moment in the mass housing campaign when Khrushchev blasted architects for not designing cheaper mass housing—a Muscovite by the name of Zhdanov outlined the troubles that "toiling automobile drivers" (*trudiashchiesia-avtomobilisty*) had with residential parking. He accused city planners of failing to set aside space in new housing districts for single-automobile garages. Pointing to the downtown Kiev district, Zhdanov complained that existing garages were being displaced by new housing projects to areas several kilometers away "to uninhabited and unkempt grounds, where there is neither water, nor electricity, where it's impossible to drive through in all weather, and where it's not entirely safe to return from at night."[36] Zhdanov warned that automobile drivers would only increase in number and called for "large, well-organized public garages" to solve the parking problem. The second best option, according to Zhdanov, would be sufficient space for single-automobile garages within five hundred to a thousand meters of housing.[37]

Zhdanov's letter suggests a strong sense of identity among car owners, reinforced by their sense of being a minority discriminated against by uncaring city planners. He complained that the Moscow city soviet's department of architectural affairs neglected "the interests of toilers, owners of light motorcars." Zhdanov even grafted working-class labels such as "toiling" onto "automobile drivers" to cast their problems as a legitimate plight worthy of immediate action. Yet his examples of fellow car owners betrayed a socially elite bias weighted toward well-educated professionals and members of the artistic intelligentsia: "workers of industry and transport, writers, doctors, artists, composers, performing artists, architects, engineers and technicians, academics."[38]

To their neighbors, car owners, their automobiles, and single-car garages dirtied new housing estates and generally got in the way of people's everyday lives. At a May 1957 residents' meeting of a newly built house on Iakovlevskii Alley in Leningrad's Moscow district, one resident, from 103 in attendance, asked for the removal of garages that had sprung up around their new house. His attempts to secure the district soviet's help in preventing these garages in the first place had been unsuccessful. The situation bothered the resident because the garages "are at the present time not completed and are in an unsanitary state." While Zhdanov identified himself and fellow drivers positively as "toiling automobile drivers," this particular resident used a less flattering moniker when referring to "the garages of independent proprietors [edinolichniki]." This term, edinolichniki, was used during collectivization in the 1930s to describe peasants who did not join collective farms. They were the only peasants who could possess horses, thereby signifying an appropriate parallel with the automobile situation on Iakovlevskii Alley. By invoking the term, the resident was making an unambiguous point: through their automobiles and garages, which dirtied the common areas of the neighborhood, car drivers went about their business at the community's expense. The resident's use of edinolichniki also suggested that car drivers used their automobiles and garages to distinguish themselves materially from their less fortunate neighbors.[39]

In the 1950s and 1960s the social meaning of the mass-produced automobile was shaped in new housing estates, and the automobile likewise played an early role in shaping neighborhood life. Along with makeshift garages, the automobile was a disruptive addition to already badly designed and incompletely built neighborhoods, and it created new social divisions within the mass housing community between those who had automobiles and those who did not. The minority who owned automobiles developed a rather strong sense of themselves as a separate, beleaguered group of urban dwellers. As Lewis Siegelbaum points out, car owners were also predominantly men, and the attention they spent on their automobiles structured the spaces of neighborhoods along gendered lines so that "garages, make-shift auto parts bazaars, and the interiors of cars themselves served as refuges from the crowded conditions of apartment dwelling."[40] Today one-car garages and automobiles are standard items in the courtyards (and sidewalks) of Russia's mass housing districts, and the association of men with automobiles has remained strong. According to one long-term resident of Moscow, the courtyard has evolved into a distinctly gendered space, and men long ago established their place in it through their automobiles.[41]

As residents' struggles with automobile drivers suggest, neighbors were not always pleased with one another's ways of creating community in mass housing estates. In a letter published in *Trud* in 1966, a Leningrader named Usanov complained that his five-year-old neighborhood on the outskirts of town had "neither a movie theater, nor a theater, nor a cafe, nor a stadium." Usanov contrasted his neighborhood with what one normally thought of as Leningrad and its "theaters and museums, gardens and parks." The hour-long commute between the older and newer parts of town compounded this spatial and cultural rupture, leaving residents with two options at the end of the workday: "Either sit at home or go to the 'casino'—this is what they call a table and two benches in our courtyard, dug into the ground right near a children's playground." The "lovers of 'kozel,' card players," became a public nuisance: "It's good, if an evening at the 'casino' ends without drunken singing, without police whistles. More often it's the opposite."[42] A *Trud* reporter expanded upon Usanov's observations that new neighborhoods created empty spaces that led to trouble if they were not channeled into socially useful places of leisure. "Nature, as is well known, does not tolerate emptiness," the reporter mused. "And therefore it is not surprising that in new housing estates the notorious 'casinos' about which comrade Usanov writes grow like poisonous mushrooms after rain."[43] This mass housing estate was not the paragon of the Soviet everyday, but neither did it lack meaningful human interaction. By setting up a casino, people were autonomously creating a community, albeit an illicit one, around a shared activity in spaces they had appropriated. Squatting in empty apartments and land plots constituted yet another way that urban residents appropriated the spaces of the Soviet city to serve their own ends and create community.

SQUATTERS' RIGHTS

As Christine Varga-Harris argues, getting a separate apartment under Khrushchev was a key entitlement in a renegotiated social contract between state and society that had lapsed under Stalin.[44] But moving to a new apartment, I would argue, was also part of a renegotiated social contract between citizens who entered a new civil state when they left communal housing for mass housing. In the ideal scenario, their new communities were not bound together by shortage and adversity, as communal apartment dwellers had been, nor by private property, which kept their counterparts in Western cities in a Hobbesian state of mutual distrust. Enacting the communist way of life, residents were supposed to enter into mass housing in a rational fashion whereby local officials assigned families to apartments in an orderly process. Residents waited their turn on waiting lists until they received the housing permit that bestowed their right to a separate apartment. The community ideally came together knowing beforehand where each family was supposed to go and that Soviet law protected each family's access to its apartment.

In practice, housing allocation could be a messy affair, and in the mid-1950s the Soviet government identified apartment "squatting" (*samovol'noe zaselenie*) as one of its major problems. Squatters took buildings before they were completed and inspected. Rather than evict squatters or prevent them from taking housing in the first place, local soviets often registered squatters as rightful residents. Government reports projected an image of new neighborhoods as landscapes of incompletely built housing already suffering from construction defects, which local officials rushed to settle, even if that meant condoning squatters.[45] In addition to taking empty apartments, squatters took land to build housing. According to the Ministry of the Communal Economy, "unauthorized builders" (*samovol'nye zastroishchiki*) were hard at work in the mid-1950s, colonizing empty plots in such cities as Kuibyshev, Saratov, Krasnodar, Sochi, and Stalingrad, as well as the Moscow and Kalinin oblasts. Local authorities failed to pursue criminal cases against these scofflaws and did not raze their illegally built homes. Not only did illegal builders "use the absence of control" to construct homes on empty land plots, these builders even asked local people's courts to register the plots as personal property. Local authorities did not contest these petitions and failed to file appeals. Particularly irksome were illegal builders' clever use of unspecified "documents," which they and people they sold their houses to effectively wielded, thereby "creat[ing] the appearance of legality" and providing builders with leverage against threats to have their homes razed.[46] Squatting in empty apartments or on land plots revealed how residents acted when the state seemed asleep at the switch, allowing them to create community on their own terms.

The Ministry of the Communal Economy proposed measures in early 1954 to crack down on squatters who took land, raze their homes, and punish local authorities who failed to stop them.[47] But in 1954 and 1955 the government overruled this ministry and instituted a conciliatory approach, spurred in part by none other than the Ministry of Internal Affairs (MVD), which wanted to register illegal builders as it did all citizens but could not under existing law. The government subsequently declared an amnesty on existing illegally built homes, adopted preventive measures, and, when those failed, simply decided to tax such squatters and let them keep their houses.[48] Adding what illegal builders had constructed to the overall housing stock was more important to the state than punishing them.

Anecdotal evidence sheds further light on the defiant nature of squatters and what brought them together as a community. In late 1956 the MVD informed the Central Committee of 131 workers and their families who squatted in a new apartment building in Moscow under cover of night. The workers were employed in housing construction, with some working for a construction firm and others working at a factory producing reinforced concrete. These families had lived together in a dormitory located one street away from the new building. Whether the workers had worked on the new building was unclear, but their close proximity suggested how frustrating it was to live in an overcrowded dormitory—with individual rooms of twenty-eight to thirty-two square meters accommodating three to four families each—while a new building was built next door. As workers in housing construction, their action suggested (rather uncomfortably for Soviet authorities) a Marxist narrative of exploited workers collectively taking back the fruits of their labor. In their dormitory and through their work, these families had already constituted a community that shared the same grievances and trusted one another enough to plan the takeover of a building and face the repercussions together. Their strategy, as far as the MVD account indicated, was to take the building and hold out until local authorities caved in.[49]

In response, the district prosecutor ordered the police to evict the squatters. Whether the police tried to use force was unclear, but whatever they did evidently failed. Local party and soviet officials tried negotiating with the squatters to get them back to their dormitory. The squatters held fast to their demands that local authorities issue them housing permits and turn on the building's water and gas. For three days they had barricaded themselves in the building and created a human barrier at its entrance with pregnant women in front, followed by women and children, and men in back. Their dramatic display of civil disobedience and the powerful symbolism evoked in its gendered organization came through even in the dry MVD report. The community's most vulnerable members held its greatest power, which the squatters were daring the police to transgress through violence. Insofar as avoiding physical removal was concerned, their strategy had thus far worked. Even the MVD wanted nothing to do with them. In response to the Moscow chief of police's request for help, the MVD explained that local authorities had not exhausted all avenues to achieve the "voluntary departure from the illegally occupied apartments" and referred them to the city procuracy if all else failed. Written during the affair, the MVD report does not tell us what eventually happened. Nonetheless, by the third day, the police had apparently chosen not to use force.[50]

Regardless of the ultimate outcome, these squatters had revealed uncomfortable truths about who had been marginalized and exploited in the quest for a separate apartment and the creation of a Soviet neighborhood. They demonstrated the desperate strategies of the excluded to form their own community through the workplace and where they lived and to put their mutual dependence on the line in unsanctioned collective action and the defense of a building held in common. This was not what Khrushchev later envisioned to be the correct or legal path to living the communist way of life. Yet these squatters' actions presaged the broader meanings of this discourse. They took over the functions of the state in building and distributing housing, creating a local community, and looking after collective property. Their move bolstered what state and society now recognized as the legitimate claim of every Soviet family, a separate apartment, while maintaining that each family had obligations before the community. These ordinary residents' actions showed how the path from the construction of new housing to its settlement and creation of a community was not always smooth and often overlapped. Construction, housing distribution, and community creation were supposed to occur separately in the ideal world of urban planning and Soviet propaganda on Khrushchev's mass housing campaign. In reality, their overlapping opened a space for ordinary residents to shape how the communist way of life—broadly understood as the ideal and harmonious relations between a single household and its community—functioned in practice.

CONCLUSION

Mass housing's glaring deficiencies allowed ordinary residents to take an active role in creating community in often unintended ways. Some joined the lowliest organs of state power, "social organizations," while others drew upon official rhetoric about the communist way of life in making their grievances heard. Their more desperate neighbors took the extraordinary step of squatting in apartments or on plots of land and then just as defiantly defended their homes and microcommunities through legal appeals and civil disobedience that fell within the official meanings of living the communist way of life. Some residents bonded over the deficiencies of neighborhood infrastructure, while others turned on their car-driving neighbors for cluttering neighborhoods with garages. In contrast to the uniformity in the aesthetics and planning of microdistricts, the mass housing community evolved into a heterogeneous body with new social divisions rooted in the ways residents made use of its public spaces and coped with its problems. Under Khrushchev, mass housing estates were a new social space where residents created community in ways that bolstered the volunteerism inherent in living the communist way of life.

To be sure, the shortcomings ordinary residents faced in Soviet mass housing illustrate the chronic failures of Khrushchev's regime to build it as intended. Examining everyday life in new mass housing estates, as shown in this essay, presents their deficiencies in incredibly vivid detail and suggests the distance that often lay between official propaganda and citizens' lived experience. The same methodology, however, can reveal other, more valuable insights into Soviet social and cultural history, particularly in a period such as Khrushchev's, when state and society underwent incredible changes from the Stalinist past. As this essay illustrates, exploring the everyday can show how officially sanctioned discourses such as the communist way of life mattered for ordinary citizens struggling to adapt to and make sense of the urban spaces they got rather than those they were supposed to have received. This methodology sharpens our understanding of the unintended ways that chronic deficiencies in the urban environment created the everyday context in which such discourses and ordinary people's actions gave meaning to one another.

NOTES

Sections of this essay originally appeared in the introduction and chapter 5 of my book, *Communism on Tomorrow Street: Mass Housing and Everyday Life after Stalin* (Washington, DC: Woodrow Wilson Center Press and Baltimore: The Johns Hopkins University Press, 2013).

I thank the Woodrow Wilson Center Press and the Johns Hopkins University Press for permission to reproduce these sections of my book in the present essay. I also thank the editors of this volume and its reviewers for their valuable suggestions to earlier versions of my essay.

1. See, for example, Alexander Vysokovskii, "Will Domesticity Return?," in *Russian Housing in the Modern Age: Design and Social History,* ed. William Brumfield and Blair Ruble (New York: Woodrow Wilson Center Press and Cambridge University Press, 1993), 289.

2. Sudhir Venkatesh, *American Project: The Rise and Fall of a Modern Ghetto* (Cambridge, Mass.: Harvard University Press, 2002).

3. Alf Lüdtke, ed., *The History of Everyday Life: Reconstructing Historical Experiences and Ways of Life,* trans. William Templer (Princeton, N.J.: Princeton University Press, 1995); Sheila Fitzpatrick, *Everyday Stalinism: Ordinary Life in Extraordinary Times* (Oxford: Berg, 2002).

4. See, for example, Victor Buchli, "Khrushchev, Modernism, and the Fight against *Petit-bourgeois* Consciousness in the Soviet Home," *Journal of Design History* 10, no. 2 (1997): 161–76; Stephen Bittner, "Remembering the Avant-Garde: Moscow Architects and the 'Rehabilitation' of Constructivism, 1961–1964," *Kritika* 2, no. 3 (2001): 553–76; Susan Reid, "The Khrushchev Kitchen: Domesticating the Scientific-Technological Revolution," *Journal of Contemporary History* 40, no. 2 (2005): 289–316; Christine Varga-Harris, "Forging Citizenship on the Home Front: Reviving the Socialist Contract and Constructing Soviet Identity during the Thaw," in *The Dilemmas of De-Stalinization: Negotiating Cultural and Social Change in the Khrushchev Era,* ed. Polly Jones (London: Routledge, 2006), 101–16; Mark Smith, *Property of Communists: The Urban Housing Program from Stalin to Khrushchev* (DeKalb: Northern Illinois University Press, 2010).

5. "Pervyi polet cheloveka v kosmicheskoe prostranstvo," *Pravda,* April 25, 1961, 1, 3–4.

6. For images of space travel, see I. Semenov, "Vsled za Gagarinym (pervomaiskaia shutka)," *Pravda,* May 1, 1961, 6. I thank Vadim Volkov for suggesting the connection between mass housing and space flight.

7. D. Burdin and Iu. Umanskaia, "Arkhitektura zhilykh kvartalov Leninskogo prospekta," *Arkhitektura SSSR,* no. 2 (1958): 12–14; I. Fomin, "Pervichnye arkhitekturno-planirovochnye kompleksy zhiloi zastroiki," *Arkhitektura SSSR,* no. 7 (1961): 21–27.

8. *Vneocherednoi XXI s"ezd kommunisticheskoi partii sovetskogo soiuza. 27 ianvaria–5 fevralia 1959 goda. Stenograficheskii otchet* (Moscow: Gosudarstvennoe izdatel'stvo politicheskoi literatury, 1959), 1:51–52.

9. "Dom za Moskovskoi zastavoi," *Leningradskaia pravda,* December 25, 1960, 2; G. Gradov, "Gorod i byt," *Izvestiia,* January 13, 1960, 2.

10. Mikhail Lifanov, *O byte pri kommunizme* (Moscow: Gosudarstvennoe izdatel'stvo politicheskoi literatury, 1961), 3–4. An updated version of Lifanov's pamphlet was published in 1963. See Mikhail Lifanov, ed., *Za kommunisticheskii byt* (Leningrad: Obshchestvo po rasprostraneniiu politicheskikh i nauchnykh znanii RSFSR, Leningradskoe otdelenie, 1963).

11. S. Frederick Starr, "Visionary Town Planning during the Cultural Revolution," in *Cultural Revolution in Russia, 1928–1931,* ed. Sheila Fitzpatrick (Bloomington: Indiana University Press, 1978), 207–40.

12. Gregory Andrusz, *Housing and Urban Development in the USSR* (Albany: State University of New York Press, 1984), 127–28.

13. A. Kuz'michev, "Dom zavtrashnego dnia," *Trud,* May 31, 1963, 2.

14. Kuz'michev, "Dom zavtrashnego dnia."

15. Aleksandr Peremyslov, *Dom budushchego (Zametki arkhitektora)* (Moscow: Gosudarstvennoe izdatel'stvo politicheskoi literatury, 1962), 8–11.

16. Susan Reid, "Women in the Home," in *Women in the Khrushchev Era,* ed. Melanie Ilič, Susan Reid, and Lynne Attwood (Basingstoke: Palgrave Press, 2004), 149–76; Christine Varga-Harris, "Constructing the Soviet Hearth: Home, Citizenship and Socialism in Russia, 1956–1964" (Ph.D. diss., University of Illinois at Urbana-Champaign, 2005), 132–86.

17. On the communal apartment's continued importance in defining communal values under Khrushchev, see Deborah Field, *Private Life and Communist Morality in Khrushchev's Russia* (New York: Peter Lang, 2007), 27–37.

18. M. Maksimov, "Zhit' khorosho, druzhno, po-kommunisticheski," *Leningradskaia pravda,* February 17, 1961, 2.

19. Alla Efremova, "Byla obyknovennaia kvartira," *Zhilishchno-kommunal'noe khoziaistvo,* no. 6 (1961): 4, 33.

20. Tsentral'nyi Gosudarstvennyi Arkhiv Sankt-Peterburga (TsGA SPb), fond 103, op. 5, d. 829, l. 90.

21. TsGA SPb, fond 103, op. 5, d. 829, ll. 90, 93.

22. TsGA SPb, fond 103, op. 5, d. 829, ll. 90–92.

23. TsGA SPb, fond 103, op. 5, d. 829, ll. 92–93.

24. TsGA SPb, fond 103, op. 5, d. 829, ll. 92–93.

25. A. Mokhova, "Raionnyi Sovet i voprosy zhilishchnogo stroitel'stva," *Pravda,* December 15, 1956, 2; I. Dmitriev, "Novyi oblik starogo raiona," *Leningradskaia pravda,* November 2, 1960, 3.

26. E. Iashmanov, "Pis'ma v redaktsiiu: Nash schet stroiteliam," *Leningradskaia pravda,* June 12, 1957, 2; M. Sharipov et al., "Zabota o byte liudei—delo bol'shoe, vazhnoe," *Pravda,* April 4, 1961, 2.

27. On social organizations, see Theodore Friedgut, *Political Participation in the USSR* (Princeton, N.J.: Princeton University Press, 1979), 235–88.

28. Steven Harris, "'I Know All the Secrets of My Neighbors': The Quest for Privacy in the Era of the Separate Apartment," in *Borders of Socialism: Private Spheres of Soviet Russia,* ed. Lewis Siegelbaum (New York: Palgrave Macmillan, 2006), 171–89.

29. Miriam Dobson, *Khrushchev's Cold Summer: Gulag Returnees, Crime, and the Fate of Reform after Stalin* (Ithaca, N.Y.: Cornell University Press, 2009), 133–55.

30. TsGA SPb, fond 103, op. 5, d. 663, ll. 79, 203.

31. TsGA SPb, fond 103, op. 5, d. 663, l. 62. Inspired by Arkadii Gaidar's 1940 story, "Timur and His Team," Timurovites were patriotic children who helped those affected by the war. On the Timurovites, see their definition in *Bol'shoi tolkovyi slovar' russkogo iazyka* (St. Petersburg: Norint, 2000), 1323.

32. On the continuum of community relations that extended from the communal apartment to broader public spaces and institutions, see Il'ia Utekhin, *Ocherki kommunal'nogo byta* (Moscow: OGI, 2001), chap. 11, "Outside the Apartment."

33. TsGA SPb, fond 7384, op. 42, d. 1002, ll. 7–8, 10.

34. TsGA SPb, fond 7384, op. 42, d. 1002, l. 9.

35. Lewis Siegelbaum, *Cars for Comrades: The Life of the Soviet Automobile* (Ithaca, N.Y.: Cornell University Press, 2008).

36. Rossiiskii Gosudarstvennyi Arkhiv Ekonomiki (RGAE), fond 339, op. 1, d. 1098, ll. 24–26.

37. RGAE, fond 339, op. 1, d. 1098, ll. 24–26.

38. RGAE, fond 339, op. 1, d. 1098, ll. 24–26.

39. TsGA SPb, fond 103, op. 5, d. 495, ll. 48–49. On independent peasants in the 1930s, see Sheila Fitzpatrick, *Stalin's Peasants: Resistance and Survival in the Russian Village after Collectivization* (Oxford: Oxford University Press, 1994), 128, 152–58.

40. Siegelbaum, *Cars for Comrades*, 7.

41. Evgeniia Pishchikova, "Moskovskii dvorik," *Moskovskie novosti*, November 29–December 6, 1998, 27. I thank Sheila Fitzpatrick for drawing my attention to this article.

42. Evgenii Nikolin, "Chelovek prishel s raboty," *Trud*, September 11, 1966, 2.

43. Nikolin, "Chelovek prishel s raboty."

44. Varga-Harris, "Forging Citizenship."

45. In 1953 the Molotov (Perm′) city soviet retroactively approved the settlement of eighty-eight unfinished buildings that squatters had taken. It approved for settlement another forty-three unfinished buildings, which presumably went to the designated residents. Similar incidents occurred in Novosibirsk and Ul′ianovsk. In Vladimir, Voronezh, and Syktyvkar, city soviets settled unfinished housing that had not passed inspection and had construction flaws that already needed to be fixed. The source for these reports was a June 21, 1954, Soviet of Ministers RSFSR decree, "On serious shortcomings in housing and civil construction in cities of the RSFSR," in Gosudarstvennyi Arkhiv Rossiiskoi Federatsii (GARF), fond A-259, op. 1, d. 663, ll. 89–90. An additional source was a 1956 report, "On improving the quality of construction," to the Central Committee and the Soviet of Ministers USSR. See Rossiiskii Gosudarstvennyi Arkhiv Noveishei Istorii, fond 5, op. 41, d. 57, ll. 2–4.

46. GARF, fond A-314, op. 3, d. 321, ll. 108–10.

47. GARF, fond A-314, op. 3, d. 321, ll. 108–10.

48. On the MVD's efforts to register land squatters, see GARF, fond A-314, op. 3, d. 321, l. 105. See also the Soviet of Ministers RSFSR draft decree in GARF, fond A-314, op. 3, d. 321, l. 107. On the government's amnesty, see the Soviet of Ministers RSFSR decree of July 3, 1954, "On measures for struggling with unauthorized construction," in GARF, fond A-259, op. 1, d. 664, l. 39. On the government's decision to tax land squatters, see the Soviet of Ministers RSFSR decree of November 4, 1955, "On the taxation of citizens who constructed buildings in an unauthorized manner on land plots that were not given to them," in GARF, fond A-259, op. 1, d. 766, ll. 59–60.

49. GARF, fond 9401, op. 2, d. 482, ll. 216–17.

50. GARF, fond 9401, op. 2, d. 482, ll. 216–17.

10

Everyday Aesthetics in the Khrushchev-Era Standard Apartment

SUSAN E. REID

The domestic and everyday, constituting the "private sphere," are commonly regarded as "the part of life you have most control over" and the least susceptible to ideological impositions.[1] The production of the domestic interior has been treated in a range of disciplines as an exercise in the production of individual or class (in particular, middle-class) identity. Studies of the modern Western home widely assume that a reflexive relation between the individual and the home is a defining attribute of modernity and consumer society;[2] indeed, the possibility of exercising agency and of what Wolfgang Braunfels calls "the freedom to participate in the design of one's own urban living environment" is seen as essential both to making living space into "home" and to making oneself.[3] Material, aesthetic, and consumption practices are crucial to the production of self in domestic space, as Leora Auslander argues: "In consumer society, everyday aesthetic practices come not only to reflect the new 'identities' of modernity, but also help to form people's sense of self, of likeness and difference."[4]

These ideas about the meaning of home privilege Western democratic capitalist contexts. The modern home that Erving Goffman, for example, envisaged as a key setting for the production of identity or "presentation of self" in his 1956 account was a middle-class house common in 1950s Britain or North America.[5] The everyday setting I will discuss here, however, is the interior of prefabricated one-family apartments that were constructed on a mass scale in the Khrushchev-era Soviet Union shortly after Goffman's study. Did these standard apartments on Soviet housing estates of the 1960s become a site for the production of self and personal meaning under socialist modernity?

This chapter will address only one small, mundane aspect of this large question: display cupboards. It draws on a research project entitled *Everyday Aesthetics in the Modern Soviet Flat,* which concerns how people made home in the 1960s in the standard spaces of separate apartments built under Khrushchev.[6] Some 108 million people—half the population of the USSR—moved out of overcrowded slums into new housing between 1956 and 1965, many of them into separate apartments with modern conveniences. The process was accelerated by a mass industrialized housing campaign launched in 1957.[7] The new apartments were not private property, yet they afforded the tenants greater "privacy" in the sense that they no longer had to conduct the intimate parts of their lives under the gaze of strangers.[8] At the same time, however, standard construction increased state control over and homogenization of living space as the party state intervened in housing conditions. While providing "private" (segregated) spaces for individual families, the *khrushchevki,* like many twentieth-century housing projects, were also conceived as a means of social engineering.[9] In addition to the physical structures and planning of urban space, which (on Marxist principles reinvigorated during the Thaw) were supposed to organize residents' consciousness and relations, extensive efforts were made to shape discursively—through advice and visual representations—the way people took up occupancy, furnished, and dwelled in their industrially built, standard apartments.[10] The project investigates the spaces for individual agency within these given, anonymous structures over which the "actors" had limited influence, addressing the relations between centrally planned, mass-produced spaces and things, on the one hand, and decentralized individual consumption choices, uses, domestic aesthetics, and handicraft, on the other. Exploring how people accommodated the physical and discursive structures of housing and homemaking, and paying special attention to everyday aesthetics and consumption, the project identifies ways in which these individuals used their apartments as the setting and material for the production of their social selves. Thereby it reflects on how the historical processes of urbanization, modernization, and social transformation, which entered a new, intense phase after Stalin, were experienced by ordinary individuals.

The project also seeks to adjudicate between two contradictory narratives concerning social processes in the Soviet Union after Stalin. There is not space here to do more than state these briefly, at the risk of oversimplification. On the one hand, there is an extension and elaboration of the Cold War tendency to deny the Soviet people any freedom for maneuver and agency, depicting them as a passive, faceless mass, duped by authority, and cowed into submission to an all-pervasive state, and to see the regulatory power of the state as extended and perfected in this period.[11] On the other, there is the thesis of increasing separation of public and private life. Vladimir Shlapentokh has argued that the mass relocation to separate apartments in the new urban housing regions—in combination with other innovations that began in this period such as ownership of television sets and private cars—was responsible for social shifts that he designates the "privatization" of life.[12] The thesis of a retreat from public values into private life has now acquired the status of orthodoxy concerning the Brezhnev era and has become part of the standard explanation for the collapse of the Soviet Union.[13] Compelling as this conclusion is, it is premature, since much work remains to produce evidence for this privatization and to define its nature and parameters. The project attempts to mediate between the two models by treating homemaking as a mutual process of accommodation between residents and standard housing whereby they made themselves at home.[14]

Sources for this research include archival documents from the 1950s and 1960s, as well as published images and texts about consumption and home decorating. However, as is often the case for research on the everyday, conventionally historical (written, printed, and archived) sources are of limited use here. With some exceptions, such as citizens' letters or comments in visitors' books, they tend to return us to policies and specialist discourses, centralized standards, regulations, designs, and production plans rather than illuminating the ways in which those impersonal structures were accommodated in individual practice in "private" space. Thus they reinforce the emphasis, in Cold War Western views of the Soviet Union, on high-level blueprints rather than individual agency and on determining structures rather than the "freedom to participate in the design of one's own urban living environment." To find decentered popular consumption, informal exchanges, and do-it-yourself ways of doing that may or may not challenge this model, we have to turn to other sources such as oral history interviews and material culture.

Semistructured, in-depth, qualitative interviews were conducted between 2004 and 2006 with residents of Khrushchev-era apartments in a number of cities of the former Soviet Union: St. Petersburg; Kaluga; two cities on the Volga, Samara and Kazan'; Kovdor and Apatity in the Far North, which were new cities in the postwar period; and the Estonian university city, Tartu. The ideal informants had moved into khrushchevki as young adults in the early 1960s when the apartments were newly built, and, now elderly, they still lived there at the time of the interviews. Almost all were women, with the exception of a few couples and some male collectors, both because the aim was to speak to the person who took responsibility for arranging and maintaining the domestic interior, a role that was conventionally female, and because of the demographic fact that more women than men have survived into their seventies and eighties. The interviews took place in their apartments and focused on domestic things, around which autobiographical stories were drawn out.

The data production also included photographing individual things and arrangements in the interior today as material for visual analysis. Clearly, such evidence has to be used with care. It prioritizes that which is visible at the time of the interview, yet, aside from the problem that homes are not museums, some of the most cherished items are not displayed but hidden away (a locket worn close to the heart, a special box kept in a clothes drawer), or they exist only in memory. They do not constitute part of the self the informant chooses to present to others.

Access to the everyday and ordinary invariably has to be opened up via the occasional and extraordinary, given that historians are largely reliant on data produced at the time, for it is the special moments that people record, store away, and recall in their own lives.[15] We tried initially to open conversations by asking to see old photographs of the interior taken when the informants first moved in, but few had photos where the interior was the main object, although it may sometimes be glimpsed as the backdrop to a family occasion. Among the exceptions I have two snapshots (undated, probably 1970s) featuring cabinets in Khrushchev-era apartments. In one, a woman opens the glass door of the cabinet as if to take china from it to lay the table. In the other, the cabinet forms the backdrop for a family scene. The photos are out of focus, black and white, and uninformative. But even such unremarkable contemporary photographic "documents" of the interior are a rarity in the albums of former Soviet citizens. Although photography was a popular hobby and was taught in neighborhood clubs and Pioneer Houses, camera ownership was far from universal in the sixties. In addition, the apartments were small and dimly lit, making it difficult to take successful photographs of anything other than details. Above all, the absence of the interior from the photographic record was a matter of priorities when film had to be bought and developed. Even if there was a keen amateur photographer in the household, he (usually) was more likely to take photographs of people or nature than of the domestic interior.[16] (Perhaps this is a matter of the conventional gendering of photography; we can only speculate whether, had women wielded the camera, they would have taken more photos of the interiors they produced and maintained.) People did not take photos of their everyday, routine activities or of the taken-for-granted settings that represented the constant environment of domestic life (or if they did, they rarely pasted them into their albums for posterity). Rather, they recorded the special occasions that punctuated the flow, marked by the presence of guests.[17]

It is not that the new domestic interior was lacking in visibility at the time. Both positive images of the "contemporary" interior of the small separate apartments under construction in the late 1950s and early 1960s and negative representations of the regressive "petit-bourgeois" domesticity it was supposed to supplant were ubiquitous in visual culture and authoritative discourse. Khrushchevki interiors were widely depicted in film and print media as well as on television. These were ideal homes, however: normative interiors designed by professionals with the aim of reforming and modernizing people's received aspirations and practice. A handful of such interior settings in the "contemporary style," produced for specific competitions and exhibitions, were photographed and appeared repeatedly in albums, popular magazines, and specialist journals.[18] Miniature modernist utopias of sophisticated contemporary taste, cleanliness, and order, representing the unpopulated vision of specialists, they are aloof from the mess and compromises of everyday living.[19] The interiors that ordinary people produced over time—as they gradually accommodated the new apartments to their needs, taste, and sense of themselves, as they grew better off, and as the availability of consumer goods increased—remained largely unrecorded.

What I present here is a "case" study, literally, in that it focuses on the cases for people's domestic displays. The photographs, out of focus as they are, dramatize the cabinet; and it is glazed cabinets or sideboards, along with their place in Soviet people's practices of making themselves at home, that I want to bring into focus here. Even these photographs are not quite "everyday": the fact that the cabinet was photographed at all indicates that it was at least momentarily the object of special attention, perhaps a new acquisition. Moreover, domestic display cases occupy a liminal position in relation to everyday functions. Special things and events, slightly removed from routine and necessity, are points where material practices in the home become more conscious, aestheticized, and invested with meaning.[20] In my project, interviewers asked (inter alia) about things that were especially valued or meaningful to informants, what they used to decorate the home or to create *uiut* (homeyness), and what they thought were generally considered "prestigious" or "fashionable." The cherished items are very often collected and displayed in the cabinet or equivalent and serve as starting points and props for informants' narratives.

A CABINET OF CONTRADICTIONS

The cabinet's presence in the khrushchevka materializes a number of contradictions between prescribed norms and practice in the 1960s. This single item of the interior allows us to explore both the axes of the public/private dichotomy that Jeff Weintraub distinguished: first, what is particular or pertains only to an individual versus what is common, collective, or affects the interests of a collectivity of individuals; and second, what is hidden or withdrawn versus what is open, revealed, or accessible.[21] We are concerned with how the apartment could become particular, such that it both "reflected" and constituted the identity of the occupants, and with how aspects of those lives were concealed or revealed: the management of

FIGURE 10.1.

Zoia's cabinet, Kaluga, 2006. Photo: Alla Bolotova for Everyday Aesthetics.
© Susan E. Reid

appearances or selective "private publicity."[22] This private publicity does
not necessarily entail rejection of what is common or mass-produced but
includes the appropriation or assimilation of such material into personally meaningful collections and its aesthetic arrangement, whereby mass-
produced material becomes part of the narrative of self.[23] The things to be
found in cabinets largely conform to a limited, conventional repertoire of
objects.[24] On the second axis, privacy is constituted not by concealment
alone but by discretion over what is concealed and what is revealed in what
circumstances and to whom. Domestic display—as the management of
appearances, the other half of which is concealment—plays a part in the
construction of privacy and the presentation of individual or household
identity for the limited "public" allowed over the threshold.

The desire to particularize standard space does not necessarily imply
the rejection of public values or a retreat from participation. The self one
makes at home is not hermetic or presocial but is a social identity, and

domestic display is a social practice, a form of intersubjective communication and culture that makes use of common codes. The contents of domestic displays—and narratives about them—are very often about relationships both within and beyond the household; they are social performances in a space somewhere between the public and the private, personal and collective, individual and common.[25]

What, for convenience, I am calling a "cabinet" embraces a number of types of cupboards that combine hidden storage for linen and clothes with open glazed shelves. The top of the cabinet, which in this period was around five feet high, was also used for display. Galina (St. Petersburg) talks about the qualities she valued in her *servant,* or sideboard:

> Interviewer: What was beautiful about it?
> Galina: First, it was fine wood, not chipboard, of course. Second, it was terribly convenient, with an incredible number of these little drawers, little shelves, and also some kind of little doors. You could get a load of stuff into it.

Galina slips fluidly from the appearance of the cabinet itself—its fine wood—to its function in managing the visual appearance of the interior. Its aesthetic value consists in the order and hierarchy it imposes on domestic things by combining the functions of display and concealment.

An item of furniture of this sort, located against one wall of the *zal* or *obshchaia komnata* (common or living room), is almost ubiquitous in the Khrushchev-era separate apartments in my sample. Many of these cabinets date stylistically from the 1960s, although in some cases they have been replaced by the larger floor-to-ceiling *stenka* (literally, "little wall") that became desirable and available in the 1970s. Much of the discussion in the interviews circulates around "special" things located in or on the cabinet or sideboard, which elevates, frames, and stages them and affords them VIP protection.[26] The cabinets today contain books and more recent acquisitions for home entertainment such as videotapes, photographs, postcard-size art reproductions, greeting cards, certificates or official letters of congratulation (for work or social service), a small toy or craft object made by a child, souvenirs, porcelain figurines, and, most commonly, tableware, both ceramic services and gilded or cut glassware. The top of the cabinet presents framed photos, crystal vases, artificial flowers, radios, and clocks, and the cabinet's entourage on the walls around it includes works of art and craft and photographs. These items and the relations between them (spatial, chronological, and associative) play an important role in narrating the self and merit separate analysis, but here space only permits us to focus on the furniture that frames them.

The presence in the khrushchevka interior of such equipment for controlling the proliferation of things and managing appearances is noteworthy, for it contravenes the prescriptions of the expert authorities, exemplifying the contradictions between the ideal material environment they envisaged, on the one hand, and the realities of Soviet production, received popular consumption practices, taste, and notions of what made a proper home, on the other. Thus it demonstrates the limits of the specialists' jurisdiction, suggesting that people weren't listening when they propounded their new norms of taste and rational, hygienic living. It also reveals a more complex negotiation between sometimes contradictory structures, dispositions, norms, and prohibitions, for example, between the modernist principles promulgated by reformist specialists after Stalin's death and the "structuring structure" of habitus and unconscious hold of tradition, which for many, especially first-generation urban dwellers, still held sway.[27]

The origins of the cabinet or commode were associated historically with the birth of the private bourgeois individual and the separation of the public and private spheres. The display and status functions of the bourgeois home were concentrated in this item of furniture, which was the "primary display of bourgeois self-fashioning."[28] Judy Attfield has argued that the glazed china cabinet ubiquitous in mid-twentieth-century British interiors served as a vestigial "front parlor"; as architects began to design mass housing with modernist open-plan interiors, the cabinet compensated for the loss of the spatial separation necessary for maintaining appearances and defining relations with visitors to the home.[29]

In the standard plan of Khrushchev-era apartments, the separation of front from back was even more radically collapsed. The new breed of Soviet architects that came to the fore with Stalin's death and Khrushchev's ascent aspired to approximate the open plan—a key feature of international modernist architecture—to the limitations of still experimental prefabrication technology and to the requirements of maximum economy and small scale. The single undivided space of the "general room," or *zal* (around eighteen square meters), had to serve a range of domestic functions, from sleeping to receiving guests. In one-room apartments all house -hold members shared a single space for these functions. In a two- or three-room apartment the zal additionally served as a passage between the entrance-service area and the back rooms, because corridors were eliminated in favor of an enfilade arrangement of rooms both to save space and costs and to achieve something like the modernist ideal of the open plan.[30] We do not have contemporaneous ethnographic data on how the plan was experienced by those moving in, but certain aspects such as the ceiling height, the enfilade plan, and the bathroom arrangements were commented on, often critically, in public consultations and visitors' books when model apartments were shown to the public at the Construction Pavilion of the All-Union Exhibition of Economic Achievements (VDNKh) between 1959 and 1961.[31] Recipients of these new apartments were unlikely to have missed a parlor they had never even dreamed of; for most, the new apartments meant more, not less, privacy and greater possibility to differentiate spaces, compared with the barracks or communal apartments from which residents came. Most of my informants vividly recalled their euphoria on receiving a new apartment, which seemed to them like a palace. Only in relation to the living conditions of a privileged elite and an aspirational ideal could the unfamiliar plan be perceived as a loss of functional segregation. Nevertheless, to impose order and hierarchy on things and manage the relations between visibility and concealment was essential not only in case of visitors but to maintain propriety among household members using the same space.[32]

The legitimacy of display, as well as of items of décor and furnishing whose primary function was dedicated to appearance rather than function and to concealment rather than transparency, was, however, in question. Already in the 1920s the cabinet's predecessor, the *bufet* or *gorka* (sideboard), had been condemned by zealous campaigners for the new Soviet way of life (*novyi byt*) because it stood for values antithetical to socialism: petit-bourgeois consciousness, individualism, the cultivation of the private sphere, competitive social display, and class aspirations.[33]

Yet despite its alien class background and tainted associations with the bourgeois commodity and private life, as Svetlana Boym notes, the cabinet in some form survived successive waves of modernist efforts to expunge it from the home.[34] Ideal representations of the "cultured" interior in the early 1950s show it dominated by a tall piece of furniture, elaborately carved, with drawers or cupboards below, a ledge at waist height covered with an embroidered cloth when not in use for serving food, and above, shelves protected by glass. The cabinet or sideboard remained an essential item of domestic equipment for representing the *kul'turnost'* (culturedness or urbanity) of the household, used to display treasured family possessions associated with eating, drinking, and hospitality.[35] Along with the *etazherka* (étagère or whatnot), a low stand of shelves decorated with embroidered napkins and used for books, these two items of furniture were, according to Victor Buchli, the primary vehicles for displaying "the private day-to-day prosperity of the immediate household, further expressing the interiority of the domestic realm."[36] In practice, according to Boym, even in communal apartments the cabinet or commode remained a site of personal pride and "a display of one's externalized interior and of the desire for individuation."[37]

In the Khrushchev era, as millions moved into new apartments, everything the cabinet stood for came under concerted attack, once again, from modernizing aesthetic specialists acting for the party-state. Decoration and display fell into disrepute along with the Stalinist style of architecture and interior decoration, which Khrushchev denounced in 1954 in favor of industrialized construction. The rejection conflated morality with aesthetics: ornament was cast as crime, just as Austrian modernist Adolf Loos had pronounced half a century earlier.[38] The reform of *byt* (everyday life) was both about introducing new, modernist principles and about rejecting the past, Stalinist as well as prerevolutionary. For reformers, display and nonfunctional decoration represented aspects of Stalinism from which the Khrushchev regime had to distance itself: wasteful extravagance and excess, privilege (associated with the concentration of resources on a few high-profile extravagant projects at the expense of mass housing), sham, and cover-up. In their place reformers promoted modernist values: a transparent, "honest" relation between function and form, structure and surface appearance.

The new aesthetic morality was not limited to the work of professional architects in designing the plan and elevation of buildings. Reformist specialists also sought to extend it into the "private" interior produced by amateurs. The modernist "contemporary style" of interior decorating that they promoted called for maximizing open space, transparency, and simplicity. Residents should only have the minimum of utilitarian, preferably multifunctional things in their apartments; only built-in storage was deemed necessary or appropriate in the new apartments because the new Soviet person was supposed not to encumber herself with fetishized, superfluous material possessions. Both to "reflect" this situation and to engineer it, free-standing cupboards of any sort were omitted from ideal interiors, such as the model room settings shown at the landmark 1961 exhibition *Iskusstvo—v byt* (Art into life). Soviet viewers of the exhibition complained, however, about the lack of cupboards and asked where they were supposed to store things.[39] Some architects and taste specialists also acknowledged that their jurisdiction was limited because, in the end, the domestic interior was produced by amateur homemakers.[40] Moreover, new residents would—and even *should*—want to attend to the aesthetics of their interior and would legitimately wish to particularize it, whereby the aesthetic element was identified with decorative, nonfunctional touches that transcended necessity and routine.[41] It was also acknowledged that, along with the provision of new homes, Soviet citizens needed consumer goods to furnish and equip them.[42]

Official statistics indicate a steep increase in the possession of most categories of furniture in the late 1950s to mid-1960s, which is symptomatic of a general rise in consumption and living standards, of which the mass move to new housing was an important part.[43] Notwithstanding the experts' equally categorical repudiation of domestic display and their mission to inculcate ascetic, modernist "good taste" in the masses, an item of furniture whose primary function was the management of appearances was part of the standard inventory produced or imported in the 1960s. Indeed, according to figures for the Russian Republic (RSFSR) cited by Steven Harris, production of bufety and servanty rose by 425 percent between 1957 and 1961, and around half of urban households might have possessed one.[44] While statistics do not distinguish according to style or model, it is likely that the increase was accounted for partly by low, lightweight furniture types in the contemporary style, whose introduction was part of a radical overhaul of furniture design and technology aimed at facilitating mass production. The rise in production indicated by official statistics is supported by my informants' recollections of acquiring new cabinets within a decade of moving into khrushchevki, that is, in the 1960s. Their remembered periodization is corroborated by the stylistic evidence of cabinets in the simple, stripped-down contemporary style, cabinets that still stand in many homes today.[45] Soviet consumers started buying low sideboards with a glass-fronted shelving unit mounted on top or a cupboard that combined storage concealed behind doors with open, glazed shelves. By the late 1960s, it was officially acknowledged by sociologists that Soviet households had more and more possessions and needed somewhere to store them, and in the following decade the cabinet was sometimes superseded by the newer furniture type, the floor-to-ceiling stenka.[46]

CONTINUITY OR CHANGE?

Thus, even as specialists conducted their modernist campaign against show, sham, accumulated clutter, and commodity fetishism in the name of the communist way of life, the material equipment for display was designed, produced, and consumed. The glazed contemporary-style cabinet or sideboard became an almost ubiquitous item of furniture in the zal of the separate apartment, an essential piece of equipment for making home and maintaining order there, and a "normal" expectation and attribute of decent, cultured living. Domestic production was swelled by imports, introducing to the Soviet Union furnishing types established for bourgeois consumption in interwar Germany and Czechoslovakia. Imports accounted for a number of those in the interiors examined in this study, especially those in St. Petersburg. Furniture from the Baltic Republics was also desirable.

In their classic study *The Meaning of Things* (1981), Mihaly Csikszentmihalyi and Eugene Rochberg-Halton found that furniture was one of the categories of domestic things that their Chicago informants most frequently cited as "special." The reasons they gave for this status associated furniture with memory value: roots, settledness, and stability.[47] Continuity with the past was the charge leveled against the bufet by Soviet reformers, first in the 1920s and again in the Khrushchev era. This had more to do with the practices and aspirations it represented than with the survival of a particular example of the category. It is true that in regard to the contents, the harbored bufety may also have represented constancy, permanence, and settledness to their owners (as positive values rather than as regrettable vestiges of a bourgeois past that should have been rooted out) since they protected precious and fragile things such as fine glassware or china from damage. A number of my informants' cabinets contained prerevolutionary Lomonosov or Kuznetsov services or the last remaining pieces of former sets, sometimes heirlooms and markers of their families' former propertied, upper-middle-class status before the Revolution. Thus the cabinets represent an alternative identity from the Soviet ones they had lived (a fairy tale of hidden nobility, princesses disguised as paupers). Galina tells of her grandmother's porcelain and art nouveau objets d'art.[48] Some informants indicated the significance of complete sets, suites, or services that had survived, which they say counted as luxury or prestigious possessions.[49]

However, in regard to the 1960s cabinet installed in khrushchevki, we should question whether this item of furniture represented continuity and memory or, on the contrary, *change:* a new way of life and a new role for the "private" interior in the construction of identity associated with the development of a Soviet form of modern consumer society. As far as the production and availability of cabinets is concerned, this was a new departure rather than a continuation of established practice. The fact that a new type of cupboard to fit the dimensions and aesthetics of the new apartments was designed and manufactured is significant, for in the planned economy the odds were stacked against innovation.[50] Production of the contemporary-style cabinet, as of other new products, required new state standards to be approved, new machinery to be installed, resources and quotas to be written into the economic plan. Similarly, the import of foreign furniture, even from COMECON countries, required special agreements and reciprocal arrangements.

Nor can consumption of this item of furniture and its presence in the new apartments be ascribed to passive reproduction of past practices. The resilience or, rather, perpetual recurrence of the display cupboard in Soviet homes cannot, for a number of reasons, simply be explained

by inertia, habitus, or continuity. First, as noted, the presence of a bufet
in Stalin-era representations was an ideal of cultured living rather than
a mass reality (although it is quite possible that many aspired to it), and
the likelihood of possessing a cabinet of some sort also varied with socio-
demographic category.[51] Many families living in communal apartments
and barracks lacked not only this item of furniture but any space in which
to put it. In the 1950s, if Soviet citizens had a bufet, it was more likely
to be a prerevolutionary piece than a Soviet-era product, given the low
level of furniture production before the introduction of the contemporary
style at the end of the decade. However, it did not necessarily have deep
personal associations or represent continuity with a family past. Given
the repeated dislocations in the lives of my informants, it was at least
as likely to have been salvaged off a dump as to have been passed down
carefully from generation to generation. (There are many accounts, both
in my interviews and elsewhere, of how even fine antique furniture was
abandoned in this period and how people acquired their furniture off the
street.)[52] Second, the cabinets in new apartments are not the same pieces
of furniture as in Stalin-era representations; instead, as indicated above,
they are new items manufactured in the 1960s in the contemporary style,
often using newly developed industrial serial production processes and
man-made materials. Third, when moving into the new apartments my
informants rarely brought old furniture with them or aspired to continue
their old furnishing practices, feeling they were inadequate—born of necessity and poverty—or that they betrayed the residents' rural origins. If
they brought an old metal bedstead to the new apartment, for example,
many soon replaced it with the new furniture type promoted as part of the
contemporary-style interior: the divan on a wooden frame, which doubled
as bed and settee.[53]

In this regard, if not in others, popular practice matched the specialists'
blueprints, although less from obedience than for reasons of the homemakers' own. When the new, small, plain apartments began to be built,
the ubiquitous advice to new residents called them to leave everything
behind and move in unencumbered by the material culture and values
of the past. While my informants generally deny any awareness of such
advice, most state that they moved in with "nothing." The reasons they
gave varied, however. A few cases conformed involuntarily to authorita-

tive discourse: the old furniture was too heavy, too cumbersome, too tall. Style and a sense of fashion—that one should move with the times—also figure. Some shared the specialists' view that a tall and ornately hand-carved sideboard was aesthetically inappropriate in the low-ceilinged, minimalist interior. Similarly, they recall how the etazherka had gone out of favor by the 1960s, although many remember it as an essential aspect of homemaking in the 1950s. The rejection of practices perceived as rural, backward, and old-fashioned is especially marked in relation to material practices of displaying photographs in the interior.[54]

The contemporary style, as promoted in publications and exhibitions, called for smooth contours without dust-catching moldings, for open-ness, transparency, and free space, and for only the minimum of necessary things. Some informants (mostly intelligentsia) reproduced aspects of the modernist criteria when explaining their choices: they wanted spacious-ness and disliked clutter or things that caught dust.[55] A number spoke of a desire to divest themselves of things (although this may have had more to do with the process of renunciation as they neared the end of their lives rather than reflecting their attitude back in the 1960s). Nataliia was made anxious by her accumulated stuff.[56] Others feared that their clutter cast them in a bad light in the interviewer's eyes and referred repeatedly to the need to get rid of it. Conversely, in her interview Diliara, a top scientist and party secretary in Kazan', conveyed a strong sense of satisfaction, self-determination, and control over the conditions of her own life, which corresponded to the uncluttered space of her interior, where everything had its place and its function in her life.[57]

Popular practices often contradicted the normative injunctions of re-formist professionals, however. Even those who claim they brought noth-ing sometimes perpetuated traditional, preindustrial practices, which were widely attacked in authoritative discourse. For example, while ad-vice literature consistently condemned rugs as atavistic dust catchers and sanctioned them only if placed on the floor, many informants continued to regard rugs as a marker of well-being and essential equipment for mak-ing the apartment cosy (*uiutno*) and hung them on the wall behind the bed or divan. Many also continued the traditional practice of arranging *shishki:* piling cushions on the bed or even divan and covering them with white lace.

Inna (St. Petersburg) reproduced the modernists' hostility toward dysfunctional display and clutter and conformed to the "correct" morality of things. She tried to divest herself of unnecessary stuff, disclaimed domestic exhibitionism, and presented herself as ambivalent toward consumption. She also disliked rugs and gave the same reason as reformers: rugs harbored dust. Yet she, too, had a cabinet (although, compared to some, it was quite sparsely populated) and longed for an antique gorka.

> I'm no lover of all these kinds of displays. There's simply nowhere to put things. . . . My dream is to buy one of those cabinets [*gorki*]. But when I look at the prices . . . I realize that this dream's never going to come true for me. And also, they don't make an awful lot of them nowadays. I like antique gorki very much. Can you picture what they are like? . . . They can be like a servant in height, but they are often curved and glazed.[58]

Inna's case may indicate that the contemporary-style cabinet was associated more with the modern than with handed-down practices of display from which she distanced herself as anachronistic. Its modernity lay partly in the fact that it could assist in producing an uncluttered interior, facilitating control over things and appearances. The reasons people gave for having made a fresh start in the new apartments corresponded to the modernist ideal of rupture with the past and unconditional embrace of the new. Some chose to divest themselves of the old for personal reasons. Galina, one of my youngest informants (born c. 1950, higher education), spoke with regret of how her mother chose to leave a fine separate apartment in the center of Leningrad for a newly built one on the outskirts in 1964 because her husband (Galina's father) had died there and she wanted to escape the memories. Here, affect and the investment of human relations in things and spaces are materialized in practices of divestment rather than retention.[59] Galina, meanwhile, regretted that her mother had given up the old apartment and disposed of their furniture, but her reasons had to do with objective quality and functionality rather than affect. (Like Inna she also reflected a more recent change in attitudes toward the very old or antique.)

> Interviewer: What did you bring with you in the way of furniture from your old apartment?
> Galina: Well, the furniture there wasn't antique, but it was quite old. My mum threw out some things, which I still regret today, because there

FIGURE 10.2.

Inna's cabinet, St. Petersburg, 2005. Photo: Ekaterina Gerasimova for
Everyday Aesthetics. © Susan E. Reid.

was a mahogany commode. . . . But then in the sixties everyone was madly moving house into these little apartments, well, many people were, anyway. And they threw stuff out. Of course, they threw out some beautiful furniture.

Interviewer: Wasn't it valued? Why did your mum throw it out?

Galina: Well, it seemed old. Of course, it may have needed restoration. But at that time there was no talk of that, about restoring old furniture. The furniture we had was perfectly fine for the time—it was some kind of Yugoslav suite, there was some kind of servant, quite beautiful, a large beautiful table, chairs, a Finnish divan, which is still going strong today and lives on at the dacha. If it wasn't so big, I think I might even have left it [here], because it is comfortable.

Most traveled light not out of a moral commitment to asceticism and change nor an aesthetic embrace of modernism but because, they say, they had nothing. Asked what they brought with them when they moved out of a communal apartment, hostel, or barracks into the separate apartment, they are dismissive of the question: what *would* they have brought! Many emphasize their utter poverty and lack of material possessions.[60] One Kaluga informant (born 1941), who moved into a new flat with her parents, portrayed the emptiness of the new apartment. Having no furniture, they made stools out of old lemon crates. In relation to this austerity she recalled a pleasurable memory of washing the floor and spreading it immediately with newspaper onto which her mother would throw hot baked potatoes, which they ate off the (clean) floor. Sometimes these claims to a ballast-free existence were hyperbole elicited by the circumstances of the interview. Informants were keen to impress on the interviewer the austerity of their lives and its difference from (moral superiority to) the post-Soviet consumerist, affluent society, often personified in their narratives by a daughter-in-law.[61] They emphasized antimaterialist Soviet values, community, and resourcefulness.[62] In the course of the interview, they often began to enumerate items of furniture they did bring with them, but these were mostly not very significant items, for many informants had long been rolling stones that gathered no moss until they finally came to rest in their khrushchevka. Their autobiographical narratives are marked by poverty, dislocation, and dispossession, providing particular cases of the common historical experiences of the Soviet Union—collectivization and dekulakization, purges, war, and the construction of new industrial cities. Salme (Tartu) recalled how her only possessions were reduced to a suitcase, which was then stolen on a train journey during one of her repeated relocations during the war.[63] Other informants included army officers demobilized in 1960 who had only the two suitcases of possessions allowed to military personnel.[64] A Kaluga woman's grandfather had been a propertied doctor before the Revolution, but her family had been dispossessed of their house, which was later (in the post-Soviet consumer boom) demolished. The only material connection to her past she had been able to preserve was her grandmother's icon—and even this she had to steal from other family members.[65]

Others explain that what little they had before the move was so broken and rotten as not to be worth bringing. Marina M. (Kaluga) explained why they left old furniture behind. They received a new apartment in 1963 because the house they lived in was condemned as unfit for habitation. She recalled that her grandfather brought his iron bedstead, but otherwise they left everything, because the derelict conditions of their former accommodation meant that any wooden furniture was rotten and riddled with woodworm: had they brought it, the worm would have spread to the new furniture. Inadvertently she reproduced the kind of rhetoric used by modernist publicists. How they would have relished the way that life wrote the book here, providing a vivid metaphor for the dangers of dragging along the ballast of the past and how it would contaminate the new, corrupting it from within!

We cannot, then, automatically explain the presence of cabinets in the new apartments by continuity—inertia, habitus, material continuity, and inheritance—nor even by the investment of personal associations in an old familiar item of furniture. Unlike Csikszentmihalyi's informants in Chicago in 1977, who named items of furniture as special because they stood for material links with roots and continuity (survival often in spite of migration and dislocation), for my subjects furniture rarely represented bonds with their family past.[66]

THE AESTHETICIZATION OF EVERYDAY LIFE

This does not mean that furniture for my respondents was any less "special" than it was for the Chicago informants, but the reasons and the meanings invested in it may differ. Specialness can be a mark of newness, perceived modernity or fashionability, and prosperity, as well as of continuity with the past, veneration, and memory.

Special efforts were required to get hold of a good-quality imported cabinet. The acquisition (along with that of the first appliances, such as a television set and refrigerator, and also a rug) is often distinctly remembered and associated with other memorable events and small traumas. One informant in Kaluga recalled how they had a cat that climbed everywhere, and they were afraid it would break the china, so they took the cat to relatives in the countryside. When they eventually bought a cupboard (*shkaf*), they wanted to get the cat back, but it had run away and died. Even more humble items could be mnemonics of (narrowly averted) disasters. Inna remembered the purchase of her kitchen table, with which the near death of a friend was associated: the friend had spotted it on sale, and in her eagerness to alert my informant to this rare purchase opportunity, she got knocked down by a motorcycle.[67]

The acquisition of the cabinet also marked the effects, in individual lives, of supraindividual (national and geopolitical) shifts. The fact that the cabinet was often of foreign origin, for example, is a sign of the times. The new global position of the Soviet Union—no longer autarkic but leader of the socialist camp, with trading partners in the socialist bloc and expanding interests in the developing world—was reflected in people's domestic interiors and everyday lives. Sometimes informants had been able to make significant purchases—a furniture suite or refrigerator—because a family member had worked abroad, for example, in developing countries where the Soviet Union was extending its interests and influence, and had earned hard currency (Aleksandra). Many of the homes of interviewees are "global assemblages": collections, compiled over time, of things whose diverse geographical origins reflect changing political geographies, foreign policy, and international relations.

Antonina, like many of my St. Petersburg intelligentsia informants, acquired East German furniture from a store in Leningrad. She still remembered that it was called Khel′ga (Helga).[68] Her "brand awareness" was typical. My subjects can also usually recall the names of their first television set and refrigerator, as well as of the improved models with which they later replaced them. Imported furniture was "prestigious" and regarded as better quality and more stylish than Soviet production. Consumer goods from the Baltic Republics shared in this prestige. While fur-

FIGURE 10.3.

Aleksandra's cabinet, St. Petersburg, 2005. Photo: Ekaterina Gerasimova for
Everyday Aesthetics. © Susan E. Reid.

nishing the apartment was at first a matter of getting whatever they could afford or get hold of, over the next decade some replaced their first stop-gaps with matching suites, which were also considered "prestigious" or "fashionable."

Galina S. (Kaluga) made reference to fashion in relation to furniture and demonstrated awareness of style and of its changes through time.[69] Inna also recalled, concerning her Helga cabinet, that it was very fashionable when she acquired it (on stylistic evidence in the 1960s): "Yes, it was the very height [literally, "chic"] of fashion." In the seventies she acquired a stenka floor-to-ceiling storage unit from Riga.[70] The successive types of display furniture—the passing of the etazherka and bufet, the arrival of the contemporary-style sideboard, and later the stenka as attributes of a "normal" (decent) lifestyle—punctuated the passage of time, relating personal experience to particular eras in collective life and historical changes.[71] Galina S. recalled the succession:

> Galina S.: We had an etazherka back then. In the past bookshelves weren't around; there was this kind of etazherka. And on every little shelf there was like an embroidered napkin. . . .
> Interviewer: So these napkins would be put on bookshelves, for example?
> Galina S.: It wasn't on bookshelves but on the etazherka.
> Interviewer: On the etazherka.
> Galina S.: And then came the stenka.[72]

Galina L. in St. Petersburg recalled that her mother updated her furniture with fashionable contemporary items from Yugoslavia and the GDR, even though her existing furniture was good quality and relatively new. By the time they moved into a new flat in 1963 the etazherka's day had passed, and they, too, had acquired a Helga cabinet with combined storage and display. She placed it in a historical succession of furniture types, showing a precise awareness of the periodization and changing fashion. It was superseded in the seventies by the popular stenka of which it was a prototype, which offered even more cupboards, drawers, and so on to accommodate the growing number of possessions in urban households.[73]

Many of my informants deny that questions of choice and taste played any part in their homemaking: they simply got whatever they could afford or came their way.[74] "Everyday aesthetics" seemed an oxymoron—beauty

and byt were incompatible. Yet their narratives, along with the arrangements in their interiors, indicate that a sense of style, fashion, and aesthetics did become an important aspect of their effort to imprint their sense of
themselves on their interior, if not immediately, then in the course of the
1960s. The acquisition of a cabinet marked a new stage in Soviet people's
lives, representing their new settledness, comfort, relative prosperity, new
opportunities to attend to domesticity, and a consciousness of how their
own interior compared to others'. It was a sign that they could now rise
above everyday necessity and survival and attend to aesthetics and presentation of self. Many had begun to see taste, fashion, or even beauty
as qualities they could, even *should,* aspire to in their apartment and to
regard the aesthetic aspect as a way both to individualize it and to realize
themselves.

Some would go to considerable lengths to find what they wanted, calling in favors, camping out in Moscow stations, or enduring other tribula-
tions.[75] Travel, first within Russia and later to the Baltic Republics and
fraternal countries, was one means to circumvent shortage and lack of
choice. Seeking to differentiate her apartment from others' apartments, a
Kaluga resident resorted to traveling to other cities to get what she wanted,
because, she explained, all the furniture produced and distributed was yellow.[76] What is noteworthy here is that aesthetic choice and the possibility
to differentiate her interior mattered sufficiently for her to make this effort.

The move to the new apartments, whose architectural austerity was
meant to inculcate in residents a new ascetic modernist taste, rational
lifestyle, and socialist consumption morality, was in practice far from con-
signing domestic display to the dustbin of bourgeois history. Although
the style of display might be updated in accordance with the modernist
aesthetic, display became *more,* not less, important, and the home became
more exhibitionary.[77] This aestheticization, epitomized by the cabinet,
was also related to changes in everyday practices, which were shaped by
the provision of separate apartments—the shift to single-family living
with one's own kitchen—as well as by changing social norms and work
patterns. First, the cabinet was separated from ordinary domestic functions as dining shifted to the kitchen. Second, the home became a place
for receiving guests and for "private" sociability.

Display presupposes a viewer; even private displays demand a "public," however small. The rise of display is associated with beginning to see home as a place to invite guests into, a private social space: what might be called, using Shlapentokh's term, the privatization of leisure and sociability. The ideas of having a home of one's own and of having somewhere to receive visitors were intimately linked in contemporary culture.[78] Authorities on home life not only accepted that people would want to make the givens of the standard architecture personally meaningful and communicative of self-image and social position—to put their new separate apartments on show and present themselves to the best advantage when receiving guests—they also encouraged and normalized this aspiration.[79]

CONCLUSION

The case of the cabinet exemplifies how common material and discursive structures are complicated by other factors, and while they condition or limit behaviors, they do not, in the end, determine them.[80] Moreover, authoritative discourses and practices were often internally contradictory and, at the same time, clashed with existing practices and norms. The people who moved into new apartments were not blank slates. The homogenizing forces of built space and specialist discourse had to contend with other structures and determinants of people's behavior, aspirations, and notions of how to dwell: tradition and unconsciously acquired dispositions or habitus. That, indeed, was why the modernizing reformists had to invest so much effort in promoting new tastes and practices and castigating the old. However, the move to new housing helped to loosen the hold of any traditions that had survived the disruptions of sovietization and war, while relatively improved selection and availability of consumer goods increased opportunities to choose the things one lived with. As Anthony Giddens notes (writing of Western modernity), in a society where tradition has more thoroughly been swept away than ever before, where large areas of a person's life are no longer set by preexisting patterns and habits, the "reflexive project of self" assumes particular importance, and the individual is continually obliged to negotiate lifestyle options. These lifestyle choices, at once constraining and emancipatory, are not merely external aspects of the individual's attitudes but "constitutive of the reflexive narrative of self"; that is, they define who the individual "is."[81]

While warning against petit-bourgeois "my-home-is-my-castle" mentalities, individualism, and fetishism, authoritative discourse nevertheless presented consumption for the home and concern with beautifying the private interior as legitimate and identified the aestheticization of the everyday environment with its particularization as a production of self. While specialists saw standardization as having positive roles to play in everyday life—routinizing everyday chores and making them more efficient, providing stability and consciousness of belonging to a group—it was an unexamined premise of much advice literature that one could and even *should* inscribe one's individuality upon the plan and walls of the new apartment. Indeed, the aesthetic organization of the domestic environment was a means to self-realization both in theory and in practice.[82] Compared to the reality (rather than the Potemkin village) of the Stalin-era interior, the move to separate apartments, the growing availability of consumer durables, and the flood of representations of tasteful modern interiors evoking a calm but sophisticated urban lifestyle together set the basis for the hypertrophy of domestic exhibitionism or private publicity. Transforming their domestic interiors into sites of conspicuous consumption and everyday aesthetics through material practices of decoration, display, and concealment, occupants made these standard spaces their own. At the same time, they made themselves at home, creating meaningful selves and coherent narratives of their lives that they could present to others on their own terms.

NOTES

An adapted version of this chapter appeared as "Everyday Aesthetics in the Khrushchev-Era Standard Apartment," *Etnofoor* 24, no. 2 (2013): 79–106.

1. Dorothee Wierling, "Everyday Life and Gender Relations," in *The History of Everyday Life: Reconstructing Historical Experiences and Ways of Life,* ed. Alf Lüdtke, trans. William Templer (Princeton, N.J.: Princeton University Press, 1995), 151; Catriona Kelly, *Refining Russia* (Oxford: Oxford University Press, 2001), xviii.

2. Daniel Miller, "Appropriating the State on the Council Estate," *Man* 23, no. 2 (1988): 353–72; Miller, ed., *Home Possessions: Material Culture behind Closed Doors* (Oxford: Berg, 2001); Miller, ed., *Acknowledging Consumption: A Review of New Studies* (New York: Routledge, 1995); S. Chevalier, "The French Two Home Project: Materialization of Family Identity," in *At Home: An Anthropology of Domestic Space*, ed. Irene Cieraad (Syracuse, N.Y.: Syracuse University Press, 1999), 83–94; Nicky Gregson, *Living with Things: Ridding, Accommodation, Dwelling* (Wantage, Oxon.: Sean Kingston Publishing, 2007); H. Dittmar, *The Social Psychology of Material Possessions: To Have Is to Be* (Hemel Hempstead: Harvester Wheatsheaf, 1992); Rachel Hurdley, "Objecting Relations: The Problem of the Gift," *Sociological Review* 55, no. 1 (2007): 124–43; S. Jackson and S. Moores, *The Politics of Domestic Consumption: Critical Readings* (Hemel Hempstead: Prentice Hall/Harvester Wheatsheaf, 1995).

3. Wolfgang Braunfels, *Urban Design in Western Europe: Regime and Architecture, 900–1900*, trans. Kenneth J. Northcott (Chicago: University of Chicago Press, 1988), 38, as cited by Blair Ruble, "From Khrushchevki to *Korobki*," in *Russian Housing in the Modern Age*, ed. William Brumfield and Blair Ruble (Cambridge: Cambridge University Press, 1993), 244.

4. Leora Auslander, "'Jewish Taste'? Jews and the Aesthetics of Everyday Life in Paris and Berlin, 1920–1942," in *Histories of Leisure*, ed. Rudy Koshar (Oxford: Berg, 2002), 300.

5. Erving Goffman, *The Presentation of Self in Everyday Life* (Edinburgh: Edinburgh University, 1956), 17–25.

6. I am indebted to the Leverhulme Trust, to the AHRC, and to my assistants, Ekaterina Gerasimova, Alla Bolotova, Sofia Chuikina, Elena Bogdanova, and Marleen Nömmela.

7. Gregory D. Andrusz, *Housing and Urban Development in the USSR* (London: Macmillan, 1984), 178, table 7.5; Timothy Sosnovy, "The Soviet Housing Situation Today," *Soviet Studies* 11, no. 1 (1959): 1–21; K. Zhukov, "Tekhnicheskaia estetika i oborudovanie kvartir," *Tekhnicheskaia estetika*, no. 2 (1964): 1; William Taubman, *Khrushchev: The Man and His Era* (New York: Free Press, 2003), 382.

8. Deborah Field, *Private Life and Communist Morality in Khrushchev's Russia* (New York: Peter Lang, 2007); Lewis Siegelbaum, ed., *Borders of Socialism: Private Spheres of Soviet Russia* (New York: Palgrave, 2006).

9. V. E. Khazanova, "Arkhitektura v poru 'Ottepeli,'" in *Ot shestidesyatykh k vos'midesyatykh: Voprosy sovremennoi kul'tury*, ed. V. E. Lebedeva (Moscow, 1991), 81.

10. For details, see Susan E. Reid, "The Khrushchev Kitchen: Domesticating the Scientific-Technological Revolution," *Journal of Contemporary History* 40, no. 2 (2005): 289–316; Reid, "The Meaning of Home: 'The Only Bit of the World You Can Have to Yourself,'" in Siegelbaum, *Borders of Socialism*, 145–70; Reid, "Communist Comfort: Socialist Modernism and the Making of Cosy Homes in the Khrushchev-Era Soviet Union," *Gender and History* 21, no. 3 (2009): 465–98.

11. Certain aspects of this process are common to the increasing power of the state and the spread of standardization with industrialization under capitalism as well as socialism. See Reid, "The Khrushchev Kitchen." For the perfection of a grid of surveillance in the Khrushchev era, see *The Collective and the Individual: A Study of Practices*, by Oleg Kharkhordin (Berkeley: University of California Press, 1999). Blair Ruble asserts that the Western alienation from residence, which Braunfels criticized, "was magnified in the Soviet Union, where all planning is done for strangers" ("From *Khrushcheby* to *Korobki*," 244).

12. Vladimir Shlapentokh, *Public and Private Life of the Soviet People: Changing Values in Post-Stalin Russia* (Oxford: Oxford University Press, 1989), 153–64.

13. See, for example, Donald J. Raleigh, *Russia's Sputnik Generation: Soviet Baby Boomers Talk about Their Lives* (Bloomington: Indiana University Press, 2006), 9. Raleigh does, however, acknowledge important correctives offered by Alexei Yurchak, *Everything Was Forever, Until It Was No More: The Last Soviet Generation* (Princeton, N.J.: Princeton University Press, 2006).

14. For the felicitous ambiguities of "accommodation," see Daniel Miller, "Accommodating," in *Contemporary Art and the Home,* ed. Colin Painter (Oxford: Berg, 2002), 115–30.

15. For crisis and the extraordinary as part of—rather than as antithetical to—the everyday, see Sheila Fitzpatrick, *Everyday Stalinism: Ordinary Life in Extraordinary Times* (New York: Oxford University Press, 1999); and Olga Shevchenko, *Crisis and the Everyday in Post-socialist Moscow* (Bloomington: Indiana University Press, 2009).

16. Interviews for *Everyday Aesthetics in the Modern Soviet Flat* (hereafter cited as *EA*): Svetlana, Apatity; married couple, Tartu, August 31, 2006; Vasilii, Kaluga; Lev, Kaluga.

17. See Igor' Narskii, *Fotokartochka na pamiat': Semeinye istorii, fotograficheskie poslaniia i sovetskoe detsvo (avtobio-istorio-graficheskii roman)* (Cheliabinsk: Entsiklopediia, 2008).

18. Model interiors produced for the 1958 furniture competition and for the exhibition *Iskusstvo—v byt* in 1961 were illustrated and described in popular and specialist periodicals. See, for example, K. Blomerius, "Pochemu malo udobnoi i deshevoi mebeli? (zametki arkhitektora)," *Sovetskaia torgovlia,* no. 9 (1959): 27–31; "V novuiu kvartiry novuiu mebel'," *Ogonek,* March 8, 1959, back cover; numerous articles in *Dekorativnoe iskusstvo SSSR;* and albums such as O. Baiar and R. Blashkevich, *Kvartira i ee ubranstvo* (Moscow: Stroiizdat, 1962).

19. Not-so-ideal homes were also represented in negative descriptions and satirical cartoons by taste reformers in the Soviet press and in rare accounts by Western observers. See, for example, Boris Brodskii, "Novyi byt i kamufliazh meshchanstva," *Dekorativnoe iskusstvo SSSR* (hereafter cited as *DI*), no. 8 (1963): 23–28; David and Vera Mace, *The Soviet Family* (London: Hutchinson, 1963), 187–88; Bruce and Beatrice Gould, "We Saw How Russians Live," *Ladies' Home Journal,* February 1957, 176; Santha Rama Rau, *My Russian Journey* (New York: Harper & Brothers, 1959), 5.

20. "Special" objects in domestic space were used to access the everyday "meaning of things" in the classic 1977 study by Mihaly Csikszentmihalyi and Eugene Rochberg-Halton, *The Meaning of Things: Domestic Symbols and the Self* (Cambridge: Cambridge University Press, 1981). See also Ian Woodward, "Domestic Object and the Taste Epiphany," *Journal of Material Culture* 6, no. 2 (2001): 115–36; Hurdley, "Objecting Relations," 124–43; Greg Noble, "Accumulating Being," *International Journal of Cultural Studies* 7, no. 2 (2004): 233–56. For an insightful study of cabinets in modern Slovakia, see Nicolette Makovicky, "Closet and Cabinet: Clutter as Cosmology," *Home Cultures* 4, no. 3 (2007): 287–310.

21. Jeff Weintraub, "The Theory and Politics of the Public/Private Distinction," and O. Kharkhordin, "Reveal and Dissimulate: A Genealogy of Private Life in Soviet Russia," both in *Public and Private in Thought and Practice,* ed. J. Weintraub and K. Kumar (Chicago: University of Chicago Press, 1996), 4–5, 333–63.

22. On public privacy and private publicity, see Katerina Gerasimova, "Public Privacy in the Soviet Communal Apartment," in *Socialist Spaces: Sites of Everyday Life in the Eastern Bloc,* ed. David Crowley and Susan E. Reid (Oxford: Berg, 2002), 207–30.

23. Svetlana Boym, *Common Places: Mythologies of Everyday Life in Russia* (Cambridge, Mass.: Harvard University Press, 1994); Miller, "Appropriating the State," 353–72.

24. Similarly, in midcentury Great Britain the Mass Observation Project found that there were certain types of things one could expect to find on a mantelpiece. See Judy Attfield,

Bringing Modernity Home: Writings on Popular Design and Material Culture (Manchester: Manchester University Press, 2007); Attfield, *Wild Things: The Material Culture of Everyday Life* (Oxford: Berg, 2000); Rachel Hurdley, "Dismantling Mantelpieces: Narrating Identities and Materialising Culture in the Home," *Sociology* 40, no. 4 (2006): 717–33. Compare Ondina F. Leal, "Popular Taste and Erudite Repertoire: The Place and Space of Television in Brazil," in Jackson and Moores, *The Politics of Domestic Consumption,* 314–20.

25. Mieke Bal, "Telling Objects: A Narrative Perspective on Collecting," in *Cultures of Collecting,* ed. John Elsner and Roger Cardinal (London: Reaktion, 1994), 97–115; Miller, "Appropriating the State," 353–72; Hurdley, "Dismantling Mantelpieces," 717–18; Hurdley, "Objecting Relations," 124–43.

26. Hurdley, "Objecting Relations," 124.

27. Pierre Bourdieu, "Structures, Habitus, Power: Basis of a Theory of Symbolic Power," in *Outline of a Theory of Practice,* trans. Richard Nice (Cambridge: Cambridge University Press, 1977); Bourdieu, *The Logic of Practice,* trans. Richard Nice (Cambridge: Polity, 1990).

28. Boym, *Common Places,* 151, 325–26nn38, 39, 44, quote at 326n39; Victor Buchli, *Archaeology of Socialism* (Oxford: Berg, 1999), 4.

29. Attfield, *Bringing Modernity Home,* 158.

30. Compare Judy Attfield, "Bringing Modernity Home: Open Plan in the British Domestic Interior," in Cieraad, *At Home,* 73–82.

31. Rossiiskii Gosudarstvennyi Arkhiv Ekonomiki (Russian State Archive of the Economy, Moscow) (RGAE fonds), Rossiiskii Gosudarstvennyi Arkhiv Nauchno-Technicheskoi Dokumentatsii (Russian State Archive of Scientific and Technical Documentation, Samara) (RGANTD), fond 127, op. 1, dd. 2175–77 (comments books for VDNKh Pavilion "Zhilishchnoe stroitel'stvo," 1960). For other examples of consultation, see Steven Harris, "Moving to the Separate Apartment: Building, Distributing, Furnishing, and Living in Urban Housing in Soviet Russia, 1950s–1960s" (Ph.D. diss., University of Chicago, 2003).

32. Interviews for *EA.*

33. Buchli, *Archaeology of Socialism,* 89.

34. Boym, *Common Places,* 152.

35. On *kul'turnost',* see Vera Dunham, *In Stalin's Time: Middle-Class Values in Soviet Literature* (New York: Cambridge University Press, 1976); Fitzpatrick, *Everyday Stalinism;* Kelly, *Refining Russia;* Jennifer Patico, *Consumption and Social Change in a Post-Soviet Middle Class* (Stanford, Calif.: Stanford University Press, 2008), 44–50.

36. Buchli, *Archaeology of Socialism,* 91.

37. Boym, *Common Places,* 151.

38. Khrushchev denounced nonfunctional surface ornament in a 1954 speech initiating the rejection of Stalinist style in architecture and interior decoration. For more detail, see Reid, "Communist Comfort."

39. Visitors' books for *Iskusstvo—v byt,* Tsentral'nyi Gosudarstvennyi Arkhiv Goroda Moskvy, formerly Tsenstral'nyi Arkhiv Literatury i Iskusstva Moskvy (TsGA Moskvy/TsALIM), fond 21, op. 1, dd. 121–25; Rossiiskii gosudarstvennyi Arkhiv Literatury i Iskusstva (Russian State Archive of Literature and Art) (RGALI), fond 2329, op. 4, dd. 1002, 1391. Viewers also criticized the lack of storage space in the model apartments shown at VDNKh: see RGAE fonds, RGANTD, fond 127, op. 1, dd. 2176–77 (e.g., l. 2). Freestanding cupboards were deemed unnecessary in numerous professional discussions: see RGALI, fond 2466, op. 2, d. 338, l. 5 (discussion of All-Union competition for furniture for one-family apartments, Cheremushki, 1958, March 20, 1959); RGALI, fond 2466, op. 2, d. 211, l. 3 (January 1957); RGALI, fond 2466, op. 2, d. 338, l. 5.

40. RGALI, fond 2329, op. 4, ed. khr. 1388, ll. 51–52 (discussion of exhibition *Iskusstvo—v byt*, June 6, 1961); Irina Voeikova, "Vasha kvartira," *Rabotnitsa*, no. 9 (1962): 30.

41. Karl Kantor, "Chelovek i zhilishche," *Iskusstvo i byt*, no. 1 (1963): 26–48; G. Liubimova, "Ratsional'noe oborudovanie kvartir," *DI*, no. 6 (1964): 15–18.

42. "Osobennosti organizatsii byta v kvartirakh novogo tipa," TSAGM (TsALIM), fond 21, op. 1, d. 123; "V novuiu kvartiry novuiu mebel'"; A. Baranov, "Sotsiologicheskie problemy zhilishcha," in *Sotsial'nye problemy zhilishcha*, ed. A. Kharchev, S. M. Verezhnov, and V. L. Ruzhzhe (Leningrad: LENZNIIEP, 1969), 16–17.

43. Harris, "Moving to the Separate Apartment," app. 1, table 26, 566.

44. Ibid., table 14, 492, and app. 1, table 26, 566; and the draft of this dissertation (with thanks to Steven Harris), "Appendix 1: Furniture Production in the RSFSR 1957–1961" (source, Gosudarstvennyi Arkhiv Rossiiskoi Federatsiia [State Archive of the Russian Federation] [GARF], fond A-259, op. 45, d. 709, l. 116); and "Appendix 2: Possession of Furniture by Families in Various Categories of Employment," undated (GARF, fond A-259, op. 42, d. 9114, l. 54).

45. See also Boym, *Common Places*, 153.

46. Baranov, "Sotsiologicheskie problemy zhilishcha," 16.

47. Csikszentmihalyi and Rochberg-Halton, *The Meaning of Things*.

48. *EA*: Galina L., St. Petersburg.

49. For example, Marina, Samara, born ca. 1960.

50. RGALI, fond 2329, op. 4, ed. khr. 1391, ll. 14, 11.

51. *Kolkhoz* and *sovkhoz* peasants were much less likely to possess a *servant* or *bufet* than were urban dwellers. Harris, "Moving to the Separate Apartment," dissertation draft, app. 2.

52. *EA*, 2007: Galina, Evgeniia; Ljubov, Tartu.

53. *EA*: Nina, Kazan'.

54. For example, *EA*: Nina, Kazan'; Marina M., Kaluga.

55. *EA*: Inna, St. Petersburg; Diliara, Kazan'. For ridding as a constitutive aspect of consumption, see Gregson, *Living with Things*.

56. Nataliia, St. Petersburg, interviewer, Ekaterina Gerasimova, for the project *Intelligentsia and Philistinism*, 2001, with thanks to Gerasimova and Timo Vihavainen; *EA*: Inga and Aleksandr, St. Petersburg.

57. *EA*: Diliara, Kazan'.

58. *EA*: Inna, St. Petersburg.

59. *EA*: Galina, St. Petersburg.

60. *EA*: Nina, Kazan'.

61. *Intelligentsia and Philistinism*: Nataliia, St. Petersburg.

62. *EA*: Nina, Kazan'.

63. *EA*: Salme, Tartu.

64. *EA*: Vladimir, Ivan, Kaluga.

65. *EA*: Anneta, Kaluga.

66. The Chicago residents had also been through many ruptures, however. Things that had survived, maintaining links with roots in spite of dislocation, counted as "special." See Csikszentmihalyi and Rochberg-Halton, *Meaning of Things*.

67. *EA*: Marina M., Kaluga, b. 1933; Inna, St. Petersburg.

68. Antonina, St. Petersburg, Gerasimova for Vihavainen, *Intelligentsia and Philistinism*, 2002.

69. *EA*: Galina S., Kaluga.

70. *EA:* Inna, St. Petersburg.

71. Compare Krisztina Fehérváry, "American Kitchens, Luxury Bathrooms, and the Search for a 'Normal' Life in Postsocialist Hungary," *Ethnos* 67, no. 3 (2002): 369–400.

72. *EA:* Galina S., Kaluga. An archival photo of an *etazherka* in a 1952 interior is reproduced in Buchli, *Archaeology of Socialism,* 91, fig. 15 (Rossiiskii Gosudarstvennyi Arkhiv Kinofotodokumentov [Russian State Archive of Cine-Photo Documents] [RGAKFD], no. 0242408).

73. *EA:* Galina L., St. Petersburg.

74. Compare Boym, *Common Places,* 155. Makovicky found similar denials among her Slovak informants, though she draws different conclusions ("Closet and Cabinet," 289, 304n2).

75. *EA:* Marina, Kaluga.

76. *EA:* Diana, Kaluga; Zinaida, Kovdor.

77. Mike Featherstone, *Consumer Culture and Postmodernism* (London: Sage, 1991), chap. 5.

78. See Reid, "Happy Housewarming," in *Petrified Utopia,* ed. Marina Balina and Evgeny Dobrenko (London: Anthem Press, 2009), 133–60.

79. For example, *Kunst ja kodu (Iskusstvo i domashnii byt),* no. 1 (1960): 28–19 of the Estonian (6–7 of the Russian translation).

80. Wierling, "Everyday Life and Gender Relations," 151.

81. Anthony Giddens, *The Transformation of Intimacy: Sexuality, Love and Eroticism in Modern Societies* (Oxford: Polity Press, 1992), 74–75; Giddens, *Modernity and Self-Identity* (Cambridge: Polity, 1991).

82. Iu. Sharov and G. Poliachek, *Vkus nado vospityvat' (besedy dlia molodezhi)* (Novosibirsk: Novosibirskoe knizhnoe izdatel'stvo, 1960), 66–79. See also M. Chereiskaia, "Zametki o khoroshem vkuse," in *Podruga,* ed. R. Saltanova and N. Kolchinskaia (Moscow: Molodaia gvardiia, 1959), 220; Liubimova, "Ratsional'noe oborudovanie kvartir," 15–18; Torshilova, "Byt," 143.

11

The Post-Soviet Kommunalka

Continuity and Difference?

ILYA UTEKHIN

Communal apartments (*kommunalki*, sing. *kommunalka*), which were emblematic of the Soviet way of life, are no longer a common urban experience in contemporary Russia. Even though these housing arrangements still exist both in the prestigious central areas and in the periphery of St. Petersburg, for the younger generation, kommunalki are considered to be media locations or sets in movies when the action denotes Soviet time. At the same time, communal apartments are the topic of numerous printed publications, documentary films, and talk shows, in which they are presented not only as a part of history and cultural memory but also as a social problem that requires mediation and redress.

Looking anthropologically at communal apartments, one can compare the various kinds of shared housing types that exist across cultures. But in order to identify and interpret the systems of meaning ascribed to communal apartments in Russia (or to favelas in Brazil), one needs a deeper understanding of the cultural context. In the post-Soviet period the meanings and functions of communal apartments have changed rapidly, but this change has been neither described nor documented in a systematic fashion. In our online virtual museum of the kommunalka, my colleagues and I made an attempt to reconstruct the ways and practices of Soviet communal apartments by analyzing the materials collected in St. Petersburg in the post-Soviet period. These included videos shot in 2006 and photographs dating from 1998 to 2007.[1] Our exhibition narrates the communal apartments as a Soviet phenomenon from the past, but it also provides illustrations of more recent developments within this system of housing. However, as far as I can judge, there are few systematic treatments of kommunalki as a post-Soviet phenomenon in the current academic literature.

The term "communal apartments" (or its Russian equivalent) may refer to a variety of homes that differ from one another in size, location, population, cleanliness, and outer appearance, but almost all of them conform to the following criteria. A communal apartment is occupied by more than a single tenant, more than one household, and these individuals share the same kitchen, toilet, and other living facilities. These features are not exclusive to communal apartments, because students' dormitories, workers' barracks, and apartments where people rent rooms from a landlord also feature similar living arrangements. In communal apartments, although there are no landlords, the housing doesn't belong to dwellers. In the USSR the authorities provided housing as part of a system of social welfare and a mechanism of control. Monthly payments subsidized by the state paid for much of the rent and the cost of housing support services provided by a state-run agency.

The inhabitants had no choice—or had a very limited choice—before they moved into a communal apartment. Correspondingly, coresidents could not select each other, and eventually they formed a heterogeneous collection of people belonging to a variety of social and ethnic groups, employed in various occupations, and engaged in different lifestyles. While some of the residents lived in poverty, others might have had well-paid jobs. Communal apartments differed from other kinds of joint communal living such as communes and kibbutzim, where residents share a common ideology or background. Students' and workers' dormitories usually shelter residents who have much more in common than residents of a communal apartment.

Neighbors were expected to take care of the public space located inside communal apartments such as corridors and kitchens, and they organized cleaning schedules, undertook small repairs, collected payments, and calculated the expenditures necessary for the maintenance of the apartment. As norms of common living had to be enforced in some way, residents needed to organize themselves and to establish procedures of management and control. They elected an apartment steward, a leader who was responsible to the housing administration for maintaining order and ensuring the timely payment of rents and fees. Even though residents had no property rights on the premises they occupied, their children and close relatives could be registered at that address and could live there for unlimited time. In fact, the right to use the premises passed from generation to generation within the family. This right was given in the form of a residency permit (*propiska*), which required the recipient to live only in the city where the permit was issued. This permit system became a powerful method of controlling the lives and movements of citizens, because access to medical care, daycare, and school was determined by place of residence. In the years of famine, even ration cards were issued by the housing authority.

Soviet-era communal apartments were a permanent residence for most of the tenants, as they had few ways to change their living quarters. If their room size was in accordance with sanitary norms, then only an increase in the number of family members or a change in their status at work would result in the allowance of additional space. Residents thus favored would be placed on the waiting list for housing so that in the future they could move to more spacious rooms or even receive a separate apartment. While residents had the right to exchange their rooms and even build a cooperative housing complex, for the vast majority their kommunalka was a permanent home they did not expect to change within their lifetime. Classic communal apartments in Leningrad were located in central districts of the city and in buildings erected before the Revolution of 1917. These were different from the kommunalki that housed more than one household in newly constructed buildings on the outskirts of the city.

The characteristics described above to a great extent had become irrelevant for communal apartments in Russia by the early twenty-first century, and today this phenomenon of shared urban housing has new forms and meanings. After 1992, as a result of the Law on Privatization of Housing adopted in 1991 and additional legislation passed in its aftermath in 1992, the privatization of urban housing was launched.[2] The renters of low-rent publicly owned housing, tenants of communal apartments among them, acquired the premises that they occupied for free, paying only a symbolic fee for the paperwork. By 2011 more than 80 percent of urban apartments had been privatized free of charge, and privatization is supposed to be ongoing until 2013. As a real estate market evolved, people began to trade their rooms so that they could acquire more than one room or apartment in their property portfolio.

In prestigious districts and historical buildings, wealthy new Russians and real estate agencies started to buy out kommunalki and convert them into huge luxury apartments. They purchased rooms from families that were living in these apartments, and these residents were then relocated to other living spaces. In smaller apartments, a family could buy the remaining rooms from their coresidents and transform their apartment into a private (*otdel'naia*, "separate") unit. The buying of kommunalki and the relocation of the original residents (*rasselenie*) led to a considerable decrease in the number of communal apartments in the historical city center, where by 2011 the percentage of the population living in communal apartments had dropped to 15 percent.[3] Despite the fact that municipal authorities in 2007 launched a special program to provide financial support for those undertaking resettlement, it would be unrealistic to assume that communal apartments will disappear completely in the near future.

Journalist Tatiana Tkachuk from Radio Liberty in a program about the kommunalki quoted a message from a resident who lacked the resources to buy an individual apartment.

> I am a doctor of sciences in physics and work at the Russian Academy of Sciences. By today's standards, I live in poverty. It so happened that by the time of transition to the "market economy" I was living in a communal apartment along with my wife, who works as a teacher in a public school, and my two children, currently in high school. Here we have two rooms, and the other resident has one. As for a separate apartment, based on my earnings, I could buy one in about eight or nine hundred years. Unfortunately, I cannot change my profession, because I am already fifty-five years old.[4]

One can find similar testimonies in the media.

In Soviet times, a highly qualified scientist who belonged to the prestigious Academy of Sciences would receive a decent salary, housing, medical care, and many social benefits. Even if the housing provided was a room in a kommunalka, people holding a degree of *kandidat nauk* (PhD) or higher had the right to more spacious housing and a separate room where they could engage in their scholarly work. The transition to a market economy destroyed the Soviet welfare system, which was partly channeled through employers. As a result, thousands of people lost their customary sources of income and social security and found themselves living below the poverty line. Many engineers, scientists, teachers, doctors, and civil employees changed the jobs for which they were qualified and were forced to pursue employment opportunities in small businesses, retail, and other emerging trades in order to survive the economic turmoil of the 1990s. Many of those who did not succeed in their attempts to find profitable jobs and opted to move out of their kommunalki received a separate apartment in exchange for their rooms as part of the resettlement process initiated by real estate agencies. By 2011 this business had slowed considerably.[5] Most of the valuable properties had been sold already, and the communal apartments that remain publicly owned are located in buildings with ruined stairways and a crumbling infrastructure, and they are usually bereft of attractive views. These apartments are often inhabited by people who demand much more than the market price for their rooms.

The most active part of the population made use of the opportunities that privatization presented, but people less adapted to the market economy mostly remained in their kommunalki. During the late socialist era, buying housing in a building cooperative was comparatively more affordable. The price of a square meter in a cooperative apartment was about equivalent to an average monthly salary. In 2011 in St. Petersburg, by contrast, the market value of a square meter in the cheapest new apartment was about five times that of the average monthly salary.[6]

The statement quoted above is a typical story about former Soviet people who still cannot find their way in the new reality of the marketplace. Their hopes had been linked to the government, the state, and the authorities—there is no suitable way to translate the Russian *gosudarstvo* into a single noun. It was the gosudarstvo that took the responsibility for providing housing and a means of subsistence to this citizen, directly or via the Academy of Sciences. The contemporary Russian state is content to assign much more responsibility to the citizens themselves in matters of employment and housing.

THE KOMMUNALKA IN MASS MEDIA DISCOURSE

On April 27, 2011, 100TV Channel, based in St. Petersburg, organized a television marathon that was dedicated to the examination of the communal apartment as a multifaceted social phenomenon. Experts, representatives of city government, and other speakers were invited to a theater, where the scene was transformed into a sort of symbolic kommunalka. Presenters led the talk with the speakers and directed a videoconference with members of Duma in Moscow, the city governor, and even residents of communal apartments in Odessa.[7] Before the marathon, during five consecutive evenings, a documentary series about kommunalki, entitled *The Communal Capital,* was screened. The title itself is revealing: in the Soviet and post-Soviet mythology, there are two capitals in this country, Moscow and St. Petersburg. St. Petersburg was traditionally regarded as the cultural capital, but as it is also known for the largest number of big communal apartments, journalists in the 1990s christened St. Petersburg "the communal capital." It is true that in Moscow, unlike in St. Petersburg, most of the communal apartments in the city center disappeared during the 1990s.

The next day, April 28, 2011, the newspaper *Vechernyi Peterburg* published an article on this event with the following subtitle: "At the 100TV marathon, citizens, bureaucrats, experts, and celebrities discussed how to get rid of the legacy of the Soviet past." The governor, Valentina Matvienko, announced her position before television audiences: "We will be working on this problem until there remains not a single communal apartment in the city." One of the key questions of the marathon was whether the tenants in kommunalki should contribute, along with authorities, to bringing this "ugly" phenomenon to an end. From what we see and read, there seems to be a consensus among the public that the era of communal apartments must come to an end. This urge to privatize all communal property is rather superficial, as it disregards the important functions of the kommunalki in present-day St. Petersburg.

People who spoke during the marathon and in the documentary series were given a caption on the screen that stated their names and the number of years that they had lived in a kommunalka. A majority of the interviewees were older and either had lived in communal apartments for many years or were still living in one. Within the framework of the TV show, the years of communal experience, so typical of Leningraders, became a sort of social capital, a base for authoritative opinions about the topic.

Typically, a newspaper or magazine article, a television program, a talk show, a documentary film, or even a documentary series that is dedicated to kommunalki will contain interesting topics and analyze the motives of the residents in a meaningful way. Most of these public presentations start with official statistics concerning the kommunalki and show how the number of these apartments has declined steadily in the recent past. Since it is very difficult to evaluate the number of inhabitants or the proportion of the total population living in communal apartments, there are very few reliable official statistics that can be cited. According to the data from the St. Petersburg city government, during 2010 the number of kommunalki in the city decreased by 2,106; currently, there are 105,000 communal apartments inhabited by around 660,000 inhabitants. Actually, in some respects these figures might be inaccurate, because it depends on the way both the apartments and the inhabitants are counted.[8] Also, there is little information available on the recent formation of communal apartments in new buildings.

TV journalists usually try to find the biggest communal apartment in the city in which to stage their programs.[9] Since it is not possible to show an apartment's actual size, what we usually see on the TV screen are clusters of doorbells at the entrance to the apartment, long winding corridors, preferably with a child riding a bicycle, women with their hair wrapped in a towel or carrying a saucepan—scenes that convey visions of intimate domesticity. These are well-known details that epitomize the Soviet communal lifestyle, and they are still relevant today. *The Communal Capital,* released in the spring of 2011, shows a monstrously large apartment, comprising thirty-four rooms in what was formerly the headquarters of the Glavpochtamt (Central Post Office). About seventy-five people are officially registered at this address, but with people moving in and out constantly, some long-term residents often cannot differentiate the guests from the tenants. Many of the residents also suffer greatly because alcoholic coresidents often invite in antisocial elements from the street.

The long hallway brings us to the kitchen, where some tenants agree to speak before the camera and where we can see the degraded state of the ceiling and walls awaiting repair and painting. Contrasting former and present inhabitants of kommunalki, *The Communal Capital* interviewed celebrities: famous actors, musicians, and writers who lived in a kommunalka during their childhood and youth. These celebrities, accompanied by the film crew, were brought to the apartment to meet their former coresidents, many of whom they hadn't seen in decades. Sometimes the celebrities found that the communal apartments of their childhood had been privatized and rebuilt. In such cases the new owners often allowed the guest to enter and see if any traces remained of the old lifestyle. Thus, in episode 1 of *The Communal Capital,* satirist Semen Altov finds that in the fifty years since he abandoned his old kommunalka, there have been no fundamental changes in his former place of residence. In one episode Altov even meets his former coresident onscreen.

Big communal apartments are often located in the central part of St. Petersburg, where the buildings often have great architectural value. Commentators often hark back to 1917 and identify the prerevolutionary owners of the building onscreen. Whenever possible, descendants of the original owners who are still living there in one of the rooms are shown along with their carefully conserved pieces of furniture, mementos, and portraits of their ancestors. Like others who are also not inclined to abandon their rooms in an apartment located in the historical city center, they feel an attachment to the place. The authors of the series show great compassion to the descendants of the former owners because of their reduced circumstances and their loyalty to their space. Despite the many problems associated with the kommunalki, many prefer to live in the heart of the city.

The television camera lingers on shabby stairways and unpainted corridors, in contrast to the bright and cozy interiors of private rooms. The footage implies that while tenants maintain the areas within their personal space responsibly, they are unable to effect improvement in the general premises, eliminate vermin and odors, and fix broken floors and columns. As *The Communal Capital* testifies, these conditions are found in building located at the very center of the city, adjacent to the grand and imposing Palace Square.

Docudrama-style reenactments of daily life within the communal apartments have certain ideological characteristics and narrate a particular vision of class struggle relating to the presence or absence of private property. The origin of disorder and dirt within these grand buildings is directly related to the appearance of victorious proletarians and communists who lacked culture, disregarded norms of "civilized" behavior, and penetrated the clean world of bourgeois apartments, bringing with them filth, violence, and destruction. The camera reveals that when private property was abolished, formerly clean entrance halls and stairways became ugly, and the walls were dirty and disfigured.

The invasion of "proletarian boorishness" into the everyday routines of the aristocracy and intelligentsia also led to unpleasant relations with coresidents. Social relations within the kommunalka have become a popular subject in the media, and the metaphoric value of communal apartments as a topic of discussion is based partly on the image of the continuous tension and provocations that emerge among people of different social classes who are forced to live together. Acute differences between coresidents have persisted into post-Soviet time, and there are few ways available to resolve tense situations. *The Communal Capital* tells the story of two residents, an air force officer and an elderly woman, who quarreled for almost twenty years. They complained about each other to the police and even submitted statements to the court. The elderly woman collected proofs to substantiate her claims in court by secretly recording her clashes with her coresident.

This is similar to another remarkable case covered by the Russian media in 2005, when residents collected evidence against each other by means of a webcam installed in the kitchen. A British newspaper also ran the story: "Puzzled by the disappearance of more than 10 lb of pork chops worth 1,075 rubles (£22.50) from their part of the fridge, a young couple, Andrei and Maria Osipov, rigged up a web camera before they left town for a few days. [Mr.] Fefelkin [the thief] later claimed to the police that he had drunkenly mistaken the couple's pork chops for his own. But the footage showed him carefully wiping his fingerprints off the fridge door with a towel. He was convicted of theft and sentenced to a year's community service."[10]

What is remarkable is the fact that surveillance by camera was being used to regulate relations between residents inside a communal apartment. In a small kommunalka where there are two or three households, the tensions between families often become more acute and dangerous than between families in big apartments. This kind of small kommunalka emerged out of the city center when a considerable number of the post-Khrushchevian three- and four-room separate apartments at times were shared by families that were unrelated by kinship ties and that had moved from bigger kommunalki or from barracks.

Human beings became aggressive and quarrelsome when squeezed into cramped premises. Heavy drinking and drug abuse also contributed to the ongoing violence often exacerbated by the peculiar habits of the residents. Thus, in episode 2 of *The Communal Capital*, Olympic champion in artistic skiing Evgenii Plushchenko, who came to St. Petersburg with his mother in the 1990s, revealed that he used to tie thread across the door of his room in order to verify if someone had entered it during their absence. The woman from whom they rented the room lived in the same apartment. She had another key made and would secretly make use of it in order to inspect their humble belongings.

The fact that relationships with coresidents were an unavoidable aspect of everyday life in communal apartments was sometimes exploited by real estate agents in their quest for privatization. The agents often arranged for one room in the apartment to be sold to a person who harassed coresidents who were unwilling to move out. The persecution continued until residents were ready to accept the terms of relocation.

In the early twenty-first century, foreigners who wished to see the everyday life of people living in kommunalki were offered guided tours. These were similar to tours available in Chinese cities and Brazilian favelas. The authors of *The Communal Capital* represent the guide not as a cross-cultural translator but rather as a repulsive character who makes his money out of the misery of his compatriots, putting on display something that should have been kept out of sight of foreigners. These tours, in the closing words of the episode, "denigrate human dignity and spoil the image of our country in the eyes of foreigners." Communal apartments are "an ugly legacy of the Soviet system," but at the same time they also represent a

Soviet motherland, a repository of nostalgic memories. The kommunalka was considered ugly in the Soviet period, but as a survival of socialism, it has become even uglier. The media refuse to recognize that communal apartments still exist and are a substantial aspect of post-Soviet reality, even if their functions are considerably different.

TOWARD A REDEFINITION OF THE KOMMUNALKA

Let us consider some examples that will help us formulate what is new about communal life in St. Petersburg in the early twenty-first century.

An announcement that was posted on a wall in the kitchen of a big communal apartment in one of the central districts of St. Petersburg in 2010 is illustrative of the new motives and attitudes of residents of communal apartments. However, the emotions it depicts, the topics that it addresses, and the style of writing are still quite traditional. Translated by Slava Paperno, it reads: "[Printed:] If the green scoop is not retuned where it belongs by Wednesday, please, I will report you to the police. [Handwritten:] And also the red spray bottle. Otherwise I'll file a report with the immigration services as well."

To understand this message, we need to know who are the senders and who is the addressee. Thus, contrary to what one might think, the author of the second, handwritten part of the message is not the same as the author of the printed part. These two tenants are indignant and are threatening to take active measures against the same unnamed addressee. As the threats reveal, the addressee's status in the apartment is highly vulnerable. The police would normally not intervene over the theft of a green scoop, nor would immigration services be involved over a disputed spray bottle, but there is something more dangerous that could make these authorities interfere.

In this rather typical case, one of the rooms was sold by the tenants who became owners after privatization. The new owner didn't buy it for himself but used it as an investment. He partitioned his spacious room into several small cubicles and rented them to migrants from Moldova who came to St. Petersburg to make a living as construction workers. In the room where one person used to live quite comfortably, now there are five residents. The landlord, who does not live in the apartment himself, did not receive permission from the other tenants before renting the room to subtenants. Had the landlord been a tenant renting the room from the state in the Soviet era, before letting anybody live in his room he would have been obliged to obtain formal permission from all the other tenants of the apartment. However, as an owner, he was formally within his rights to dispose of his property as he saw fit. Moreover, the landlord could place up to fifteen migrant workers in a crowded room and disregard official sanitary norms within the limits of his private property. Nevertheless, the tenants went to court, claiming that the partitions were installed illegally and should be removed. Although the court supported the coresidents' claims, the defendant refused to obey the court decision.

The landlord also committed other violations of the legal norms. First, he did not conclude a formal agreement of rent with his tenants, nor did he pay taxes from the income that he was receiving. It is hard to estimate the market volume of communal rooms in St. Petersburg, but it is a considerable figure. In almost every apartment there are residents renting from owners or subletting from permanent residents. Practically all these activities continue, as they did in the past, in an economic gray zone outside of state fiscal surveillance. Second, the room owner most probably did not register the Moldovans as officially living at this address. Those migrants who have do not have legal papers avoid meetings with authorities, as each encounter leads to the extraction of bribes and other payments.

Hence, for the migrant workers the threat of calling the police is very real. The reference to immigration services is probably a joke that underlines the illegal status of the residents. This text shows that the new category of residents in St. Petersburg kommunalki are temporary, underprivileged, and illegal migrants who are barely tolerated by other residents. One of the problems in this situation is how to involve the new residents in the internal economy of the apartments, for instance, assigning them cleaning duties and other responsibilities. Trusting someone to help with the cleaning also grants them certain rights.

Another interesting document has to do with apartment cleaning, which is supposed to be performed in turn by the residents. In other publications I have analyzed the cleaning duties and the rules and instructions invented by the tenants and placed in the public space of the apartment. These rules, while regulating the use of shared facilities such as the washroom and the kitchen, were also tools of ranking that updated the hierarchy in the apartment, regulated relations among coresidents, and prevented abuse. The rules implied a definite unnamed addressee: a person who was regarded as a potential transgressor. The rules that we quote below differ stylistically:

Those on duty for apartment cleaning should
- mop with a wet rag the kitchen, washroom, and lavatory floors
- scour the sinks in the kitchen, the washroom, and the lavatory
- scour the toilet
- wash the shower (the shower itself) and the walls and remove hairs from the strainer
- wipe clean the stove and all the surfaces in the kitchen
- wash the rug from the hallway in the washing machine in case it needs cleaning
- wipe the walls in the shower and the lavatory[11]

This text could have appeared in a students' residence, issued by the administration. The list of requirements is quite impersonal and purely pragmatic, aimed at preserving cleanliness in the apartment. There are no traces of the author's wish to make the text play a role in coresidents' relations. In this case, the apartment is smaller, but it is also populated mostly by temporary residents renting from absentee owners.

Generally, in today's communal apartments there is more privacy than was customary in Soviet times. Since most tenants have mobile phones, the common landline telephone is rarely used. High-speed Internet connection is available in most apartments in St. Petersburg, and so communication with the outside world and media consumption are no longer linked with the public space of the apartment. At the same time, the living standard of some residents allows them to eat outside, and even if they cook, they might prefer to do it in a microwave oven inside their rooms. This means that the kitchen is no longer necessarily the center of activities in the apartment: people dedicate less time to cooking in the common kitchen and do not need to visit it often, especially if they are unwilling to socialize. We noticed the beginning of the process of privatization of everyday life in kommunalki during the years of perestroika in the 1980s, when trash removal became a private affair of a household, and common trash buckets were rarely used.

In the last few years municipal rent payments have been increased to cover all the expenses of service providers in apartments. Payments have remained subsidized only for a small part of the population. Although the quality of services has not improved significantly, housing administrations have discovered that a large share of tenants do not pay their bills on time—if they pay at all. Most of them are not the owners but hold a "social rent agreement," which is reserved for less privileged groups. This creates additional tension. Although the legislation allows evictions for nonpayment of rent, residents do not take these threats seriously, because eviction and relocation are rarely used. Housing administrations have resorted to desperate measures to get the debts paid. They offer delinquent residents an opportunity to work with the janitors to discharge their debts through service. Some housing authorities publish the names of debtors along with the sums owed on the entrance door in an attempt to induce shame through public condemnation.

To expose debtors to shame is in fact to treat all the residents of a building as the residents of a single communal apartment, as if to say: "Look, these people are freeloaders for whom you pay from your pocket, and if something is wrong with cleaning or repairs, it is because of their delinquency." This reminds me of the monthly payment calculation tables for electricity expenditure that were issued and displayed on the kitchen wall in the big kommunalka with the names of those who had paid removed from the list.

These measures proved to be less than efficient, but the idea that the residents of a house can be treated as a community of coresidents eventually had far-reaching consequences. As the management of housing stock in the city is still largely in the hands of municipalities, residents are reluctant to pay the bills for poor and inadequate services offered by the city and its contractors.

The rapid, free-of-charge privatization of apartments therefore in many ways lies at the heart of the fundamental problems in the Russian Federation's housing sector. Privatization was not accompanied by the creation of an adequate legal framework that was relevant to the new situation, nor was it accompanied by a systematic analysis of the variety of organizational

forms for the management and maintenance of the housing stock.[12] One of
the possible organizational forms of management and maintenance is the
owners' association (in Russian, "tovarishchestvo sobstvennikov zhil'ia")
as an alternative to the zhek.[13] Owners' associations are usually formed in
buildings where a few kommunalki remain. For mixed-ownership houses,
the zhek is the dominant form of management. It excludes residents from
participation and control, except for futile calls to take part in a *subbotnik,* or, as we have seen above, exposing debtors to shame before their
coresidents.[14]

Projecting kommunalka relations on a wider environment leads to a
situation in which neighbors in the same building or, more often, on the
same stairway behave as if they were living together even though they live
in separate apartments.[15] As in the kommunalka, they lack the authority
to regulate their arguments with their neighbors. Thus, the following message placed on the door of an apartment in 2010 was one step in a chain of
incidents and gestures between the residents of two private apartments on
the same stairway. The authors of the message were two female students:

> If you throw down the snow once again on our laundry, which is dried on
> the balcony, and if your dogs again disturb us with their noise and bark-
> ing, or if you let your dogs loose upon us when we come to complain about
> your behavior, we will call the police.
> [Signed:] Your neighbors from below[16]

When two or more persons who know each other decide to rent an
apartment together, this living arrangement does not constitute a kommunalka. There are many small apartments shared by more than two, where
the tenants rent rooms from the owner (or different owners) independently. The landlords usually live elsewhere and only appear to collect the
monthly rent. These are kommunalki. Few of those who own the rooms
live in them, and if they don't wish to rent the rooms, they simply keep the
rooms closed, waiting for an opportunity to sell them. In fact, we often see
closed rooms within communal apartments.

The kommunalki are thus becoming emptier, in spite of the fact that
many people are queuing for rooms. The waiting list for housing moves
slowly: people who received rent-controlled apartments from the city in

2010 had been on the waiting list since the late 1980s. The city government of St. Petersburg has launched a target program to support the privatization of communal apartments, but this is an inefficient program. The decrease in the number of kommunalki is mostly due to the demolition of apartment buildings in good neighborhoods in order to facilitate new construction. Even when the residents of former apartments have been relocated, their living conditions have not improved significantly, as they have been provided with the same amount of living space in a room or an apartment in a remote area of the city that lacks access to employment opportunities.

In conclusion, it is apparent that while more than one household living together in one apartment and sharing the kitchen and toilets still constitutes the basic definition for a communal apartment in the post-Soviet era, it differs substantially from the classic Soviet kommunalka in terms of ownership, living arrangements, profile of the residents, and stability of residential patterns. In today's apartments, unlike those in Soviet times, at least half of all rooms are privately owned. Only those residents who have a special social rent agreement have their monthly payments subsidized by the state. In the contemporary real estate market, affluent people do not live in communal apartments. Moreover, people who rent a room in a kommunalka from its owner do so out of choice and not in response to a bureaucratic command.

In today's apartments residents do not elect a steward to oversee living arrangements, nor do all residents take part in household chores, as some prefer to hire private services for cleaning duties. Many residents who sublet from room owners in communal apartments lack residency permits, and few are registered to live in the apartment. On the other hand, room owners who do have legal registration papers often live elsewhere. As a result, unlike in Soviet times, when most residents of communal apartments were permanent, today at least half of the inhabitants are temporary residents, renting rooms from the owners or from those who have social rent agreements. Coresidents do not share the same premises for years, as they used to. The social and economic nature of the kommunalki has changed substantially in post-Soviet times. As a living unit, the communal apartments were highly regulated during the Soviet era, but in post-Soviet

Russia the kommunalka has become one of the cheapest and most accessible forms of housing and one that partly evades control and surveillance by the state.

NOTES

1. Ilya Utekhin, Alice Nakhimovsky, Slava Paperno, and Nancy Ries, *Communal Living in Russia: A Virtual Museum of Soviet Everyday Life,* http://kommunalka.colgate.edu/index.cfm.

2. Jane Zavisca, "The Political Cost of Property Booms," *Comparative European Politics* 6, no. 3 (September 2008): 365–86.

3. Before privatization, almost half the population lived in kommunalki in the central districts.

4. See http://www.svobodanews.ru/content/transcript/24201246.html, May 26, 2002.

5. The human aspects of *rasselenie* have been investigated in *pereSTROIKA—umBAU einer Wohnung* (pereSTROIKA—reCONSTRUCTION of a flat), a documentary film by Christiane Buechner, 2008.

6. My estimation for 2006 was ten times, so for the last few years the economic crisis has contributed to freezing real estate prices.

7. Odessa, currently in Ukraine but with a mostly Russian-speaking population, was famous for its communal apartments.

8. As I tried to show in my monograph *Ocherki kommunal'nogo byta* (Essays on communal life) (OGI Moscow, 2004), even for a single apartment during Soviet times there was no easy way to say how many people lived there. The number of those who were taken into account in the calculation of payments and expenditures for electricity, gas, telephone, and small repairs is not the same, because the number of officially registered might differ from the number of those who actually lived there, and the status of those who actually lived there might vary. These days, a considerable part of what goes on in communal apartments evades official statistics. The latest existing aggregate data on the number of kommunalki are from 1999; at that time there were officially 746,000 communal apartments in Russia.

9. After the virtual museum of Soviet everyday life was launched, journalists researching this topic tried to contact me and ask for advice, with particular interest in the biggest kommunalka in the city. My knowledge also comes from the producers of NTV Channel, who in late 1998 reported from the apartment that was described by the city housing administration as the largest remaining apartment of that type. Since then, the tenants of that apartment have gotten tired of being celebrities, and they do not let cameras enter anymore.

10. Nick Holdsworth and Colin Freeman, "Caught on Webcam: A Thief—and Grim End of a Soviet Dream," *Telegraph,* November 20, 2005.

11. The Russian original was provided by Sveta Erpyleva, to whom I express my gratitude.

12. Gert Gundersen, *The Housing Sector in the Russian Federation,* Barents Urban Survey 2009, http://www.northernexperiments.net/index.php?/Housing/.

13. The word *zhek* is a Russian acronym for "zhilishchno-ekspluatatsionnaya kontora" (housing management office). It is used to refer to the offices that might actually have a different official name because the name has changed more than once during recent attempts

at reform. The reforms aimed at introducing competition to the highly inefficient communal service sector failed in part because of the fierce opposition of some local authorities and zhek management not wishing to lose their guaranteed source of income. In St. Petersburg on the district level, local authorities even launched a campaign to explain to residents the dangers of abandoning the services of zhek and switching to alternative providers.

14. In the USSR, each year the Saturday (Russian, *subbota*) closest to Vladimir Lenin's birthday on April 22 was designated as a day of voluntary labor. The population had to dedicate part of their holiday to working for free, most often performing cleaning services at their workplace. Currently, the tradition is being renewed so that citizens take part in cleaning work in courtyards and streets, symbolically sharing the responsibility for order and cleanliness.

15. See chapter 11 in Utekhin, *Ocherki kommunal'nogo byta,* for a brief discussion of the phenomenon of projecting kommunalka relations onto a wider environment.

16. The Russian original goes like this: Если вы еще раз скинете снег на наше белье, которое сушится на балконе, и если еще ваши собаки будут нам мешать своим топотом и лаем, и если вы будете пускать на нас своих собак, когда мы приходим жаловаться на ваше поведение, то мы вызовем милицию!!!

PART IV.
MYTH, MEMORY, AND THE HISTORY
OF EVERYDAY LIFE

12

Everyday Stalinism in Transition-Era Film

PETER C. POZEFSKY

In a 1997 roundtable chaired by Liubov Arkus, editor of the film journal *SEANS*, several of Russia's leading critics examined the body of
late Soviet and post-Soviet films on the history of Stalinism. While the
participants expressed a variety of opinions regarding the artistic merits
of individual works, they seemed to agree that most of the films did not
convey an authentic or ethically challenging version of history and expressed the concern that commercial films, which had come to dominate
the post-Soviet film market, lacked the capacity to do so.[1]

Films such as Evgenii Tsimabl's *Zashchitnik Sedov* (Defense Counsel
Sedov, 1988) with a clear, critical view of Stalinist repression were a small
minority that received little attention. More typically, high-profile films
either avoided explicit representations of political violence, distorted it
beyond recognition through the use of the surreal and grotesque, or, most
disconcerting, attenuated its impact and meaning by a generally nostalgic
depiction of the period. In the words of Sergei Dobrotvorskii, a participant
in the *SEANS* roundtable, genre films, "constructed on the basis of mass
mystification and mythology . . . are not only incompatible with historical
truth, they are antithetical to it."[2]

This essay will argue that, to the contrary, transition-era films on the
history of Stalinism taken collectively represent a serious attempt at historical thinking. It will do so by considering a group of ideologically and
artistically diverse films set in the Stalin years, by unpacking the common
devices by which they seek to give history meaning, and by making analo-

gies to the historiography of everyday life, with which the cycle shares a thematic focus. I would argue further that it is the emphasis on everyday life—in which the routines of ordinary people overshadow well-studied events and the decisions of leaders—that has confounded critics who have based their judgments concerning the qualities of individual films on implicit and unexamined comparisons with more traditional and explicitly political forms of historical narrative.

Given the emphasis on everyday life, the reaction by Arkus and her colleagues to the body of films about Stalin is perhaps not so surprising. In the first place, when the history of everyday life was initially applied to the study of totalitarian societies in Western Europe, its complication of national narratives by the relegation of politics to the background and its emphasis on "little people" and history at the local level was the source of controversy. Most visible in this respect was the criticism of the history of everyday life in Nazi Germany in the "Historians' Debate."[3] In the second place, this approach to history was new to Russia in the transition era. I do not mean to suggest that Russian filmmakers were influenced by academic histories of everyday life but rather that a significant number of transition-era films on the history of Stalinism depict analogous subject matter and that our understanding of these films can be enhanced by an appreciation of everyday life as a distinctive subject for historical inquiry. It is in the spirit of analogy that this study of history on film borrows its title from a landmark work in the historiography of Stalinism, Sheila Fitzpatrick's *Everyday Stalinism: Ordinary Life in Extraordinary Times*.

Likewise, the political context in which these films were produced is critical to understanding their significance as forms of ideological expression. In the late 1980s, citizens of Russia and other Soviet Republics rushed to fill in the "white spots" in their country's history. This public conversation about the Soviet past, which lasted well into the 1990s, concentrated largely on the Stalin period. It did so because the years of Stalin's rule were widely perceived as the fulcrum of Soviet history and because their mixed legacy of achievement, terror, and loss continued to generate controversy. Moreover, in spite of its historical content, this discourse was directed at the present as much as the past. The rejection of Stalinism was part of the intellectual arsenal of liberal reformers. Likewise, conservatives put forward laudatory or, more typically, ambivalent views of Stalin that balanced an acknowledgment of "problems" with accomplishments such as victory in World War II and the emergence of the Soviet Union as a global power.[4]

Filmmakers contributed to this discussion in important ways. Over the course of the 1980s and 1990s, they produced many films set in the Stalin period. The group of Stalin films that Arkus and her peers examine in their critical survey is extensive and influential enough to be described as a cycle. While the focus of highly visible films within this cycle on everyday life represents an artistic choice, it too has a sociopolitical context. The emphasis parallels the popular concern with everyday life in transition-era Russia that social scientists have tied to revolutionary change in general and, more specifically, to the material and emotional struggles Russians faced as they attempted to adapt themselves to the collapse of the Soviet Union and destabilizing economic conditions.[5] My analysis of conventions underlying representations of everyday life in this cycle will use examples drawn from a group of well-known transition-era films. They include Aleksei German's *Moi drug Ivan Lapshin* (My friend Ivan Lapshin, 1984), Semen Aranovich's *Ia sluzhil v okhrane Stalina ili opyt v dokumentarnoi myfologii* (I served in Stalin's bodyguard; or, An experiment in documentary mythology, 1989), Andrei Konchalovsky's *The Inner Circle* (1991), Ivan Dykhovichnyi's *Prorva* (Moscow parade, 1992), Nikita Mikhalkov's *Utomlennye solntsem* (Burnt by the sun, 1994), Sergei Livnev's *Serp i molot* (Hammer and sickle, 1994), Pavel Chukhrai's *Vor* (The thief, 1997), and a second film by German, *Khrustalev, mashinu!* (Khrustalev, my car!, 1998).[6]

FRAMING EVERYDAY LIFE: THE OPPOSITION BETWEEN THE ORDINARY AND THE EXTRAORDINARY

One way that directors of films in the transition-era Stalin cycle have called attention to everyday life has been by contrasting it with its opposite, with what I refer to as extraordinary life. If the former includes ordinary people and that which is regular, routine, and repeated in their lives,[7] the latter includes a small elite and singular events of national or international significance. Unexpectedly, even films that focus primarily on the elite highlight this distinction by offering insights on the relationship between those elites and ordinary people. The fact that the distinction between ordinary and extraordinary life rarely advances a core narrative (and, therefore, could be considered an artistically superfluous element of a popular medium that values economy of expression) suggests that explanations for its presence might best be pursued in the realm of ideology.

For example, Nikita Mikhalkov's *Utomlennye solntsem* is a film about extraordinary life. It is set in an elite dacha settlement and portrays its affluent, well-connected inhabitants at rest. In spite of a tragic ending, the tone is generally nostalgic. The fictional hero, Sergei Kotov, a legendary Red Army division commander, Civil War–era hero, and friend of Stalin, is dignified, tall, handsome, and surrounded by a beautiful family. In addition, the film climaxes with an extraordinary event in the arrest of this eminent figure. However, the ordinary and everyday make brief but critical appearances in the film.

In an early scene, a squadron of tanks involved in a large-scale military exercise threatens to trample the cultivated fields adjacent to the compounds of the powerful. Peasants, representatives of ordinary people, appear in the background as they attempt to shield their livelihood from senseless destruction. To this end, they enlist Kotov's help. By impressing a young commander and winning the support of friends in high places, he succeeds in diverting the tanks. While relishing the adulation that comes from defending "the people," he nonetheless confides in his wife that he regrets having stood in the way of the tanks. In spite of his heroic gesture, his loyalties are to the army and not the peasants.

Another of the film's encounters with the everyday involves a nameless truck driver who serves as a double for the hero in that their fates are both connected and shared. Like the peasants' story, the presence of the truck driver's story is somewhat surprising in that it plays no role in the tale of Kotov's demise. Unable to find an address for a delivery to a location not far from the division commander's dacha, he asks passersby for assistance. No one is able or willing to help him. As a result of his clumsily exaggerated gestures and proletarian speech, his repeated failures appear comic. However, in the film's final moments, they turn serious. The truck driver asks directions of the chauffeur of an official limousine. At first he is not aware of the fact that this is the car in which agents of the People's Commissariat for Internal Affairs (NKVD) are ferrying the recently arrested Kotov to Moscow. When it becomes clear to those agents that the truck driver has recognized their prisoner, he is executed on the spot. The viewer is left to imagine Kotov's own death, which is reported in titles at the end of the film.

Aleksei German's *Khrustalev, mashinu!* also focuses on a member of the elite. Like Division Commander Kotov, Dr. Gen. Yuri Klensky is a high-ranking official with a proletarian "double." Fedya Aramyshev is a stoker in a fur shop not far from Klensky's apartment. Like the truck driver of *Utomlennye solntsem*, Aramyshev, as a result of awkward gestures and distinctly working-class speech patterns, appears comic, especially in relation to the tall, dignified protagonist. And, like the truck driver, he plays the role of accidental witness. After inadvertently observing NKVD agents tailing Klensky, he is arrested and sent to a labor camp. Klensky is arrested shortly thereafter.

Years later, at the time of his release from prison, Aramyshev encounters Klensky on a train hundreds of miles from the Moscow neighborhood in which the two once lived and worked. Both have been transformed by the experience of incarceration, yet, in contrast to viewers, they are unaware of the circumstances that unite them. At that meeting, the former doctor general, who has undergone his own ordeal at the hands of the NKVD, watches with bemused indifference as several of his acquaintances, also drifters, beat Aramyshev. They appear to do so for no apparent reason other than the fact that they can get away with it. Aramyshev cries. The blows are arbitrary, the violent outburst is demeaning as well as painful. Most important for our purposes, the encounters of Kotov and Klensky with ordinary people divert attention from a core narrative of the protagonist's demise in a way that highlights two aspects of an interpretation of history: on the one hand, the idea that under Stalin the elite and ordinary people shared a common fate and, on the other, the idea of the elite's indifference to the impact of its conduct upon ordinary people.

THE PROLETARIAN GAZE AS ASPECT OF EVERYDAY LIFE AND POINT OF MEDIATION BETWEEN EVERYDAY AND EXTRAORDINARY LIFE

Through the device of doubling, films in the Stalin cycle that focus on the elite call attention to the connection between the extraordinary and the everyday. Films in the Stalin cycle that focus on ordinary people make this connection in a different but no less significant manner. They place ordinary people in proximity to the elite in ways that sharpen the distinction between everyday life and extraordinary life while making a relationship to extraordinary life a key element of everyday life. This is done by highlighting ordinary people's perceptions of the elite and their interactions with it. Let me discuss these perceptions and interactions as they are depicted in two very different films, Andrei Konchalovsky's *The Inner Circle* and Semen Aranovich's documentary, *Ia sluzhil v okhrane Stalina ili opyt v dokumentarnoi myfologii.*

The Inner Circle is the story of Stalin's projectionist. In contrast to the heroic, larger-than-life Colonel Kotov, Ivan Sanshin is an ordinary person. Raised in a village and then orphaned, this Russian Everyman served as a soldier in the Civil War before working as a projectionist for the NKVD. When the projectionist who shows movies for Stalin's nocturnal entertainments with the Politburo is removed, Sanshin is placed in a position from which he can observe Stalin's "inner circle."

At several points in the film, we observe him observing his exalted employers. From his concealed position inside a projection booth, he ponders the unfathomable gap that separates him from the members of the Politburo, whom he regards as though they were gods. Their habits, manners, and interactions become an obsession. Moreover, this obsession infantilizes him, leaving him unable to think for himself, to make personal decisions on his own, or even to engage in sexual relations with his wife. In a dream sequence, he discusses intimate aspects of his marriage with an avuncular Stalin. Sanshin appears to long for the leader's approval. In another sequence, he watches Stalin reprimand Kliment Yefremovich Voroshilov. Later that day, Sanshin removes Voroshilov's portrait from its privileged position on the wall of his bedroom. Sanshin has internalized the regime. One might view this frame of mind as the symptom of a personal pathology were it not shared with other characters in the film and treated as normal.

While Sanshin's physical proximity to the inner circle is unusual for an ordinary person, his very ordinariness suggests the typicality of his fascination with the leaders. It also adds to the attractiveness of the subject matter from an historical point of view in that it suggests a causal link between looking at the elite and a mode of everyday life. One can imagine

other ordinary people sharing Sanshin's inclinations although lacking
his extraordinary access. They would need to satisfy their own need to
see (and somehow understand) the leaders indirectly through posters,
portraits, photos, and newsreels or directly, but from a distance, at parades
and other staged spectacles.

The proletarian gaze as an element of the cinematic representation
of everyday Stalinism is also apparent in *Ia sluzhil v okhrane Stalina ili
opyt v dokumentarnoi myfologii*. Semen Aranovich's glasnost-era documentary focuses on the filmed recollections of Aleksei Rybin, an agent of
the NKVD who served in Stalin's personal security detail. Like Sanshin,
Rybin is an ordinary person unusual only in his direct access to the inner
circle. In the film he discusses his work in the NKVD, but, more important, he tells stories about the members of the Politburo whose lives he
once observed. A montage of historic photographs supplements his personal narrative. Many if not most of the images that the director employs
in this montage, like the subject matter of Rybin's tales, concern everyday
life, albeit the everyday lives of the extraordinary people who live in the
Kremlin.

Rybin's Stalin is remarkably similar to Sanshin's. As Rybin saw it, Stalin lived simply, eschewed luxury, sang songs, told jokes, looked after his
friends, and liked to take care of himself rather than be served. Taken together, Rybin's anecdotes draw a picture of Stalin as a kind of "regular guy"
or idealized "muzhik." The environment in which Stalin lived and worked
with his inner circle is likewise presented in nostalgic tones. For Rybin, the
present does not measure up to the past. The most frequently repeated of
the photographs from the director's montage is of Stalin's mother ladling
soup from a tureen. The image of this commonplace activity, with no apparent relationship to Rybin's narrative except as an echo of his interest
in the mundane aspects of the leaders' lives, serves to reinforce the link
between Stalinism and the everyday.

As Rybin's personal story of his life inside the inner circle progresses,
the director allows the audience to view more and more of him physically.
In this way, it comes to see evidence of his everyday life as well. At first,
Rybin is invisible. We hear his disembodied voice as we view the historic
photographs supplied by the director. Later we see his eyes, followed by
a face whose most prominent feature is a set of crudely manufactured

gold teeth. Only gradually do we see the rest of his body. He wears a non-descript civilian suit with World War II–era combat ribbons. Then we are shown his bedroom. The camera zooms into the green geometrically patterned wallpaper behind him and the modest furnishings of his small apartment, all recognizable elements of a traditional Soviet lifestyle. Without commentary, the camera zooms in on Rybin's ailing wife. She lies listlessly on the bed in the apartment's single room. The bed is only a few feet away from the desk at which Rybin sits as he narrates his story. This progression of images transforms Rybin from a source illuminating Aranovich's study of Stalin to the director's actual subject.

Following the conclusion of Rybin's personal narrative, we see him at work in a new context in the glasnost-era present in which the movie was filmed. Long retired from the NKVD, he teaches music to children. Accordion in hand, surrounded by young pupils, he translates his personal Stalinism into pedagogy and, through this pedagogy, transmits his ideals to the next generation. Instruction in Russian folk music becomes an opportunity for imparting the traditional virtues that he had absorbed, like Sanshin, by watching the leaders. By this point in the film, it has become evident that the documentary, initially presented to the audience as a history of Stalin from the perspective of an eyewitness, is actually a study of contemporary Stalinism. The context in which Aranovich makes the persistence of Stalinism comprehensible is not so much history (e.g., the narrative of Rybin's work with the NKVD or the insights revealed by his direct observations of Stalin's inner circle) as it is a mode of everyday life in the present (and recognizable in the wallpaper, gold teeth, combat ribbons, material hardship, and traditional music) that both sustains Stalinism as an ideology and makes its presence visible.

The idea of the gaze of the Everyman as a point of mediation between everyday life and extraordinary life is no less important in *Ia sluzhil v okhrane Stalina ili opyt v dokumentarnoi myfologii* than in *The Inner Circle*. Like the image of Stalin's mother serving soup, a shot of Rybin's eyes is repeated many times. As Rybin speaks of his duties as an NKVD agent protecting Stalin from terrorists, we look straight into his eyes. We are led to imagine him looking out for "enemies" in the 1930s or even to imagine him watching us.[8]

This repetition of the image of Rybin's eyes calls attention to the proletarian gaze, while its intimation of the idea of surveillance appears as a trace of Stalinism in the present. Still more important, Rybin's story is the product of this gaze or, more precisely, of his having watched Stalin's entourage from close quarters. Like Sanshin, Rybin is preoccupied by the routines of the members of the Politburo and sees in Stalin's conduct a guide for his own. For example, Stalin's relationship with his close subordinates—or so the film implies—becomes a model for human relations (humble but firm) that Rybin follows in teaching music to young children. It also interferes with his intimate life. Sanshin's obsession renders him impotent. Rybin's wife, as we learn, does not know her husband's real name but has instead lived with his alias. In this context, the proletarian gaze once again mediates between the everyday and the extraordinary. On one side is an ordinary person, on the other, the leaders whose actions help to structure everyday life.

THE SPACE OF EVERYDAY LIFE AND LIFE ON THE PERIPHERY

In a move reminiscent of postmodern tendencies in geography, history, and the social sciences more generally, films in the Stalin cycle also write the history of everyday life by mapping its key spaces. Moreover, while the most visually striking aspect of this effort is the re-creation of the small, self-contained worlds that ordinary people inhabited (including apartments and towns), the directors also use a variety of mapping techniques to situate local stories on a broader field. Textured representations of society at the ground level are contextualized by references to a larger picture in a way that either explains or renders problematic the relationship between everyday life and the larger course of Soviet history. The pairing of extraordinary people with proletarian doubles and the representation of ordinary people viewing the leaders of the Soviet Union represent only two ways in which the films connect the micro and macro.

This connection is drawn spatially in a particularly interesting way in Aleksei German's *Moi drug Ivan Lapshin,* which presents a picture of the early 1930s that in addition to highlighting everyday life rather than extraordinary life illuminates the geographical periphery at the expense of the center.[9] The film is set in the imaginary Unchansk, a small city on the Volga described by the narrator as on the edge of the country. Removed from the leaders, decision making, and wealth of Moscow, Unchansk is by definition a site of everyday life rather than extraordinary life. The film closely examines the lives of its ordinary characters, who are situated in relation to larger developments (developments in the center) in part by the unfocused observations of the narrator, who, speaking in the cinematic present, summons the memory of his father's generation, in part by snippets of dialogue whose oblique references to high politics link the characters to events on the national stage, and in part by photographs of leaders that provide stable historical references.[10] The latter serve as the chronological equivalents of establishing shots in a film that lacks them. Most notable in this regard is an official portrait of Sergei Kirov that hangs in Lapshin's bedroom (another hangs in the interrogation room of the police station). Its position, unframed, crooked, tattered, and posted next to the protagonist's bed, suggests that the portrait is of personal significance, that Lapshin, from Leningrad in the short stories on which the film was based, may have felt a genuine connection to Kirov.[11]

This particular image of Kirov also tells us that the events in the film probably took place when he was still an important leader, before his assassination in 1934. The fact that there is no portrait of Stalin in a bedroom that contains other political images suggests that at this point in time it was still possible to imagine an alternative Soviet future (one with a diminished role for Stalin and, consequently, for terror). This optimism, which Lapshin shares with roommates and colleagues, is presented by German's narrator as a characteristic of a generation that came of age in the Civil War, had not yet experienced the ultimate consequences of Stalinism, and still had access to the myth of Kirov as an alternative to Stalin. The optimism is perhaps best expressed in Lapshin's motto: "We'll clean out the land, plant a garden, and take a stroll together in that garden."[12] In other words, we are living in difficult times. We may be compelled by circumstances to undertake unpleasant or even morally questionable work, but our efforts will serve as the foundation for something better that we will soon experience for ourselves.

The most prominent portrait of Stalin appears only at the very end of the film, as a visual afterthought. It is posted to the front of a tram charging forward in a manner that figuratively repudiates Lapshin's vision for the future by restoring Stalin to the center stage of history. It is meant to make it clear to the film's intended audience of Soviet citizens in the early

1980s that the optimism of their fathers and grandfathers was misplaced. Lapshin would not live to stroll in his garden. Nonetheless, the rich depiction of Lapshin's idealism and his attempts to construct a satisfying private life in dire circumstances makes it clear that even as his life was constrained by its material and political contexts, it was not fully determined by them. German's history of everyday life on film achieves what some historians have seen as a crucial objective of the history of everyday life: it challenges historical narratives constructed on a larger scale by considering phenomena so small as to be outside their purview and using them to address the question of the boundaries between the public and private or, as historian Natalia Pushkareva, describes it, the question of how "individual intention [is] inscribed in a system of collective compulsion."[13]

TOPOI OF EVERYDAY LIFE

In other films in the Stalin cycle, the topoi of everyday Stalinism are defined not so much by a political geography that calls attention to distance from (or proximity to) political power but by mapping the actual sites of everyday life and by contrasting those sites with spaces on their perimeter. More precisely, the sites of everyday life can be viewed as part of a spatial continuum. As defined by Pushkareva in her remarks at the conference on which this collection of papers is based, "Everyday life is outside work and outside holidays but somehow exists in between."[14]

Let's examine this continuum beginning with the spaces of work and leisure that, in Pushkareva's view, may not be part of everyday life but nonetheless frame it. In some sense, the protagonists of the films within the Stalin cycle are defined by their occupations. We watch Sanshin the projectionist show movies in the Kremlin. In an early scene he exhibits his extraordinary skills working with the machinery, changing reels with his eyes averted. Later he impresses Stalin himself by taking apart a Soviet-made projector while explaining the strengths and weaknesses of its key components. In an important work-related scene from *Moi drug Ivan Lapshin*, Lapshin interrogates a murder suspect, and, in another, he hunts down a group of bandits in a village on the outskirts of Unchansk. Lapshin at work impresses with his selflessness and physical courage but also with a thoughtless display of brutality. Although he is a member of the militia who pursues the criminal element rather than political criminals, his violent conduct calls to mind NKVD operations of the same period. In a similar fashion, other protagonists in the Stalin cycle attend to their work, Gen. Yuri Klensky supervises his Kremlin clinic, and Tolyan of *Vor* commits robberies. Their social status and identity are to a certain degree a function of their occupation.

Still, within the context of the Stalin cycle, work is secondary. Most important, work occupies a narrow band of time and space and is depicted as alienating. Sanshin's life is destroyed by his work. Lapshin's heroism is diminished by brutality. Klensky is stalked by the NKVD in his own clinic. The workplace is almost always rigidly hierarchical and tainted by menace. Someone is invariably about to be ridiculed, chided, or punished. And given the importance of certain forms of work within the ideology of the workers' state, it is significant that work is not represented as meaningful or productive. The historically most significant forms of everyday work, industrial and agricultural labor, are deemphasized within the context of the cinematic memory of the period. An exception here is Sergei Livnev's *Serp i molot*, in which the main character, Evdokim, is a Stakhanovite construction worker and his wife a champion tractor driver. However, the film is the exception that proves the rule in that this heroic depiction of labor is distinctly ironic. Its value is deconstructed, mocked, and derided.

Another key topos in the Stalin cycle is the parade ground, which represents leisure but also public life. Like work, it stands on the boundary of the communal apartment, which is the key space of everyday life. Both *The Inner Circle* and Ivan Dykhovichnyi's *Prorva* begin with documentary footage of Stalin-era parades that is spliced into footage of actors on a set shot in the transition era. The narrative of *Moi drug Ivan Lapshin* is punctuated by brass bands in place of parades. The bands play a smaller but noticeable role in making public spaces festive in the same director's *Khrustalev, mashinu! Utomlennye solntsem* takes place amidst preparations for a festival celebrating Stalin's balloonists. What is it that happens in these festivities to which films in the Stalin cycle call attention? In the spectacle of the parade, the state demonstrates its power through its capacity to mobilize and organize the population. This is best illustrated in the synchronized movements of huge columns of soldiers, athletes, and musicians that all end in a ritualized adoration of the regime. The cinematic representation of public (urban) spaces such as the Moscow subway or skyscrapers in the Moscow skyline or VDNKh (Exhibition of the Achievement of the National Economy) or a central square set for a spectacular event such as Stalin's funeral may stand in for the parade ground, calling attention in somewhat different ways to the regime's attempts to reinvent the forms of life and its desire to create an impression of its transformative power.

Perhaps the most interesting visual representations of public space in the 1930s appear in *Prorva,* a film about the elite in which the everyday life of ordinary people appears in the background. In contrast to the gritty, realist images of urban life found in other transition-era films set in Stalin-era cities, the Moscow of *Prorva* is filled with splendid public architecture. Good-humored, elegantly attired passersby stride through the well-manicured parks and gilded fountains of downtown Moscow. Here, nostalgic memories of the Soviet Union under Stalin appear as a glittering reality whose imperial splendor is based in part on the actual forms of Stalinist architecture, in part upon the regime's aspirations, in part upon a fictional glamour derived from an odd hybrid of Hollywood's golden age grafted onto Soviet memory, and in part upon archetypal memories of a happy youth. The town square in Lapshin's Unchansk with its new archway is also the site of happy memories, but, in contrast to *Prorva,* one in which the warm feelings and nostalgia are the product of a memory of noble aspirations rather than an idealization of the built environment.

The newly constructed archway abutting Unchansk's central square and the square itself are in reality quite homely, but, as the narrator of *Moi drug Ivan Lapshin* remarks in the opening lines of the movie, Lapshin and his friends celebrate it nonetheless. They understand that they must make do with what they have. Here the effect is the inverse of that in *Prorva.* Warm feelings are associated not with grandeur but with the heroic ways in which ordinary people cope with difficult circumstances. What is impressive to the film's narrator in the present day is not the memory of a glorious epoch but the memory of the optimism of a generation that struggled as well as the utopian ideals embodied in the attempts to transform public space.[15]

However, public spaces, like working spaces, do not typically serve as the centerpieces of films in the Stalin cycle. Instead, public space provides a backdrop for scenes set within living spaces that explore everyday life or, more specifically, the impact of the regime on private life. Just as everyday life is defined in relation to extraordinary life, the favored site of everyday Stalinism on film, the communal apartment, is defined in part in opposition to work and public spaces such as the parade ground. Personal and family dramas unfold on a small, human scale inside communal apartments. How do the representations of parades and public space more generally provide part of the context for this examination? In the first place, they provide a contrast—the contrast between the grandeur of public life (or, in *Moi drug Ivan Lapshin,* the grandeur to which it aspired) and the poverty evident in the living spaces of ordinary people. In the second place, the contrast between the orderly parade or the monumental architectural ensemble and the disordered social life of the communal apartment suggests that in spite of the regime's pretensions, private life could not be manipulated as easily or effectively as it imagined.

More precisely, in contrast to the one-dimensional public life represented on the parade ground, social life inside the communal apartment is complex. Spatially, the cinematic representation of the Stalin-era communal apartment has three layers. There is the outer layer, the layer of the common spaces in which several families interact and in which moments of social solidarity alternate with moments of tension, conflict, and schism. Like the parade ground outside, this outer layer is the site of social rituals, most notably the festive dinner among neighbors, a key trope in the Stalin cycle. Through the sharing of toasts, songs, jokes, and food, members of the collective enact an ideal of communal solidarity and publicly commit themselves to the official values of the world outside.

The next layer is composed of bedrooms in which the life of individual families unfolds. These families are at times unified by the harshness of the world outside the bedroom door just as at other times they are divided by the tensions it exerts. These tensions are intensified by the differing ideas of individual family members about how to respond to them. And finally, there is the layer of the individual, which, because it has no well-defined space of its own, is more difficult to describe. It can unfold anywhere in which the resident of a communal apartment enjoys a rare moment of privacy. It may even occur behind the locked door of a toilet or in another empty communal space. In spite of crowds outside and crowdedness inside, in spite of the fictions of communal solidarity and moments of genuine intimacy with family and friends, the film hero has a rich and active inner life and typically suffers alone. Tensions on all three levels (common spaces, family spaces, private spaces) belie the false unanimity of the parade ground and the fragility of the communal solidarity toasted at festive meals. The public crowds the private but does not stifle it.

SOCIAL RELATIONS, SOCIAL PRACTICES, AND EVERYDAY LIFE

In "Energizing the Everyday," historians Alf Lüdtke and Sheila Fitzpatrick examine social relations under totalitarian regimes. In opposition to Hannah Arendt's hypothesis that "totalitarian domination" atomizes society, they argue that its impact is more complex. Yes, the regime breaks down certain relationships, but, notably, it supports others.[16] The question of relationships under totalitarianism is as important in the cinematic depictions of everyday Stalinism as it is for historians of everyday life. Like Fitzpatrick and Lüdtke, the filmmakers complicate the idea of social isolation in oppressive regimes by pointing to the existence of various forms of sociability.

Most of the fiction films in the Stalin cycle are historical melodramas. They look at the lives of their heroes and heroines as they are shaped by historical events. The melodramas emphasize two different types of social relations. Some focus on romance, others on the relations between parents and children.[17] Nonetheless, there is a common metanarrative whose most distinctive feature is that it is highly gendered and that it turns the history of Stalinism into a personal story about social relationships.

The films' central characters are typically male. (This is unusual in that within the genre of melodrama, male-oriented plots are the exception rather than the rule.) The focus, moreover, is on fathers and heterosexual male lovers, who, within the melodramatic narrative, are crushed by Stalinism. Consequently, the impact of the regime on society is personalized and figured metaphorically as the destruction of masculinity. In the romances, as analyzed by Susan Larsen, this takes a particularly misogynistic form. Protagonist males are destroyed by hypermasculine, sexually voracious women, who personify the qualities of a predatory regime.[18] The family melodramas feature a different kind of stereotypic woman, highly feminine, good, but passive, innocent of any association with the regime. Moreover, as in the melodramatic romances, the female

roles are secondary. Mothers are overshadowed by fathers (or father sur-
rogates such as stepfathers), who are themselves destroyed because Stalin,
the father of all nations, tolerates no rivals to his paternalized authority.
In the family melodramas, there is a contemporary frame. Grown-up children in the transition-era present come to understand the tragic nature
of childhood under Stalin, but by then it is too late. The damage to their
own lives and the larger society has already been done. The clock cannot
be turned backward.[19]

Thus, the focus of films in the Stalin cycle is on relations between parents and children or between lovers and the ways that those relations are
warped or destroyed by the regime. However, significant if secondary
attention is given to the depiction of other types of social relations. Moreover, these secondary relations are conveyed in a more socially realistic
and historically complex light than the primary ones, which are structured to a much higher degree by generic formulas. It is in these relationships, including relationships with neighbors (often fellow residents of a
communal apartment), relationships with coworkers (often outside the
workplace), and a variety of social transactions and interactions in other
environments that we can look for the complexity in social relationships
that Fitzpatrick and Lüdtke pursue in their history of everyday life under
Stalin. Moreover, these relationships, typically represented in highly ambivalent terms, are best examined as they unfold through a small number
of social rituals and in a limited number of social spaces.

The sociability of the communal apartment is one such field of ambivalent relations. In *Vor*, the residents in a communal apartment welcome
Tolyan, the handsome thief disguised as an officer, and his pseudofamily.
Within days, the formerly homeless refugees seem grounded in the apartment's routines and relations. At some level, they have been embraced. At
the same time, Sanya, the young son of Tolyan's fictive wife, is hounded as
an outsider by neighborhood children, and his difficulty adhering to the
norms and routines of communal life, with its informal but strictly enforced rules about lights, toilets, and faucets, discredits the family. Tolyan,
meanwhile, exploits the goodwill of his new neighbors to rob them.

Similarly ambivalent dynamics play a role in the communal apartment
inhabited by Ivan Sanshin and his wife, Anastasia, in *The Inner Circle*.
Some of the neighbors, jealous of the high-ranking Jewish officer Aaron
Gubelmen, with his foreign goods and political connections, denounce

him. An elderly professor hides in his room. He considers all social contact dangerous for an intellectual. A slight, elderly woman, the prerevolutionary owner of the apartment (before it was communalized), is ostracized by its other residents as a result of her bourgeois origins. Still, the collective gathers to celebrate holidays and provides solidarity and warmth, which serve as a kind of counterbalance to political fears and material hardship. For example, Anastasia seeks to adopt Katya Gubelman following her parents' arrest in spite of prohibitions regarding contact with the children of "enemies of the people."

At times, the proximity of everyday life in a communal apartment breeds an intimacy that approaches the familiar. Neighbors support each other in moments of difficulty, while numbers add a festive quality to holiday meals and even to the daily routines of laundry, dishwashing, and mealtime. A common sense of hardship breeds solidarity and compassion. In this sense, the cinematic representation of friendly neighbors in the Stalin years echoes the yearning for forms of social solidarity (real or imagined) projected on the past that are typical of the transition era.[20] However, at other times, the intimacy engendered by this proximity seems inappropriate and demeaning. Inside the collective, there are petty jealousies and rivalries enflamed by the lack of adequate personal space, by material need and a concomitant greed and envy, by efforts to establish hierarchies, and by a political climate in which denunciation offers an opportunity to avenge perceived slights and to make material gains through the acquisition of either a job or a living space made vacant by an arrest.

While officials are nearly always treated as callous and self-serving, interactions with strangers and fellow workers have the ambivalent quality of relations in a communal apartment. Anastasia, the wife of the projectionist protagonist of *The Inner Circle*, finds work at an orphanage for children of class enemies so that she can keep track of her orphaned neighbor, Katya. When her ruse is discovered, her supervisor strikes her viciously in front of the children and her fellow employees. Moments later, the two speak as old friends. Abusive one moment, the boss provides comfort and support the next. At least in private, the expansiveness of the Russian soul trumps fear and respect for a social hierarchy.

The relationship between characters and the regime is also painted in ambivalent tones. Like historians, the directors of films in the Stalin cycle ferret out patterns: they look for and find in everyday people and everyday life willful collaboration, naive or passive complicity, and forms of resistance ranging from simple awareness of official injustice to direct action. Most often the directors find hidden in the conduct of individuals or revealed in the unpacking of social rituals a personal appropriation of Stalinist norms and ideology. These contradictory impulses and inclinations may even be embodied in a single character. Vor's Tolyan is amoral and outside ideology, yet he engages in manipulation and abuse that mirrors that of Stalin, whose image is tattooed on his chest. The police investigator Lapshin's motives are unimpeachable. He is a true believer who wishes to do his part in the establishment of socialism by ridding Unchansk of banditry. He displays extraordinary physical courage in the conduct of his duties, although he is depicted as having nothing to gain. In this sense at least, he is not a careerist. Nonetheless, his use of violence in pursuit of common criminals is shocking and justified by the same utopianism that, at times, justifies its use by the state against supposed enemies. Meanwhile, as mentioned, Anastasia Sanshina, wife of Ivan, ignores the prohibitions against associating with the children of class enemies in favor of her maternal instincts. Ivan himself is something of a child. At times he appears a true believer, at times, an opportunist. At other times, he is simply too frightened to act on humane impulses. Nonetheless, he balks at the idea of denunciations. Ultimately, as a result of bitter experience, he abjures his Stalinist past. Although a figure from extraordinary rather than ordinary life, Colonel Kotov fits within the same pattern of ambivalence and complexity. A believer, complicit in Stalin's Terror, he is also an idealist and patriot. Good and evil are intertwined as characters grapple with their beliefs, needs, and a combination of social and ideological pressures.

CONCLUSIONS: NOSTALGIA AND THE
IDEOLOGY OF EVERYDAY LIFE

As with the representation of social relations, the overall interpretation of the Stalin years conveyed in the Stalin cycle is highly ambivalent. On the one hand, the arc of melodrama is such that by the end of the films in the cycle, the regime has been unmasked and its moral authority called into question. Emerging from childlike innocence, central characters come to understand its dark side. Usually, the protagonists arrive at this understanding too late to save themselves or their loved ones. Terror, hidden as anxiety and violence, intimated but previously invisible, reveals itself for what it is. Kotov is beaten. Anastasia Sanshina is raped. Klensky is sodomized. Evdokim (of *Serp i molot*) is shot.

On the other hand, the films betray a nostalgia for what was supposedly lost in the decades following Stalin's death. Most notable here is regret for the loss of the optimism and sense of purpose that came with a belief in utopia, as well as the feelings of security that resulted from an unquestioning confidence in the social and political order. In spite of the bleak circumstances in which he lives, Lapshin believes that his generation will soon cover the tundra with gardens and orchards and live to enjoy them, a vision shared by Evdokim. Division Commander Kotov believes that his daughter Nadia will live in a world in which children, spared of war and demeaning forms of labor, will have soft, pretty feet forever.

In addition, the films find in the Stalin years a sense of social cohesion that is meant to stand in stark contrast to the unbridled individualism of the transition period. Within the context of this myth, people suffered under Stalin, but at least they suffered together. This comforting feeling of solidarity somehow exists alongside of representations of life in communal apartments that call attention to overcrowding, material deprivation, and the simmering rage that these conditions engendered, representations that also comment on the extreme loneliness of heroes and heroines. The bittersweet attitude of the Stalin cycle is effectively summed up by the critic Victor Demin, who, in a review of *Moi drug Ivan Lapshin*, observes: "These people lived worse than us, but they were better than us."[21] And Anthony Anemone finds in this same film great "sympathy for the characters and their faith in a radiant future," even as the film exposes the crudity of Stalinist politics, art, and morals.[22]

The patina of nostalgia is disturbing in representations of the history of Stalin and Stalinism, as it seems exculpatory, a distraction from criticism of the violence perpetrated by the regime or, at the very least, a devaluing of its human cost. It is the ambivalence in the depiction of the period that has made leading critics such as Arkus of *SEANS* and Daniil Dondurei of *Iskusstvo kino* deeply uncomfortable and to press for screen adaptations

of the morally uncompromising work of writers such as Aleksander Solzhenitsyn and Varlam Shalamov.[23] Moreover, the ambivalence in interpretation of the period within the Stalin cycle is heightened by the focus
on everyday life and the historical perspective that often accompanies it.
As recorded in criticisms leveled against historians of everyday life in the
German Historians' Debate, the emphasis on the everyday has the potential to relegate to the background the decisions of policy makers and the
most violent acts of the regime while bringing attention to the theme of
the suffering of ordinary people. Consequently, the idea of victimization
trumps any notion of individual or collective responsibility. This optic,
which has led some German social historians to reject the idea of the
history of everyday life altogether, is itself heightened by the popularity
within the Stalin cycle of the trope of childhood (associated with innocence and victimization) and by the genre of melodrama, both of which
direct the cinematic examination of Stalinism toward private life and away
from politics.[24]

However, from the vantage point of the present day, it is possible to
see some constructive aspects of the Stalin cycle that were probably not
apparent to Arkus and her fellow panelists when they leveled their criticisms more than a decade ago. Most important, by early 1997, when the
transcript of the critical discussion in *SEANS* appeared, the Stalin cycle
was all but over, with some important exceptions (notably, *Khrustalev, mashinu!*). This is not to say that popular interest in Stalin has disappeared or
that his power as a cultural symbol has in any way diminished. In a recent
article, Daniil Dondurei has argued that, to the contrary, Stalin remains a
national obsession.[25] Nonetheless, criticism of Stalin and Stalinism within
commercial cinema has all but disappeared. The questioning of the epoch
engaged in by the films within the transition-era Stalin cycle may have
been limited, but it was more probing than what came before or after.
Moreover, the research conducted by film scholars and theorists since the
early 1990s on such themes as post-Communist nostalgia and postmodern
retro makes it possible to see how the cycle may have been more successful
in illuminating the question of Stalinism for the public than Arkus and
her peers recognized.

One of the most striking and important conclusions from the literature
on post-Communist nostalgia, as expressed by Maya Nadkarni and Olga

Shevchenko in a comprehensive article on the subject, has been that this nostalgia has many sources and multiple meanings. The term may refer to nostalgia for an epoch, for the idealism of those who lived through it, or for objects and social practices associated with it. Nostalgia need not involve the hallmark of political reaction, the aspiration to resurrect the past. To the contrary, in their opinion, nostalgia more typically arises from an acute awareness of the fact that the gulf between past and present is unbridgeable. Although in some instances nostalgia may provide a foundation for reactionary politics, it is just as likely if not more likely to be a response to an inchoate sense of loss in the present, to be a criticism of the present, or simply to convey regret for the loss of childhood innocence.[26] In short, nostalgia in a film about the Stalin period need not be read as a longing for the return of Stalin and Stalinism.

In an essay on retro in contemporary cinema, Oleg Kovalov speaks of nostalgia in another manner that seems apt for understanding its appearance in contemporary Russian cinema. For Kovalov, nostalgia in retro films is less part of an ideology than it is a rhetorical device. Retro cinema seeks to engage in a dialogue with society about the past and, in doing so, to unsettle prevailing myths, which are often nostalgic. Somewhat paradoxically, although retro is not nostalgic itself, it relies on nostalgia. Kovalov observes: "As if accepting the mass conception of the shape of the past and lulling the viewer to sleep with pretty pictures from his youth, retro thrusts a sharp spike into his consciousness, forcing him to see something that he had never noticed before in the idyllic past."[27] Within retro, nostalgia acts as an anesthetic, an unfortunate but necessary prelude to engagement. It is the familiar, comforting, and, therefore, entertaining dimension of history that prepares an audience mentally to consider history's troubling aspect. That aspect of the past may be introduced into an otherwise nostalgic setting like a "sharp spike," briefly and unexpectedly, within the context of a disturbing scene or incident—such as the moments in which an NKVD agent delivers sharp blows to Kotov's face, in which Lapshin shoots his human quarry in cold blood, or in which Tolyan first uses the appearance of respectability supplied by his false family and stolen uniform to rob his neighbors.

In short, the dissociation of central characters from culpability in the worst of Stalinism creates a space for popular films to discuss the Stalin years seriously with a large audience. Kovalov persuasively argues that cinematic retro's use of nostalgia involves a pragmatic but morally defensible compromise with truth. This compromise accepts the ideological limitations inherent in the forms of commercially driven popular culture in order to convey history with some seriousness to a mass audience.

Moreover, not only do films in the transition-era Stalin cycle attempt to introduce a morally challenging (if limited) history of the Stalin years to the public, but, in their attention to the everyday lives of ordinary people, they also attempt the politically delicate task of including the public in the history of totalitarianism in a manner analogous to that attempted by historians in histories of everyday life. For a combination of aesthetic, political, and economic reasons, films in the Stalin cycle typically avoid direct criticisms of Stalinism. However, it should be noted that just as there is little outright condemnation of Stalinism in most of the films examined here, neither is there exculpation or praise. Moreover, implicit in the transition-era Stalin cycle's layered representations of social spaces, in the complex, ambivalent depiction of social relations and private life, in the balancing of the nostalgic and the horrific, and in the attempts to make symbolic connections between the micro and macro in history is a rejection of the notion of individual conduct as determined entirely by political or material circumstance. In this cinema of everyday life, "little people" are often victimized, but they are not simply victims. Along with the leaders whom they observe or for whom they serve as doubles, they both experience the full import of history and bear some responsibility for its direction. In spite of the distressing equivocations and evasions of individual films, the Stalin cycle's explorations of the everyday offer critical insights into the lives of ordinary people and their place in history.

NOTES

1. Liubov Arkus et al., "Tema," *Seans* 14 (1996), http://seance.ru/n/14/istoriya/tema/.

2. Ibid.

3. For a discussion of this debate, see M. Nolan, "The *Historikerstreit* and Social History," *New German Critique* 44 (Spring–Summer 1988).

4. Stephen F. Cohen, "The Stalin Question since Stalin," in *Rethinking the Soviet Experience: Politics and History since 1917* (New York: Oxford University Press, 1985).

5. Michael Burawoy and Katherine Verdery, introduction to *Uncertain Transition: Ethnographies of Change in the Post-Socialist World* (Lanham, Md.: Rowman and Littlefield,

1999), 2–3; and Olga Shevchenko, *Crisis and the Everyday in Postsocialist Moscow* (Bloomington: Indiana University Press, 2009), 7–8.

6. *The Inner Circle,* produced in Hollywood, is included because it was made by one of Russia's best-known directors and was treated by influential Russian critics as a Russian film.

7. Alf Lüdtke, "Introduction: What Is the History of Everyday Life and Who Are Its Practitioners?," in *The History of Everyday Life: Reconstructing Historical Experiences and Ways of Life* (Princeton, N.J.: Princeton University Press, 1995), 3, 5.

8. Boym, "Stalin's Cinematic Charisma: Between History and Nostalgia," *Slavic Review* 51, no. 3 (1992): 538.

9. Benjamin Rifkin, "The Reinterpretation of History in German's Film *My Friend Ivan Lapshin:* Shifts in Center and Periphery," *Slavic Review* 51, no. 3 (1992). On the significance of this shift to the periphery in the history of everyday life, see Lüdtke, "Introduction," 4–5.

10. On the opposition between center and periphery in *My Friend Ivan Lapshin,* see Rifkin, "The Reinterpretation of History."

11. Iurii German, "Lapshin," in *Sobranie sochineniia v shesti tomakh,* vol. 6 (Leningrad: Khudozhestvennaia literatura, 1975–77).

12. As cited in Rifkin, "The Reinterpretation of History," 441. See also Anthony Anemone, *"Moi Drug Ivan Lapshin/My Friend Ivan Lapshin,"* in *The Cinema of Russia and the Former Soviet Union,* ed. Birgit Beumers (London: Wallflower Press, 2007), 208; François Niney, "L'avenir Radié," *Cahiers du cinéma,* no. 427 (1990).

13. N. L. Pushkareva, "Chastnaia zhizn' i problema povsednevnosti glazami istorika," in *Goroda evropeiskoi rossii kontsa XV—pervoi poloviny XIX veka: Materialy mezhdunarodnoi nauchno-prakticheskoi konferentsii 25–28 aprelia 2002 Goda, Tver—Kashin—Kaliazin,* ed. S. O. Shmidt (Tver, 2002), 50. For the role of individual agency in microhistory, see Giovanni Levi, "On Microhistory," in *New Perspectives on Historical Writing,* ed. Peter Burke (University Park: Pennsylvania State University Press, 1992).

14. Natalia Pushkareva, "'We Don't Talk about Ourselves': Memory of Everyday Things by Women Academics," paper delivered at the conference "Everyday Life in Russia and the Soviet Union," Indiana University, May 2010.

15. Maya Nadkarni and Olga Shevchenko, "The Politics of Nostalgia: A Case for Comparative Analysis of Post-Socialist Practices," *Ab Imperio,* no. 2 (2004): 492–95.

16. Sheila Fitzpatrick and Alf Lüdtke, "Energizing the Everyday: On the Making and Breaking of Social Bonds in Nazism and Stalinism," in *Beyond Totalitarianism: Stalinism and Nazism Compared,* ed. Sheila Fitzpatrick and Michael Geyer (Cambridge: Cambridge University Press, 2009), 267.

17. Susan Larsen, "Melodramatic Masculinity, National Identity, and the Stalinist Past in Postsoviet Cinema," *Studies in 20th Century Literature* 24, no. 1 (2000); Peter Pozefsky, "Childhood and the Representation of the History of Stalinism in Russian Cinema of the Transition," *Studies in Russian and Soviet Cinema* 4, no. 1 (2010).

18. Larsen, "Melodramatic Masculinity," 107–109.

19. Pozefsky, "Childhood."

20. See, for example, David Ransel's research on transition-era Russia as described in his contribution to this volume.

21. As cited in Elena Stishova, "Konets tsitaty," *Iskusstvo kino,* no. 1 (2000), http://www.old.kinoart.ru/2000/1/2.html.

22. Anemone, *"Moi Drug Ivan Lapshin/My Friend Ivan Lapshin,"* 207.

23. For example, Arkus discusses film adaptations of the fiction of outspokenly anti-Stalinist authors such as Aleksandr Solzhenitsyn and Varlam Shalamov as an attractive

alternative to the existing body of Stalin films, an idea first proposed by Daniil Dondurei, editor of *Iskusstvo kino*. See Arkus et al., "Tema."

24. Nolan, "The *Historikerstreit*," 75. Carlo Ginzburg speaks of the reconciliation between the micro and the macro as the greatest challenge facing microhistorians ("Micro History: Two or Three Things I Know about It," *Critical Inquiry* 20, no. 1 [1993]: 24–28).

25. Daniil Dondurei, "Mif o Staline: Tekhnicheskoe vosproizvodstvo," *Iskusstvo kino*, no. 4 (2010), http://kinoart.ru/2010/n4-article3.html.

26. Nadkarni and Shevchenko, "The Politics of Nostalgia."

27. Oleg Kovalov, "S chego nachinaetsia proshloe?," *SEANS* 33–34 (2008), http://seance.ru/n/33-34/crossroad33-34/s-chego-nachinaetsya-proshloe/.

13

Totality Decomposed

Objectalizing Late Socialism in Post-Soviet Biochronicles

SERGUEI OUSHAKINE

> For us art means the creation of new things. This is what determines
> our gravitation toward realism, weightiness [*k vesy*], volume, toward the
> earth. . . . Every organized work—be it a house, a poem or a picture—is a
> thing with a purpose; it is not meant to lead people away from life but to
> help them to organize it. . . . Abandon declarations and refutations as soon
> as possible, make things!
> —El Lissitsky, "Blokada Rossii konchaetsia," 1922

In his short essay "The Stage Set of the Epoch," Boris Eikhenbaum, a Russian formalist, explained the ubiquity of nonfiction literature in early Soviet Russia by suggesting that the material of postrevolutionary daily life (*byt*) was still too one-dimensional to be used as the content for such literary constructions as drama or novel. Its very "topicality" prevented the new order of things from fitting the stylistic and narrative constraints of the plot. To become "plot-able" (*siuzhetosposobnym*), to evolve into a full-fledged narrative, daily life of the present had to undergo a "preliminary literary framing": an internally coherent story (*fabula*) can be achieved through organizing the raw life material according to some *external* logic, be it the logic of time (as in chronicles), biography (as in memoirs), space (as in travelogues), or events (as in reportage, sketch, *ocherk*).[1]

It was hardly surprising, Eikhenbaum noted, that the framework of biographic chronicle provided the most popular literary "container" for emotionally charged bits and pieces of the new life under construction.

The present unfolded not as a combination of purposeful *processes* but as an open-ended portrayal of *people* "constructing their own life" (stroiash-chikh svoiu sud'bu).[2] The object of aesthetic experience in this case was not the formal organization of the material but the material itself.[3]

Since the second half of the 1990s, Russia has been experiencing a simi-lar explosion of the genre of biographic chronicle. In a situation where socialist forms of employment have been abandoned and new narrative conventions have only begun to take shape, memoirs, diaries, and per-sonal correspondence convey a sense of historical materiality through descriptions of details and objects.[4] Literature has been a major source of these "ego-documents," with increasing contributions by feature films and television projects.

Several documentaries made by prominent Russian filmmakers during the last fifteen years suggest that the popularity of biographic chronicles is not a temporary artistic fashion but an expanding tendency. For instance, in 1997 Viktor Kosakovskii finished his *Sreda. 19.07.61* (Wednesday, July 19, 1961, 1997, 93 mins., BB, Docstudios, Roskomkino), in which he set out to film all those people (fifty males and fifty-one females) who were born on the same date (July 19, 1961) and in the same place (Leningrad) as the filmmaker himself. Kosakovskii ultimately managed to locate only seventy individuals, and *Sreda* presents them as a succession of indepen-dent visual fragments (cinegrams), which have their own structures and which could be assembled in multiple ways.[5] Linked narratively only by the birth date of their subjects, these visual sequences did not merge into a coherent biography of the cohort. Yet this cinegrammatic depiction does create a diverse mosaic of the generational environment, highlighting the ambiguity of the title: *sreda* in Russian means not only "Wednesday" but also "milieu, setting, inhabited space."

In a very different way, another important Russian documentarian, Sergei Mirochnichenko (b. 1955), has continued his longitudinal project. For his *Born in the USSR*, every seven years Mirochnichenko interviews and films the same group of people who went to school in 1991, when the Soviet Union was about to collapse, and who are now scattered all over the world. The project is a long-term collaboration with the BBC. To date, three films have been released: *7 Up in the Soviet Union* (1991), *14 Up Born in the USSR* (1998), and *Born in the USSR: 21 Up* (2005).[6]

It is Vitalii Manskii, a prominent Russian documentarian, who has been using the biochronicle format most intensively. His *Chastnye khroniki. Monolog* (Private chronicles: Monologue, 1999, 86 mins.) and *Nasha Rodina* (Gagarin's pioneers, 2005, 100 mins., Vertov Studio) directly and forcefully address the fate of the last Soviet generation. The goal of his other ambitious documentary project, *Russia—the Beginning* (2001), is to record the life of the generation born in the first year of the new millennium. The opening installment presents twenty-six episodes about women giving birth to these children. Filmed in different parts of the country, these stories of beginnings are intended as a panoramic preface to the documentary study of the generation. Like Mirochnichenko's *Born in the USSR,* the project is a version of extended cinematic observation: the crew plans to revisit these children every several years in order to produce in the end a continuous ensemble of disjointed generational narratives.

Still too topical to succumb to a proper literary reframing, these cinegrams of Soviet and post-Soviet experience often present a blend of political clichés and everyday objects, "a Beef Stroganoff of platitudes [*poshlostei*]," as Eisenstein called it.[7] There is, however, a major difference between the fascination with records of "raw life" in Dziga Vertov's *kinopravda* of the 1920s and the documentation of late Soviet and post-Soviet byt in the 1990s. While catching "the crunch of the old bones of everyday existence," the new generation of Russian documentarians openly resists Vertov's appeal to produce an organized "whole." The postcommunist decoding of the Soviet world is not intent upon discovering a new, solid basis underneath the ephemeral superstructure of daily life. Rather, the point of these new Russian documentaries is to demonstrate the absence of any *coherent* Soviet totality by "defocusing" it.[8] What unites the various elements in these retrospective pictures of Soviet life is not its ideology but its calendar.

A change of medium—the shift from Soviet cinema theaters to post-Soviet TV sets—also played a role in this reluctance to commit to a homogenizing plot: the television format had its own narrative and visual requirements. Overall, the change of the medium stimulated more individualizing approaches. Formal experiments with camera work, sound, lighting, and editing became more prominent. Preoccupation with audience (and ratings) also resulted in a noticeable shift toward more human-oriented issues. Such traditional Soviet topics as the history of the working class and the peasantry and detailed documentary studies of major political events have almost disappeared.[9]

Abandoning altogether the monumental style of late Soviet documentary epics, many new documental films reproduced instead the deliberately fragmented structure of the newsreel. Documentary plots are usually divided into a series of relatively independent semantic segments. For instance, in Loznitsa's *Portrait* (2002, 28 mins., St. Petersburg Documentary Film Studio), cinegrams of motionless people replace one another, as if in a slide show. In Kosakovskii's *Sreda,* separate cinegrams have no visual connection either. Kino-things are combined without producing a coherent—or even predictable—whole.

The narrative autonomy of cinegrams is often underscored structurally. Transitions from one to another are not masked but emphasized. The bridging role of fade-ins and fade-outs is radically diminished. Lev Roshal', a film scholar, describes this visual texture of Russian documentaries as "consciously torn."[10] To highlight discontinuity, some post-Soviet documentarians frequently punctuate the film by specially designed transition elements that separate (and link) the chapters of the film. This visual "curtain" (*shtorka*), as Kosakovskii called it, however, is devoid of the informative function that original intertitles performed in silent films.[11] The purpose of this curtain today is not to inform the viewer but to maintain the rhythmic structure of the spectacle. Semantic motion is realized through a series of visual stops.

The structural salience of jump cuts and segment breaks is emphasized further by the visual foregrounding of the object. The television format tends to privilege close-up and medium shots. As a result, the on-screen space is often visually shortened. The background plane and the depiction of the context give place to talking heads and macroshots of things. Late Soviet byt becomes equated with exaggerated detail taken out of its primary web of everyday relations.

In what follows I explore two important visual projects of the late 1990s—Vitaly Manskii's documentary *Chastnye khroniki. Monolog* and Dzhanik Faiziev and Leonid Parfenov's forty-three-episode TV series *Namedni* (Lately, 1997–2004). I intend to show how these filmmakers decompose the visual legacy of monolithic and totalizing late socialism. In these documentaries, the last three decades of the USSR emerge as a "tangible time" (*predmetnoe vremia*), to use Viktor Shklovskii's term.[12] Each project achieves a certain degree of temporal and spatial granularity of the period by breaking late Soviet history into material units of meaningful analytic and everyday experience. Autonomous and usually disconnected, these kino-things of sorts bring with them no coherent story. In fact, through their concreteness, they decontextualize identities and destabilize dominant narratives of socialism while simultaneously producing a grounding effect of mnemonic and historical palpability.

Following the insightful work of André Green, I will refer to this tendency to transform "epistemophilia into an object" as *objectalism*.[13] Objects are called upon to differentiate—to puncture and anchor—periods, processes, or events of the past. However, a constant shift of emphasis from the semantic linkage to physical texture, the perpetual play between indexicality and materiality of these embodiments of the Soviet, provides no final closure but only reveals a ceaseless slide down the signifying chain.[14]

Despite its fascination with the object, objectalism of post-Soviet filmmakers is neither objective nor fetishistic. In a peculiar fashion, it absorbs and transforms earlier forms of object-driven strategies of symbolization. In many respects, post-Soviet objectalization of the recent past is not dissimilar to the factographic experiments of Russian avant-garde artists in the 1920s. Both want to move away from the stifling monumentality of old forms of visual narration. Both share the same desire to "render reality visible without interference or mediation."[15] Both envision the object as a primary site of investment and collective experience. However, there is a clear reluctance among post-Soviet documentarians to follow Sergei Tret'iakov's famous suggestion to leave behind the *trials and travails* of the individual "within a system of objects" and explore instead "the object proceeding through the system of people."[16] As I will demonstrate, Tret'iakov's idea of "the biography of the thing" is still alive in post-Soviet Russia. But the suggested move from "comrades to commodities" has been slowed by the persistent questioning of the very premise about the *systemic* organization of people and objects in the Soviet universe.[17]

There is another important predecessor of post-Soviet objectalism. The distancing of Russian documentarians from emotionality and ideological exuberance, their attachment to the concrete and the material, and their tendency to isolate things of the past share the social and aesthetic disillusionment of the Neue Sachlichkeit movement (aka New Objectivity or New Sobriety) in interwar Germany. However, the post-Soviet edition of New Sobriety could not be further removed from the Weimar artists' attempts to respond to a new *"rappel à l'ordre"* with endless classifications and typecasting of the material world. Instead, the material world of everyday socialism is presented as a dazzling cacophony of things, events, and people, as an example of "programmatic instability" of clashing, inverted, and/or superimposed narratives, as a result of "mechanical operations that systematically produce disassociation in space and time," if only cinematically.[18]

In spite of their profound resistance to the narrative closure and continualist perception, objectalizing strategies of representational disjunction have produced an effective compositional structure for their disparate kino-things. The sequencing of autonomous visual objects was arranged chronologically: newsreels have reappeared as biographic chronicles, as a genre of the generational documentary. In an idiosyncratic way, these *biochronicles* combine the post-Soviet fascination with the visual authenticity of life-caught-unawares and the equally powerful striving to find a way to organize disjointed objects of Soviet and post-Soviet life in a plausible constellation. Chroniclers visualize past and current events as a life account of the last Soviet generation and radically dislodge Soviet "kino-epics" and "kino-monuments," with their emphasis on industrial successes and class achievements.

While weak in plot, these postsocialist projects are by no means nonartistic. *Kinopravda* meets here a postmodern "montage of daily life exciters."[19] As I will show, the intricate interweaving of scattered visual elements becomes the main technique that establishes and emphasizes cultural disjunction. Creative audio and visual editing allowed the new generation of Russian filmmakers to reaccess and reconfigure not only the available stock of visual representations of late Soviet life but also the basic assumptions about this life itself.

FIGURE 13.1.

A curtain from *Private Chronicles* (1999)—Leonid Brezhnev and
Mikhail Suslov kissing.

NAMEDNI: FIELD NOTES OF THE ERA

We have made things that still keep us beholden.
We reject the old [order], but we do not disavow it.
— Viktor Shklovskii, "Tetiva," 1970

Given the increasing prominence of television for post-Soviet documentary, it is only logical that a new trend of biochronicles was most vividly manifested by a TV series. In March 1997, NTV channel began broad-
casting a massive project—*Namedni. Nasha Era. 1961–1991* (Lately: Our
Era, 1961–1991)—produced by the film director Dzhanik Faiziev (b. 1961)
and the TV journalist Leonid Parfenov (b. 1960).[20] For several months in
a row, NTV ran weekly a documentary account of a particular calendar
year. In these forty-minute episodes, old Soviet footage of political events,

A curtain from *Namedni* (1997) that segments the narrative without providing
any additional information.

clips from film and animation, and musical videos were interspersed with
comments by post-Soviet experts: two cinema stars (Renata Litvinova
and Tat'iana Drubich), a journalist (Anatolii Streliannyi), a politician
(Egor Gaidar), and a pundit (Sergei Karaganov).

Through his voice-over and on-camera presence, Parfenov, the anchor
and author, lent the series (some) illusion of cinematic consistency. The
creators of the forty-three-episode series billed it as an "encyclopedia of
Soviet life."[21] The slogan with which Parfenov began every episode of the
series summed up the project as a collection of "events, people, and phenomena that have defined a way of life. Without this, it is hard to imagine
us, let alone—to understand."

In the series, Parfenov never explained why he had decided to begin
in 1961. Two other biographical accounts that appeared around the same
time—Manskii's *Chastnye khroniki* and Kosakovskii's *Sreda*—likewise

used 1961 as their point of departure. In a 2005 documentary about his classmates from a provincial secondary school, Manskii came up with the term "Gagarin's pioneers" to describe the generation born around 1961. Gagarin, in fact, figures in the first episode of *Namedni,* but his role is no more significant than that of others. In fact, the collection of kino-things assembled by Parfenov for the first episode suggests that the year was seen as an important watershed that significantly distinguished different historical periods in Soviet history. The year started with the introduction of new ruble bills that would be in circulation for the rest of the Soviet period. Moreover, the year witnessed the Bay of Pigs invasion and the erection of the Berlin Wall. In addition, in 1961 the Communist Party adopted its new program, promising the achievement of fully fledged communism by 1980, and Stalin's body was removed from Lenin's tomb (and buried right next to it). In other words, 1961 marked a significant break with the Stalinist past, a break accompanied by the adoption of new (Communist) goals. A signpost for the new era, the year also became an imaginary starting point for constructing a biographical account of the last generation, whose perceptions, approaches, and dispositions were fundamentally shaped by Soviet reality.

Often credited with discovering a new "postmodernist" way of visualizing history by "fusing the cultural avant-garde with television," as one critic put it, *Namedni,* in fact, was not that original.[22] Indeed, late Soviet documentary actively utilized the format of chronicle for narrating the history of the country. For instance, in 1977 a large group of filmmakers produced a state-sponsored "video cycle," *Nasha biografiia* (Our biography, 1977, Ekran, Moscow), in which sixty episodes covered the sixty-year history of the Soviet state (one year per episode). *Nasha biografiia*—not unlike Faiziev and Parfenov's *Namedni*—combined different genres and media (on-screen commentaries, archival footage, poetry, music, film, and the like) to re-create a sense of historical authenticity. A loyal cultural functionary, Galina Shergova, the artistic director of the cycle, saw the series as a "dialogue with history," as a cinematic way of fleshing out the "fuzzy shadows of memory." Symptomatically, such a dialogue often relied on the objectalization of history: reconstructed props of byt acted as a bridge connecting the present with the graspable past. For example, in the episode about the year 1928, the authors re-created a typical living

room of the time and used it as a literal stage set of the period to interview people who had been active in 1928 and to talk to representatives of
younger generations who were invited to temporarily "inhabit" a (fake)
living space of the past.[23]

The ideological climate of late socialism provided an overarching epic
framework that could easily absorb the everyday and the heroic. Despite
its title, *Nasha biografiia* was construed not as a biographic chronicle of a
specific generation but as a "biography" of the October Revolution: the
series was dedicated to the sixtieth anniversary of the event. Revolutionary pathos and revolutionary teleology, in other words, were used as a form
of emplotment of the byt that had been so elusive in Eikhenbaum's time.

Faiziev and Parfenov's rendition of the era of late socialism completely
erased such traces of teleology, revolutionary or otherwise. From this
point of view, *Namedni*'s synchronic narrative was indeed a cinegrammatic
story of stagnation (*zastoi*), for it documented a period of immobility—
both semantic and social. This abandonment of the purposeful (narrative)
progression activated other dynamics. Syntax drove the semantic motion
of *Namedni*. Ideas unrolled on the screen through the "montage of attractions," a montage of "arbitrarily selected independent . . . effects" aimed at
producing "certain emotional shocks," as Eisenstein put it.[24]

Radical thematic incompatibility of segments became the rule. Thematic shifts were presented as clashes of cinegrams, the length of each
segment varying from thirty seconds to three minutes. The first episode
of the series, for example, included the following array of people, events,
and phenomena (in the order of their appearance on the screen): the introduction of new paper money; the birth of six puppies to Strelka, one
of the two dogs that had been sent into space in 1960; the forceful (and
universal) introduction of corn by Khrushchev; the smashing success of
the science fiction film *Chelovek-amphibiia* (Aqua-Man); Gagarin's flight;
a new hobby—sculptures made from tree roots and branches; stiletto-heel
shoes; the Bay of Pigs invasion; the beginning of the mass construction of
prefabricated panel housing (*khrushchevki*); the decline of operetta, and
its last star, Tat'iana Shmyga; the construction of the Bratsk hydroelectric
power station; the opening of the Palace of Congresses in the Kremlin;
Valerii Brumel's achievements in sport; the Twenty-Second Congress of

FIGURE 13.3.

To avoid visually static footage, Faiziev and Parfenov often split the screen,
running two mirror images at the same time. Delegates of the Twenty-Second
Party Congress listen to Khrushchev's speech.

the Communist Party and its new program; the burial of Stalin's body; the
first publication of the collected works of Il'ia Il'f and Evgenii Petrov; the
black market in currency and the court trial of the hard currency dealer
Ian Rokotov; the first meeting of the nonaligned movement in Belgrade;
the international popularity of the Soviet clown Oleg Popov; Nikita and
Nina Khrushchev's official meeting with John and Jacqueline Kennedy;
the song "Do the Russians Want War?" by Evgenii Evtushenko and Eduard
Kolmanovskii; the Berlin crisis; Leonid Gaidai's comedies and the trio of
slapstick comedians, Vitsin-Nikulin-Morgunov, who starred in them.

The proportion of the political and the everyday would fluctuate from
one episode to another. The 1960s and the 1970s, with their often unexpected combinations of daily routine and political rituals, would be re-

placed in *Namedni* by the predominantly political perestroika years of the 1980s. In the 1990s the visual pendulum of the series shifted again, and new forms of daily life would become the main focus of the project.

Despite the differences in theme and duration, all these stories fit into the structural mold of the chronicle. Entry logs of sorts, these visual and narrative molecules of *Namedni* provided a diverse table of primary elements of late Soviet life; yet none of these episodes presented an in-depth analysis of an event, a personality, or a phenomenon. Objects and people would pop up for a minute or two in the Soviet space of *Namedni* only to disappear forever. None of them determined the other. The transformation of a chronicle into a story was deliberately frustrated: no object was emphasized, no motif was privileged, no diachronic logic was hinted at. The meaning of sequencing did not determine (nor did it derive from) the meaning of cinegrams.[25] Conducting an on-screen inventory of Soviet life, producing a diverse list of its objects seemed to be the ultimate goal. Decomposition of the available visual stock, a persistent assault on any form of narrative linearity was its main method.

On-screen commentaries likewise offered no conclusions. Parfenov and his experts did not redefine history by grafting new judgments onto old visual records. Rather, commentaries and records coexisted in the series without undermining each other. With the same candor Parfenov would read a joke of the period, an official statement from *Pravda* about a series of public protests against the Soviet troops staged in Czechoslovakia in 1969, and a report that the USSR was the world's biggest producer of shoes (three pairs per capita). Commentators, of course, knew that all 155 kilometers of the Berlin Wall would eventually come down, but this knowledge did not influence their story about the original decision. They also knew that the year 1980 would be marked by the Olympic Games in Moscow, not by the beginning of full-fledged communism Khrushchev had promised. This knowledge, however, manifested itself only in a slight change of intonation, tacitly offsetting the excessive enthusiasm of Khrushchev's party program. The synchronic approach to history was realized here as a temporal mimicry: "fuzzy shadows of memory" were used as an invitation to revisit and reconnect with objects of the time, not to restore (or denounce) them.

FIGURE 13.4.

A curtain from *Namedni*. In the still, Leonid Parfenov digitally inhabits
the era (behind Leonid Brezhnev). A mechanical calendar (*right top corner*)
says: "Rotate slowly."

Many reviewers of the first installment of *Namedni* (*1961–1972*) deemed
the project a failure precisely because of Parfenov's decision *not* to provide
a clear-cut message that could guide the audience through the uneasy
process of comprehending "our era." Expecting a completed story with
an obvious message, if not a verdict, these critics found the chronicle too
disorganized, and they dismissed *Namedni* as the vanity show of a TV
star.[26] Some perceived deconstruction as destruction.[27]

Today, more than ten years after the premiere of *Namedni*, this critique
seems utterly misplaced. As the urgency of distancing from the Soviet
past, so characteristic for the mid-1990s, subsided, it becomes more and
more apparent that *Namedni* was neither an "alternative" version of late
Soviet history nor "a search for truth in its multiplicity."[28] Instead, it was
a search for multiplicity itself; an effective attempt to document the polyphonic texture of a society that had been routinely reduced to its most

authoritarian genres. Politically, it was a search for a framework in which the story about the Helsinki Watch group in Moscow would not look alien next to a report about a new version of the Soviet anthem (1977). Culturally, it was the quest for a narrative structure in which the popularity of Il'ia Glazunov's folk-pop paintings could be placed side by side with the overwhelming success of Paul Mauriat's French orchestra and the West German disco group Boney M (1978). Field notes of the era, *Namedni* was preoccupied with the process of inscription that could turn the "flow of action and discourses" into visual elements.[29] Detailed interpretations of these kino-things were left for a different project.

What was important about these decomposing cinegrams of reality, though, was their counterhegemonic effect. By attributing the same historical value to all late Soviet discourses and artifacts, *Namedni* openly questioned the established hierarchy of practices and representations without suggesting a new one. As Parfenov put it in one of his interviews: "All newsmakers are equal."[30]

The setting of Parfenov's on-camera appearance made this point even more obvious. Each episode of the series started and ended with a scene in a library room with the anchor surrounded by cabinets with catalog drawers. Events and discourses of the past, the setting seemed to suggest, were not just equal in their importance (all are catalog cards now), they also all became the property of history.

The same search for multiplicity was realized syntagmatically. The screen was often divided into two or three or four sections, presenting different cinegrams at the same time. As if making a programmatic point about the value of interpretation, in some cases, two identical visual segments would run on the screen simultaneously, with one of them being flipped 180 degrees vertically. Such "radical reversibility" of the footage not only forced the viewer to choose his or her own trajectory of reading but also—and perhaps more importantly—upset the orienting function of the horizon of history itself.[31] History, as this visual metaphor implied, could be easily read in many directions and perceived from many points of view.

Yet *Namedni* was not just a whimsical reconstruction of the late Soviet period but also a dialogue with the past. It was an invitation to achieve an almost tactile, hands-on sense of historical experience, not to learn

FIGURE 13.5.

Documenting multiplicity, 1963. The Twist is the dance of the day in the
USSR. Although officials disapproved of it, the dance is nonetheless
performed everywhere: on a construction site during a lunch break (*top right*),
in a dancing hall (*left*), and during a wedding (*bottom right*).

history's lessons. At times this materiological desire for "raw" objects of
the past was realized in *Namedni* quite literally. Each episode of the series
contained a few segments with Parfenov revisiting the place of the event
described in the story. The coverage of the Berlin crisis ends with Parfenov
in front of the last—memorialized—remains of the Wall. The story about
the U.S. invasion of the Bay of Pigs includes a scene with the anchor walking down the Cuban beach. The account of Khrushchev's speech to the
Twenty-Second Party Congress was accompanied by a segment with Parfenov delivering parts of the speech from the historical podium of the
Palace of Congresses in the Kremlin.

In *Namedni*, Soviet history was not a new stage set built to display the
biography of the Revolution. It was an authentic location that could be
reinhabited—albeit belatedly—in order to convert a heavily ideologized

and clichéd period into one's own era. To highlight his approach, Parfenov often used the same method of objectalizing decomposition: a panoramic view of a large industrial site or a historical location would have a barely noticeable dot far in the background. Then the camera would rapidly zoom in, turning the "dot" into a close-up shot of the anchor. The visual disposition would be reversed: an overwhelming historical location suddenly would acquire a human dimension by becoming Parfenov's own background. The temporal distance between the past and the present would be overcome—at least partially—by shortening space and by radically inverting the perspective.

Remarkably, in this postsocialist attempt to get in touch with events and phenomena that had vanished, Soviet ideology was neither whitewashed nor denounced. But by decomposing the period to its elementary particles, Faiziev and Parfenov convincingly revealed that dreams about non-Soviet or even anti-Soviet enclaves that could be carved out of the Soviet space were just that: dreams. Without ideological signposts, political borders, and cultural boundaries, all these cinegrammatic shards of actually existing socialism—from the Cultural Revolution in China to the Soviet obsession with amber jewelry (1966); from the first Soviet automobile, the Lada, to Angela Davis (1971); from the death of Vladimir Vysotskii to the murder of John Lennon (1980)—became part and parcel of the late Soviet text, with Lennon and Lenin on the same page—or, to be more precise, on the same screen. Archival footage made this coexistence believable; the chronological approach made it graspable.

By decomposing the realm of the Soviet life, *Namedni* significantly reformatted the traditional picture of late socialism. Perhaps the biggest historical achievement of the visual archaeology of the Soviet life undertaken in *Namedni* was one persistently conveyed point. Approaching any information through the human subject (*pokazyvat' "cherez cheloveka"*), Parfenov compellingly demonstrated that late socialism was the period when private life ceased to be a privilege of the Soviet *nomenklatura*.[32] For the first time in the Soviet period, institutional and organizational frameworks such as separate apartments and two-day weekends made private life possible for a large group of people. It was a profoundly Soviet way of life, but it had a degree of privacy that earlier Soviet generations had never experienced.

This poetics of the everyday significantly determines the aesthetic and thematic preferences of the generation born in the early 1960s. Just as World War II became the organizing plot for the Thaw generation, and the chaos of the 1990s is used as a master narrative by people born in the early 1970s, for the generation of Brezhnev's zastoi the intricacies and pit-falls of daily life provided a historical and experiential interface in their dialogue with history and the present. In this respect, the story about new ruble bills chosen by Parfenov to open both the series and the era is highly symbolic. One of the dominant features of late socialism was indeed a chronically frustrated desire to exchange banknotes for consumer goods. These monetary signs of unfulfilled demands would disappear together with the period. Introduced in 1991, new, post-Soviet money would signify the arrival of new regimes of consumption.

The importance of the everyday, however, should not be reduced to consumption only. Weary of the excessive emotional self-exposure of the Thaw's *shestidesiatniki,* the generation of zastoi would also find in the world of material objects an important refuge from the world of inflated ideas. For instance, when showing footage of Gagarin's official walk on the runway of a Moscow airport soon after his space trip, Parfenov did not miss a chance to point out the untied laces on Gagarin's shoe. It is exactly these details of the everyday that would often provide in *Namedni* a precarious counterpoint to the grand Soviet rituals and gestures.

Namedni's decidedly multimedia nature and implicit ironic distanc-ing from the past attracted a serious and loyal audience.[33] After Parfenov converted the TV program into a book format, all three of the *Namedni* volumes published so far not only have become best sellers but also have drawn praise from the traditionally snippy critics.[34] For almost two de-cades Parfenov has remained an author whose pioneering electronic and print projects have been defining the intellectual and aesthetic develop-ment of Russian media. *Namedni*'s model of working with archival evi-dence and historical artifacts had an immense impact on the scope and form of the post-Soviet documentary, too. In short, Faiziev and Parfenov created with *Namedni* a new visual and narrative paradigm. With their cinegrammatic assemblages they consciously broke down the boundar-ies between the private and the political; they intentionally merged high and low cultures; they convincingly reminded their audience about the affective importance of montage; they rejected any attempts to fit their material into a unifying plot; and they deliberately refused to commit themselves to any form of ideological or aesthetic closure. The materiality of the object and grid points of chronology appeared to be the only consistent principles that bound together the otherwise disparate molecules of actually existing socialism.

"BECOMING SOVIET MADE NO SENSE"

[It] looks like a chronicle of events, but it acts like a drama.
—Sergei Eisenstein, "O stroenii veshchei," 1939

Faiziev and Parfenov's playful experimentation with details and fragments of late socialism predictably provoked charges of neo-Soviet nostalgia or, at least, of a revisionist rewriting of recent history.[35] Defending his aesthetic and thematic approach, Parfenov spelled out his position in several interviews. "I had no nostalgia whatsoever," maintained the journalist:

> That epoch had all kinds of things, but overall it was a pretty frightening [strashnaia] period. Under the leadership of the sweet petty bourgeois Brezhnev, the country moved nowhere.... Worse than that, it was an epoch with no initiative. And a lot of people drank themselves to death: their attempts at self-realization failed; and they considered themselves—not without a good reason—a lost generation. Timelessness, the lack of any big ideas, which were still around in Khrushchev's period ... all that had a detrimental impact on several generations. This is what matters most.[36]

The scope and rhythm of Namedni's chronicles and their structural fragmentation made any consistent reading of "our era," if not impossible, then at least nontransparent. A coherent story required a different "preliminary treatment" of visual and textual documents. To go beyond striking visual effects, field notes of the late Soviet period needed a literary framework that would be able to translate the records of the era into a convincing plot: construction had to be turned into a composition.

From this point of view, Manskii's internationally acclaimed Chastnye khroniki was a successful operation of emplotment in which visual shards and slivers of the period were reworked into a developing story. In Chast-

nye khroniki, the "detrimental impact" of the era emphasized by Parfenov took the shape of an extensive obituary for the last and lost Soviet generation. Formally, the transformation of the chronicle into a tale was achieved through the superimposition of three different texts: the amateur footage of the time (the chronicles themselves), the off-screen commentary written in the late 1990s (the "monologue"), and a haunting musical soundtrack composed for the film.

The film was a product of intense collective collaboration: Manskii's authorship of *Chastnye khroniki* is only true in part. Igor Iarkevich (b. 1962), a writer from Moscow, created the witty and ironic life story, and Aleksandr Tsekalo (b. 1961), a popular comedian from Ukraine, lent his voice to this monologue. Aleksei Aigi (b. 1971), a Moscow violinist and the leader of the musical group 4′33, composed a captivating minimalist score. Finally, and most importantly, the visual narrative of the film itself was a meticulous montage of autonomous cinegrams, which were shot between the 1960s and the 1980s by more than a hundred people all over the Soviet Union.

The idea to produce such a film developed gradually. In 1995 Manskii, already known for his interest in archival footage, worked as a producer at Ren-TV, an independent Moscow television station with a national audience. Allegedly, *Chastnye khroniki* started with a film reel that a friend brought to Manskii. The reel contained amateur footage from the 1960s with bits and pieces of somebody else's private life: kids running around, half-dressed adults, parties and drunken guests. Manskii broadcast a brief episode from the reel on Ren-TV, asking those who recognized themselves in the footage to contact him. Shortly after the broadcast, Manskii received about two dozen phone calls from such diverse places as Voronezh, Novokuznetsk, and Vladivostok. All these people claimed that the episode was a part of their own private life. This reaction, improbable as it was, prompted Manskii to organize a campaign called "The Private Life of a Big Country." Through Ren-TV, he asked people to send in their old reels for a newly established archive of amateur footage of the late Soviet period. The campaign met with an enthusiastic response: Manskii received more than five thousand hours of recordings, and for three years Ren-TV broadcast excerpts of this footage under the title *Chastnye khroniki.*[37]

It was precisely this amateur factory of late Soviet facts that provided Manskii with a stock of visual material for his own *Chastnye khroniki.* In 1999 he assembled some facts about the private life of a big country into a single story. Dozens of visual bits and pieces were surgically stitched into a fictitious biochronicle of an "average Soviet man." The protagonist's off-screen voice privatized this visual material, turning a collection of disjointed kino-things into a personal video-album accompanied by the commentaries of its "owner."

The time frame of this biography roughly paralleled the late Soviet period: the protagonist was born in April 1961 and vanished in August 1986. Following each year of the protagonist's life, *Chastnye khroniki* exhibited and explained life under late socialism. Each year had its own episode and consisted of several large "chapters" that unpacked the meaning of major rituals and symbols of Soviet life: the first day at school, meetings of young pioneers, trips to the South, rock-and-roll parties, student summer construction teams, and so on.

The combination of two distinctive forms of narration—silent visual records and an oral life history—produced a significant narrative effect.[38] Structured as a video-chronicle—every year was introduced by and concluded with its own "curtain"—the film, however, had all the qualities of a bildungsroman. Reinforced by the music, the film's monologue meaningfully "clarified" or "dramatized" visual scenes. This bildungsroman had a negative dynamic, though. The monologue transformed the traditional story of personal growth and self-development into an account of the protagonist's gradual disintegration and ultimate collapse.[39]

As a documentary, Manskii's *Chastnye khroniki* was, of course, a fabrication, a masterful montage of a biography that was never lived. Yet the power of the film had little to do with the authenticity of its monologue. As Manskii himself explained in an interview, "the documentarian could be biased, but chronicle is impartial [*bespristrastna*]."[40] Fictitious linkages and commentaries simplified the perception of the footage. But this artful organization of previously disconnected archival materials could not undermine the quality of historical documents of the era. And it was precisely this "raw life"—not the problematic composition of the film—that attracted a lot of interest. In their responses, audiences and critics animatedly described moments of recognition of "daily life exciters" recorded by somebody else's camera.[41] At the same time, very few wanted to identify with the protagonist's monologue. It is perhaps Dmitrii Bykov, a literary critic, who framed this position most tellingly. Reproducing the argument and phrase of Boris Eikhenbaum, Bykov cast the verdict: in *Chastnye khroniki* "the visual story is raped by the text."[42]

This polarized response reflected, in part, a basic Soviet tension between the world of material objects and the world of articulated ideas. There was another important reason, too. Forced to homogenize the visual story, Manskii could no longer rely on the montage of colliding cinegrams. Instead of juxtaposing video segments, Manskii created a semantic dissonance between the visual narrative and the soundtrack. Sometimes the monologue contradicted the footage it was supposed to annotate. Occasionally, it would turn itself into a freestanding manifesto. This counterpointal relationship between image and sound was amplified by a profound affective incongruence: the remarkable impersonality of the visual story radically contrasted with the intimacy emphasized in the monologue. The tone was set in the opening scene: Carried by his mother, the protagonist appeared on the steps of a Soviet maternity ward as a swaddled newborn baby. The protagonist's name was not disclosed, yet the viewer was informed that it was a "standard" Soviet name. The name of the hometown and other "individual" details were not specified either. The protagonist's date of birth ("one day before Gagarin's flight") remained the only personally specific information.

Given the type of footage used in *Chastnye khroniki,* this namelessness of both the protagonist and his environment is understandable. The lack of prominent individual features is, first of all, a consequence of the composite nature of the film. As I have mentioned, most chapters ("a holiday," "a demonstration," "a wedding," "a funeral," "a party," etc.) were created through an elaborate suturing of totally independent cinegrams, originally not connected by space or even time. Yet even with this stitching, many scenes are quite short, lasting several seconds only. The intensity of this rapid visual succession of frames has its own semantic effect: faces change too quickly to leave any meaningful impression. Moreover, many compound chapters present people through long- and medium-length shots. Close-up shots are rare, and depictions of settings tend to dominate the portrayal of people. With a few exceptions, individuals are usually filmed in groups or as a part of a landscape with mountains, lakes, and the like. Creating distance, this representational strategy upsets any stable identification of the viewer with the protagonist (or his parents). The protagonist's progression in age, that is to say, his constant physical changes, impedes any possibility of a consistent visual identity even further. Cinematically, the bildungsroman of *Chastnye khroniki* is a *roman* without a visible hero.

Certainly, such thwarted identification is more than just an unexpected outcome of formal technicalities. In *Namedni,* Parfenov had to produce a cacophony of cinegrams in order to unleash the period's latent polyphony and, simultaneously, to avoid the privileging of any new dominant theme, event, or person. In *Chastnye khroniki,* by forcing his visual, vocal, and musical narratives in a contrapuntal—almost adversarial—interaction, Manskii similarly suppressed the possibility of any lasting identification with the period in order to convey the facelessness of the time. The faceless and nameless protagonist functions in this context as the Jakobsonian shifter: the main purpose of the protagonist's "I" is not to present the speaking subject but instead to identify the context, to switch the flow of discourse from one theme or thing to another.[43]

Significantly, Manskii refrained from presenting the depersonalizing effect of late Soviet collectivity through traditional images of Soviet citizens parading in uniform rows through the country's main squares. Instead, he achieved the same semantic effect by constantly exposing the lack of anything idiosyncratic about Soviet citizens' privacy. People's personal rituals, objects, and spaces were decidedly uniform. Nothing went beyond the limits of the expected. Nobody crossed the boundaries of the predictable. The same semolina porridge (*mannaia kasha*) was fed to every baby around the country. The same film by Andrei Tarkovskii was watched (and discussed) by all the Soviet intelligentsia. Strikingly, *Chastnye khroniki* is a biography of people who failed both to create distinctive lifestyles and to recognize the lack of this distinctiveness.[44] It is a life story of an anonymous Soviet man born to a family of "bright representatives of the gray Soviet intelligentsia," as the off-screen commentary put it.

This visual dissolution of the late Soviet subject was compensated by an expected move toward objectalizing. Instead of a biographical account of a person who "builds his own fate" (as Eikhenbaum would have it), *Chastnye khroniki* becomes the story of a material world in which a fate-building process never occurred. Members of the last Soviet generation did not just dissolve in the air; they dispersed in the material fabric of late Soviet *byt*. While depersonalizing the subject, Manskii objectalized history. Knowingly or unknowingly, the documentarian seemed to follow the suggestion of the Moscow theater director Nikolai Foregger not to reduce the development of the plot to "acting characters" only but also to use "acting things" (*deistvuiushchie veshchi*)—animated as well as nonanimated objects—to convey "the tangibility [*osiazaemost'*] of all collisions."[45] People might be silent in *Chastnye khroniki,* but every object has a story to tell. Rituals themselves might be dreary, but the stories behind them are not. Thus, the wedding of friends of the protagonist's parents is used to remind the audience that it was not only the civil act of marriage that was pointedly and almost universally supported by the pronatalist state. In many cultures, the extraordinariness of an event is usually marked by the extraordinariness of consumption; yet in a country of perennial shortages, this convention was hard to follow without the help of the state. As a result, throughout the country, brides and grooms were officially entitled to some purchasing privileges. Special "Newlywed Salons" were designed to supply betrothed couples with some crucial ritual attributes that were unavailable in regular stores: wedding rings, Czech or Yugoslav shoes, or white shirts, for example. On their wedding day couples could even rent (for four hours) the ultimate sign of late socialist success: a Chaika, the Soviet-made limousine normally reserved for high-level government officials and diplomats. The decision to marry might have been private, the episode seems to suggest, but the actual process of marrying cemented many times (and on many levels) the crucial link between the state and the couple.

Things chronicled in the film are far from being "objects of affection." Eliciting nostalgic sentiments is not their goal; nor are they meant to decode the present or to inspire reflections about the future. Instead, like a good ethnographer, Manskii uses every object for re-creating the polyphonic structure of a world that has vanished. Often, these kino-things collapse metonymy and metaphor. Fragments of daily life lead metonymically to the original whole, but they also point metaphorically toward nonobvious connections and comparisons. For example, a durable lamb coat (*tsigeikovaia shuba*) of the baby-protagonist—its "life expectancy exceeds the life expectancy of its owner," as he remarks—serves in *Chastnye khroniki* as an entry point for a story about Russia's long winters.

The coat also acts as a bridge to a segment that muses on the Russians' famous ability to ignore any confessional or calendar differences in order to merge Christmas and New Year's Eve celebrations into a three-week holiday.[46] Taken together, these objects and events endlessly drawn in time—everlasting coats, everlasting winters, and everlasting holidays— work as a compound symbol for a life in which the passage of time was made irrelevant by the permanence of things. Zastoi as an absence of movement emerged also as a period that erased major distinctions—political, social, sartorial, or even climatic: "The USSR was a country of winter," the monologue concluded.

Covering predominantly the same historical and cultural terrain as Parfenov's *Namedni*, Manskii's *Chastnye khroniki* goes beyond a mere inventory of people and events. While similarly relying on objectalization as its main method of reconfiguring the past, the film also decomposes Soviet totality by documenting its semantic instability. It is a montage film in which everything seems to be connected—however plausibly—with everything else; but everything has at least two meanings here. For instance, a visual segment about a high school drama studio quickly morphs into an oral narrative about late Soviet performance, double game, duplicity, and, finally, a lack of any moral foundation. In a similar fashion, a segment about pioneer camps deconstructs the very notions of separation and protection. The episode starts with a cinegram of children separated from their parents by the camp's tall fence. Within seconds, this story about a "preserve [*zapovednik*] for kids" evolves into a cinegram about the dacha. Also a preserve of sorts, the dacha is described as a "territory of one's own, with no plans and deadlines; with the state left behind the fence."

Theater as a form of life or play, fence as a symbol of containment or freedom—such transmutation of objects and reversals of meaning are typical for *Chastnye khroniki* as a whole. The story of stagnation, the film is also a story about a profound crisis of representation in late Soviet society, a crisis in which ossified rituals, symbols, and taxonomies failed to guarantee semantic stability. As the film demonstrates again and again, by imposing their structure on daily life, these rituals and symbols could successfully distribute people and things throughout Soviet space—either to a construction site in the Far East or to a *subbotnik* nearby. Yet these routines and procedures did not determine the outcome of such distribution. The mandatory attendance at an official November march (*demonstratsiia*) was turned into a dancing party. The compulsory participation at an institutional subbotnik in April would be used as an occasion for collective drinking.

Contrary to the usual picture of late Soviet society, *Chastnye khroniki* demonstrates the surprisingly limited role of politics in private life. As a separate, autonomous sphere, politics (and the official world in general) is almost completely absent in *Chastnye khroniki*. The personal and the political did not oppose each other in the film; in fact, in many cases, these two allegedly distinctive worlds were not even differentiated. For instance, a story about Jewish emigration in the early 1970s is personalized in the film in a segment about the Jewish boyfriend of the protagonist's mother. The news about the boyfriend's decision to leave for Canada, however, is immediately turned into a story about the famous series between Soviet and Canadian ice hockey teams and the role of sport in the USSR in general (the year 1972). While objectalizing history, *Chastnye khroniki* used acting things to proliferate links and connections, not to create a well-organized political taxonomy.

Of course, it would have been naive to expect from amateur filmmakers of the period any extensive coverage of political gatherings, whether party conferences or dissident meetings. Given the relatively high costs of such filmmaking, it is also reasonable to suspect that people filmed situations that they wanted to remember: they filmed events and things that were not that ordinary. And this is, perhaps, the most essential contribution of the film. Without any sentimentality and pity, *Chastnye khroniki* underscores again and again the sobering predictability of supposedly *extraordinary* events and rituals that were voluntarily exposed for the camera. These slices of daily life had almost nothing that could even remotely deviate from the basic canons of Soviet life. As Zara Abdullaeva, a Russian film scholar put it, the film made clear that the long-cherished desire to create a safe distance from the political regime, to maintain a gap between the official and the underground (ofitsioz i podpol'e), was only a "self-gratifying delusion" (samouteshenie).[47] As Chastnye khroniki shows, the last Soviet generation—even when left alone—would still voluntarily mock rituals of baptizing (the year 1978) and regret a missed opportunity to visit Lenin's residence in a town called Gor'kii (1970).

It is not that Chastnye khroniki completely erased social and aesthetic borders between the world of politics and the private world; rather, it reinforced the fact that such standard binaries as "public versus private" and "official versus unofficial" consistently fail to explain in any meaningful way the kind of life that the last Soviet generation actually lived. The official and the unofficial could easily trade places in the Soviet time. With no difficulty, the public could quickly morph into the private, and vice versa. Depending on the context, the same bulky Chaika acted both as a status symbol of the Soviet nomenklatura and as the dream vehicle of Soviet newlyweds. The world of material objects united the official and unofficial spheres in a way that ideological schemes could neither predict nor reflect.

Manskii highlighted this amalgamated state of late Soviet life even further by using "curtains" to introduce a set of visual editorial comments. Each curtain is unique: against a black background, white digits indicate the year (1961, 1962, etc.), while a combination of photos and video provides an indexical link to a significant event of the year. Thematically disconnected from the materials that preceded and followed them, these "curtailed" images create a peculiar mosaic of the period. Political icons are interspersed with celebrities of the time.[48] Snapshots of major political events (the Prague Spring, 1968; the Afghan War, 1982) are followed by excerpts from private video archives. Like in Parfenov's Namedni, late socialism emerges in Chastnye khroniki as a multilayered and multivocal visual text. As both projects vividly suggest, the problem of late socialism was not so much a lack of cultural or intellectual diversity but a radically constrained ability to translate this diversity into a meaningful individualized action.

This plurality discovered post-factum could hardly be attributed to Manskii's romantic nostalgia for things Soviet. Clarifying his own attitude to the protagonist, Manskii explained: "I do not know whether the life of our hero was useless. But I do know that he was prepared for a life that had nothing in common with the life we have now. Imagine an intelligence agent who has been trained to go to China but who ends up in the USA instead. He does not know a word and does not have the slightest idea how to find his way out. Likewise, becoming Soviet [*sovetskaia podgotovka*] made no sense, either."[49]

As the film progresses, the anti-Soviet tenor of its monologue grows stronger.[50] And the internal vacuity of the discourse (and life) rooted in negation becomes more prominent. By the end of the film, scenes of "everlasting drinking" develop into the dominant feature of *Chastnye khroniki* until the viewer is informed that the protagonist drowned in the Black Sea aboard the tourist cruiser *Admiral Nakhimov,* which sank near Novorossiisk in August 1986. Manskii's fictitious last Soviet man disappeared with the period, and his monologue, as it turns out, was a postmortem message of a lost Soviet ghost, faceless and timeless. The last line of this ghost of late socialism, though, was "It seems to me that I am still alive."

Starting in the 1990s, studies of everyday life brought attention to fields and forms of activity that previously remained outside the scope of academic studies. Following the work of Michel de Certeau and Pierre Bourdieu, many scholars have pointed out the autonomizing potential of daily routines and structures. The everyday is often conceptualized, if not as a form of tactical resistance to the pressure of dominant political and cultural forces, then, at least, as a creative way of avoiding such pressure. Manskii's *Chastnye khroniki* provides a different way to conceptualize private life that has not yet become a visible part of this fascination with the mundane. Late Soviet byt reveals here its darker side. Far from being a refuge or a ground for resistance, this byt "stifles life in its tight, hard mold."[51]

In his poignant essay "On a Generation That Squandered Its Poets," Roman Jakobson claimed that it was precisely this "stagnating slime" of byt that had propelled the generation of the Russian Revolution toward radical political and aesthetic gestures. Abjecting the "alien rubbish offered by the established order of things," this generation "strained toward the future," only to realize by the end of the 1920s that it had completely missed its present. Writing on the occasion of Maiakovsky's death, Jakobson drew this sad conclusion: "All we had were compelling songs of the future; and suddenly these songs are no longer part of the dynamic of his-

FIGURE 13.6.

A squandered generation: in one scene of *Chastnye khroniki. Monolog,* the camera focuses on a poster on the wall, cutting the sign in such a way that for several moments the viewer can see above and behind people's heads the word *Sovki,* a derogatory description of those who were born in the Soviet Union. The full sign (*Sovkino,* an abbreviation for "Soviet cinema") will be revealed briefly only much later. A still from *Chastnye khroniki. Monolog.*

tory, but have been transformed into historic-literary facts. When singers have been killed and their songs have been dragged into a museum and pinned to the wall of the past, the generation they represent is even more desolate, orphaned, and lost—impoverished in the most real sense of the word."[52]

Bringing history full circle, *Chastnye khroniki* documented yet another biography of a lost and impoverished generation, a generation that gradually forgot its "songs" and lost the view of its bright future. All it had instead was "the swamp of byt," a set of ossified daily routines that kept the generation busy but that provided little meaning to the life it had squandered.

* * *

It is tempting to see in the two documentaries that I have described here yet another attempt to attach a new "human face" to the deceased body of Soviet socialism. The biochronic format of these projects would certainly make such a reading possible. Yet throughout the article I have been suggesting that these renewed attempts to "humanize" socialism could also be understood as a response to the dominant tendency to perceive late Soviet society as a culture in which cynical double-dealers were dominated by state control. The "discovery" of private life in the USSR undertaken in *Namedni* and *Chastnye khroniki* does not excuse political oppressions or whitewash the ideological constraints of the period. But it does not rely on these practices of domination to turn the raw life of late socialism into a coherent story, either.

Decomposing the visual legacy of socialism, the last Soviet generation of filmmakers pointedly avoids unifying frameworks and overarching conclusions. Their new sobriety tends to privilege the concrete. And their engagement with history leans toward the tangible. Rooted in personally experienced socialism, the objectalism of these chroniclers often takes the shape of a decidedly discordant narrative. Strategies of disjunction and practices of dissonance become their main way of linking incompatible objects and concepts. However, by locating the facts of their chronicles within the biographical account of the generation, post-Soviet documentarians managed to overcome the gap between the document and documentary, between the object and the plot that split apart early generations of Soviet filmmakers. Their final product is not a story. It is not even a proper biography. It is a list of things and events. It is an inventory of objects and people. Yet without their catalogs of these crucial phenomena, it is hard to imagine late Soviet culture now, let alone—understand it.

NOTES

A longer version of this essay was originally published in the *Russian Review* 69, no. 4 (October 2010): 638–69. I thank the *Russian Review* for permission to reproduce an abridged version of the article.

1. Boris Eikhenbaum, "Dekoratsiia epokhi," in his *Moi vremennik* (St. Petersburg, 2001), 129–30.

2. Ibid., 130.

3. Viktor Shklovskii, *Za 60 let: Raboty v kino* (Moscow: Iskusstvo, 1985), 103.

4. This increasing importance of the detail in rendering the unstable meaning of post-Soviet changes is discussed at length in Sergei Alex. Oushakine, "Aesthetics without Law: Cinematic Bandits in Post-Soviet Space," *Slavic and East European Journal* 51, no. 2 (2007): 357–90. On emplotment, see Hayden White, *Metahistory: The Historical Imagination in Nineteenth Century Europe* (Baltimore, Md.: Johns Hopkins University Press, 1973), 7–11. See also Viktor Shklovsky, *The Energy of Delusion: A Book on Plot* (Champaign: University of Illinois Press, 2007), 110–51.

5. For more on the usage of cinegrams, see Bernard Tschumi, *Cinegram Folie: Le Parc de la Villette, Paris, Nineteenth Arrondissement* (Princeton, N.J.: Princeton Architectural Press, 1987), vi.

6. For details on *Born in the USSR,* see Maria Beiker, "Rozhdennye v SSSR: Siuzhet v razvitii," *BBCRussian.com* at http://news.bbc.co.uk/hi/russian/news/newsid_6251000 /6251376.stm.

7. Sergei Eizenshtein, "Zametki kasatel'no teatra," in *Mnemozina: Dokumenty i fakty iz istorii otechestvennogo teatra XX v,* no. 2, ed. V. V. Ivanov (Moscow: GITIS, 2000), 232.

8. Lars von Trier, "Defocus," in *Dogme Uncut: Lars von Trier, Thomas Vinterberg, and the Gang That Took on Hollywood,* by Jack Stevenson (Santa Monica, Calif.: Santa Monica Press, 2003), 86.

9. Mal'kova, "Kinopravda vne 'kommunisticheskoi rashifrovki mira,'" in *Dokumental'noe kino epokhi reformatorstva,* ed. G. Dolmatovskaia and G. Kopalina (Moscow: Materik, 2001), 14.

10. Lev Roshal', "Khlebnyi den' neigrovogo kino," in Dolmatovskaia and Kopalina, *Dokumental'noe kino epokhi reformatorstva,* 88.

11. Viktor Kosakovskii, "Stop. Spasibo. Prozhito," *SEANS* 32 (2008), http://seance.ru /n/32/vertigo32/stop-spasibo-prozhito/.

12. Viktor Shklovskii, "Tetiva: O neskhodstve skhodnogo," in his *Sobranie sochinenii v trekh tomakh* (Moscow: Khudozhestvennaia literatura, 1974), 3:548.

13. André Green, *The Work of the Negative* (London: Free Association Books, 1999), 238.

14. Jacques Lacan, *Écrits: A Selection* (New York: Norton, 1977), 154.

15. Benjamin H. D. Buchloh, "From Faktura to Factography," *October* 30 (1984): 103.

16. Sergei Tret'iakov, "The Biography of the Object," *October* 118 (2006): 62.

17. Ekaterina Degot, "Ot tovara k tovarishchu: K estetike nerynochnogo predmeta," in *Pamiat' tela: Nizhnee bel'e sovetskoi epokhi. Katalog vystavki. 7 noiabria 2000–31 ianvaria 2001* (Moscow: Gosudarstvennyi muzei istorii Sankt-Peterburg, 2000), 8–19.

18. Bernard Tschumi, *Architecture and Disjunction* (Cambridge, Mass.: MIT Press, 1994), 203, 213.

19. See Sergei Eisenstein, "Nabroski k stat'e," in *Eizenshtein: Popytka teatra. Stat'i. Publikatsii,* ed. Vladimir Zabrodin (Moscow: Eĭzenshteĭn-tsentr, 2005), 249.

20. The series was supplemented later by post-Soviet episodes and rebranded as *Namedni. Nasha Era. 1961–2003.* The project is available as a DVD set (eleven discs) published by NTV-Channel in 2004.

21. Newspapers also reported that it was the most expensive documentary project on Russian TV of the time. See, for example, Anton Charkin, "Leonid Parfenov: Ia nikomu ne pytaius' zadurit' golovu," *Novaia gazeta,* April 6, 1998.

22. Boris Kagarlitskii, "Podryvniki i dekonstruktory," *Nezavisimaia gazeta*, July 23, 1998.

23. Galina Shergova, *Ekho slova: Zapiski o zvuchashchei publitsistike* (Moscow: Iskusstvo, 1986), 148.

24. Sergei Eisenstein, *Film Sense* (New York: Harcourt Brace Jovanovich, 1947), 232, 230.

25. Tschumi, *Cinegram Folie*, 12.

26. Oleg Davydov and Igor Zotov, "Zakat Parfenova," *Nezavisimaia gazeta*, June 7, 1997; Anastasia Boichenko, "Obyknovennyi snobizm," *Moskovskii komsomolets*, March 3, 1998.

27. See Mal'kova, "Kinopravda," 15.

28. Shklovsky, *Energy of Delusion*, 178.

29. James Clifford, "Notes on (Field)notes," in *Fieldnotes: The Making of Anthropology*, ed. Roger Sanjek (Ithaca, N.Y.: Cornell University Press, 1990), 51.

30. Charkin, "Leonid Parfenov."

31. Yve-Alain Bois, "El Lissitzky: Radical Reversibility," *Art in America* 36, no. 4 (1988): 188.

32. Leonid Parfenov, "Ia ne rabotaiu s 'kholodnym nosom,'" *Zvezda*, no. 10 (2002); Denis Korsakov, "Leonid Parfenov: Brezhnev byl normal'nym obyvatelem. I liudiam pozvolil stat' takimi," *Komsomol'skaia pravda*, December 12, 2006.

33. *Namedni*'s highest TV ratings were among viewers age fifteen to thirty-nine; the series was the least popular among those who were fifty-five and older (Anna Filimonova, Leonid Parfenov, "Ia—otdel'no," *Moskovskie novosti*, June 19, 2001, 23).

34. Leonid Parfenov, *Namedni*, vol. 1: 1961–1970; vol. 2: 1971–1980; vol. 3: 1981–1990 (Moscow, 2009).

35. For a sophisticated example of this critique, see Kagarlitskii, "Podryvniki i dekonstruktory." See also Aleksandr Vasil'ev, "Nadys' sluchilas' nasha era," *Nezavisimaia gazeta*, March 7, 1997.

36. Korsakov, "Leonid Parfenov," 5.

37. Viktoriia Petrova, "Lichnaia zhizn' sovetskoi obshchestvennosti," *Izvestiia*, October 1, 1999; Andrei Gamalov, "Govorit i pokazyvaet Kreml'," *Profil* 24 (2001).

38. With some rare exceptions, there is almost no original soundtrack in *Chastnye khroniki*.

39. Viktor Matizen, "Nadgrobnyi pamiatnik sovku (1986–1961=25)," *Novye izvestiia*, December 5, 1999.

40. Zara Abdullaeva, "Vitalii Manskii: Drugie mesta pamiati (O ponimanii khroniki i istorii v dokumental'nom kino)," *Novoe literaturnoe obozrenie* 4 (2005): 419.

41. See a collection of critics' responses in *SEANS* 27–28, http://seance.ru/n/27-28/perekrestok/manskiy/chastnyie-hroniki/.

42. Dmitrii Bykov, "Chastnye khroniki. Monolog," *Iskusstvo kino*, no. 11 (1999); Eikhenbaum, "Dekoratsii epokhi," 132.

43. Roman Jakobson, "Shifters, Verbal Categories, and the Russian Verb," in his *Selected Writings*, 7 vols. (1–5, 7–8) (The Hague: Mouton, 1971), 2:131–32.

44. Zara Abdullaeva, *Real'noe kino* (Moscow: Tri Kvadrata, 2003), 264.

45. Nikolai Foregger, "P'esa. Siuzhet. Triuk," in *Mnemozina: Dokumenty i fakty iz istorii russkogo teatra XX veka*, ed. V. V. Ivanov (Moscow: GITIS, 1996), 67.

46. The holiday starts with the "Western" Christmas on December 25, continues through the New Year and the Orthodox Christmas (January 7), and ends on January 13, when the old (Julian) New Year is celebrated.

47. Abdullaeva, "Vitalii Manskii," 428.

48. Gagarin in 1961, Khrushchev in 1962, Kennedy in 1963, Martin Luther King, Jr., in 1967, Mao in 1970, the figure skaters Liudmila Pakhomova and Aleksandr Gorshkov in 1976, pop star Alla Pugacheva in 1983, and Princess Diana in 1984.

49. Matizen, "Real'noe kino."

50. The film was even used as a part of an antinostalgia campaign during the parliamentary elections in December 1999. See Viktor Matizen, "Dokumental'nyi vybor Rossii," *Novye izvestiia*, December 12, 1999.

51. Roman Jakobson, "On a Generation That Squandered Its Poets," in his *Language in Literature* (Cambridge, Mass.: Belknap Press, 1987), 277.

52. Ibid., 300.

14

Everyday Life and the Ties That Bind in Liudmila Ulitskaia's Medea and Her Children

BENJAMIN SUTCLIFFE

"It is a wonderful feeling, belonging to Medea's family, a family so large that you can't know all its members by sight, and they merge into a vista of things that happened, things that didn't, and things that are yet to come."[1] This utopian vision of kinship concludes the novel *Medeia i ee deti* (*Medea and Her Children*, 1996) by the contemporary author Liudmila Ulitskaia. The ending, a favorite for citation by critics, explains the enormous popularity this Booker Prize–winning author has with intellectuals and ordinary readers: such positive reception comes in great part from the connections between family and *byt* (everyday life) uniting her oeuvre. These links reveal everyday life to be a network of small, ethical decisions that together oppose the brutality of the twentieth century. For Ulitskaia, byt is both practical morality and small-scale history, an implicit challenge to the overarching lies of the Soviet state. *Medea and Her Children* portrays the quotidian as heavily influenced by the body (whether erotic or ailing) and family: these factors recall the writing of Iurii Trifonov and women's prose of the perestroika years.[2]

The plot of *Medea and Her Children* is not particularly striking: childless widow Medea lives in the Crimea, and a multitude of relatives visit her every summer. Their changing network of marriages, affairs, and friendships is the background for two intergenerational love triangles that together run from the postwar era to the late 1970s. Such narratives of family spanning the Soviet experience have become the dominant narrative of post-Stalinist writing, especially since 1991, when what Serguei Oushakine terms "rhetoric of kinship" used relations between relatives to describe the recent past. It is likewise no coincidence that the main plot takes place during the Brezhnev era, when byt seemed to stretch off into a limitless horizon of sameness against which family joys and conflicts stood out.[3]

It is Medea herself who makes this novel remarkable. Ulitskaia's work sharply differentiates its protagonist from her original mythological namesake: Medea Mendez (née Sinoply) has no children of her own (but is greatly concerned with others') and uses time and forgiveness to overcome betrayal. Treachery may be either personal or cultural, as the protagonist shows when sheltering Ravil Yusupov, a descendant of the Crimean Tatars deported decades earlier by a vengeful Stalin. She, like Euripides's Medea, is a foreigner. In the novel, however, she acts as an emissary from a culture of humanism, implying that ethics are more important than ethnicity.[4]

This moral hierarchy indicates Medea's abiding belief in the tolerance and contemplation that unite Ulitskaia's positive protagonists. Such abstract virtues are grounded in the link between byt and family that provides the novel its title, plot, and oft-quoted ending. It is the focus on everyday existence as an arena for these values that makes *Medea and Her Children* resemble a genre long lionized by the intelligentsia and common readers: the family chronicle.[5]

Oddly enough, the family chronicle lacks sustained theoretical treatment from Slavists, despite the genre's central place in Russian letters. Robert Stephens, describing kinship and fiction, posits several axioms that can be used to bind *Medea and Her Children* to this type of literature: using multiple generations to describe history; the long-lasting effects of familial conflict; and lineage and doom as inheritance. Examining Ulitskaia's novel, Irina Savkina for her part characterizes the family chronicle as making kinship into a fortress against the hostile forces of history.[6] Indeed, the antagonism between family and history runs through twentieth-century Russian literature and is one of the basic divisions between public and private life. Ulitskaia's contribution to the family chronicle is a profound element of ambivalence that stems from the paradoxical legacy Stephens identifies. Medea's network of kinship (with the childless protagonist at its center) stabilizes its members through everyday interactions, a shared past, and the peculiar rituals of Medea's home. However, the tragic interactions of two sets of characters—including Medea—lead to hurt, estrangement, and the suicide of one relative, suggesting a far less supportive image of the family.[7]

This bifurcated image of kinship as support and tragedy distinguishes *Medea and Her Children* from most previous family chronicles. Predecessors tend to be more polarized, either upholding relatives as a bastion of support (e.g., family ties in Tolstoi's *War and Peace*) or depicting them as a nexus of doom (as in Liudmila Petrushevskaia's grim minichronicle *The Time: Night* [Vremia noch']). Ulitskaia's novel argues that the family and the quotidian it forms may bring either hope or despair.[8]

MEDEA: EVERYDAY LIFE AND THE FAMILIAL

Despite her provocative name, Medea is a creature of the ordinary and unnoticed flow of usual events.[9] During the course of the novel she only leaves the Crimea twice, with both journeys linked to crises that disrupt the twinned constants of daily life and family. Geographical location connotes stability, a pairing whose presence (or absence) informs the family chronicle. Medea supports her relatives and the narrative with domestic ritual, cyclicality, and a sense of the archaic as a part of daily life. Evocation of the past would seem to dislocate the limitless present that is the provenance of byt, yet in the context of the protagonist's life, both elements exist harmoniously. This peace quietly distinguishes itself from the turmoil of the Soviet Union's ideological campaigns and conflicts.[10]

Home creates its own traditions, whose logic has sometimes been lost. A number of peculiar rules govern Medea's household and apply to the multitude of relatives who visit during the warm Crimean summer. Some of these strictures originate in Medea's peculiar nature; others have no discernible source: "Taciturn by nature, Medea was particularly short on conversation in the mornings. Everyone knew this and saved up their questions for her until evening. . . . It was one of the customs of the house that nobody could go to the well after sundown. Out of respect for Medea this and other inexplicable laws were observed by all visitors, and the more inexplicable the law, the more force it had" (37).

Both the "inexplicable" nature of these laws and the rationale for en-
forcing them emanate from Medea. In an early, formative discussion of
the novel, Svetlana Timina comments on Medea's special sense of order
as a symbol of byt in its positive sense: ritualized stasis that promotes
temporal and geographical stability in the often turbid lives of her relatives. Such constancy resists the chaos of the twentieth century, much of
which, the novel implies, comes from Soviet repression. *Medea and Her
Children* presents an apolitical quotidian that critiques a predacious state,
the same state Ulitskaia's novel *Zelenyi shater* (*Imago,* 2011) explicitly at-
tacks by lauding the everyday heroism of the dissident movement.[11]

The yearly arrival and departure of these family members lends Medea's
life a cyclicality linked to her location near the coast. Having lived entirely in the Crimea, she has roots in the land despite the change of governments (tsarist, provisional, Red, White, German, Romanian). What
results is a basic opposition that reasserts the novel's affinity with the
family chronicle: hearth versus state. Medea's home is a constant, outlast-
ing governments that prove temporary yet cause problems as inevitable as
the changing seasons. The novel's epilogue, set in 1995, shows that, while
Medea has died, her home and many of her relatives have survived the
Soviet regime (201, 309). Within the protagonist's home, everyday routine
allows its owner and visitors to survive manifold tragedies. Medea is not
only a link to bygone times, she is the past surviving in the present, a key
trope that Iurii Lotman and Boris Uspenskii chart throughout Russian
history.[12] It is no coincidence that the narrative begins by noting that
Medea is an archaic figure and the last pure-blooded Greek in Crimea
(4, 3).[13]

The allure of the aged resonates with Ulitskaia's other works. Medea's
old-fashioned appearance and the idiosyncrasies that come with living
alone connect her to a series of positive older protagonists in the author's
oeuvre.[14] The author notes that Medea is a memorial to the inspiring older
women in Ulitskaia's life, including her own grandmother. These women
belong to a generation that matured before 1917 and thus had their own
values. Medea's worldview is certainly pre-Soviet: for her, church and
family are the sole stable ethical referents (with the latter prone to error,
as we discover).[15]

In the context of Ulitskaia's work, Medea is a maternal elder who embodies everyday tradition. Her life shows that the minute actions constituting byt yield enormous significance. This assessment is not new: one predecessor is the focus on "little things" that Barbara Heldt ascribes to late-Soviet women's prose. In *Medea and Her Children,* however, seemingly minor actions have a sacred as well as a quotidian dimension. In this sense, Ulitskaia's novel embodies the Tolstoyan ethics of everyday life made famous by Bakhtin, Gary Saul Morson, and Caryl Emerson. Medea's household consists of daily rituals that together provide a worldview protecting the hearth from the social turmoil inimical to the family chronicle.[16] Medea is not the only one in the novel who reads the quotidian as a sign of larger cultural values. The mother of Elena, Medea's closest childhood friend, is won over by the habits of Medea's family and decides that her aristocratic daughter has found an appropriate companion (26).[17]

Nora, a timid lodger next door, also views everyday actions as an indicator of the viability of a family. Looking at Medea's relatives,

> Nora felt a pang when she thought of her own mother, prematurely aged, her swollen white legs lined with blue veins, hysterically and frantically embattled with the evils of old age, her constant tearful demands and ultimatums, her insistent advice and recommendations.
>
> "Lord, what incredibly normal human relationships. There's nobody demanding anything from anyone else, not even the children," she sighed. (83)

The next moment one of these very same children bursts in, outraged at some passing injustice. The narrative none too subtly qualifies Nora's idealized image of Medea's home, yet her underlying assessment is correct. Medea successfully establishes an everyday atmosphere of understanding and cooperation.

Family and byt implicate *bytie,* that realm of spiritual and intellectual significance that Russian culture opposes to the quotidian. Ulitskaia's oeuvre consistently erases the boundaries between the two: Samuel, who served with the Red Army during the Civil War, falls in love with Medea in great part because she sees him as a person, not a hero. For him, everyday existence is more important than participation in the Bolsheviks' bloodthirsty effort to transform society. Ivan Isaevich, a humble man from an

Old Believer family who marries Medea's sister, Sandra, also associates family, byt, and bytie.[18]

> [Ivan Isaevich] was touched by her prayerful sigh, but only much later, when he was already [Sandra's] husband, did he realize that the crucial point was the amazingly simple way she had solved the problem which had tormented him all his life. For him the worship of a righteous God simply could not be reconciled with the living of an unrighteous life, but [Sandra] brought everything together in a splendidly straightforward way: she painted her lips and dressed to kill, and could throw herself into having fun with total abandon, but when the time came, she would sigh and weep and pray, and suddenly give generous help to someone in need. (139)

Sandra is far from sinless, as her last husband senses and the narrative will make clear. However, Ivan Isaevich values the broader implications of byt, that is, being at peace with self and God.

The protagonist models this flexible spirituality. Although Medea is Greek Orthodox, Judaism plays a significant role in the novel, continuing a trend evident in Ulitskaia's prose and plays, with their connections between Jews and the family. In the last year of his life, Samuel, who abandoned Zionism for Marxism in his youth, returns to his cultural ancestry and reads the book of Leviticus. Its seemingly obscure precepts reveal a network of everyday advice needed to maintain order in the house of God and humanity. Samuel realizes that only Medea, with her odd habits and humble spirituality, is living according to the laws she has set for herself (194–95). His epiphany is key to Ulitskaia's work: as the author has noted and a wide range of her positive characters demonstrate, orthopraxis (correct living) is more important than orthodoxy.[19]

Medea puts forth a similar but more modest idea. Visiting Elena in Tashkent, she recalls that the religious instruction passed down from her mother has allowed her to lead a Christian life. In doing so, she need not trouble herself with "philosophical questions which it is by no means essential for each individual to try to resolve" (224). Instead, she continues, one must live according to the knowledge that nothing can turn evil into good and that many people have strayed from righteousness. This is the closest Medea ever comes to voicing an ethical system reflected in her orthopraxis of everyday life, where it is the individual who is ultimately responsible.[20] Repudiation of flawed group morality also recalls the upbringing of both Medea and Elena. These women, who came of age before 1917, use their archaic worldviews, ethics, and habits to subtly reject the "new" and mistaken mindset that accompanied the Revolution. Such an assessment and its religious overtones unite Ulitskaia's characters with the *shestidesiatniki* she admires, while the implied difference in generations recalls the family chronicle. Like Trifonov, she stresses the crucial nature of individual ethical actions, which are ultimately incompatible with Soviet collective values.[21]

Medea embodies the past at the level of symbol as well as practice. Her small house has a number of well-loved objects, echoing the author's own inability to give up cherished but broken things until she puts them in a work of fiction.[22] The most striking image of this phenomenon is Medea's trunk: "The small leather trunk bound with strips of molded wood, lined inside with glued white-and-pink striped calico, full of partitioned boxes which interacted ingeniously to form a series of little shelves and compartments, had once belonged to Elena Stepanyan. . . . It was a true family archive, and like any worthwhile archive, it concealed secrets not to be made public before the time was ripe" (182–83). The trunk, inherited from Elena's mother, has been the envy of generations of girls believing it to be full of treasure. Instead, it harbors pieces of jewelry and odds and ends as well as important or once-meaningful documents.

The trunk is a "true family archive," one that places the ossified remnants of past byt in the hands of Medea as caretaker. This symbol links the novel to a rich history of such repositories, first in the nineteenth century and then in post-Stalinist prose's attempt to make sense of a distorted past. *Medea and Her Children* domesticates this effort, placing it in the center of Medea's home, hidden in plain view. Its central yet unobtrusive place suggests the importance of family, history, and everyday life throughout the author's oeuvre.[23]

FAMILY AS HOPE AND DOOM: MEDEA AND HER "CHILDREN"

The ties between relatives create a structure centering on the summer of 1977 at Medea's house in the Crimea. In their assessment of the novel, critics have privileged the positive side of this family as evidenced by their fondness for the work's closing paragraph and its evocation of an expanding family. This conclusion, however, comes after Masha's suicide and funeral, events inseparable from the complexities of kinship.

Generations overlap to both good and bad effect in the novel. In a genetic sense, Medea has received her qualities from her grandfather Harlampy, who bequeathed his male heirs energy and a love of building, while "in the women, as in Medea, it turned into thrift, a heightened interest in material things, and a practical resourcefulness" (6). The narrator observes that the family would have been a good genetic study, with Medea the obvious choice to undertake it. True to the genre of the family chronicle, virtues and vices pass from one set of children to the next along with physical similarities. Medea's family, however, is not a closed system. It is under threat from chaos, whether this disorder is external (the hostile forces of history that Savkina notes) or inherent in human interactions (within as well as outside the family). In one sense the novel's plot is a prolonged and inconclusive battle with these two threats.[24]

As her nephew Georgii reminds Masha, Medea sees family as the highest secular authority. Characters' mistrust of the state is easy to understand: one of Medea's brothers was killed by the Reds during the Civil War, and the other was dispatched by the Whites. During the Great Patriotic War the Communists murdered a third brother and the Fascists a fourth. The Crimean setting of the novel, with its shifting governments, provides ample evidence for the destruction wreaked by politics, yet the strength in everyday connections between Medea's relatives allows her home to become an exemplar of kindness that can transcend the horrors of the twentieth century (51).[25]

Family shapes Medea's world, and Medea shapes her family. While the narrator wonders what kind of love a childless woman can have for others' children, the novel depicts this mysterious attachment as the centripetal force that holds the relatives together (7). Medea's authority comes from a combination of respect and habit and is as unquestioned as the place her house occupies in the Crimean landscape. In the context of post-Soviet writing and the cult of kinship Oushakine observes, such voluntary affection from family members contrasts with the maternal monsters Liudmila Petrushevskaia has penned. Ulitskaia herself amplifies this difference, noting that while Petrushevskaia is a specialist in destruction, she promotes preservation. Medea's creator associates her with the intelligentsia ethic of safeguarding values against a cruel and unthinking society. For Medea, this protection relies on the axioms of understanding and non-interference. As is typical for Ulitskaia's fiction, such an abstract world-view is implemented through everyday actions, which in turn critique deeply mistaken Soviet policies.[26]

Medea does not attempt to isolate the clan from the outside world. Indeed, one of her family's peculiarities is that it is simultaneously self-preserving and open. New members can and do join, as long as they abide by the principles Medea received from her parents. The result is kinship that models not perfection but hope, comforting both its members and readers wearied by the poverty and uncertainty of 1990s life and the Soviet legacy of the Great Family, which had seen the state as omnipotent patriarch.[27]

Kinship, however, has a darker side. The plot of *Medea and Her Children* coalesces around two conflicts: the estrangement between Medea and Sandra and the affair between Masha and Valerii Butonov, which ends with Masha's suicide. These familial disasters occur because of two love triangles spanning three generations—together they constitute a counter-narrative of doom alongside the supportive relations of Medea's family.[28]

The first love triangle involves Medea, Samuel, and Sandra. In the summer of 1946, at the height of the closeness between the two sisters, Sandra has an affair with Samuel. The result is Nike, a multiple insult for Medea, who is infertile and does not discover the betrayal until a year after her husband has died (199, 212). The tragedy is first alluded to in the main plot when Medea finds the ring Sandra lost that year; this seemingly small discovery transpires at the beginning of the summer that will destroy Masha's life (74–75, 200).

Medea, uncovering Sandra and Samuel's betrayal, does not see her sister for almost twenty-five years. Her first reaction is to leave the Crimea for a visit to Elena in Tashkent (200, 207). On the train ride she hears a variety of responses to Stalin's recent death. Jenne Powers notes how the Soviet people are experiencing a betrayal that echoes Medea's: during the course of the Thaw, they will discover that their past is built on lies and muted pain (209–10).[29]

Nike, the daughter of Sandra and Samuel, plays her own disastrous role. After the sudden death of Masha's parents and the insane accusations of the girl's grandmother, it is Nike who becomes a sort of second mother to Masha. Surrounding her with love and protection, she counteracts the misplaced guilt that drove Masha to unconsciously attempt suicide while she was with her grandparents. As with Sandra and Medea, Masha and Nike are dissimilar: Masha is brooding and introverted, while Nike is relaxed and enjoys meeting new people (men in particular). Unlike Nike, Masha views life as ruled by moments when fate reveals itself. This combines with a series of vivid dreams after she discovers that her lover, Butonov, is also having an affair with Nike. In a return to the fear and hopelessness of the period following her parents' death, she kills herself by jumping out of the window (158–59, 231, 301–302).[30]

Family is both stability and the basis for destruction, an internal parallel to the external dangers Savkina identifies as the antagonist in the family chronicle. Ulitskaia amplifies this theme in the work that won her the Booker Prize, *Kazus Kukotskogo* (*The Kukotskii Case*, 2001). The novel describes the decline of the Kukotskiis, an intelligentsia family whose members have gradually lost their connections to one another. *Medea and Her Children* depicts the dislocation and death that may come from family problems. *The Kukotskii Case,* in a similar vein, describes an intact family that has been hollowed out by misunderstanding and lack of communication. Masha's grandparents contain a hint of this theme: the husband uses his high-ranking military post to avoid his wife, who torments Masha and blames the girl for the death of her parents (152). In both novels the uncaring family is essentially lifeless, a truism inherited from the more pessimistic moments in Trifonov's work and the nineteenth-century family chronicle.[31]

BROADENING THE FAMILY: EVERYDAY UNDERSTANDING

Tragedy both sunders and supports in *Medea and Her Children*. Ulitskaia suggests that a response to misfortune based on forgiveness and recognition of past mistakes can to a certain extent heal the past. This banal observation becomes more valuable when distinguishing it from the strengthening of emotional ties through manipulation, as occurs with Petrushevskaia's grotesquely tight-knit families, themselves an indicator that the Great Family of Soviet society was decaying.[32]

Masha's suicide and the ensuing funeral draw Medea to the one person, Sandra, whom she has not forgiven throughout the novel (305–307). The service and wake, while following Greek Orthodox tradition, bring together a multitude of different confessions and ethnicities. This scenario has already occurred in the novel with the unusual combination of guests that commemorated Samuel's death decades ago.

> [Sandra] came with Sergei, Fyodor with Georgii and Natasha, brother Dimitry with his son Gvidas from Lithuania, and all the men of the family from Tbilisi. . . . Medea did not allow any baking of pies or a big funeral party. There was traditional kutiya with rice, raisins and honey, there was bread, cheese, a bowl of Central Asian greens, and hardboiled eggs. When Natasha asked Medea why she had arranged it this way, she replied: "He was a Jew, Natasha, and Jews don't have funeral parties at all. . . . I don't like our parties where people always eat and drink too much. Let it be this way." (196–97)

Despite being a strictly observant Christian, Medea melds the Orthodox wake with Jewish tradition. The third element present is a natural reluctance to promote the overindulgence alien to her own upbringing and values.

The multiethnic funeral is a favorite moment for the author, as *Veselye pokhorony* (*The Funeral Party,* 1997) demonstrates. The scene that gives the novel its name brings together a motley set of guests in the melting pot of New York's Russian diaspora. It is significant that this coming together occurs outside the USSR: friends and relatives have replaced the false unity of the Great Family. These gatherings reflect the main theme underlying Ulitskaia's oeuvre: kinship is based on personal ethics, tolerance, and understanding. These common values are ultimately more important than biology and shape the author's reworking of the family chronicle. Blood ties for their part may draw relatives together in gladness (Medea's home) or in sorrow, as the generational overlap of Sandra and Nike shows.[33]

In the final paragraph of *Medea and Her Children,* the protagonist's kin stretch from past to future, united by a byt consisting of tolerance and support. Ulitskaia crafts this epilogue as a coda reinforcing the central message that everyone belongs to the human family. It is in this spirit that Ravil Yusupov, the son of deported Tatars, reappears in the narrative to claim his surprisingly appropriate legacy: Medea's house. Medea has willed him her property, and this action closes the circle, as Ravil was the first "guest" to appear in the narrative (309–10). Medea's home, conveyed to the reader via its habits, happiness, and sadness, shows how kindness can join generations just as easily as can sorrow. The diffused nature of quotidian existence reveals the tolerance and forgiveness that make Medea's house a home and her family a function of ethical as well as physical affinity.[34]

NOTES

I thank Vitaly Chernetsky (University of Kansas) and Elizabeth Skomp (University of the South) for their comments on an early draft of this chapter. The chapter also benefited from suggestions made at the "Everyday Life in Russia and the Soviet Union" workshop at Indiana University in May 2010. At the Association for Slavic, East European, and Eurasian Studies meeting (November 18–21, 2010), the panel "The Familiar and Familial in the Works of Liudmila Ulitskaia" likewise provided useful ideas.

1. Ludmila Ulitskaya, *Medea and Her Children,* trans. Arch Tait (New York: Schocken, 2002), 312. Hereafter cited in the text.

2. Throughout this discussion I use a range of necessarily imprecise synonyms for *byt:* "everyday life," "daily life," and "quotidian." My reasoning is more stylistic than scholarly, since byt, as other authors in this volume have shown, is more than merely a combination of the terms listed above. For one of the key discussions of byt, see Iurii Lotman, *Besedy o russkoi kul'ture: Byt i traditsii russkogo dvorianstva (XVIII–nachalo XIX veka)* (St. Petersburg: Iskusstvo-SPB, 1994), 10. A number of critics cite the conclusion of the novel, for example, A. Baranova, "Semeinaia problematika v sovremennom psikhologicheskom romane (L. Ulitskaia, Medeia i ee deti)," http://mith.ru/epic/lito1.htm, accessed August 2, 2013; and Irina Savkina, "Rod/dom: Semeinaia khronika Liudmily Ulitskoi i Vasiliia Aksenova," in *Semeinye uzy: Modeli dlia sborki,* comp. and ed. Sergei Ushakin (Moscow: Novoe literaturnoe obozrenie, 2004), 1:173.

3. Sergei Ushakin, "Mesto-imeni-ia: Sem'ia kak sposob organizatsii zhizni," in *Semeinye uzy: Modeli dlia sborki,* comp. and ed. Sergei Ushakin (Moscow: Novoe literaturnoe obozrenie, 2004), 1:10. On the appearance of eternal sameness, see Alexei Yurchak, *Everything Was Forever, Until It Was No More: The Last Soviet Generation* (Princeton, N.J.: Princeton University Press, 2005), 1.

4. Anja Grothe, "Medusa, Cassandra, Medea: Re-inscribing Myth in Contemporary German and Russian Women's Writing," PhD diss., City University of New York, 2000, 267–68. For a description of Medea acting as an emissary from a culture of humanism, see Ulitskaya, *Medea and Her Children,* 8–12.

5. Boris Pasternak's *Doctor Zhivago* and Iurii Trifonov's *House on the Embankment* are two foundational family narratives from the Soviet era. Vasilii Aksenov's *Generations of Winter* is a post-Soviet example that Savkina perceptively links to *Medea and Her Children* in its juxtaposition of kinship with a foreboding external environment (see Savkina, "Rod/dom").

6. For a key discussion of family and literature, see Robert Stephens, *The Family Saga in the South: Generations and Destinies* (Baton Rouge: Louisiana State University Press, 1995), 3–6. Jenne Powers drew my attention to this reference. Stephens draws on Robert Boyers, "The Family Novel," in *Excursions: Selected Literary Essays* (Port Washington: Kennikat Press, 1977), 6–7. See also Savkina, "Rod/dom," 157. For one example of the opposing viewpoint, see Leonid Bakhnov, "Genio loci," *Druzhba narodov*, no. 8 (1996): 179. Bakhnov disqualifies *Medea and Her Children* based on a nonlinear narrative and narratorial subjectivity. The first claim has more merit than the second, which would decimate the ranks of the "classic" family chronicle, which includes Sergei Aksakov's appropriately titled *Family Chronicle* and, in a darker sense, Fedor Dostoevskii's *Demons*.

7. On the division between public and private as a function of family and home, see the seminal work by Georges Duby, "Private Power, Public Power," in *A History of Private Life*, ed. Philippe Ariès and Georges Duby, 3 vols. (Cambridge, Mass.: Belknap Press, 1988), 2:1–31. This division is more nuanced in the Soviet context, as Ilya Utekhin and Deborah Field note in this volume.

8. Helena Goscilo provides a helpful discussion of Petrushevskaia's work in Helena Goscilo, *Dehexing Sex: Russian Womanhood during and after Glasnost* (Ann Arbor: University of Michigan Press, 1996), 18–21. For an overview of the ambiguity of byt and its tumultuous relationship with literature, see Benjamin Sutcliffe, *The Prose of Life: Russian Women Writers from Khrushchev to Putin* (Madison: University of Wisconsin Press, 2009), 7–12.

9. Along with the novel's final paragraph, another commonplace for commentary is the juxtaposition between Ulitskaia's Medea and her more famous namesake. See, for example, Svitlana Korshunova, "Intertekstual'nyi analiz v romane L. Ulitskoi 'Medeia i ee deti,'" *Pitanna literaturoznavstva*, no. 77 (2009): 156. Another critic asserts that the novel's title is a polemic against "Medea," an earlier (and horrific) story by Petrushevskaia. See N. Egorova, "Mifopoeticheskie obrazy v romane L. Ulitskoi 'Medeia i ee deti,'" in *Khudozhestvennyi tekst i kul'tura: Materialy shestoi mezhdunarodnoi nauchnoi konferentsii* (Vladimir: Vladimir State Pedagogical University, 2006), 333.

10. Stephens, *The Family Saga*, 4. On ritual, cyclicality, and the archaic, see T. Prokhorova's intriguing discussion "Osobennosti proiavleniia mifologicheskogo soznaniia v khudozhestvennoi strukture romana L. Ulitskoi 'Medeia i ee deti,'" in *Russkii roman XX veka: Dukhovnyi mir i poetika zhanra. Sbornik nauchnykh trudov*, ed. A. Vaniukov (Saratov: Saratov University, 2001), 289. One critic argues that only harmony can create a real home: I. V. Davidenko, "Kontsept 'dom' v romane L. Ulitskoi 'Medeia i ee deti,'" in *Dni nauki: Sbornik nauchnykh materialov nauchno-prakticheskoi konferentsii prepodavatelei i studentov*, ed. A. A. Maslak, issue 7, pt. 1 (Slaviansk-na-Kubani: Slaviansk-na-Kubani State Pedagogical Institute, 2008), 15.

11. Svetlana Timina, "Ritmy vechnosti: Roman Liudmily Ulitskoi *Medeia i ee deti*," in *Perom i prelest'iu: Zhenshchiny v panteone russkoi literatury. Sbornik statei*, ed. Wanda Laszczak and Daria Ambroziak (Opole: Wydawca Dariusz Karbowiak, 1999), 152; Liudmila Ulitskaia, *Zelenyi shater* (Moscow: Eksmo, 2011). Arch Tait is currently preparing an English translation of this novel; it will be published with the title *Imago*.

12. Iurii Lotman and Boris Uspenskii, "Binary Models in the Dynamics of Russian Culture (to the End of the Eighteenth Century)," in *The Semiotics of Russian Cultural History: Essays by Iurii M. Lotman, Lidiia Ia. Ginsburg, Boris A. Uspenskii*, ed. Alexander Nakhimovsky and Alice Nakhimovsky (Ithaca, N.Y.: Cornell University Press, 1985), 31.

13. The other Greeks were presumably deported by Stalin, but Medea was saved by her Sephardic husband's last name.

14. Lilia's Jewish grandparents in "March 1953" conjoin familial support and the imparting of religious tradition, both of which the narrative opposes to Stalinism. In another story, "The Great Teacher," Gena discovers after his grandmother's death that she was involved with the Optyna Monastery and had saved some of his relatives from starvation (Ludmila Ulitskaya, "March 1953," in *Present Imperfect: Stories by Russian Women*, ed. Ayesha Kagal and Natasha Perova [Boulder: Westview, 1996], 11–15; "Velikii uchitel'," in *Liudi nashego tsaria* [Moscow: Eksmo, 2005], 51–53).

15. Liudmila Ulitskaia, "Korzina, kartina, kartonka," interview with Liudmila Ulitskaia by Iana Zhiliaeva, *Moskovskii komsomolets,* January 30, 1999, 3; Baranova, "Semeinaia problematika." For a discussion of how these women embody pre-1917 ideas and implicitly challenge Soviet conceptions of history, see the intriguing study by Jenne Powers, "Novel Histories: Repudiation of Soviet Historiography in the Works of Iurii Trifonov, Vladimir Makanin, and Liudmila Ulitskaia," PhD diss., University of North Carolina at Chapel Hill, 2009, 157. See also her volume of memoirs, *Sviashchennyi musor* (Moscow: Astrel', 2012), and "Mladshaia shestidesiatnitsa," interview with Liudmila Ulitskaia by Mariia Sedykh, *Obshchaia gazeta,* May 16, 2002, 8. Ulitskaia notes the substantial overlapping of her own life and the historical eras (late 1940s to early 1980s) dominating her works: Liudmila Ulitskaia, interview by Elizabeth Skomp and Benjamin Sutcliffe, e-mail, June 17, 2011.

16. Barbara Heldt, "Gynoglasnost: Writing the Feminine," in *Perestroika and Soviet Women,* ed. Mary Buckley (Cambridge: Cambridge University Press, 1992), 169. Concerning Tolstoi, Bakhtin, and the ethics of the everyday, see Gary Saul Morson and Caryl Emerson, *Mikhail Bakhtin: Creation of a Prosaics* (Stanford, Calif.: Stanford University Press, 1990), 25.

17. For a number of interesting observations on Medea's extended family, see Ol'ga Berezkina, "Issledovanie istorii rasshirennoi sem'i na materiale romana L. Ulitskoi 'Medeia i ee deti,'" *Zhurnal prakticheskoi psikhologii i psikhoanaliza,* no. 4 (December 2005), http://psyjournal.ru/psyjournal/articles/detail.php?ID=2679, accessed August 2, 2013.

18. For a good outline of the differences between *byt* and *bytie,* see Hutchings, *Russian Modernism,* 38; Elena Gorskaia, "Männerbilder in Werk Ljudmila Ulickajas: Die Verschiebung von Genderrolen," M.A. thesis, University of Vienna, 2000, 74.

19. For one of the first discussions of Ulitskaia, ethnicity, and family, see Tat'iana Kazarina, "Bednye rodstvenniki," *Preobrazhenie,* no. 4 (1996): 171. On the crucial concept of orthopraxis, see Ulitskaia, "Mladshaia shestidesiatnitsa," 8. This tendency is evident in the protagonist of her novel *Daniel Stein, Interpreter,* who creates a community built on truth yet attacked by the three religions (Judaism, Christianity, Islam) he brings together. See Benjamin Sutcliffe, "Liudmila Ulitskaia's Literature of Tolerance," *Russian Review,* no. 3 (2009).

20. The implicit opposition between everyday life and "philosophy" recalls what Henri Lefebvre sees as the antagonistic relationship between the two, where philosophy vainly attempts to control the unruly quotidian (*Everyday Life in the Modern World,* trans. Sacha Rabinowitz [New York: Harper & Row, 1971], 12).

21. Ulitskaia, "Mladshaia shestidesiatnitsa," 8. On the family chronicle's representation of divergent and degraded family values, see Stephens, *The Family Saga,* 4. Ulitskaia does not explicitly frame the quotidian as resistance to the status quo, yet Medea's rejection of politics comprises a low-level critique of a state that endeavored to imbue byt with ideology. For a crucial discussion of everyday life versus power, see Michel de Certeau, *The Practice of Everyday Life,* trans. Steven Rendall (Berkeley: University of California Press, 1984).

22. Ulitskaia, "Korzina, kartina, kartonka."

23. Pechorin's trunk in *A Hero of Our Time* is the most famous example in nineteenth-century Russian prose, while Iurii Dombrovskii's *The Keeper of Antiquities* applies this idea to picking up the pieces after Stalinism's assault on present and past. My characterization of everyday objects as "hidden in plain view" comes from the foundational book of the same name: Gary Saul Morson, *Hidden in Plain View: Narrative and Creative Potentials in "War and Peace"* (Stanford, Calif.: Stanford University Press, 1988).

24. Prokhorova, "Osobennosti proiavleniia mifologicheskogo soznaniia," 290.

25. On the connections between kindness, home, and history in the novel, see Tat'iana Rovenskaia, "Arkhetip doma v novoi zhenskoi proze, ili Kommunal'noe zhitie i kommunal'nye tela," *Inoi vzgliad,* no. 3 (2001): 26.

26. The most notorious example Petrushevskaia's prose provides is the narrator of *The Time: Night,* who ruins her family by attempting to save it. On the perceived difference between Ulitskaia and Petrushevskaia, see Liudmila Ulitskaia, "Dumala, ne dozhivu do finala svoego poslednego romana," interview with Maksim Chizhikov, *Komsomol'skaia pravda,* February 22, 2008, http://www.kp.ru/daily/24053/104935, accessed August 2, 2013. Her thoughts on Petrushevskaia's works are not wholly negative: see Ulitskaia, interview by Skomp and Sutcliffe.

27. Berezkina, "Issledovanie istorii rasshirennoi sem'i"; Baranova, "Semeinaia problematika." For the most influential analysis of the Great Family, which is depicted as a potent metaphor for Stalinism, see Katerina Clark, *The Soviet Novel: History as Ritual* (Chicago: University of Chicago Press, 1980), 114, 115.

28. On the relationship between the novel's plot and these two factors, see Berezkina, "Issledovanie istorii rasshirennoi sem'i."

29. Powers, "Novel Histories," 193.

30. It is no coincidence that Masha's grandparents are members of the Stalinist elite. Throughout Ulitskaia's oeuvre this group exemplifies the corruption and lack of individual responsibility tainting Soviet society as a whole. See, for example, the doomed privileged family in Liudmila Ulitskaia, "Pisatel'skaia doch'" (The writer's daughter), in *Liudi nashego tsaria* (Moscow: Eksmo, 2005).

31. On the problem of estrangement in the intact family, see Berezkina, "Issledovanie istorii rasshirennoi sem'i." For a discussion of family and history as reflected in the body, see Benjamin Sutcliffe, "Mother, Daughter, History: Embodying the Past in Liudmila Ulitskaia's *Sonechka* and *The Case of Kukotskii*," *Slavic and East European Journal* 4 (2009); and Elizabeth Skomp and Benjamin Sutcliffe, "Liudmila Ulitskaia's Art of Tolerance," manuscript in progress.

32. On the decline of the Great Family, see Helena Goscilo and Yana Hashamova, "Cinepaternity: The Psyche and Its Heritage," in *Cinepaternity: Fathers and Sons in Soviet and Post-Soviet Film,* ed. Helena Goscilo and Yana Hashamova (Bloomington: Indiana University Press, 2010), 14.

33. Ludmila Ulitskaya, *The Funeral Party,* trans. Cathy Porter, ed. Arch Tait (New York: Schocken, 2001), 145–49.

34. On the epilogue as coda, see Powers, "Novel Histories," 185.

PART V.
COMING HOME: TRANSNATIONAL CONNECTIONS

15

Sino-Soviet Every Day

Chinese Revolutionaries in Moscow Military Schools,
1927–1930

ELIZABETH MCGUIRE

One evening in the middle of January 1928, ninety-four Chinese students rushed headlong through downtown Moscow from the school where they were receiving military training to the headquarters of the Communist International, the governing body of global revolution. Having beaten up several of their classmates and threatened their schoolmaster, they were seized by the sort of whirling fury that is generally associated with intense moments of popular revolution. The Chinese gusting through Moscow's wintry streets were determined to reach the highest power in the land (in the world, as far as they were concerned) to protest—what?

Judging by statements they made in the run-up to their outburst, the ingredients of their outrage included dismay at the failures of the revolution back in China and dissatisfaction with Soviet management of Chinese affairs, as well as the more proximate irritation with their daily lives in Russia, where they were disgruntled about everything: their teachers, their food, their classes, and each other.

If revolution is supposed to upend everyday life by rearranging the political and social order that structures it, altering even time itself so thoroughly that a change in calendars seems fitting, then international revolution is a phenomenon even more counterpoised to the everyday. If revolution changes time, then international revolution transcends space as well, erasing traditional boundaries and creating new maps of the world, at least in the imaginations of the people who fight for it. Historically speaking, "global revolution" is a particularly tricky phenomenon: even the people who fought for it and believed in the unity of theory and practice could not agree on where "international" revolution could occur, or had to occur, to be considered a global phenomenon.

This lack of specificity fueled an ambient sense of revolutionary expectation that was perhaps never so potent as in the 1920s. In the early part of the decade the Bolsheviks focused most of their attention on revolutionary movements in Europe. But as uprisings there fizzled, attention gradually turned to China. A major protest movement in May 1919 radicalized many young people there, and by 1921 some of these had coalesced into a small, nascent Communist Party under the watchful eye of the Comintern. At the same time, the Comintern also spent considerable resources to assist China's other, more established revolutionary party: Sun Yatsen's Nationalists, led after Sun's death in 1924 by Chiang Kaishek. As in other countries, the USSR simultaneously promoted revolution in China and pursued traditional objectives like diplomatic recognition and territorial claims. The dual nature of Soviet involvement in China and disagreements about the Comintern's China policy led to controversy over the efficacy of Soviet involvement in China.

This controversy continues today in the historiography of Sino-Soviet relations, which often focuses largely on military, political, and revolutionary strategy in the abstract. With some notable exceptions, the history of "Sino-Soviet relations" usually belongs to the realm of the geopolitical or the ideological and is not considered part of Soviet (or Chinese) social history, much less histories of everyday life in Russia.[1]

The story of the ninety-four Chinese, however, points to something quite different: Sino-Soviet relations had a social history, which encompassed, among other things, the everyday experiences of Chinese revolutionaries in Russia. They lived parts of their lives in specific spaces and times in which the Soviet and Chinese revolutions crossed paths—not only in China or in the Soviet far east but also in Moscow and other central Soviet cities. Chinese in Moscow or St. Petersburg included rank-and-file Communists and Nationalists, luminaries from both parties, and their spouses, lovers, and children. Working, studying, and living in Soviet organizations, face to face with Soviet people on a daily basis, these people were actually "Sino-Soviet every day."

Beginning in the early 1920s and continuing up to the Chinese Cultural Revolution, with a brief intermission during the Second World War, waves of Chinese came to Moscow with abstract notions of communist ideals and left with concrete experiences of Soviet reality. In the early 1920s, the first group of would-be communists came, like many radicals in the early stages of a revolutionary movement, full of romantic revolutionary notions. Sino-Soviet education at this point focused largely on imparting a "revolutionary liberal arts education" that included heavy doses of Lenin, *Pravda,* and the Russian language. By 1925 large numbers of both Communists and Nationalists were being educated in a special university in Moscow, Sun Yatsen University, which promoted the Soviet concept of a united front between Chinese Communists and Nationalists.

But by 1927, when the events described in this chapter took place, Chiang Kaishek had turned on his erstwhile Communist allies, massacring hundreds. The Comintern and the Chinese Communists came to the conclusion that what Chinese Communists needed most was a military education, and as Chiang's anticommunist campaign intensified, the Soviet Union seemed the only safe place to receive it.

The result was a rather singular experience in the long history of Soviet education for the Chinese. The military recruits were, in some ways, a more fascinating group. Plucked off the streets of China and dropped in Moscow, they were barraged daily with a confusing array of physical, political, cultural, and emotional challenges. The military recruits were less intellectually and less politically sophisticated than their predecessors, who came to Moscow with more impressive political and cultural credentials, were in the Soviet Union long enough to absorb Soviet factional struggles, and learned how to parse, compartmentalize, or mobilize their everyday experiences in terms of Sino-Soviet politics. They did not have the political, intellectual, or cultural training they needed to mediate their ideas, experiences, and feelings. Whether the food they ate influenced their attitudes toward their inchoate understanding of Stalin's China policy or Stalin's China policy affected their digestion is hard to say.

Yet the ninety-four Chinese throw into sharp relief a fundamental challenge that the international revolutionary movement never really met. How effective, really, was the universal ideology, the geopolitical justifications, or the cross-cultural conventions that were supposed to help international revolutionaries work together effectively on an everyday basis? The explosion of conflict and the ultimate closure of the military courses illustrate how disagreement over policy and cross-cultural friction combined and were intertwined in the minds of the foot soldiers of international revolution, catalyzing numerous small acts of resistance that could and did foil the Comintern's grand strategies.

BACKDROP

The ninety-four rabble-rousing Chinese students described here as well as the larger cohort of post-1927 recruits differed from earlier groups of Chinese revolutionaries in Moscow in that their main focus was military studies. Soviet education for the Chinese had always had a military component—through the late 1920s this was accomplished through training in summer camps—but mostly these students were learning the ABCs of Communism, examining the history of global revolution and revolution in "the East," and acquiring "white-collar" revolutionary skills like agitation and propaganda.[2]

Chiang Kaishek's 1927 about-face and massacre of Communists was shocking, and it immediately changed the entire tenor of Soviet-Chinese revolutionary relations not only in China but also in Moscow.[3] For the first time, policy toward China took center stage in Soviet domestic politics, as Trotsky blamed Stalin for the 1927 debacle and Stalin maneuvered to control the political damage.

At the same time, it changed the terms upon which Chinese students came to Moscow. Before 1927, the students who had enrolled in these schools had often made the long journey to Moscow with great enthusiasm, fueled by high hopes for a Soviet-style revolution in China. Students in the earlier, idealistic cohorts included leading lights of the Chinese revolution such as Liu Shaoqi (Mao's number two man until the Cultural Revolution), Deng Xiaoping, and even, ironically, Chiang Kaishek's son and future president of Taiwan, Chiang Chingkuo, who was one of the very first students to enroll at Sun Yatsen University in 1925 at the age of fifteen. He was still there in 1927 at the time of the April massacre in China, and—perhaps carried away by the anger of his communist classmates or perhaps pressured by the Soviet authorities—he immediately and publicly denounced his father. Chingkuo stayed on in the Soviet Union for the very military training that was intended to defeat his own father's rule.[4]

As Chiang Kaishek intensified his anticommunist campaign, the Chinese Communist Party and the Comintern worked hard to quickly round up as many loyal communists as possible for transfer to the Soviet Union. In late 1927 and early 1928, hundreds of young Chinese communists were hastily chosen and transported to Moscow for military training. The reason was simple: their lives were in danger, and they needed to learn how to protect themselves. There were several hundred of them, and they were to attend the new "military-political short courses" run by Communist Eastern University.

With an operation so clearly driven by international communist realpolitik, it would be easy to assume that it was quite a serious matter: rigorous and effective training of diligent young foot soldiers by stern Soviet drillmasters. The reality couldn't have been more different.

PLAYERS AND OPENING SCENE: SINO-SOVIET FOOT SOLDIERS AND THEIR SOVIET COMMANDER

In their muddled urgency to gather and transport Chinese communists to Moscow, Soviet and Chinese authorities ended up selecting a good many unwilling, dispirited, or even unwitting trainees. One young person who was sent to Moscow in the spring of 1927 for military training recalled being ordered by the party in China to come to a certain meeting spot; only after the student arrived did it become apparent that those gathered were getting on a boat; only after the group was on the boat was it clear that the boat was headed for the Soviet Union.[5]

Other military recruits thought they were being sent to study at the renowned Sun Yatsen University but got stuck in the military courses instead. Such students immediately began writing letters, begging to be transferred. One student wrote a petition, in English, that read: "We four girls just coming from China ask to be allowed to study revolutionary theories in the Chinese Workers University named Sun Yat-Sen, simply because, the first, that our bodies are not strong enough to be good soldiers."[6] Female recruits weren't the only ones to object to military training: one young man who had come from a Chinese university refused to wear a uniform and burst into tears when he was denied a transfer out of the military courses. Another student announced that uniforms "weren't for him" and that only workers and peasants should have to "meet bullets."[7]

Even new arrivals convinced of the importance of military education were, nonetheless, the most dispirited group of Chinese who had yet come to the USSR to study. One student remembers how desperate many revolutionaries back in China were at that point:

> They were forced to beg for their living on the streets and await arrest and execution [by Chiang's forces].... One solution to this problem was to send some of us to Moscow. We were all very excited about the prospect of learning to use weapons. After the catastrophic defeat the Revolution had just suffered, the idea that armed force was the ultimately decisive factor in any situation was very appealing to us, we were in no position to make a deeper analysis of the causes of the defeat. The facts were only too clear, in less than six months we had watched one military man after another switch from leading the revolution to opposing it. In quick succession they had shamelessly and bloodily deceived us. We were like abandoned concubines, or pitiful and impotent old-fashioned scholars. It was natural that we should draw the conclusion that to achieve victory in the Revolution we ourselves should take up arms.[8]

Going all the way to Moscow just to learn how to shoot a gun or to save your own skin, however, implied that the trip was a grim necessity, not an exciting adventure.

Another serious problem with the new recruits was their health. Chinese students in Moscow had always suffered a variety of ailments due to changes in climate and diet and to the intensity of daily life in the capital of world revolution, but the academic nature of their prior studies meant that they could still benefit from the experience. The new military trainees had to meet higher physical standards. A number of students were deemed physically unfit for the military camp that had been set up for them during the summer of 1927 and instead were settled in a nearby village.[9]

If the students chosen for military training were not always ideal, neither was the man picked to oversee their training. Rather than tapping one of the dozens of seasoned military advisors with experience in China, the head of Communist Eastern University wrote to the head of Tolmachev Military-Political Academy in Leningrad requesting one of its graduates to lead the new military courses for the Chinese. The Tolmachev Academy suggested a young man named Malyshev, who was about to step into one of the most frustrating, difficult, and completely forgotten bit parts in the history of Sino-Soviet relations. Malyshev was to graduate that spring, he was at the top of his class, he had been studying Chinese for three years, and he intended a career in the Soviet far east. Now he was to be paid 225 rubles a month to run a summer military camp in the Moscow suburbs for five hundred soon-to-arrive Chinese and a quarrelsome contingent of those yanked from the other Moscow schools.[10]

Malyshev took charge of the summer camp for the Chinese with op-timism and enthusiasm. There were problems, to be sure: the students who had been deemed physically unfit for military training and had been settled in a nearby village came to be a major thorn in his side because of their open ties with the students in a camp whose very existence was supposed to be a secret. Particularly vexing were their liaisons with local women, often initiated under the impeccable pretext of Russian-language practice but quickly the source of local gossip.[11] Another problem was the cultural gap between Soviet and Chinese concepts of the martial arts. Many students rejected the study of military tactics and demanded more time spent on marching drills, which Soviet officials attributed (with a certain disdain) to the fact that Chinese generals had recruits spend most of their time on such drills.[12]

Still, the camp was deemed a relative success. Trainees who completed the summer course covered military tactics, subversive activities, military hygiene, and topography, as well as the more prosaic physical education, political literacy, math, and newspaper-reading courses. Camp officials reported that the students showed overwhelming enthusiasm for learn-ing how to shoot.[13] In August, to conclude the camp's activities, Malyshev organized a two-day jubilee, with parades, movies, games, and banquets.[14] Nothing in particular about the 1927 summer camp foreshadowed the problems to come, potential conflicts perhaps masked by the novelty of the situation for both sides and the general haze of summer in the Moscow countryside.

TENSIONS BUILD

Come fall, some students from the summer camp were sent home or to other universities, but a large contingent remained. And in September 1927, a second big batch of students arrived from China, refugees of Chiang's ever more repressive policies. To accommodate the several hundred Chinese students who would have pushed past the breaking point enrollments in the existing classes at Sun Yatsen University (renamed Communist University for the Workers of China after 1927) or Communist Eastern University, special, regular-term military-political courses were organized just for them at Communist Eastern University.[15]

By the fall of 1927, defeats of Chinese Communists by the increasingly powerful Nationalists had shifted the tide of public opinion in Moscow about China in general and Moscow's Chinese population in particular. In 1926 and early 1927, revolutionary success in China had caused ordinary Muscovites to warmly embrace the Chinese in their midst: some students recalled being surrounded by girls whenever they went to the movies, and others remembered Russians being courteous in the extreme, offering them seats on busses and invitations to dance parties.[16] The Soviet government, too, had bestowed privileges on Chinese students: Sun Yatsen University was extraordinarily well funded, and the students enjoyed a scandalously high standard of living for Moscow at that time.

Now, however, a new attitude on the part of Soviet authorities was reflected in a peculiar, one-time physical exam in the fall of 1927 that one student recalled in retrospect as a bad omen: the Soviet secret police spent a week physically measuring all the Chinese at his school in great detail.[17] The exam caused resentment. "Would the Russians use this record to hound us for the rest of our lives. . . . Jokingly, we said that we had now given ourselves body and soul to the Russians."[18] At the same time, attitudes of ordinary Russians on the streets had changed dramatically after Chiang Kaishek's reversal; a new arrival that fall remembers having a tomato thrown at him, a far cry from the warm glow of public approval earlier in the year.[19] The large influx of Chinese Communist refugees/military trainees lowered Soviet tolerance and generosity.

Paranoia and ambivalence about the Chinese in Moscow may have reflected a shift in Soviet attitudes toward China more generally, but this coincided with real changes in Moscow's Chinese student community specifically. For one thing, because of the need to bring large numbers of Chinese to the relative safety of Moscow, the Chinese student community in Moscow was bigger than ever, a diverse, unruly band of would-be revolutionaries that reflected a Chinese revolution that had spun out of control and fragmented. Moreover, because the Soviet Union was none too efficient in processing people for departure, Chinese students accumulated in a sedimentary fashion.[20]

Meanwhile, throughout the fall of 1927, students would hear news of a series of failed uprisings—news that could only increase their overall disillusionment. Just as many were leaving China, they would have heard of the August 1 Nanchang Uprising. Nanchang was a failed attempt by Communists to seize the capital city of Jiangxi province.[21] It occurred on the first day of the August plenum of the CPSU, at which Stalin attacked Trotsky and Zinoviev and Trotsky accused Stalin of timing the Nanchang uprising to coincide with the plenum. Students who had been chosen to come to Moscow for short-term military education, then, seemed to be training not for participation in a well-planned campaign where victory was possible but rather for a scattered offensive of poorly planned, ill-fated rebellions driven as much by Soviet domestic politics as by the exigencies of the Chinese revolution.

Some Chinese students in Moscow who had been there for several years actually became Trotskyists, partly in anger about a China policy that many attributed to Stalin. In a remarkable instance of public protest, the Chinese had flashed an oppositionist banner right outside the Lenin mausoleum as they passed in a procession to celebrate the tenth anniversary of the October Revolution.[22] Yet the Chinese Trotskyists were an elite group, of sorts: they knew enough about the Soviet political scene to express themselves in its idiom.

The more recent arrivals at Malyshev's military-political courses were a different story. On the one hand, they tended to be less experienced, more recent recruits to the Chinese Communist Party. On the other hand, they hadn't been in the Soviet Union long enough to be politicized in Soviet terms either. They were, of course, aware of revolutionary developments in China and upon arrival in the Soviet Union began to learn very quickly about Soviet factional struggles, especially since more experienced students who took sides in Soviet factional battles vied for their support. These preexisting factions efficiently mapped their large-scale political views onto everyday life in their schools, taking sides and fomenting disputes about pedagogical questions: Is it OK for students to spend so much energy studying the Russian language? Should Russian be taught at all? Are the teachers qualified? Are personal issues like love triangles and fistfights fair game as targets for political reeducation? New recruits could comprehend these issues more clearly than they could make out what it meant to be a Trotskyist or a Stalinist, and they navigated politics on the basis of their preexisting experiences in the revolutionary movement in China and their everyday experiences. Both frustrated them in ways that made them deceptively easy targets for political agitators; it proved difficult for anyone to control them.

From the point of view of the Soviet authorities, their offenses ran from the minor to the catastrophic—but then, the Soviet authorities weren't exactly in a position to appreciate the humor in the situation. These supposedly disciplined soldiers of revolution were always getting drunk, fighting, bringing women back to their dorms, or doing all three at once. And they were eternally coming late to breakfast because they'd been out the night before, acting as if their excuses were perfectly understandable. The administration was forced to report that Nechaev (most Chinese were given Russian names upon their arrival in Moscow) was stealing socks from the school inventory and that Dudkin had gotten into a fight with his classmate during shooting lessons and had actually tried to use his weapon. Moreover, the students were rude to the workers in the cafeteria and to the university staff in general. They complained incessantly about the food. Their refusal to eat cheese and fish and their demands for meat and rice were exactly the sort of nuts-and-bolts cross-cultural conflict for which higher-ups had little patience.[23]

The pedagogical effectiveness of the military courses was also questionable. Tolstoy the translator (who had undoubtedly come to Russia several years before Nechaev and Dudkin and was therefore in a position to translate for them) was overworked, but, then, so were all the translators, which was a serious problem in the short courses. Both Russians and Chinese objected to the translators, who were deemed irresponsible.[24] Since students arrived on a rolling basis, coursework was often disjointed, and students continued to complain bitterly through the fall of 1927 about poor instruction of key subjects like topography and a shortage of rifles for shooting practice.[25] These issues suggested to students a lack of Soviet support for the Chinese revolution, and the resultant resentment mingled with their preexisting sense of outrage over failed uprisings in China. Neither of these factors—dissatisfaction with daily life in Moscow or criticism of the Comintern's China policy—was an independent variable; they commingled and were codependent.

THE BREAKING POINT

Malyshev, the aspiring commander of far eastern revolution, became the scapegoat for the students' dissatisfactions. They called him a "red imperialist" and accused him of all manner of treachery, imagining that he was plotting to take over the Chinese revolution himself and accusing any-one who defended him of being his "running dog." They scrawled "Down with Malyshev" on the walls, wrote letters directly to the Comintern's Eastern Section, and made so much trouble that finally, on January 3, 1928, Malyshev called a meeting for all the students to air their grievances.[26]

The meeting lasted four whole days, and over 120 students got up to speak. Malyshev tried to keep control: he opened the meeting with a con-ciliatory speech and allowed the session to go on until the students had ex-hausted their energies denouncing and defending themselves, Malyshev, and the school. One student made an impassioned appeal on his own be-half: "It's not true that I drank wine in the sickroom and brought a woman in there. This should be investigated, and if it's true, let them shoot me!" Malyshev had the last word: "Critics forget I'm a member of the party, am constantly controlled by the party, and receive my working instructions according to the party line. I am not a dictator, who can independently decide all questions against the will of the party."[27]

The meeting failed to pacify the students, so two weeks later the rector of Communist Eastern University gave them a stern lecture, putting up for a vote resolutions in support of school policies. The resolutions carried, but the confrontation riled the students all the more. At this point, the students began to behave like so many characters from a comic novella, perhaps by Gogol: they ate dinner and then went looking for Malyshev. When they found him, they "made obstructions and caused a riot." Having trapped and harassed their schoolmaster, they were still not satisfied, so they decided, right then and there, to march to the Comintern offices. They began rounding up students to go with them, beating up people who refused. Ultimately, ninety-four students marched, rowdy and defiant, to Comintern headquarters.[28]

While they were marching, the rest of the students got together and made a resolution denouncing them. Somebody from the Comintern's Eastern Section met the marchers, asked them to appoint a delegation to voice their complaints, and sent the rest home. In the end, the only consequence was that four students were excluded from the party, leaving the rest in confusion and turmoil. The school's daily operations continued only nominally; emotionally, the institution had come to a standstill. The students' protest caused such consternation and disagreement among the higher-ups overseeing their training that it stymied the entire apparatus of large-scale military training for Chinese in Moscow. A series of investigations began, which ended in the closure of the school.

DENOUEMENT

At the end of the school year the so-called short courses were disbanded, and Malyshev divided the students into six different groups: sixty-nine students were deemed politically trained, reliable, and prepared in military terms for return to China; twenty-eight of the most disciplined and "brave" were chosen for special training in "military sabotage"; ninety-seven students who were judged politically educated but in need of further military training were sent to Soviet military schools; forty-one were labeled poor students and politically unverified and sent to Sun Yatsen University; eight even less reliable students were sent to work among the Chinese population in the Soviet far east; and finally, thirty people remained whose fate was left unspecified but who were considered "without a doubt completely politically unreliable" and about whom detailed materials had been gathered.[29]

Mostly, it appears, Malyshev's will was done—remarkably, thirty-five thousand rubles had been envisioned for the training in sabotage—except that the list of thirty "completely unreliable" students whom Malyshev wished to punish was progressively whittled down until only two students, whose fate is unknown, remained. The sixty-nine students who were supposed to return to China were held back because the Comintern's International Liaisons Department (its most secretive department, in charge of espionage and communication between the Comintern and the Soviet secret police) couldn't deal with them until September, no doubt causing further dissatisfaction.[30]

STRAGGLERS AND HOLDOVERS

The end of the short courses was not, however, the absolute end of military training for Chinese in Soviet Russia. At least two hundred Chinese Communists were chosen from among the student body in Moscow as well as from among the ranks back in China to attend existing Soviet military schools—mostly Red Army artillery, infantry, engineering, and communications schools in Moscow.[31] In some cases, these students were alone or with just a handful of other Chinese; a few schools had enough Chinese students to form a proper "Chinese section." These students were real exceptions to the pre–World War II rule for Chinese communist students in Soviet Russia: they attended Soviet schools alongside regular Soviet people rather than institutions designed for foreigners. Their experiences imparted a deeper sense of Soviet Russia than they could glean in their former schools.

Ironically, the most prominent example was Chiang Chingkuo, who was sent along with some other Chinese students to exactly the place whence their detested teacher, Malyshev, had come: Tolmachev Military-Political Academy. In his published memoirs, Chingkuo recalled with affection his teacher for battle tactics at Tolmachev, whose red-and-white-checkered family history clearly resonated with Chingkuo's own.

The teacher was the son of a tsarist aristocrat who had graduated from military school and had been a leader of the Eighth Army during World

War I.[32] After the Revolution he had fought with the Whites, but in 1919 he had been captured by the Red Army and convinced to advise them. There he saw, as Chiang recalled, how "people who had received no military training could be officers and people who had no battle experience could wage war, and he thought it was really strange." Eventually, he became the leader of a Red Army division, where he served until he learned, one day, that his army was supposed to attack a White division that contained his own younger brother. At this point, Chiang's teacher deserted the Reds but was nevertheless captured along with his brother's troops and jailed, subsequently becoming a teacher. Chiang asked him whether or not he believed in communism, and his teacher answered, "Hard to say, but whoever wants to topple Soviet power is hoping in vain."[33] Experiences and conversations like this gave a more complex and nuanced understanding of life in the Soviet Union to the handful of Chinese who had them.

Not only were high-ranking Chinese like Chiang held in the Soviet Union for safekeeping, but regular students were kept on as well. Among the most fascinating cases were those students who were deemed politically reliable enough for further clandestine training and operations.

In Khabarovsk, for example, an underground camp was founded to educate Chinese in special operations. Yet even here the everyday reality did not match the glamorous expectations. One student who was sent there wrote back to his old Russian commander in Moscow, reporting the utter pointlessness of the so-called training. In February 1930 there were about fifty-eight Chinese in the camp, and they were supposed to be learning bomb making, radio communications, and dynamite laying. But the instructors were recent graduates of Russian military academies who had had even less education in such topics than their Chinese students had had in Moscow over the course of their time in summer camps, military schools, or the Communist Eastern University short courses. Dissatisfied, the fifty-eight Chinese spent their time doing lots of "gymnastics" and collected between themselves seventy rubles to purchase their own radio equipment with which to practice. They also considered buying the chemicals they would need to conduct bomb-making experiments, but they couldn't figure out how to find suppliers.[34]

To relieve their boredom, they paid careful attention to international politics, following revolutionary activity in China and Europe. In this way, an everyday existence in which time passed with excruciating regularity and space was delimited with suffocating exactitude became suffused with consciousness of a global revolution whose possibilities in space and time were breathtaking. "Everyone has the same imaginary idea—that we are all in storage!" the student exclaimed. "Even though it's just a joke, still it contains some real dissatisfaction. Let's get home! . . . If there is no chance of us going home, I wonder if you couldn't have me sent to the area along the Chinese Eastern Railway [in northeastern China] to do spy work."[35] This student's request couldn't have been more timely: in the summer of 1929 a warlord cooperating with Chiang Kaishek had seized control of the railroad, prompting the Soviet Union to invade Manchuria in late 1929 to retake control of it.

RESULTS? TOP-SECRET IRONIES OF THE EVERYDAY

Other Chinese *were* sent to do underground work in borderlands like Xinjiang. This was exactly the sort of work that the military training was supposed to enable Chinese to accomplish. Although military training in the Soviet Union no doubt supplied the Chinese Communists with some capable leaders who were key to future military successes,[36] Comintern archives provide parallel plotlines that verge on the absurd.

As with all such operations, it was the blunders that got reported. In September 1930, a former Moscow Artillery School student wrote in utter exasperation from a Soviet prison in a small border town called Osh (present-day Kyrgyzstan) to beg for help from the Chinese delegation in Moscow.[37] In late 1929, he and five other Chinese students had been ordered to return to China via Xinjiang in order to "lead guerrilla warfare." They were thrilled, "because it meant we'd be able to put all we'd learned about the theory and practice of armed insurrection in the October Revolution to use in China." Their superiors issued them new clothes, gave them thirty American dollars, and put them on a train to Tashkent. There they were met and taken to the border on horseback—and that, as far as the Soviet authorities were concerned, was that.

Not knowing what else to do, they set out on foot through the snowy mountains that lay between them and Kashgar. "Climbing this mountain in the snow with luggage and not knowing the road it goes without saying was really hard," the student wrote. They decided to hire a horse, at which point they were arrested by Chinese border guards. They said what they had been told to say—that they were Chinese traders in Moscow—and they also made a slew of anti-Soviet statements, but the Xinjiang government didn't believe them. The student enumerated all the reasons why not: "1. We were all young, 20–30, we didn't look like people who did business in Moscow, we looked like students, 2. We were all wearing the same new clothes, our suitcases were all about the same, we all had the same stuff, 3. We didn't have passports, and we didn't have passports to GO to Russia, 4. The people who go to Moscow to do business are usually from China's three northern provinces, whereas we are southerners, and southerners are usually revolutionaries . . ." and the list went on.

The Xinjiang government jailed them, then let them live on their own for a while under close supervision. They tried, nevertheless, to make contacts with Soviet agents. One of them applied to study in a special radio technology school (where they tried to do organizational work with the students) and was admitted. But since they could find no trace of any sort of Soviet party organization in Xinjiang, the others decided to return to Moscow. The Xinjiang government gave them permission to leave, but only with a chaperone, who would contact the Chinese embassy in Moscow and investigate their real status. The minute they got to the border near Tashkent they gave their chaperone the slip and went straight to the offices of the Soviet police in Osh . . . where they were promptly arrested by the very Soviet authorities to whom they were fleeing.[38]

So much for "putting all they had learned about the theory and practice of armed insurrection in the October Revolution to use in China." When or how these students ever left the prison, much less the Soviet Union, is unknown.

CONCLUSION

These stories of Chinese in Soviet military schools show not only how silly the sinister can be but also how easily grand strategies of international revolution could be caught in quagmires of prosaic detail. China was one of the few geopolitically significant countries in the world where revolution was even a remote possibility, so the stakes were high—as were the actual monetary costs. Moreover, in the period following Chiang's 1927 reversal, China policy actually became a serious issue in Soviet domestic politics, as both Stalin and Trotsky used it as a proxy in their struggle for power. Each and every Chinese student or activist brought to the Soviet Union in the aftermath of Chiang Kaishek's 1927 reversal was considered to be a precious resource—a scarce shard of raw material to be processed into a highly refined final product, a person capable of fighting effectively for communism in an increasingly dangerous environment.

Yet, however important a Soviet-trained Chinese communist army may have been strategically or theoretically for the international revolutionary movement, in this particular case grandiose objectives and serious considerations were so irrelevant as to make them absurd, even funny. Bad food, good sex, lame teachers, inappropriate clothing, overbearing administrators, excessive booze, the air of petty rebellion that wafts through any group of young people cooped up together—the ordinary complaints of foreign exchange students—made a mockery of the serious considerations of international revolution. Moreover, material details like food, supplies, and translators in Moscow, and then again clothes, maps, cash, and documents once students were given their marching orders, really mattered, and the failure to provide them undermined international revolution both objectively and symbolically.

Students were imbued with revolutionary ardor and thought constantly about the revolution back in China—why else would they have such determination to learn how to fight and feel such fury about the nature of their Soviet education? Yet their smoldering resentments were stoked by the conditions of daily life in Moscow. They *didn't* have enough rifles or bomb-making equipment; their teachers *were* inexperienced; and they *did* mingle with ordinary Soviet people. They found it difficult if not impossible to fulfill the overdetermined political and military expectations for them, and nothing about the organization of their daily lives worked against this defeatist tendency. No wonder they exploded in a fury of confusion and frustration.

The protest of the ninety-four Chinese and its consequences showed how the theoretically unified aspirations of international revolution were contested not only in China but also in Moscow, where everyday difficulties and cross-cultural irritations lent specificity to generalized dissatisfaction. In this case, ultimately, the grand hopes of the Comintern and even CPSU leaders like Trotsky and Stalin were undermined, held hostage, and occasionally imprisoned by everyday obstacles.

NOTES

Research for this article was completed in tandem with research for my book manuscript, "The Sino-Soviet Romance: How Chinese Communists Fell in Love with the Russian Revolution," which tells the stories of six prominent Chinese revolutionaries who traveled to the Soviet Union and whose lives were emblematic of Sino-Soviet relations writ large against the background of ongoing Soviet efforts to educate Chinese radicals in Moscow. The manuscript is a revision of my dissertation, "The Sino-Soviet Romance: How Chinese Communists Fell in Love with Russia, Russians, and the Russian Revolution," University of California, Berkeley, 2010.

1. Exceptions include a pioneering, comparative social history, Smith, *Revolution and the People in Russia and China* (Cambridge: Cambridge University Press, 2008) as well as relatively new research into Russian-Chinese literary relations, such as Mark Gamsa, *The Chinese Translation of Russian Literature: Three Studies* (Leiden: Brill, 2008); Gamsa, *The Reading of Russian Literature in China: A Moral Example and Manual of Practice* (New York: Palgrave Macmillan, 2010); He Donghui, "Coming of Age in the Brave New World: The Changing Reception of the Soviet Novel, *How the Steel Was Tempered,* in the People's Republic of China," in *China Learns from the Soviet Union, 1949–Present,* ed. Thomas Bernstein and Li Hua-yu (Lanham, Md.: Rowman & Littlefield, 2010), which also includes several other articles about Sino-Soviet cultural exchange in the post-1949 period. In Chinese, see Chen Jianhua, *Er shi shiji Zhong E wenxue guanxi* (Chinese-Russian literary relations in the twentieth century) (Beijing: Gao deng jiaoyu chu ban she, 2002). An older Russian treatment is M. E. Shneider, *Russkaia klassika v Kitae: Perevody, otsenki, tvorcheskoe osvoenie* (The Russian classic in China: Translations, evaluations, creative assimilation) (Moscow: Izdatel'stvo "Nauka" glavnaia redaktsiia vostochnoi literatury, 1977). See also Lorenz Luthi, *The Sino-Soviet Split: Cold War in the Communist World* (Princeton, N.J.: Princeton University Press, 2008) and Sergey Radchenko, *Two Suns in the Heavens: The Sino-Soviet Struggle for Supremacy, 1962–1967* (Washington, D.C., and Stanford, Calif.: Woodrow Wilson Center Press and Stanford University Press, 2009). Both of these books are based on extensive use of newly opened archives and focus on the geopolitical and ideological elements of the Sino-Soviet relationship. Classic accounts of the early period include Robert North, *Moscow and Chinese Communists* (Stanford, Calif.: Stanford University Press, 1963); Allen S. Whiting, *Soviet Policies in China, 1917–1924* (New York: Columbia University Press, 1954); Maurice Meisner, *Li Tachao and the Origins of Chinese Marxism,* Harvard East Asian Series 27 (Cambridge, Mass.: Harvard University Press, 1967); Benjamin Schwartz, *Chinese Communism and the Rise of Mao* (Cambridge, Mass.: Harvard University Press, 1979); and Arif Dirlik, *The Origins of Chinese Communism* (New York: Oxford University Press, 1989).

2. The Soviet government also organized and funded the so-called Whampoa military academy in Guangdong for members of the Chinese Nationalist Party, which the Comintern considered a stronger revolutionary party than the Chinese Communists.

3. One of the most useful treatments of the run-up and aftermath to the 1927 debacle is Mechthild Leutner, ed., *The Chinese Revolution in the 1920s: Between Triumph and Disaster* (London: Routledge Curzon, 2002).

4. Yu Minling, "E guo dangan zhong de liu su xuesheng Jiang Jingguo" (Russian exchange student Jiang Jingguo according to Soviet archives), *Zhongyang yanjiu yuan jindai shi yanjiu suo jikan* (Bulletin of the Institute of Modern History, Academia Sinica) 29 (June 1998). Chapters 6 and 7 of my book manuscript focus on Chiang Chingkuo in the USSR.

5. Fang Xuemin, "Guanyu qu Sulian Dongfang Daxue xuexi de huiyi" (A memoir about going to study at the Soviet Eastern University), *Dang shi zi liao cong kan* (Journal of party history), no. 1 (1980): 104–105.

6. Russian State Archive for Social and Political History, Moscow (RGASPI), fond 532, op. 1, d. 35, l. 184. For other such letters from girls, see pages 198–200. In fact, it seems that there was some sort of mix-up with a group of young women students; see RGASPI, fond 532, op. 1, d. 35, l. 177.

7. RGASPI, fond 532, op. 2, d. 97, l. 110a. His statement didn't go over too well with the workers and peasants who made up the majority of the students in the courses and who demanded that he be punished.

8. Wang Fanxi, *Memoirs of a Chinese Revolutionary*, trans. Gregor Benton (New York: Columbia University Press, 1991), 42.

9. RGASPI, fond 532, op. 1, d. 39, l. 111.

10. RGASPI, fond 532, op. 1, d. 39, ll. 9, 19, 34.

11. RGASPI, fond 532, op. 1, d. 39, l. 111.

12. RGASPI, fond 532, op. 1, d. 52, l. 4.

13. RGASPI, fond 532, op. 1, d. 39, l. 55. "In general the Chinese at the present demand that we teach them, chiefly, practical things: preparing bombs, blowing up bridges, shooting from revolvers, using side-arms. They ask that we teach them how to work conspiratorially, how to approach work in the army. A big question, which we haven't completely worked out is the question of the underground techniques. This is the main demand of the participants, which they put forward at all meetings, in all their speeches, everywhere they can."

14. RGASPI, fond 532, op. 1, d. 413, ll. 4–8.

15. RGASPI files on the founding of the courses.

16. Yueh Sheng, *Sun Yat-sen University in Moscow and the Chinese Revolution: A Personal Account* (Lawrence: University of Kansas, Center for East Asian Studies, 1971), 118–20; Jiang Jingguo, *Wo zai Sulian de shenghuo* (My life in the Soviet Union) (Shanghai: Qianfeng chubanshe, 1947), 6–7.

17. Yueh Sheng, *Sun Yat-sen University*, 48.

18. Ibid.

19. Wang Fanxi, *Memoirs*, 44.

20. RGASPI, fond 1, op. 532, d. 35, ll. 117–18. Holding Chinese students back and preventing their return to China for various reasons was common throughout the 1920s and early 1930s.

21. Bruce Elleman, *Moscow and the Emergence of Communist Power in China, 1925–30: The Nanchang Uprising and the Birth of the Red Army* (London: Routledge, 2009), 122–38.

22. Alexander Pantsov, *The Bolsheviks and the Chinese Revolution, 1919–1927* (Richmond, Surrey: Curzon Press, 2000), 183. This book contains a useful overview of Soviet educational initiatives for the Chinese and a detailed study of Chinese Trotskyists in the Soviet Union.

23. RGASPI, fond 532, op. 1, d. 409, ll. 5a, 56, 71–86, 114, 166, 212. Nechaev was the name not only of this Chinese student but also of a famous Russian nihilist of the 1860s. Dudkin was the name of a character from Bely's symbolist novel about revolutionary terrorism, *Petersburg*. Ironically for this story, Bely's Dudkin felt he was possessed by some sort of eastern demonism. On this, see Adam Weiner, *By Authors Possessed: The Demonic Novel in Russia* (Evanston, Ill.: Northwestern University Press, 1988), 167–68. On a student refusing to eat cheese, see RGASPI, fond 532, op. 2, d. 97, l. 110a (in a sentence that Bely himself might have written): "A second fact: one of these comrades, having been in the cafeteria, didn't want to eat cheese and demanded to exchange it, but the *dezhurnaia* refused, so he banged on the table."

24. RGASPI, fond 532, op. 1, d. 409, l. 161, and RGASPI, fond 532, op. 1, d. 35, ll. 181, 192 are examples of complaints about translators: "The translation work is really bad, only 50% or less is translated into Chinese, and the translators fight with the teachers, the questions and answers don't correspond." More complaints from higher-ups: RGASPI, fond 532, op. 1, d. 413, l. 57.

25. RGASPI doc.

26. RGASPI, fond 532, op. 2, d. 97, ll. 112–23.

27. RGASPI, fond 532, op. 1, d. 413, ll. 14–19 are the notes from Malyshev's speech, and pages 21–41 record the students' comments in shorthand in Russian.

28. RGASPI, fond 532, op. 2, d. 97, l. 111a recalls this incident from a different perspective, noting especially how the rowdy students beat the others up.

29. RGASPI, fond 532, op. 1, d. 413, ll. 74–76.

30. RGASPI, fond 532, op. 1, d. 413, ll. 77–80.

31. Kui Song, "1925–1932 nian zai Sulian jun xiao xuexi de Zhongguo xueyuan diaocha biao (zhi yi)" (A Chinese researcher's investigation of military studies in the Soviet Union, 1925–1932 [part one]), *Jun shi lishi* (Journal of military history), no. 1 (1994): 44–45. This PLA history journal article gives a list of 229 Chinese who attended military schools in the Soviet Union, almost all between 1927 and 1930; only one came before 1927, and only a dozen left after 1930; one was in Kiev, another in Kaliningrad, but the rest were in Moscow or at Tolmachev. Most studied for about two years. This list does not include students who ended up in Taiwan. Shi Zhe (who later became one of Mao's translators) recalls that there were fifty or sixty nationalist military students studying with him in Kiev for two years, until after Chiang Kaishek's 1927 reversal, at which point he himself was sent to a Moscow military engineering school. Shi Zhe, *Zai lishi juren de shenbian* (By the side of a great man of history) (Beijing: Zhongyang wenxian chubanshe, 1991), 14–28.

32. Who this person actually was is hard to say. In his Chinese-language memoir, Jiang doesn't call the teacher by name. In his English-language version, he says his "instructor in tactics" was "General Malshev, who was a full general in the Czar's Army." And he claims that "Marshal Tukashevsky was my instructor in military strategy." Ray Cline, *Jiang Jing-guo Remembered* (Washington, D.C.: United States Global Strategy Council, 1989), 164. But there is something not quite right here: many Chinese memoirs garble Russian names or use the name of one person for another. In this case, it seems possible that Jiang was substituting Malyshev—who in fact had come from Tolmachev—for his real teacher's name, which he couldn't remember, and then misspelling it as Malshev. In fact, Malyshev got called all kinds

of things in memoirs—in English, see Wang Fanxi, who called him "Maslov" (*Memoirs,* 62). Here again, Shi Zhe's experience in military school is similar: he seems to have had more substantial relationships with his teachers than the average students at Communist Eastern University or SYSU describe (*Zai lishi juren de shenbian,* 16–20).

33. Jiang Jingguo, *Wo zai Sulian de shenghuo,* 21–29.

34. RGASPI, fond 514, op. 1, d. 602, ll. 7–100b.

35. RGASPI, fond 514, op. 1, d. 602, ll. 7–100b.

36. Kui Song, "1925–1932 nian zai Sulian," was an effort to uncover real data about the Soviet roots of the PLA, listing people who had studied in Soviet military schools, including several well-known PLA leaders.

37. RGASPI, fond 514, op. 1, d. 604, ll. 98–1060b. This letter is the source for the following paragraphs relating this incident.

38. RGASPI, fond 514, op. 1, d. 604, ll. 98–1060b. For another, somewhat similar story, see RGASPI, fond 495, op. 152, d. 155, ll. 1–3, which is a Mongolian security services report dated October 10, 1935, describing the arrival of a group of "illegal" Chinese party workers in Mongolia.

16

Coming Home Soviet Style

The Reintegration of Afghan Veterans
into Soviet Everyday Life

KAREN PETRONE

On August 22, 1990, *Komsomol'skaia pravda* reported that Afghan veteran V. Shumkov "waited for an apartment, but one was not assigned to him." Given the perennial shortage of housing in the Soviet Union, this situation was quite typical, but Shumkov's reaction to his plight was not: "He poured gasoline on himself and lit himself on fire. He died in the emergency room."[1] This simultaneous enactment of protest and suicidal violence brings together several currents in late Soviet life: material shortages, the pain and suffering of a generation of men trained to commit violence and traumatized by their war experience in Afghanistan, the expectation that Soviet society owed its veterans privileges and compensation in exchange for their service on behalf of the Soviet Union, and the marginalization of Afghan veterans in late Soviet society. This essay explores, in particular, the expectations of Afghan veterans that in return for their service to the state they would receive material compensation, improvements in everyday life, and respect, and the veterans' reactions when the late-Soviet state and its citizens did not live up to their part of the bargain as the soldiers understood it.

The conceptual framework of everyday life offers a significant, but rarely studied, window into military service and its aftermath. The military as an institution claimed substantially more control over every aspect of the daily life of its subjects than did civilian life. Conscription pulled soldiers out of their normal milieu, sent them to new places, determined virtually every aspect of their daily routines, trained them in the systematic use of violence, and exposed them to life-threatening danger. While not quite as totalizing as prison life, military life constrained individual everyday choices to a very significant degree. Military regimes set soldiers apart from their civilian peers and defined soldiers' experiences as qualitatively different from those left at home. Just as combat experiences left their imprint on soldiers, so, too, did the routines of barracks life, army food, new social configurations, and the dislocation from home shape the soldiers' lives.

Because of the extreme nature of military life (especially during wartime), there has often been tension surrounding the return of the soldier to "regular" everyday life. The reintegration of the soldier into peacetime society was complicated by his sense of alienation from his civilian peers. Often these tensions played out along gendered lines, with the soldiers resenting the women who stayed at home, safe in the rear, and who now could not understand the changes that war had wrought upon the soldiers' minds and bodies. Soviet veterans struggled to make the transition from a highly regimented and dangerous daily life to one that was shaped by ordinary work and leisure. They left their tightly organized peer group (one might even say "brutally organized" through strict military discipline, hazing, and *dedovshchina*—the systematic abuse of new recruits by senior soldiers) for life among people who had little idea what these soldiers had experienced during their time in the army.

This distinction between the soldier and the civilian was heightened in the Soviet Union by the state's elevation of the soldier and the veteran as model citizens, honored for their sacrifice on behalf of the motherland. Throughout Soviet (and Russian) history, there has been a strong connection between military service, citizenship, and the receipt of material privileges and concessions as well as honor and status. Joshua Sanborn demonstrates that the successful Soviet mobilization of soldiers during the Civil War was based on an informal "contract" in which the state acknowledged that, in return for military service, soldiers "deserved to have their family's welfare protected by the state in their absence, to receive a promise of respect from state authorities, and to be granted privileges in relation to their non-warrior fellow citizens."[2] This contract also, in theory, included care and support for veterans who came home from war with physical and mental wounds. Soviet veterans had to fight hard, however, to receive what they had been promised. Due to the severe economic crises of the Soviet state in the 1920s, the central government could not afford to provide relief for perhaps over two million mentally and physically disabled veterans from World War I and the Civil War, never mind benefits for healthy veterans.[3] Nor did veterans gain a particularly high level of prestige.

Although both the number of war invalids eligible for pensions and the size of the pensions increased steadily throughout the 1920s and 1930s to almost two hundred thousand pensioners in 1939, only a small fraction of war invalids received pensions or placement in invalid homes and work cooperatives. The Soviet state's failure to live up to its obligations to soldiers did not escape the notice of the military. As the commander of the Moscow Garrison and the Moscow Military District wrote in a secret report to the Central Committee in the late 1920s: "The position of disabled persons cannot but affect the morale of the Red Army. Invalids appearing on crutches without hands, legs, starving and ill-clad as a result of being denied legal aid produces a painful impression and comprises a significant agitator against Soviet power."[4] Although officials were concerned that inadequate aid to war invalids would threaten current Red Army morale, the majority, if not the vast majority, of disabled veterans were nonetheless denied compensation.

Soviet World War II veterans also had to wage a long campaign to gain their rights and benefits after they defeated the Germans. As Mark Edele has shown, these veterans lobbied the state for benefits for over thirty years after mass demobilization and received institutionalized status as an entitlement group only in 1978.[5] By the 1980s, World War II veterans had succeeded in obtaining special *l'goty* (privileges) such as access to special stores and "personal privileges such as free housing, free or heavily discounted food packages, cars, medicine, health-care, and transportation, and other in-kind benefits," but this generosity to the veterans and recognition of their special status had taken decades to establish.[6]

Afghan veterans' expectations were raised by the example of the benefits and honor accorded to the World War II generation before them. Given the hard-fought nature of the World War II veterans' battle to gain benefits and the vast difference in heroic status between the victorious World War II veterans and the Afghan veterans who had been trapped in a secret and brutal counterinsurgency against enemies they had difficulty defining, these expectations were not likely to be fulfilled. World War II veterans were jealous of their hard-fought concessions and did not want to share the elevated status and material benefits for which they had worked so long with the seemingly upstart Afghan veterans. One veteran from Leningrad, M. Tikhonov, complained in a letter that was published in *Pravda* on November 25, 1987: "It is fundamentally incorrect to put the soldiers who served in Afghanistan on the same footing as participants in the Great Patriotic War. During the 1,418 days and nights of the Patriotic War, we fought against fascism and destroyed it. What can that have in common with Afghanistan? Nothing. So why have they been given equal rights with us?"[7] This kind of resentment made homecoming even more difficult.

The long Soviet silence about the war in Afghanistan led to both a fundamental lack of understanding on the part of the Soviet public and rapid disillusionment once ugly details about the war began to emerge during the glasnost era, beginning in 1985. It was not only World War II veterans who challenged the status of Afghan veterans. One Afghan veteran complained about the attitude of the younger generation toward the Afghan veterans: "Officially we have the same status as the World War II vets. The only difference is, they were defenders of the Fatherland, whereas we're seen as the Germans—one young lad actually said that to me!"[8] The Afghan veterans were doubly disadvantaged. Given the economic constraints of the late Brezhnev and Gorbachev periods, they would have had difficulties receiving their entitlements even in a war that was both in the public eye and heroic. Because of the Soviet population's earlier lack of awareness about the war and the growing perceptions that the war was a "political mistake" and that the Afghan soldiers were murderers, their struggle was even harder.[9]

By the early 1990s, these popular perceptions produced a "wave of hatred," against Afghan veterans.[10] Strangely enough, the veterans of the Afghan war came to be known as "Afghantsy," or Afghans. This nomenclature blended the very identities of the Soviet soldiers and the people whom they were supposed to be helping in international brotherhood. As was the case for American soldiers during the Vietnam War, the unpopularity of the war rubbed off on the veterans, and soon the glasnost era Soviet press began to write about the Afghan veterans in the trope of the dangerous veteran who brought the violence of war home with him. Although popular reactions in the Soviet Union were rarely as extreme as in the United States, where Vietnam veterans were sometimes spat upon and called "baby killers," negative depictions of the veterans complicated popular attitudes toward them as they sought to gain benefits after returning home.[11] These unfavorable images of the Afghantsy raised the question of whether they were deserving of benefits after all.

Because of a steady stream of Soviet anti-American propaganda in the 1960s and 1970s, the roles of American soldiers in the Vietnam War and the troubled homecoming of American soldiers was a familiar topic to a Soviet audience. As more information about the war in Afghanistan became available in the Soviet press starting in 1985, it did not take long for Soviets, Americans, and Europeans to begin to compare the two wars and their aftermaths.[12] The mid-1980s saw a rise in people-to-people diplomacy, and during a trip to the Soviet Union, Diana Glasgow of the Earthstewards Network in Seattle, Washington, met Soviet Afghan veterans who were seeking assistance "in order to meet a variety of postwar challenges." She organized a delegation of American Vietnam veterans, psychologists, and a prosthetic specialist to meet with Afghan veterans and Soviet health experts in September 1988. Several other delegations followed, and the participants discovered that they had much in common and much to learn from the way that American experts had helped veterans.[13]

Soviet Afghan veteran Vladislav Tamarov was one of the participants in these exchanges. He described the meeting of the Afghan and Vietnam veterans at the airport during the Americans' second visit: "Almost none of them spoke Russian, and only a few of us spoke English. Within five minutes we knew we had found friends, even more than that—blood brothers by blood. How did we understand each other? I don't know. But they understood us a lot better than our own people did." Tamarov's dramatic statement that the soldiers who fought in Vietnam, much vilified in the Soviet press, understood the Afghan veterans better than their own people strengthened his belief that Afghanistan was the Soviet Union's Vietnam. Tamarov implied that the instant connection of the veterans stemmed from their commonality of experience both during the wars and in their homecomings. These visits also demonstrated to Soviet Afghan veterans that much more could be done to help them adjust to civilian life than was being done in the Soviet Union at the time.[14]

The notion of a complex moral and economic exchange between the state and the veterans continued into the post-Soviet period. Serguei Oushakine, in his ethnography of Chechen veterans in the post-Soviet period, has noted how "the theme of compensation, benefits, privileges, and money emerged alongside the theme of patriotic duty," with veterans feeling that they had "already paid our Motherland in full," while "the state has not settled the account [with us.]"[15] Many Afghan veterans likewise felt that they had been shortchanged in the interaction between state and soldier. One military adviser from the Afghan war articulated this frustration. "Society is good at *doing* things, 'giving' medical help, pensions, flats. But all this so-called giving has been paid for in very expensive currency. Our blood."[16] As the Soviet Union crumbled, even this unequal and inadequate "giving" became difficult for the state.

The growing inadequacy of the exchange between the state and the soldiers came at a time when the Soviet economy struggled to supply its citizens with basic material necessities. One of the hallmarks of the late Soviet period was the increasing inability of the socialist production and distribution system to provide for the needs of Soviet citizens, leading to widespread corruption, a burgeoning black market, and the use of informal networks to gain access to coveted goods.[17] Soviet soldiers in Afghanistan were profoundly affected by these economic trends. The failures of the state to fulfill its part of the bargain in relation to the Afghan soldiers began in Afghanistan. Supply was poor, and the soldiers found themselves lacking food, clothing, and basic equipment.

In memoirs written in the late 1980s and early 1990s, soldiers reported going hungry. One soldier who weighed eighty kilos when he joined the army lost nineteen kilos because of the "dried potatoes that you could've used to caulk the windows, the sort of bread that broke my teeth when I ate it, porridge that looked most of all like something left in the toilet bowl." This soldier concluded, "For me, all of Afghanistan was one single heartburn. I don't even know from what it finally derived: spoiled bread or moldy cigarettes."[18] Another infantry soldier recalled, "I myself had to open up meat that was butchered in 1941 or 1953. Even that kind of meat would've been a great treat for us, because we were fed lard instead of meat. If you turned a piece of lard upside down on the plate, on the other side you could always see a row of bristles." After the war, this soldier complained that he "never succeeded" in reaching his "normal weight."[19] A key aspect of the war experience, then, for many Soviet soldiers was physical deprivation because of an inadequate diet. This failure to nourish the soldiers adequately affected their health negatively in the long term.

The lack of nutritious food also led to behaviors that damaged both the soldiers and the war effort. One nurse recalled, "They were dying for three roubles a month—that was a private's pay. Three roubles, meat crawling with worms, and scraps of rotten fish. We all had scurvy, I lost all my front teeth. So they sold their blankets and bought opium, or something sweet to eat, or some foreign gimmicks."[20] Another veteran reported being punished for selling a "huge tub of butter . . . over the fence to some Afghans." He did this to buy food, because "army food was so bad that we tried to buy extra food in the commissary, or from the Afghans themselves."[21] This vicious cycle of wartime shortages, leading to theft and corruption and then to even greater shortages, was hardly exclusive to the Afghantsy or to the Brezhnev period. In fact, similar tales of failures in supply, corrupt officers, and looting of the civilian population were standard in Russia's modern wars (and not just in Russia's). What is striking is that in the 1980s, the soldiers faced this cycle of shortage and corruption both in Afghanistan and when they arrived home. This situation led to a widespread disregard for the law in both places.

As in the Soviet Union, shortages were exacerbated because soldiers stole everything they could get their hands on in the barracks to trade with the Afghans. As one soldier reported, "Everyone traded, officers as well as the rest of us, heroes as well as cowards. Knives, bowls, spoons, forks, mugs, stools, hammers, they all got nicked from the canteen and the barracks. Bayonets disappeared from their automatics, mirrors from cars, spare parts, medals. . . . You could sell anything."[22] Because the state was not supplying or compensating the soldiers adequately, the soldiers felt justified in appropriating state property for their own ends.

The soldiers' struggles for the necessities of daily life took place in an environment that was strange to the soldiers: a marketplace where luxury and other desirable goods were widely available to those who could afford to purchase them from Afghan vendors. One soldier remarked: "In an Afghan market you could see everything between heaven and earth, beginning with a Toyota and modern stereo equipment and ending with little nuts and screws."[23] Another soldier explained: "We saw that the stores were bulging with goods—Japanese electronics and all sorts of things that you couldn't even dream of at home in the Soviet Union. All that was just eyewash, though. Very few Afghans could buy those goods."[24] The latter soldier embraced a class-based critique of capitalist consumption, pointing out that such luxury goods were out of the reach of ordinary people both in Afghanistan and the Soviet Union. Yet the open display of stores "bulging with goods" raised possibilities in the minds of soldiers that could not be entertained in the Soviet Union, as goods in special closed stores for the party elite and foreigners were not accessible to ordinary people.

Hierarchies of consumption reigned both in the Soviet Union and in Afghanistan. Soldiers complained that officers were particularly focused on acquiring luxury items: "An all-encompassing moral corruption prevailed in our officer corps. Everyone had an incomprehensible urge to grab for himself as much as possible: cassette tape players, blue jeans, leather jackets, drugs. They got those things by doing business." The soldier was disgusted by the avarice of the officers and contemptuous of "doing business" as a form of becoming rich at the expense of others. At the same time, he bemoaned how "all-encompassing that degeneration was. It seemed that the only thing that people thought about was grabbing things for themselves, from the lowest rank of the hierarchy all the way to the top."[25] He and several other Soviet citizens witnessing events in Afghanistan recognized the disjuncture between the idealistic words of proletarian brotherhood that supposedly defined their mission and the crass everyday behavior of Soviet soldiers and officers. While this soldier saw as despicable the officers who sent home a Mercedes-Benz or got into a drunken brawl as they carried home large numbers of cassette recorders, he recognized that all of the troops were implicated in such behavior.

This disregard for state property inevitably undermined Soviet military efforts and worsened the shortages of basic supplies. Just as in the Soviet Union, the actions that citizens took to address economic shortages created a spiral of worsening conditions and led to the humiliation of the soldiers, many of whom were dying for a country that could not even supply them with such basic necessities as food and underwear or with housing and a job when they returned home.

The transition of Soviet veterans returning home from Afghanistan was also complicated by the fact that after 1985 the Soviet Union was in the process of a thoroughgoing economic reform under Gorbachev's perestroika, or "restructuring." New economic opportunities such as cooperative for-profit private businesses were opening up for the first time; simultaneously, the Communist Party sought to reinvigorate Communist ideology by emphasizing the heroic nature of reform. The upheaval of the reforms, far from improving production and distribution, actually exacerbated some of the economic problems facing the country, making shortages more common at the same time that new economic ventures were taking off. The veterans returned to a country that was seeking a new path and was unsure of the direction in which it was heading.

Soviet official representations of the war in the early days of Gorbachev's reform era sought to heroize the returning veterans as the exemplars of the kind of selfless idealism that would be necessary to make perestroika work. Aleksandr Drobotov, a thirty-three-year-old investigator from the city of Togliatti whose specialization was the investigation of the theft of state property through embezzlement or abuse of office, wrote a letter to *Komsomol'skaia pravda* in which he described meeting Anatolii, a young veteran who had recently returned from a year-and-a-half-long tour of duty in Afghanistan. The investigator was in awe of the veteran, who had "not cooled down from the white heat of revolution; he had been refashioned and reshaped by it."[26] Drobotov believed that war provided the revolutionary heat that transformed Afghan veterans into a new (and presumably better) generation of men, the "new Soviet men" of perestroika. Drobotov played off of the official framing of Afghanistan as an "internationalist" and, therefore, revolutionary duty to indicate the necessity for moral revolution at home.

Drobotov claimed that because Anatolii had served in Afghanistan, he had overcome a base desire for material things. Anatolii had fought in numerous battles and had lost a dear friend, a "comrade-in-arms," to sniper fire in one of those battles. Because of these experiences, he had given up his "laziness and idleness" and was now completely different from his materialistic girlfriend and his circle of male friends at home. According to the letter, the veteran's "pre-Army friends were chasing after fine clothes and new musical recordings; someone was about to buy a car." And his girlfriend took him shopping for "brand-name" clothes so that he would "measure up." The veteran asked in response, "What did my comrade die for? Was it really for these speculators, for these satisfied self-seekers, who are content with everything? Why is that battle going on 'there'? So we can live like this afterwards? To grab and covet, to get drunk?"[27]

The letter writer utilized the trope of the alienation of the veteran from the home front, bolstered by the misogynistic image of the cold, ambitious girlfriend questioning the veteran's masculinity, for his own particular purpose. According to Drobotov, it was the veteran's disgust at the pursuit of the material that made him question why he had fought in Afghanistan. If he and his fallen comrades sacrificed themselves in Afghanistan, then those at home, both men and women, should also sacrifice on behalf of a higher purpose. The veteran spurned the material in search of the elevated truths of self-sacrifice and service to his country; the letter writer raised up the veteran as an example of both the self-sacrifice and the rejection of materialism that were necessary to eradicate corruption in the system.

But Drobotov's admiration of the veteran was tempered by a more ominous revelation: the veteran planned to call upon a group of fellow Afghan veterans to enact vigilante justice upon a corrupt official whom the investigator had failed to bring to justice through the regular channels.[28] The white heat of revolutionary tempering and the exposure to violent conflict in Afghanistan led Afghan veterans to bring the violence of Afghanistan home. Their frustrations with those who did not appreciate their sacrifices might be resolved through the targeted use of violence. If they were now hardened revolutionaries fighting against the lazy and materialistic Soviet population, then revolutionary violence was both sanctioned and necessary. In this letter we see both the admiration of the Afghantsy for their sacrifice and the fear of how their wartime transformations might affect Soviet society back home. This letter also reveals a dilemma of perestroika: How could reforms gain traction if the Soviet population was complacent? Would "revolutionary" violence be required to enact reforms?

What Drobotov's letter failed to capture was that the Afghan veterans were faced with the problem of whether to acquire goods that might be sold on the black market from the moment that they arrived in Afghanistan. Soldiers had access to all kinds of foreign goods (either through looting or purchase), and they could easily bring those goods back with them to the Soviet Union. Many soldiers brought back carpets, jewelry, and what seemed to be the most coveted prize: a foreign cassette player. The "grabbing" and "coveting" were not just going on inside the Soviet Union. While this phenomenon disgusted some soldiers, every Soviet soldier, like every Soviet citizen at home, was engaged in "illegal" buying and selling that undermined both the idealism of the mission in Afghanistan and the idealism needed for reform at home.

Other soldiers' accounts from interviews conducted in the late 1980s echo the words of the veteran whom Drobotov met. One private in the signal corps who lost an arm in the war recorded the reaction of his friends when he returned home: "I met some old friends. 'Did you bring back a sheepskin? A Japanese cassette player? What, nothing? Are you sure you were in Afghanistan?' I only wish I'd brought my gun back with me!" This soldier expressed his sense of alienation from those at home and the fantasy of violence against those who did not understand the ordeal of the Afghan veterans. The soldiers who were motivated by something beyond the material expressed their frustration with their peers' material expectations in violent terms. Like Anatolii, this veteran entertained the possibility of violence as a solution to his disillusionment at home.

This soldier also expressed disgust at the avarice of his fellow soldiers after "seeing planes take off for home with a cargo of zinc coffins, plus suitcases full of leather jackets, jeans, women's underwear, China tea."[29] For this soldier, no material goods could ever make up for his lost arm and his lost comrades in Afghanistan. The juxtaposition of the zinc coffins containing the bodies of the dead soldiers and the luxury goods being taken home to enjoy was, to him, profoundly disgusting. Unlike in the letter in Komsomol'skaia pravda, there was no redemption through the possibility of revolutionary transformation of society. The only possible solution was further violence.

After he returned home, another soldier, a private and a gunner, was tortured by the question, "What did my best mate die for? For these fat speculators and black marketers you see everywhere? It's all wrong here, and I feel like a stranger in my own country." This quote is striking in its similarity to Drobotov's 1986 letter to *Pravda,* which seems to have captured the attitude of at least some Afghan veterans but then used it to call for revolutionary action on behalf of perestroika, a position that most Afghan veterans would not endorse. The returning veterans found the economic breakdown in late-Soviet society and its ubiquitous petty corruption to be extremely galling because they did not deem their fellow countrymen worthy of the sacrifices the soldiers had made. The veterans were angry at a state that did not provide adequate care for them, at Soviet citizens who were too engaged in their day-to-day activities of getting and spending to honor the veterans' sacrifice, and at their fellow veterans who enriched themselves while their comrades died. These feelings are certainly not exclusive to Soviet Afghan veterans. One can find similar reactions among American Iraq and Afghanistan veterans today. What made Soviet veterans' plight particularly difficult was the degree of breakdown in the economic system in the mid-1980s and the impact of first secrecy and then glasnost on Soviet public opinion about the war.

Once Soviet veterans returned home, some of the most acute problems of veterans had to do with satisfying their basic material needs. Disabled veterans complained of discrimination in housing, and other veterans "decried the public indifference or even resentment shown veterans when they come home and apply for jobs or apartments."[30] One veteran interviewed at the turn of the 1990s complained about the state's broken promises and lamented the loss of his health because of the Afghan war: "The Afghan war veterans were promised benefits and allowances. We haven't heard about them. Now nine years have passed since I returned from Afghanistan. I still don't have a place to live. . . . I went to work in a mine because you can retire from that ten years earlier." This veteran did not think that he would be able to make it to the regular retirement age of sixty, because "my health will never last that long."[31] The veterans suffered because the state, in the waning days of the Soviet Union, could not fulfill its commitments to the Afghan soldiers.

An officer (a sapper) who lost both legs in an explosion complained about the quality of Soviet prostheses. "Have you ever tried our Soviet-manufactured prostheses? I've heard that abroad, people with artificial limbs go skiing, play tennis and dance. Why don't the authorities use foreign currency to buy decent arms and legs instead of wasting it on French cosmetics, subsidized Cuban sugar, or Moroccan oranges?"[32] Here the officer indicts the government for two different kinds of failures: the inability to organize production in a way that competes with the West, and the skewed priorities of a state that would import luxuries and grant aid to other countries before it helped the soldiers who had sacrificed their health for the country.

The officer also lost his sight in the explosion that took his legs. Because of his disabilities, he was given piecework manufacturing to do at home, but he complained bitterly about the indignity of this: "I'd like to write a book about the way an officer can be reduced to a housebound wreck, earning his bread assembling lamp-sockets and wall-plugs, about a hundred a day, or putting the metal bits on the ends of shoelaces. . . . He ties string-bags, and glues little boxes—the sort of work he used to think only lunatics did."[33] The state's system of compensation for disabled veterans did not take into account individual talents and abilities but rather assigned menial at-home labor to those no longer mobile enough to go out to work. From a statistical point of view, this was a disabled veteran who had received compensation and a new livelihood. From the officer's point of view, he was relegated to the same status as "lunatic," despite his previous skilled work and respected role as an officer and a sapper. This officer felt that even when the state did its best, it could never make up for the consequences of the war in Afghanistan.

Another officer described his frustration with the Soviet population. Because those around them don't "want to know" what happened in Afghanistan, the young veterans struggled with finding "moral values for themselves." Some fantasized about murdering these "know-nothings" who wanted to spit in the veterans' faces, accusing them, "You bastards! You killed and robbed and now you expect special privileges?" The officer complained: "We're expected to take all the blame, *and* to accept that everything we went through was for nothing."[34] This officer drew a direct connection between the people accusing Afghan veterans of committing unjustified violence and society's unwillingness to grant them the same privileges that World War II veterans were receiving. Furthermore, he described the young veterans' fantasies of violence against their accusers, showing how violence and the threat of violence were ever present as both the cause of the problem and the potential solution to the problem. In a society in which personal ties and networks substantially influenced the distribution of goods and services, one can imagine that the population's ill-will toward and mistrust of the Afghan veterans could easily translate into difficulties in gaining jobs, housing, and other benefits. It was not just state mandates that were decisive in determining veterans' well-being.

In their day-to-day activities, Afghan veterans had to assert themselves in order to access the privileges they felt they had earned through their wartime service. One Afghan veteran witnessed a confrontation between another veteran and civilians waiting in line for oranges. The veteran "came straight up to the counter," cutting the line. An "athletic" boy of seventeen who was at the front of the line "said something to the fellow through clenched teeth. The old woman behind him joined in and began to scold halfheartedly. In a flash, the guy turned around and shoved a certificate under the boy's nose. 'Here, look. I have the right. I spilled blood in Afghanistan while you were here.'"[35] The everyday activity of buying food precipitated a dispute over the soldier's right to receive goods without having to wait in line. And, undoubtedly, this kind of interaction occurred frequently when young, seemingly healthy veterans claimed the same rights as World War II veterans.[36] The Afghan veterans had to choose on a daily basis whether to confront their fellow citizens in order to claim their rights. Many simple interactions were therefore fraught with tension. Equally telling is the veteran's explanation about why he had the right to cut the line. He did not invoke his service to the state or the sacrifice of being put in harm's way. Rather, he recounted "spilling blood" on the citizens' behalf. This veteran himself raised the issue that the Afghantsy were killers, but here traumatic (and perhaps guilt-inducing) experience served as justification for compensation.

But even when Soviet citizens acknowledged the right of the veterans to privileges, the veterans did not always receive this acknowledgment with gratitude. The same embittered officer who was angry that Soviet citizens blamed veterans for the violence in Afghanistan was appalled at a sign at a new perestroika-era cooperative pay toilet. This toilet was opened in one of Moscow's railway stations as a private enterprise. The sign announced, "Children up to 7 years, invalids, veterans of World War II and wars of liberation—free." The "young lad" who ran the toilet was pleased to be offering this benefit to veterans, but the officer responded irately, "'So my father went through the whole war, and I spent two years with my mouth full of Afghan sand, just so we could piss for nothing in your toilet?' I said. I hated that boy more than I hated anyone all the time I was in Afghan. *He* had decided to pay *me*."[37] This unexpected reaction reveals the complexities of the veterans' attitudes. They felt that the people back home were in their debt, yet this debt could never be paid to them, because any attempt to do so trivialized their sacrifice. They wanted to claim what they considered owed to them, but the notion that someone was "giving" them anything infuriated them. They could never be adequately paid back for what they had given to the Soviet Union, and attempts to try to pay them back were met with hostility, hatred, and fantasies of violent retribution.

There was a broad consensus that had developed throughout the Soviet period that the state should give its veterans privileges and respect in exchange for their service, yet the state was rarely able to fulfill its part of the bargain, and from 1917 onward, veterans had to fight for the privileges and respect that the state had promised. In the case of the Afghan veterans, there were several impediments blocking this exchange of material goods for service. The first was the failing production and distribution system, which did not enable the Soviet economy to supply the soldiers efficiently or provide for material goods and services upon their return. But this economic aspect of late Soviet culture was only one layer of the complex set of exchanges between the Soviet population and the veterans.

Another aspect of the exchange was based on the perceptions of the disillusioned Soviet population. When the war in Afghanistan went from secret to public, the population rejected Soviet involvement in a senseless foreign war. And as the glasnost press revealed some of the brutalities perpetrated by Soviet soldiers in their counterinsurgency war in Afghanistan, the population increasingly saw the returning soldiers as murderers of innocent Afghans. Some of the difficulties faced by veterans occurred because the population remained relatively indifferent to their plight, and social networks that might have been employed on veterans' behalf remained unutilized. Under these circumstances some Afghan veterans reached out to American veterans of the Vietnam War who had endured a similarly complex homecoming. In doing so, veterans indicted both the Soviet population and the government for failing to understand them and pointed to the superior benefits and services available to veterans in the

United States. By embracing a former enemy, these veterans underscored the inadequacy of the Soviet response to their sacrifices.

Even in cases when the state and its citizens did their best to provide compensation, benefits, and privileges to the Afghan veterans, some veterans perceived this compensation to be inadequate. The veterans did not want the charity of others, since they had earned these rights and privileges with their blood, their limbs, and their lives. In sum, at the economic level, the social level, and the moral or personal level, the system of exchange between Afghan veterans and the state was broken. Ominously, the Afghan veterans envisioned violence as a currency with which they could redefine this broken exchange. Some veterans directed this violence against themselves in drug abuse, alcoholism, and suicide. The glasnost press also recognized the Afghan veterans' potential for committing violence against others, associating the veterans with disorder and criminal activity in late-Soviet and post-Soviet society. The failures of the Soviet and post-Soviet systems to address the everyday needs and expectations of both Afghan soldiers in the field and returning veterans, and soldiers' frustration with everyday life both in Afghanistan and at home, led to the violence of war penetrating the psyche and sometimes the security of the Russian home front.

NOTES

1. Quoted in E. Ia. Tarshis, "Problemy sotsial'noi reabilitatsii uchastnikov voiny v Afganistane v materialakh pressy," in *Problemy sotsial'noi reabilitatsii uchastnikov voiny v Afganistane, 1979–1989 gg.*, ed. A. V. Kinsburskii and M. N. Topalov (Moscow: Institut sotsiologii RAN, 1993), 30. This extreme form of protest, in modern times most closely associated with Buddhist protests in South Vietnam and with Vietnam antiwar protests, spread to Eastern Europe after the invasion of Czechoslovakia. In 1978 a Crimean Tatar named Musa Mamut, who was arrested for living in Crimea without a residence permit after returning from the Stalin-era mass deportation, set himself on fire. Shumkov was not the last Russian veteran to take his life by self-immolation because he was not given an apartment. In 2010 an eighty-six-year-old World War II veteran living in a nursing home committed suicide by self-immolation because he "was believed to be upset about being unable to obtain an apartment of his own, which he had sought under a program providing housing for World War II veterans." Eight other residents of the nursing home were also killed in the fire. See http://www.cbsnews.com/stories/2010/08/30/world/main6818971.shtml.

2. Joshua Sanborn, *Drafting the Russian Nation: Military Conscription, Total War, and Mass Politics, 1905–1925* (DeKalb: Northern Illinois University Press, 2003), 50.

3. This analysis is based on Karen Petrone, *The Great War in Russian Memory* (Bloomington: Indiana University Press, 2011), 120–21. See also Vincent Comerchero, "From Outcasts to Allies: Red Army Veterans and the Soviet State from the Introduction of the New Economic Policy through the First Five Year Plan" (PhD diss., Indiana University, 1997), 203; Emily E. Pyle, "Village Social Relations and the Reception of Soldiers' Family Aid Policies in Russia, 1912–1921" (PhD diss., University of Chicago, 1997), 310–11; Catherine Merridale, *Night of Stone: Death and Memory in Twentieth-Century Russia* (New York: Viking Press, 2000), 117.

4. Comerchero, *From Outcasts to Allies,* 212–13.

5. Mark Edele, "Soviet Veterans as an Entitlement Group, 1945–1955," *Slavic Review* 65, no. 1 (Spring 2006): 111.

6. Serguei Alex. Oushakine, *The Patriotism of Despair: Nation, War and Loss in Russia* (Ithaca, N.Y.: Cornell University Press, 2009), 165.

7. A. Simurov and P. Studenikin, "Returning to What Was Printed: 'There Is No Gratitude in Their Hearts,'" *Current Digest of the Soviet Press* 39, no. 48, December 30, 1987, 6.

8. "Private, Grenadier Battalion," in *Zinky Boys: Soviet Voices from the Afghanistan War,* ed. Svetlana Alexievich (New York: W. W. Norton, 1992), 19. The title of the collection *Zinky Boys* refers to the fact that the dead from Afghanistan were sent home in zinc coffins.

9. "1st Lieutenant i/c Mortar Platoon," in Alexievich, *Zinky Boys,* 95.

10. A. V. Kinsburskii and M. N. Topalov, "Teoreticheskie aspekty izucheniia problem sotsial'noe reabilitatsii veteranov voiny v Afganistane," in Kinsburskii and Topalov, *Problemy sotsial'noi reabilitatsii,* 8; N. Engver, in *Radikal,* no. 3 (1991), quoted in Tarshis, "Problemy sotsial'noi reabilitatsii," 31.

11. See Bob Greene, *Homecoming* (New York: G. P. Putnam's Sons, 1989), for firsthand accounts of soldiers arriving home to spitting and taunts.

12. Hartwig Nathe, "Afghanistan War Veterans: 'What's the Point of It All?' The Soviet Union Has to Deal with Disenchanted Soldiers Frustrated by a Far-Away Conflict," *Sun Sentinel,* March 23, 1986, http://articles.sun-sentinel.com/1986-03-23/features/8601180076_1 _afghanistan-veterans-soldiers-soviet-union, accessed on August 3, 2012; Bill Keller, "Soviet Afghanistan Veterans Call for End of Neglect and for Honor," *New York Times,* November 22, 1987, http://www.nytimes.com/1987/11/22/world/soviet-afghanistan-veterans-call-for -end-of-neglect-and-for-honor.html?pagewanted=all&src=pm, accessed August 4, 2012.

13. Walter H. Capps, *The Unfinished War: Vietnam and the American Conscience,* rev. ed. (Boston: Beacon Press, 1990), 163–66, quote on 163.

14. Vladislav Tamarov, *Afghanistan: A Russian Soldier's Story,* trans. Naomi Marcus, Marianne Clark Trangen, and Vladislav Tamarov (Berkeley: Ten Speed Press, 2001), originally published as *Afghanistan: Soviet Vietnam* (San Francisco: Mercury House, 1992).

15. Oushakine, *The Patriotism of Despair,* 165.

16. "A Military Adviser," in Alexievich, *Zinky Boys,* 36.

17. See James R. Millar, "The Little Deal: Brezhnev's Contribution to Acquisitive Socialism," *Slavic Review* 44, no. 4 (Winter 1985): 694–706.

18. "Yuri Yurchenko," in *The Soldiers' Story: Soviet Veterans Remember the Afghan War,* ed. Anna Heinamaa, Maija Leppanen, and Yuri Yurchenko, trans. A. D. Haun (Berkeley: International and Area Studies, University of California, 1994), 18–19.

19. "Aleksandr Lavrov," in Heinamaa, Leppanen, and Yurchenko, *The Soldiers' Story,* 60.

20. "Nurse," in Alexievich, *Zinky Boys,* 26.

21. Tamarov, *Afghanistan,* 94.

22. "Private, Grenadier Battalion," in Alexievich, *Zinky Boys*, 18.

23. "Vladimir Rudoi," in Heinamaa, Leppanen, and Yurchenko, *The Soldiers' Story*, 47.

24. "Nikolai Knyazev," in Heinamaa, Leppanen, and Yurchenko, *The Soldiers' Story*, 48.

25. "Yuri Yurchenko," in Heinamaa, Leppanen, and Yurchenko, *The Soldiers' Story*, 16–17. See also "Yuri Khlusov," in Heinamaa, Leppanen, and Yurchenko, *The Soldiers' Story*, 32.

26. *Komsomol'skaia pravda*, January 8, 1986, 4, *Current Digest of the Soviet Press* 38, no. 1 (1986): 1.

27. Ibid., 2.

28. Ibid., 3. A similar incident, in which a veteran who was trying to fight a "trade mafia" landed in prison, was recorded in *Komsomol'skaia Pravda* on March 30, 1990 (Tarshis, "Problemy sotsial'noi reabilitatsii," 30).

29. "Private, Signals Corps," in Alexievich, *Zinky Boys*, 56.

30. *New York Times*, November 22, 1987.

31. "Yuri Tinkov," in Heinamaa, Leppanen, and Yurchenko, *The Soldiers' Story*, 13.

32. "1st Lieutenant i/c Mortar Platoon," in Alexievich, *Zinky Boys*, 95.

33. Ibid., 99.

34. "1st Lieutenant, Battery Commander," in Alexievich, *Zinky Boys*, 113.

35. Tamarov, *Afghanistan*, 133.

36. When there were significant shortages of goods, there was also some popular resentment of World War II veterans who claimed their right to be served "outside of the line."

37. "1st Lieutenant, Battery Commander," in Alexievich, *Zinky Boys*, 113.

17

Everyday Life in Transnational Perspective
Consumption and Consumerism, 1917–1939

CHOI CHATTERJEE

I have measured out my life with coffee spoons.
—T. S. Eliot, *The Love Song of J. Alfred Prufrock,* 1920

Love's boat has smashed against the daily grind.
—Vladimir Mayakovsky, *Past One O'clock,* 1930

Amoeba-like lines were straightened out in shops and cafeterias, and an effort was made to unclog the service and distribution process—to this day a major psychic scourge to foreign residents in the Soviet Union.
—Richard Stites, *Revolutionary Dreams,* 1989

Following the revolution of 1917, a sizable community of intrepid Americans, both male and female, traveled to the Soviet Union to report on the birth of a newly emerging civilization. There was an historical reason for this interest, as in the preceding decades scores of writers, journalists, engineers, businessmen, and tourists had toured this vast and strange land called the Russian Empire and recorded their impressions of the people and the civilizations in which those people lived.[1] Travel literature on Russia, both popular and academic, was already an established literary genre, and publishing companies in the United States devoted specialized series to reportage about the empire. The Soviet authorities courted well-known American intellectuals and journalists in the hopes that they would give the revolution a glowing bill of health, and organizations such as the International Association of Revolutionary Writers (MOPR), the All Union Society for Cultural Relations with Foreign

Countries (VOKS), and subsequently the Foreign Tourist (Intourist) were specifically created by the Soviet government to "manage" the travel experiences of the visitors. While Europeans were equally fascinated by the socialist experiment in the Soviet Union, American visitors soon outnumbered them. Also, American intellectuals, artists, journalists, scholars, and tourists wrote copiously about their Soviet experiences. The flood of publications was so voluminous and influential that during these early decades of the twentieth century the United States emerged as one of the leading centers of knowledge production about the Soviet Union.[2]

Over the years, historians and foreign policy experts have produced many excellent studies on the diplomatic, economic, and intellectual connections between Russia and the United States, and recently the field has been reenergized both by the ending of the Cold War and by the opening of Soviet-era archives.[3] But rather than scrutinize these travel accounts for their historical accuracy in representing conditions in the Soviet Union or probe the ideological inclinations of the travelers and the motivations of their hosts, I will analyze American experiences within the material culture of Soviet socialism from 1917 to the onset of the Second World War in 1939. While writing this essay, I have been strongly influenced by both postcolonial and postsocialist scholarship that has fundamentally retheorized the trope of the cultural encounter in the modern world and forced us to rethink the ways in which the "West" constructs other peoples and produces knowledge about their cultures.[4] But postcolonial scholarship has been more concerned with Western intellectual representations of the Orient and less with the actual conditions of the physical encounter between the traveler and the native, the terrain where lives intertwine and new meanings are generated. For the most part, scholars have evinced little interest in understanding the everyday life experiences within which Western travelers formed their systems of knowledge about others.[5]

In contrast to the previous inattention to the quotidian, I present a coterminous reading of American travel writing about the Soviet Union, one that is grounded in the material conditions of daily life in both empires. Such an approach illuminates the many ways in which petty annoyances, the unfamiliar nature of daily routines in a new country, and the stress of adjusting to alien surroundings color our perspective, influence our judgments, and shape our evaluations of other cultures.

American representations of the Soviet Union were fundamentally shaped by their preconceptions of what should constitute the material conditions of modernity. As such, visiting Americans found it difficult to countenance what they perceived to be a complete disregard for the needs and requirements of the consumer. Travelers criticized the chronic short-ages of material goods, the poor quality of food products and consumer goods, the uncomfortable living arrangements, and the hostile attitudes of sales personnel and staff at stores, restaurants, and hotels. Ultimately, even pro-Soviet Americans, those passionately committed to the Bolshe-vik experiment, had to filter the utopia of their dreams through the fine mesh of what they perceived to be the unnatural "everyday life" of a so-cialist society. By means of their political commentary and travel writing, Americans established a powerful intellectual framework that contained persuasive rhetorical devices and tropes that described the Soviet sys-tem of distribution and consumption. In the eyes of these observers, the Soviet inability to institute the modern practices of a consumer society threw a dark shadow over its other attempts to create a socialist civiliza-tion. This evaluative framework, established in the interwar period, had considerable staying power and continues to influence our retrospective judgments about the Soviet Union after its collapse in 1991.

One travels to escape from the realm of the everyday and to abandon the repetitive actions that govern our daily existence. And although the juxtaposition of travel and everyday life appears to be counterintuitive, our exotic journeys to distant places necessarily entail daily rituals that ensure the reproduction of our selves. Bodily experiences are interpreted through cultural codes that govern our existence, but these norms are neither static nor time bound. While American travelers brought a host of cultural assumptions about what should constitute the material culture of modernity, for the most part they were quick to learn the differences between capitalist societies of mass consumption and what they perceived to be socialist deprivation. And within a reasonably short period of time they acquired the everyday skills and ethnographic information necessary to survive "as Americans" within the Soviet socialist system.

Americans learned to stand in line patiently, to barter goods, to bargain for fair prices in the black market, and to stock up on daily necessities in anticipation of shortages. They also became inured to sharing cramped physical quarters and scarce commodities. Many broke the law as they exchanged foreign currency for rubles on the black market.[6] As they mastered the Soviet practices of using *sviazi* (connections) as well as *blat* (judicious gift giving) in order to procure housing, summer dachas, travel and work permits, and food and drink, they also began to appreciate the power of the state.[7] They soon learned to regard influential Soviet bureaucrats as significant sources of material largesse and cultural patronage. These skills of survival were often shared among their fellow Americans and other Westerners as a sort of oral lore, rarely systematized, but recorded laconically in travel accounts.[8] The travel knowledge that Americans acquired while negotiating the terrain of Soviet socialism was translated into metaphors and images used to describe the material culture of the Soviet Union. American commentators, both on the right and the left, perceived everyday life in the Soviet Union as fundamentally anomalous, as devoid of moral and ethical meaning even for the native inhabitants of the Soviet Union, and for the most part they represented Soviet consumption and retail practices as an aberrational form of modernity.[9]

THE AMERICAN CONSUMER REVOLUTION AND SOCIALIST CONSUMPTION

While framing the Soviet-American encounter, one must remember that the two civilizations were also representatives of two radically new regimes of consumption in world history. In the early twentieth century, the United States was beginning to experience the full flood of the modern consumer revolution. Although easy credit was yet to reach significant sections of working-class households, comparatively high wages and installment payment plans enabled workers to buy mass-produced goods such as labor-saving appliances, disposable articles of personal hygiene, ready-made clothing, canned and packaged food, radios, and even automobiles. During this period, large corporations as well as the U.S. government were concerned with promoting the purchasing power of American consumers. Town planners emphasized the building of suburban homes large enough to furnish them with consumer goods, and new suburban communities were built with convenient access to shopping centers. By the late 1920s, half of American homes had indoor plumbing, and a third had access to electricity.

Chain variety stores and large department stores such as Woolworth's, Macy's, and Filene's created new norms of consumerism by means of commercial advertising in print and film media. The Sears & Roebuck mail-order business, a milestone in the new consumer culture, delivered coveted goods to the more remote parts of the country. American cities developed massive spaces for the merchandizing of goods, larger in scope than the more genteel shopping arcades and department stores established in Paris, Milan, London, and St. Petersburg during the eighteenth and nineteenth centuries. Department stores offered what was until then considered the unimaginable: goods of standardized quality and a guaranteed return policy if they were found defective. Rising living standards in the United States, coupled with a massive influx of imported goods, meant that American consumers had unprecedented access to a dazzling array of goods from around the world.

The U.S. government and the Bureau of Commerce helped with the distribution of goods that American factories were producing in ever-increasing quantities by building roads and highways, promoting railroad construction, controlling labor unions, and creating a highly efficient postal system that helped mail-order businesses. Aggressive imperial policies, market penetration by large American corporations, and the evangelism of Protestant missionaries in the Caribbean, Central America, South America, the Pacific Islands, and parts of Asia helped spread the American norms of consumption beyond the Western Hemisphere.[10] From the 1910s onward European notions of high bourgeois consumption were soon challenged by the onslaught of American goods, services, and what American marketing experts called "best practices." The idea of a democratic polity that was based on facilitating mass access to ever-widening spheres of material consumption was finding purchase in American society at large and would soon make significant inroads in Europe, especially during the postwar era.[11]

Scholars have challenged our twentieth-century notions of the consumer as a politically passive and socially alienated individual who is taught to desire commercial products and services through blatant propaganda and manipulative advertising.[12] They have argued that through much of American history, and especially during the late nineteenth and twentieth centuries, citizens expressed their civic consciousness and political engagement through acts of consumption and by organizing associations of consumers and consumer activists. Activists and consumer leagues protested against unfair labor practices and unsafe and unsanitary products, and they leveraged their buying power as consumers to force changes in the politics of production.[13] Members of the Progressive movement such as labor unionists, journalists, academics, consumer activists, socialists, and religious groups, while deeply critical of untrammeled industrialization, fought for the expansion of individual wealth and consumption rather than the nationalization of private property.[14]

Progressives and their political heirs demanded the creation of a welfare state that would enable a more equitable distribution of goods and resources among the various social classes rather than the dismantling of the American system of privatized industrial production and mass consumption. As Edmund Wilson observed rather wistfully, "It is probably impossible for an American . . . to imagine Russia correctly . . . and if he is an advocate of socialism and a reader of 'U.S.S.R. in Construction,' he is likely to imagine the Soviet Union as simply the United States plus his ideal of socialism."[15] Americans, as avid consumers of mass-produced goods, accustomed to the standardized conveniences of a rapidly modernizing economy, and schooled in the notion that the customer is always right, trained a set of culturally coded lenses on Soviet material conditions.

The Soviet Union transitioned from a mixed aristocratic/bourgeois regime of consumption among the elites and an emerging consumer economy based primarily in the cities to state control of production, distribution, and consumption. In the imperial period the bulk of the peasant households had limited engagement with the market except for the purchase of kerosene, matches, tobacco, and sometimes vodka. While the thrifty Russian peasant bought few ready-made goods, articles of mass consumption such as cigarettes, soap, bottled beer, and cheap books were beginning to feature in worker households in the cities in the early twentieth century.[16] As recent historiography has demonstrated, the intelligentsia's aversion to the market served to strengthen the Bolshevik predilection for state control of the economy.[17] From 1918 to 1927 the state made fitful attempts to control the market, and there was an uneasy Bolshevik coexistence with the private retail sector, the black market, and the essentially privately owned peasant economy. But with the Stalinist revolution the state gained control of larger sectors of the economy and sought to institute a modern system of socialist distribution and consumption. The collapse of the private retail system led to the rationing of bread and other daily necessities during the First Five-Year Plan. During this period, there was widespread deprivation, enormous scarcity of food and consumer products in the cities, and starvation and even famine in the countryside. The black market, which had served visiting foreigners so well in the 1920s, was drastically limited; instead, Americans were steered toward the Torgsin (*Torgovlia s inostrantsami*, 1931–36) stores.[18] These expensive state-run stores sold groceries, clothing, antiques, and artworks for foreign currency only. Other shopping venues included the Insnab (*Inostranets snabzheniie*), which were created in 1932 for foreign workers and specialists. Visiting journalists and intellectuals also seemed to have access to *kommissionyi* stores for secondhand goods and antiques.

Rationing was officially ended with the inception of the Second Five-Year Plan, and there was a concerted effort to increase production of foodstuffs and consumer goods and create sites of cultured socialist consumption such as cafés, emporiums, and opulent Gastronom food department stores in Moscow and Leningrad. The production of clothes, shoes, and furniture increased, and there was even a drive to mass-produce luxury items such as caviar, chocolates, champagne, and gramophones. In the quest for social distinction, Soviet women were encouraged to dress well, acquire permanents and manicures, and even decorate their apartments with tasteful knickknacks.[19] But, as we know, Americans, even working-class ones who fled the Depression-era United States for employment in the USSR, reported on the massive shortages of consumer goods and food items in the Soviet Union. American dissatisfaction with Soviet retail and distribution systems transcended class affiliations, as both elite and working-class travelers were astounded by the myriad inconveniences that seemed to be embedded in the very system. Fellow travelers and those sympathetic to socialism were hard-pressed to understand and explain why unemployed workers in the depression-ridden countries of Western Europe and the United States dressed better and had higher living standards than their Soviet counterparts.[20]

Bertha Markoosha Fischer, returning émigrée and avid partisan of the Russian Revolution, while acknowledging the increased availability of consumer goods and services during the 1930s, still felt that the supply never was commensurate with the demand.[21] In her letters to her husband, the well-known journalist Louis Fischer, she complained bitterly about the lack of food and basic medicines for children. While she bought expensive butter and vegetables for her two sons, she herself subsisted on a diet of cheap kasha. She repeatedly begged Fischer to bring chocolates, face cream, stockings, and children's clothes from the United States.[22] Markoosha Fischer's correspondence is an interesting compendium of political commentary on the achievements of the revolutionary state interlaced with diatribes against the conditions of daily life in the Soviet Union. In a letter dated August 9, 1929, Markoosha Fischer confessed that the problems of daily life, the lack of good food and warm clothes, and the limited access to medical care were preventing her from sustaining a larger vision of the communist revolution.

While American visitors were frustrated by the living conditions in the Soviet Union, they admired party efforts to create a welfare state that included massive expenditures on institutions of art and culture. Fischer, despite her many complaints, constantly saw plays and ballets and reveled in her social life in Moscow. In a letter dated February 14, 1931, she confessed that she didn't want to travel back to the United States with her husband: "But I fear America. I am so different from all your friends over there, I hate those parties, and the eternal conversations about sex and marriage and all the things which are so settled and done with (wrong or right) by us. And life seems so flat there."[23]

Americans were particularly drawn to the artistic innovations and lively cultural life in the Soviet Union that existed despite the omnipresent censorship and repression. Once in the United States, returning travelers became vocal proponents of state subsidy for the arts.[24] State funding for the arts, cultural production, and higher education was still rare in the United States during the 1920s and 1930s, and philanthropic organizations such as the Carnegie Foundation and subsequently the Rockefeller Foundation were just beginning to fund research in the social sciences and the humanities. During the New Deal the Roosevelt administration employed artists, musicians, actors, and intellectuals through five organizations that were administered by the Works Progress Administration, but due to political unpopularity, these were scaled back considerably in 1939 and officially ended in 1942. Even while they deplored the heavy-handed Soviet censorship, American travelers realized that the state had an important role to play in the production and preservation of culture, as well as in the creation and maintenance of an intelligentsia. Edmund Wilson, Theodore Dreiser, and Eugene Lyons, among others, perceptively noted that the privileges of journalists and intellectuals in the Soviet Union were primarily material ones and that Soviet intellectuals had access to better standards of housing, clothes, food, vacation homes and clubs, and cars.

THE KNOWLEDGE NECESSARY TO SURVIVE EVERYDAY LIFE IN THE SOVIET UNION

In the late imperial era, American travelers had been favorably impressed by the efficient travel amenities, the extensive choice of consumer goods, and the excellent quality of food in the Russian Empire.[25] The themes of an exuberant Russian hospitality and the overabundance of food and drinks pervade the pages of the American travel literature from the imperial era. After the revolution of 1917, while Russians retained their famed hospitality, much of the American writing about Soviet Russia described the absence of food, the search for food, and the shared strategies of food procurement. Americans suffered greatly while sojourning in revolutionary Russia, and the concern with food and complaints about bodily discomfort were omnipresent in the texts. Most Americans, even the ones sympathetic to the revolution, complained of hunger, cold weather, inadequate heating, faulty plumbing, and pervasive filth. Food prices rose during the years of civil war, and one paid exorbitant prices for skimpy and tasteless meals. Visitors to the Soviet Union packed large stores of canned food in anticipation of hunger and privations.[26]

Travel in the Soviet Union produced new rituals of food consumption and encouraged the pooling of resources among visitors. And increasingly through much of the twentieth century, Americans often became sources of food and consumer goods for their Soviet friends. As the Civil War progressed, Americans found themselves in privileged positions compared to their beleaguered hosts. While the massive American relief operations that Herbert Hoover instituted in 1921 to deal with the aftermath of the famine have been well documented, we know little about the countless instances of American generosity and kindness or how these acts were interpreted by their hosts. Frank Golder, noted historian and archivist, trudged two miles in the snow to anonymously deliver packages of white flour, tea, sugar, rice, and other scarce food products to impoverished friends in Moscow on a cold Christmas morning in 1921.[27]

To some observers the romance of the revolution often trumped the unbearable conditions of everyday life in Soviet Russia, and these material privations were understood as necessary consequences of war and revolution. John Reed, famous journalist and left-wing activist, in his worldwide best seller, *Ten Days That Shook the World*, enthusiastically celebrated the ability of Russian workers to ignore hunger pangs and endure cold and continuous sleep deprivation in their quest to build a revolution. In fact, Reed made a concerted effort to remake himself as a Bolshevik, as someone who bore extended prison sentences uncomplainingly and was ready to give his life for the cause of the revolution.[28] But Reed was extraordinary in his dedication and his ability to rise above the quotidian. Another left-leaning idealist, the famous dancer Isadora Duncan, realized that she would never develop the requisite Bolshevik stoicism in the face of deprivation. And even John Scott, in his classic account of Magnitogorsk, reported with palpable relief on improvements in living conditions during the Second Five-Year Plan and the wider availability of consumer goods.[29]

In the 1920s American visitors complained continually of the poor service at the hotels in Moscow, the ubiquity of bedbugs, and the unsanitary bathrooms, and they criticized the monotonous and unappetizing meals.[30] Even a hardcore idealist such as Isadora Duncan, who migrated to the Soviet Union in the hopes that the Soviet government would help her found a school for orphaned children, was severely disillusioned by the conditions. Duncan went to the Soviet Union with the firm belief that through the medium of dance she would fashion Soviet children into citizens of a socialist world order. Her fascination with the Soviets stemmed from a disdain for what she claimed was a shallow, profit-minded, and materialistic bourgeois culture where the artist had to prostitute herself in order to perform her art. Duncan's flight to Russia was intended to be a grand gesture of renunciation of the material world and a rededication of her art to the common people. Ignoring dire warnings of hunger and misery in Russia, she arrived with her adopted daughter and a French maid(!) in 1921.

As soon as Duncan entered the Soviet Union, the talk about art and revolution was subsumed under a narrow concern with the quotidian. Duncan's account reads like a cautionary tale to other starry-eyed idealists who mistakenly believed that it was possible for the spirit to triumph over the flesh. Upon her arrival in Moscow, Duncan and her entourage found that the Soviet government had forgotten to send them an escort or even arrange for a hotel. The rooms at the Savoy Hotel were poorly furnished, and while they lacked pillows and bed linen, they contained an abundance of flies and rats.[31] Coffee was hard to find, and soon Duncan and her entourage were thinking longingly of New York, London, or Paris, where coffee with fresh cream was readily available.[32] When Duncan was invited to spend a week at the country cottage of a dedicated Russian communist, she discovered that she could not bear to sleep on the floor, drink goat's milk, or eat the rough food that was offered.[33] Wandering in the cold, rainy, Moscow weather with a communist, she said, "I found, after meeting others, that a real communist is indifferent to heat or cold or hunger or any material sufferings. As the early Christian martyrs, they live so entirely in ideas that they simply don't notice these things."[34]

Another sympathetic traveler, Margaret Bourke-White, associate editor of *Fortune* magazine and an ardent advocate of labor rights, created a stunning visual record of the First Five-Year Plan with her glamorous photographs of Soviet industrialization.[35] Although VOKS officials privately condemned her work as superficial, they also realized that Bourke-White's photographs broadcast favorable images of the Soviet Union to a global public. But in her travel narrative she continuously contrasted American plenitude with Soviet scarcity, never once acknowledging the impact of the Depression in the United States or the widespread existence of hunger and poverty. Bourke-White noted that shoes were rarely to be found in the Soviet Union, ice cream was a precious commodity, and chocolate was simply unavailable. Bourke-White, who never ate sweets in the United States, developed an absolute craving for sugar, and whenever she found it, she would devour it on the spot. Early in her account, her interpreter, Lydia

Petrovna, asked her why American women dieted. As the two women shared monotonous meals comprised mostly of American cans of baked beans, which Bourke-White provided, Lydia was hard-pressed to imagine a world where women suffered hunger by choice. Indeed, the concept of self-imposed hunger must have seemed particularly obscene in the context of the widespread famine that resulted from the collectivization of the Soviet countryside.

Bourke-White, like other American visitors, realized that when the availability of food was not guaranteed, it became an important and precious resource. And the act of eating, when enacted in a communal and convivial manner, acquired a deep cultural significance that it had lacked back home. At a party with young Russians, Bourke-White realized that her hosts had saved their meager rations for weeks in order to provide a special snack of crackers and wine. In the Soviet Union she realized that the ease of life in the United States, with its widespread availability of food, clean water, and communication services, was actually an anomaly and not the norm. When returning to "civilization," Bourke-White confessed that on the train to Berlin she managed to consume eight eggs at one sitting. Stories such as these established an important trope of the widespread scarcity of goods and provisions within the Soviet system.

While shopping for food and necessities became extremely difficult during the Soviet era, the collapsed state of the Soviet economy allowed visiting Americans unprecedented access to luxury goods and artworks. Not only could Americans shop at special hard currency Soviet stores, they also purchased lavishly on the black market and funneled a brisk transatlantic trade in imperial art and artifacts. Margaret Bourke-White proudly reported in 1931 that she picked up a sixteenth-century icon for a fraction of its value, and she managed to smuggle it out of the country.[36] Joseph Davies, American ambassador to the Soviet Union, and his wife, Marjorie Post, heiress in her own right, acquired a large collection of Russian art and antiques from the kommissionnyi stores and art museums with the help of conniving Soviet authorities.[37] At the other end of the spectrum there was a deep Soviet fascination with ordinary American articles of consumption, such as ready-made clothes, stockings, canned food, candy, and chocolates. Indeed, American identity became inextricably tied to the possession of articles of mass consumption. However, in the Soviet context these were not viewed as disposable goods but as articles that had innate value. Lydia Petrovna asked Bourke-White for the rims around food cans, which she then ingeniously turned into a brace-let. After leaving the Soviet Union, Bourke-White sent back a real gold bracelet for Lydia Petrovna so that she could wear it instead of the bracelet fashioned from cans of baked beans.

Ella Winter, left-leaning journalist and wife of the famous radical Lincoln Steffens, candidly acknowledged: "Not all the young people in the USSR have the disregard for material welfare that most young communists show. Girls especially feel the lack of goods intensely. They want nice clothes, good cosmetics, silk stockings. They envy foreigners. Some have devel-oped an almost pathological desire for the good-quality clothes that they have been deprived of. I have had them feel feverishly my foreign clothes, hat, frock, sample the material, stroke the silk, almost pull my underwear from under my blouse in their frenzied hunger."[38] The journalist Anne O'Hare McCormick was besieged by women wanting to know "where they could duplicate an old American tailored suit or a pair of shoes bought in a Balkan town."[39] And Markoosha Fischer wrote that she could have made money by conducting people through her household, which was furnished with cheap American devices that her husband had brought back from the United States: "A hook which did not get rusty from humidity, a new can opener, a potato peeler, a dish cloth which did not discolor—these never ceased to arouse the amazement of our Soviet visitors."[40] American travel narratives at these moments read like orientalist European accounts that contrasted naive natives with the more sophisticated and civilized travel-ers.[41] And like the colonial literature, American representations of Soviet material poverty and hunger for consumer goods played an important political function during the twentieth century.

STATE PATRONAGE

While Ludmilla Stern and David Caute have accused the Soviet gov-ernment of bribing American intellectuals with royalties from transla-tions, large lecture tours, lavish dinners, and well-organized excursions, files from both VOKS and Intourist tell the other part of the story.[42] The correspondence from both organizations contains detailed requests by visiting Americans for tickets to theaters and concerts, excursions to various Soviet institutions and museums, fully funded trips to different parts of the country, access to research materials, employment opportunities, and requests for room and board while sojourning in the Soviet Union.[43] While VOKS understood the value of gaining favorable publicity through the medium of these important dignitaries, and thus most of the requests were granted, at the same time there was a cynical awareness that foreigners often feigned enthusiasm for the achievements of the Soviet state while visiting the country and then displayed intense anti-Soviet sentiments when back in their own countries.[44] Theodore Dreiser, the famous American writer, represented a classic case of the Soviet quandary.[45]

Dreiser was initially invited to attend the commemoration of the tenth year of the October Revolution in 1928, but he stayed on for several months afterward and traveled extensively through the country. Dreiser signed a generous contract for the translation of his works into Russian and was guaranteed substantial royalties. But Dreiser was not an easy guest, and he complained loudly and vociferously to Olga Kameneva, the head of VOKS, about the terrible travel conditions and poor amenities in the Soviet Union. Dreiser subsequently wrote about his experiences in a book entitled *Dreiser Looks at Russia*.[46] However, once he returned to the United States, Dreiser became an ardent defender of the Soviet Union, and his articles and books facilitated the flow of American tourists to the Soviet Union.[47]

We become aware of Dreiser's suffering very early in his narrative, and as he travels around the Soviet Union, he appears completely oblivious to the fact that the country had just experienced the depredations of the First World War, a bloody civil war, allied military intervention, an international blockade, and a complete breakdown of industrial and agricultural production. The greater Russian tragedy is eclipsed by the minute descriptions of his travails. He avers, "Never have I seen a land more poorly equipped with the aids and ways and means of . . . comforting the citizen or the traveler" (56). He complains bitterly about the lack of cleanliness, which is so un-American, and he believes that it has less to do with poverty than with a general Russian unconcern with hygiene (59). He makes repeated references to "stocky sweaty smelly bodies" and the "half-stifling

Asiatic odor" that pervades the wretched houses of the peasants (84, 133). The furnishings in Soviet hotel rooms are threadbare, the bed linen is insufficient, bathtubs and washstands are unavailable, and the water is invariably cold (60). When Dreiser is invited to the house of Eisenstein, one of the most brilliant and influential film directors of the twentieth century, upon entry he is helplessly fixated by Eisenstein's bed: "I remarked that he had the largest and most comfortable looking bed that I had seen in Russia, and I envied him the same, I having thus far seen only narrow and most uncomfortable looking ones" (206). Eisenstein explains that he had bought the bed from an American farming commune near Moscow.

Dreiser is even surprised that Tolstoy, the Russian apostle of anti-materialism, lived in such simplicity at Yasnaia Poliana and that his dressing gown was of such poor quality. And in general, Dreiser has little to say about Tolstoy's literature and focuses almost exclusively on the spartan and uncomfortable surroundings that Tolstoy inhabited (210). He is savagely critical of Soviet restaurants, the poor furniture, and the mismatched clothes of the patrons, and he even claims that "there is almost no such thing as good cooking in Soviet Russia" (63). Finally, what upsets Dreiser the most is the sight of a hearse in a funeral procession that carries an open casket: "For all you can think of now is why not a box of sufficient depth, in an enclosed hearse? And reticence? Seclusion? Evasion of this gruesome thing even though it must be?" (240). Dreiser seems unable to contemplate life stripped to its bare essentials, human bodily functions rendered transparent in communal kitchens and shared bathrooms, devoid of the aesthetic privacy of bourgeois civilization.

But what makes this travel account so fascinating is not simply its parochial and even orientalist condemnation of another civilization. Dreiser in his narrative simultaneously engages in critiquing American culture or the lack thereof. Even as he bemoans the absence of physical comfort in Soviet Russia, Dreiser, like John Reed, Isadora Duncan, and Bertha Markoosha Fischer, praises the Russian capacity for abstract thought and intellectual discourse. Dreiser uses the intellectuality of Russians as a stick with which to belabor his fellow Americans. He criticizes the American obsession with materialism and comments on the indifference of his fellow citizens to art and culture. Thus he writes: "For we are so wholly materialistic, so in the main, utterly puerile mentally. But in Russia, how different! God the swish and talk of actual, serious, generous, non-material, highly spiritual mentation!" (260). Dreiser's travel writing has a didactic intent: it is intended to goad the bourgeois audience at home to slough off their cocoon of prosperity and engage more seriously in the realm of the intellect. It is the traditional lament of the American intelligentsia, their complaints about being isolated in a culture of Babbittry and materialism. But Dreiser's obsessive concern with his own physical discomfort while traveling in the Soviet Union ends up valorizing the very system he tries to critique in America.

While Dreiser was seemingly impervious to the complicated arrangements that were made to ensure his comfort,[48] other American travelers in the 1930s became increasingly conscious of their own privileged position in the Soviet Union, as well as the political compromises that they sometimes had to make in order to benefit from the state-sanctioned system of rewards. Walter Duranty, Pulitzer Prize–winning journalist for the *New York Times,* possibly maintained his luxurious lifestyle in Moscow, assisted by a team of assistants and servants, by justifying Stalinist policies of collectivization and industrialization to audiences in the West.[49] But others such as Eugene Lyons and Louis Fischer increasingly grew pessimistic about the vitality of the Soviet revolution.[50] It was not only the repressive tactics of the Stalinist regime, the brutal methods of collectivization, and the attendant famine that made them question their previous idealism. They were also deeply perturbed by the growing inequality and the desperation engendered by unequal access to food that they witnessed in the Soviet countryside in the 1930s. Paradoxically, as material conditions improved in the Soviet Union, visiting Americans became even more critical about the debased quality of the living conditions of the masses of workers and peasants and contrasted it negatively with the elite lifestyles of members of the party, the Red Army, the security services, and the intelligentsia.[51]

CONCLUSION

American travel literature on everyday living conditions in the Soviet Union reveals several narrative strategies. In the first and the most obvious reading through the sources, I found conspicuous use of orientalist language, which travelers used to criticize the poor quality of goods

and services and the difficult and burdensome living conditions.[52] These
graphic accounts effectively conveyed the inadequacies of the socialist
retail and distribution system to a large English-speaking public throughout the world. The islands of material privilege that the travelers described
were further proof that the socialist ideals of equality were being per-
verted in the Soviet Union. American travelers also were increasingly
guilt-stricken that their own material resources were far greater than those
of their hosts, and this led to the creation of complicated social relationships and tensions with Russian friends and colleagues.[53] At the same
time, Americans were forced to rely increasingly on the Soviet state to
ensure their own comfort while traveling in the Soviet Union. Throughout
the 1920s and 1930s, Western travelers availed themselves of hotels, guest-
houses, apartments, free excursions, and subsidized trips to the theater and
museums. They also employed servants to stand in line at stores, take care
of household needs, drive their cars, and babysit their children.[54] They
shopped at special stores and frequented the large hotels in Moscow, especially the bar at the Metropole, which served excellent food and featured
beautiful barmaids willing to dance with foreigners. While perceptive
Americans noted the ways in which citizens of the Soviet Union suffered
within the system, accommodated themselves to the myriad inconveniences that it inflicted on them, and on occasion even benefited from it,
by and large Americans saw the socialist system as an abnormal state of
affairs, validated neither by the new consumerism they themselves had
experienced at home nor by the capitalist mode of human interactions.[55]

While political affiliation dictated American reactions to both the Bolshevik revolution and Stalinist policies, most travelers, whether on the left
or on the right, evinced a deep concern with the physical suffering that
they witnessed while traveling in the Soviet Union. Those on the right
cited the terrible material conditions of Soviet existence to advocate a
return to capitalism and what they considered to be a natural economic
order. They argued that without the right to private property, an individual was helpless in the face of the oppressive power of the state. More
pragmatic advocates of modernization initially believed that despite the
hardships imposed by state-sponsored industrialization and collectivization, these policies would ultimately bring material prosperity to the
masses. When this failed to materialize, even erstwhile fellow travelers

such as William Chamberlin, Eugene Lyons, and Louis Fischer assumed an anti-Stalinist position.

The narratives of those sympathetic to leftist ideology performed a double function. Observers such as John Reed and Theodore Dreiser praised Russian spirituality and the Russian capacity to subordinate the needs of the individual to the imaginative demands of a communitarian future. But even as they commemorated the indomitable Bolshevik spirit and ability to rise above the quotidian, their subtext of physical hardships often captured the attention of American readers.

Descriptions of endless lines, the search for daily bread and sausage, cramped living quarters, unhygienic communal kitchens and bathrooms, ubiquitous bedbugs, rude attendants in stores and hotels, and the lack of soap and toilet paper: these were memorable pictures of the Soviet Union that stayed in the American public memory.[56] The emphasis on bodily discomfort in Soviet Russia was so pervasive a trope in American travel literature that it found its way into popular culture through films such as *Ninotchka* (1939), *Comrade X* (1940), and *Silk Stockings* (1957). The impossible conditions of daily life were featured prominently in movies, jokes, and fiction about the Soviet Union. In the American imagination, Soviet material culture and everyday life represented a grotesque distortion of modernity. Images of the Soviet other helped legitimize American modes of consumerism and consumption through much of the twentieth century. Above all, negative references to socialist means of distribution normalized conceptions of a world political order based on safeguarding the rights of consumers rather than protecting the interests of the producers. Ultimately, American standards of consumption, which had acquired global significance in the latter part of the twentieth century, played a major role in hastening the demise of the Soviet Union and the socialist world.[57]

NOTES

1. John Gaddis, *Russia, the Soviet Union and the United States: An Interpretive History* (New York: Wiley, 1978); A. V. Golubev et al., eds., *Rossiia i zapad: Formirovanie vneshne-politicheskikh stereotipov v soznanii rossiiskogo obshchestva pervoi poloviny XX veka* (Lewiston, N.Y.: Edwin Mellen Press, 1999); Sergei Zhuravlev, *"Malen'kie liudi" i "bol'shaia istoriia"*:

Inostrantsy moskovskogo Elektrozavoda v sovetskom obshchestve 1920-x-1930-xgg (Moscow: ROSSPEN, 2000).

2. Peter Filene, *Americans and the Soviet Experiment, 1917–1933* (Cambridge, Mass.: Harvard University Press, 1967); David Foglesong, *The American Mission and the "Evil Empire": The Crusade for a Free Russia since 1881* (New York: Cambridge University Press, 2007).

3. David Charles Engerman, *Modernization from the Other Shore: American Intellectuals and the Romance of Russian Development* (Cambridge, Mass.: Harvard University Press, 2003); Michael David-Fox, *Showcasing the Great Experiment: Cultural Diplomacy and Western Visitors to the Soviet Union, 1929–1941* (New York: Oxford University Press, 2012).

4. Sharad Chari and Katherine Verdery, "Thinking between the Posts: Postcolonialism, Postsocialism, and Ethnography after the Cold War," *Comparative Studies in Society and History* 51, no. 1 (2009): 6–39; Larry Wolff, *Inventing Eastern Europe: The Map of Civilization on the Mind of Enlightenment* (Stanford, Calif.: Stanford University Press, 1994).

5. Mary Louise Pratt, *Imperial Eyes: Travel Writing and Transculturation* (London: Routledge, 1992); Edward Said, *Orientalism* (New York: Vintage, 1978); Dipesh Chakrabarty, *Provincializing Europe: Postcolonial Thought and Historical Difference* (Princeton, N.J.: Princeton University Press, 2000).

6. See James E. Abbe, *I Photograph Russia* (New York: R. M. McBride and Co., 1935), 78–79.

7. Anthropologist Alena V. Ledeneva explained *blat* as "the use of personal networks for obtaining goods and services in short supply and for circumventing formal procedures" (*How Russia Really Works: The Informal Practices That Shaped Post-Soviet Politics and Business* [Ithaca, N.Y.: Cornell University Press, 2006], 1).

8. Frank Costigliola, "'The Invisible Wall': Personal and Cultural Origins of the Cold War," *New England Journal of History* 64, no. 1 (Fall 2007): 190–213; "'Unceasing Pressure for Penetration': Gender, Pathology and Emotion in George Kennan's Formation," *Journal of American History* 83, no. 4 (March 1997): 1309–39.

9. While André Gide in his infamous tract *Return from the U.S.S.R.* (New York: A. A. Knopf, 1937) was also critical of the quality of Russian food products and consumer goods, he was intellectually supportive of the socialist system of production and distribution (19–22).

10. Emily Rosenberg, *Spreading the American Dream: American Economic and Cultural Expansion, 1890–1945* (New York: Hill and Wang, 1982); Frank Ninkovich, *Global Dawn: The Cultural Foundations of American Internationalism, 1865–1890* (Cambridge, Mass.: Harvard University Press, 2009).

11. William Leach, *Land of Desire: Merchants, Power, and the Rise of a New American Culture* (New York: Pantheon Books, 1993); Lizabeth Cohen, *A Consumers' Republic: The Politics of Mass Consumption in Postwar America* (New York: Knopf, 2003); Gary Cross, *An All-Consuming Century: Why Commercialism Won in Modern America* (New York: Columbia University Press, 2000); Victoria de Grazia, *Irresistible Empire: America's Advance through Twentieth Century Europe* (Cambridge, Mass.: Harvard University Press, 2005); Kristin Hoganson, *Consumers' Imperium: The Global Production of American Domesticity, 1865–1920* (Chapel Hill: University of North Carolina Press, 2007).

12. Thorstein Veblen, *Theory of the Leisure Class* (New York: Modern Library, 1912); Herbert Marcuse, *One-Dimensional Man* (Boston: Beacon Press, 1964). See also Martyn J. Lee, ed., *The Consumer Society Reader* (Malden, Mass.: Blackwell, 2000) for a range of critical theories on consumption and consumerism.

13. T. H. Breen, *The Marketplace of Revolution: How Consumer Politics Shaped American Independence* (New York: Oxford University Press, 2004); Lawrence B. Glickman, *Buying*

Power: A History of Consumer Activism in America (Chicago: University of Chicago Press, 2009).

14. Lawrence B. Glickman, *A Living Wage: American Workers and the Making of Consumer Society* (Ithaca, N.Y.: Cornell University Press, 1997).

15. Edmund Wilson, *Travels in Two Democracies* (New York: Harcourt, Brace and Co., 1936), 162.

16. Peter Gatrell, *The Tsarist Economy, 1850–1917* (New York: St. Martin's Press, 1986); Paul Gregory, *An Economic History of Russia: From Emancipation to the First Five Year Plan* (Princeton, N.J.: Princeton University Press, 1994); Margery Hilton, *Selling to the Masses: Retailing in Russia, 1880–1930* (Pittsburgh: University of Pittsburgh Press, 2012).

17. Peter Holquist, *Making War, Forging Revolution: Russia's Continuum of Crisis, 1914–1921* (Cambridge, Mass.: Harvard University Press, 2002); Lars Lih, *Bread of Authority in Russia, 1914–1921* (Berkeley: University of California Press, 1990).

18. Elena Osokina, *Zoloto dlia industrializatsii: TORGSIN* (Moscow: ROSSPEN, 2009).

19. Jukka Gronow, *Caviar with Champagne: Common Luxury and the Ideals of Good Life in Stalinist Russia* (New York: Berg, 2003); Sheila Fitzpatrick, *Everyday Stalinism: Ordinary Life in Extraordinary Times* (Oxford: Berg, 2002); Julie Hessler, *A Social History of Soviet Trade Policy, Retail Practices and Consumption, 1917–1953* (Princeton, N.J.: Princeton University Press, 2004); Elena Osokina, *Our Daily Bread: Socialist Distribution and the Art of Survival in Stalin's Russia, 1927–1941* (Armonk, N.Y.: M. E. Sharpe, 2001); Amy Randall, *Soviet Dream World of Retail, Trade and Consumption in the 1930s* (New York: Palgrave Macmillan, 2008).

20. Mary Leder, *My Life in Stalinist Russia: An American Woman Looks Back* (Bloomington: Indiana University Press, 2001); John Scott, *Behind the Urals in Russia's City of Steel* (Bloomington: Indiana University Press, 1989).

21. Bertha Markoosha Fischer, *My Lives in Russia* (New York: Harper and Bros., 1944), 113.

22. Box 41, folder 1, correspondence from 1929 to 1931, Louis Fischer Papers, Mudd Library, Princeton University.

23. Ibid.

24. Lynn Mally, "The Americanization of the Soviet Living Newspaper," in *Carl Beck Papers in Russian and East European Studies*, no. 1903 (Pittsburgh: University of Pittsburgh Press, 2008), 1–40.

25. Isabel Hapgood, *Russian Rambles* (New York: Arno Press, 1970); Edna Dean Proctor, *A Russian Journey* (Boston: J. R. Osgood and Co., 1872).

26. Choi Chatterjee, "Odds and Ends of the Russian Revolution: Gender and American Travel Narratives of 1917," *Journal of Women's History*, no. 4 (Winter 2008): 10–33.

27. Frank A. Golder, "Christmas, 1921," *Independent*, December 24, 1927, 626; Bernard Patenaude, *The Big Show in Bololand: The American Relief Administration and the Famine of 1921* (Stanford, Calif.: Stanford University Press, 2002).

28. John Reed, *Ten Days That Shook the World* (New York: St. Martin's Press, 1997); Eric Homberger, *John Reed* (New York: Manchester University Press, 1990).

29. Scott, *Behind the Urals*.

30. George Sylvester Viereck, "Russia Marks Time," *Saturday Evening Post*, November 30, 1929, 14–15, 94.

31. See also Dorothy Thompson, *The New Russia* (New York: H. Holt and Company, 1928), 24–27.

32. Irma Duncan and Allan Ross MacDougal, *Isadora Duncan's Russian Days and Her Last Years in France* (New York: Covici, Friede, 1929), 28–29.

33. Ibid., 67–70.

34. Ibid., 35.

35. Margaret Bourke-White, *Eyes on Russia* (New York: Simon and Schuster, 1931).

36. James Abbe, the first to photograph Stalin, traded his wife's silk stockings for an heirloom samovar. *I Photograph Russia,* 316.

37. Robert C. Williams, *Russian Art and American Money, 1900–1940* (Cambridge, Mass.: Harvard University Press, 1980); Anne Odom and Wendy Salmond, eds., *Treasures into Tractors: The Selling of Russia's Cultural Heritage, 1918–1938* (Seattle: University of Washington Press, 2009).

38. Ella Winter, *Red Virtue* (New York: Harcourt, Brace and Co., 1933), 45.

39. Anne O'Hare McCormick, *The Hammer and the Scythe* (New York: A. A. Knopf, 1928), 35.

40. Markoosha Fischer, *My Lives in Russia,* 113. Pro-Soviet fellow traveler Lamont Corliss reported that a Russian barber thought his very "ordinary American comb is so superior that he wants to buy it" (Lamont Corliss and Margot Corliss, *Russia by Day: A Travel Diary* [New York: Covici, Friede, 1933], 233).

41. See Aleksandr Etkind, *Tolkovanie puteshestvii: Rossiia i Amerika v travelogakh i intertekstakh* (Moscow: Novoe literaturnoe obozrenie, 2001).

42. David Caute, *The Fellow-Travellers: Intellectual Friends of Communism* (New Haven, Conn.: Yale University Press, 1988); Ludmila Stern, *Western Intellectuals and the Soviet Union, 1920–1940: From Red Square to Left Bank* (London: Routledge, 2007).

43. State Archive of the Russian Federation (GARF), fond 5283 (VOKS), op. 3, d. 66 contains numerous letters from Americans to Olga Kameneva.

44. GARF, fond 5283, op. 8, d. 158, ll. 1–5 (Otdela priema inostrantsev za 1932 g).

45. Michael David-Fox, "Troinaia dvusmyslennost': Teodor Draizer v sovetskoi Rossii (1927–1928): Palomnichestvo, pokhozhee na obvinitel'nuiu rech'," in *Kul'turnye issledovaniia, ed.* Alexander Etkind and Pavel Lysakov (St. Petersburg: Evropeiskii Universitet, 2006), 290–319.

46. Theodore Dreiser, *Dreiser Looks at Russia* (New York: H. Liveright, 1928). Hereafter cited in the text.

47. Norman Saul, *Friends or Foes? The United States and Russia 1921–1941* (Lawrence: University Press of Kansas, 2006), 193–97.

48. Ruth Kennel, *Theodore Dreiser and the Soviet Union, 1927–1945* (New York: International Publishers, 1969).

49. Walter Duranty, *I Write as I Please* (New York: Simon and Schuster, 1935); James W. Crowl, *Angels in Stalin's Paradise* (Washington, D.C.: University Press of America, 1982).

50. Eugene Lyons, *Assignment in Utopia* (New Brunswick, N.J.: Transaction Publishers, 1991); Richard Crossman, ed., *The God That Failed* (New York: Harper, 1949).

51. Louis Fischer, *Life and Death of Stalin* (New York: Harper, 1952), 77, 130–32.

52. While orientalism is commonly used to refer to European descriptions of the Middle East and Asia during the colonial period, Larry Wolff and Aleksandr Etkind have thoughtfully refashioned Edward Said's formulations in their analysis of Western descriptions of Russia. Larry Wolff, *Inventing Eastern Europe: The Map of Civilization on the Mind of Enlightenment* (Stanford, Calif.: Stanford University Press, 1994); Etkind, *Tolkovanie puteshestvii.* See also Maria Todorova's excellent work in this vein, *Imagining the Balkans* (New York: Oxford University Press, 1997).

53. Barbara Walker, "Pollution and Purification in the Moscow Human Rights Networks of the 1960s and 1970s," *Slavic Review* 68, no. 2 (Summer 2009): 376–95.

54. Linton Wells, *Blood on the Moon: The Autobiography of Linton Wells* (Boston: Houghton Mifflin Co., 1937), 333–56.

55. According to Elena Osokina, left-wing foreign workers, engineers, and specialists were equally disenchanted with Soviet living conditions (*Our Daily Bread,* 82–101).

56. African American writer and poet Langston Hughes wrote that Lincoln Steffens advised him to take soap and toilet paper for himself and silk stockings for the girls for his Soviet journey. See *I Wonder as I Wander* (New York: Rinehart, 1956), 65–66; William Chamberlin, *Russia's Iron Age* (Boston: Little, Brown, 1934), 108–28; Christopher Mari, *No Soap and the Soviet* (Plainfield, N.J.: Red Ram Press, 1936).

57. Slavenka Drakulić, *How We Survived Communism and Even Laughed* (London: Hutchinson, 1992); Alexei Yurchak, *Everything Was Forever, Until It Was No More: The Last Soviet Generation* (Princeton, N.J.: Princeton University Press, 2006); György Péteri, ed., *Imagining the West in Eastern Europe and the Soviet Union* (Pittsburgh: University of Pittsburgh Press, 2010).

Afterword

SHEILA FITZPATRICK

*B*yt (everyday life) is a "swamp," according to one contemporary Russian view, keeping people busy in "a set of ossified daily routines" that fail to provide meaning to life.[1] It was this byt that wrecked the poet Mayakovsky, or so he claimed in a farewell poem when he killed himself in 1930. For idealistic Communists of the 1920s, byt, and more particularly the *meshchanskii byt* of petty bourgeois philistines, was the great threat to the revolution.

The swamp metaphor could also be applied to the everyday as a preoccupation of historians, so fluid and amorphous is the concept. It is a realm defined by what it is not: *not* the realm of states, institutions, structures, purposes, ideologies, grand designs but what is left when you take those things away. Some scholars understand the everyday as more or less synonymous with private life, others in terms of resistance to power or the individual's ways of coping with an externally regulated world. As a historian's strategy, studying the everyday is a good way of subverting assumptions made on the basis of formal political and social structures and codified ideologies. Just as microhistory shows us how surprisingly different the experience of a particular individual can be from the "big-picture" generalizations about life in his or her era, class, and cohort, so the history of the everyday shows us how people live in the interstices between the various disciplinary structures that dominate their lives.[2]

The present volume is distinguished by its exploration of three innovative approaches to the everyday: interdisciplinary, longue durée, and transnational. My comments in this brief afterword will focus on the insights that these three approaches afford and the paths for future exploration that lie ahead.

MIXING DISCIPLINES AND GENRES

One of the daunting things about the everyday for an academic historian is that other genres often do the job better. Memoirs have a capacity for re-creating lived experience that is hard to equal in a scholarly work, and so do fiction and film. We may recognize this implicitly in our teaching (does anyone teach the Gulag section in Soviet history courses without setting at least one of the great memoirs as class reading?), but we prefer to ignore this in our scholarly work—as demonstrated, for example, in our reflex habit of citing theorists like Hannah Arendt on the totalitarian everyday, regardless of the fact that the key texts shaping the perceptions of our readers are George Orwell's fictions, *Animal Farm* and *1984*. Of course, the Orwell books have the particular problem as a scholarly source that the direct personal experience he drew on was not the Soviet Union under Stalin but his own British boarding school,[3] but that is irrelevant to the general public and does not change the fact that it is within the Orwellian template of Soviet everyday life that readers are going to read our work. Things are more straightforward with fictional work like the satirical stories of Zoshchenko and Voinovich, which capture the everyday contradictions and absurdities of their times better than any historian has ever done. We scholarly historians do our best to convey the texture of the times through extensive quotation from memoirs and contemporary texts, but it's surely rare for us to make our readers feel that they are actually living in the period, as readers of Hilary Mantel's *Wolf Hall* may do for sixteenth-century England, Georgette Heyer's legions of followers for her Regency romances, or viewers of the television series *Jewel in the Crown* for the end of the British Raj in India. Moreover, there is the additional problem that not all artistic works, including and perhaps particularly the greatest, lend themselves to quotation.[4]

Of course, vivid re-creation of the past is not our only goal in writing everyday history. We are also trying to understand it analytically, in which case fiction and film may constitute data on how people lived, along with, say, social statistics and court proceedings. Four of the contributions to this volume take specific works of literature (Skomp, Sutcliffe) or film (Pozefsky, Oushakine) as the subject of analysis. So did one of the most remarkable and idiosyncratic scholarly works ever written in our field: Vera Dunham's *In Stalin's Time,* in which she evoked and commented upon postwar Soviet everyday life on the basis of what she called "middle-brow" Soviet fiction of the postwar period.[5] Dunham's book, however, is not just an attempt to summarize the content and tone of other people's literary work; it is an authorial interpretation of a particular way of life and culture for which this particular body of data happens to serve. Francis Spufford went one step further and offered his authorial interpretation of the Khrushchev period in the form of a (research-based) novel, acknowl-edging his debt to scholarly work on the Soviet everyday.[6]

It is hard, perhaps even dishonest, to keep studies of near-contemporary everyday history free of the author's own experiences and subjectivity. An-thropologists, the original academic investigators of the everyday, started off with the dubious assumption that they could be "participant-observers" of foreign communities without actually affecting the action but have since given up the pretense of invisibility. They, along with literary schol-ars, have been quicker than historians to introduce themselves as char-acters and/or data sources in their own scholarly stories. Alexei Yurchak, though not a character in his late Stalinist everyday, clearly draws on his own personal experience as well as other "objective" data; Sergei Zhuk, similarly, is describing a world he knew intimately, as well as one he has researched.[7] One cannot imagine a work like Nataliia Lebina's *Entsiklo-pediia banal'nostei,* combining mockery with a tinge of nostalgia, being compiled by anyone for whom those "banalities" were not part of personal experience.[8] The same goes for Petr Vail and Aleksandr Genis's lavishly illustrated and imaginatively formatted book on the Thaw,[9] written in the style of the Soviet new journalism of the 1960s but having much in com-mon with the kind of film biodocumentaries discussed by Oushakine in this volume. Recent works like Svetlana Boym's *Common Places* and Rachel Polonsky's *Molotov's Magic Lantern* blur the boundary between memoir and scholarship.[10]

Subjectivity may mean introducing a truly individual and quirky au-thorial personality, like Elif Batuman's *The Possessed,* a work of ambiguous

genre in which observation of the post-Soviet everyday is one component.[11] More often, however, just one subjective brush, or at least a fairly
limited palette, is used by scholars to paint the picture of a particular
everyday, as well as by subjects recalling it. Authors and subjects alike
tend to narrate their wartime everyday histories as stories of popular endurance and heroism. *The world we have lost* became shorthand for a whole
genre of nostalgic evocations of preindustrial England. In a post-Soviet
context, nostalgia may be a more complex emotion, as in Boym's work,[12]
but it is scarcely less prevalent.

After the collapse of Communism, nostalgia for the old artifacts of
Soviet-style life was manifest throughout the former Soviet bloc. In the
second half of the 1990s, the Russian television series *Staraia kvartira* presented the events, popular songs, and characteristic artifacts of the late
Soviet period year by year, with moderators and studio audience joined
in affectionate, only occasionally ironic, remembrance. In East Germany
(for which the term *Ostalgie* was coined),[13] nostalgia for the artifacts of
Communism found its reflection in oral histories, scholarly works, and
films like Wolfgang Becker's 2003 *Good Bye Lenin!*

THE LONGUE DURÉE

It is not easy to find ways of handling the everyday that allow for change
over time. The classic "everyday" books written in the interwar period by
museum curator and historian Marjorie Quennell and her architect husband, C. H. B. Quennell, dealt with the everyday by epochs (*Everyday Life
in Roman Britain*), but within the epochs, life was as static as the "period
rooms" she would later create in the Geffrye Museum in London.[14] We
are inclined to see the everyday as the backdrop for the dynamic action of
histoire évènementielle, something like the "tradition" that is often invoked
as a foil to "change." It was, of course, this conception of byt that made the
Bolshevik revolutionaries so fearful of it.

But everyday life changes. If, as Iurii Lotman suggests, rules laid down
from above are constantly negotiated and transformed in local application,[15] then major changes in the state's rules must surely produce corresponding changes in everyday practices. One has only to think of the
impact of government-mandated rationing in the Soviet Union in the early

1930s or Britain during the Second World War to see how this happens. Stephen Lovell's history of the dacha in Russia is a fine (but rare) example of a study of an everyday institution changing over time.[16]

One subset of everyday studies focuses on adaptation of everyday patterns in the wake of a major event—war, collectivization, national disasters like the Japanese tsunami of 2011. My *Stalin's Peasants* and *Everyday Stalinism* both fall into this category, the precipitating event being collectivization in the first case and Stalin's "great break" and the end of NEP in the second.[17] Anthropologists have had a field day with the last of Russia's great twentieth-century crises, the collapse of the Soviet Union, which was not only an "unmaking" of the Soviet everyday but the beginning of the creation of a new one.[18] The Second World War and its aftermath have been the subject of a few "everyday" studies, although, thanks perhaps to Elena Zubkova's influential work, the dominant emphasis has been on change in the realm of social psychology rather than everyday practices.[19] The everyday aspect of the Great Purges, another watershed event, has its historians,[20] but none of them have so far addressed the question of how the practices of everyday urban life, especially elite life, changed in response to them. (To be sure, this would have its peculiar difficulties because the war came so soon after the Purges: everyday life changes, but not necessarily at the same speed as histoire évènementielle.)

The Soviet communal apartment has been one of the central objects of attention in everyday studies.[21] In this volume, Steven Harris discusses the impact of Khrushchev's new housing policy, which resulted in the move of millions of urban families out of communal and into separate apartments, and Ilya Utekhin investigates how life in the remaining communal apartments changed as a result of the collapse of communism in 1991. One could imagine a similarly rich series of studies of child-bearing and marital strategies related first to the 1936 ban on abortion and second to its repeal in the mid-1950s.[22] Brian Lapierre has explored the impact on family life of the expansion of the definition of the crime of hooliganism to cover actions committed behind the closed doors of the (now separate) apartment as well as on the street.[23] The classic work on the "double bind" of work and family is Natalia Baranskaia's *A Week Like Any Other*, which formally belongs to the genre of fiction, though it was widely read as a social-issue text and is surely based on personal experience.[24]

Things, so prominent in the first generation of everyday life works by pioneering authors like Marjorie Quennell, have been relatively neglected in Russian twentieth-century everyday studies,[25] perhaps because scholars have been mainly struck by their absence and scarcity. We have Lewis Siegelbaum's history of cars, some recent work on the impact of television on people's lives, and scattered information from oral histories on various kinds of consumer goods available in the 1930s,[26] but the washing-machine and the refrigerator, which came into mass use in the Khrushchev period, not to mention the long-delayed arrival of the plastic bag, still await their historian. In a Western context, writing on the history of things often focuses on continuity, as objects pass down through family generations.[27] Even post-Soviet Russia seems to have produced few such studies, however, and in the Soviet period such continuity was probably exceptional, even after new inheritance laws in the 1940s made the transmission of personal property through generations easier.[28] Few objects passed down through many generations, elite apartments were furnished out of state warehouses, and the prevailing ethos of the prewar period discouraged expression of attachment to things.[29]

On the other hand, the story of *discontinuities* of ownership in twentieth-century Russia offers rich possibilities: objects confiscated or seized during the revolution or during dekulakization (the drive against "kulaks," alleged exploiters of other peasants, at the beginning of the 1930s) and their subsequent fate; elite dachas repossessed by the state during the Great Purges; objects, including apartments, lost during the war; and postwar attempts at recovery. Susan Reid tells us that when people moved out of communal apartments into separate ones, they often discarded their old furniture (inappropriate, too big and heavy) and bought new. Impressionistically, the collapse of communism seems to have provoked a new round of discarding and the buying of Western items in Russia, especially state-of-the-art modern bathrooms.[30] One can't help wondering what happened to the old stuff. There are histories of secondhand stores (*komissionnye*) and pawnshops (*lombardy*) still to be written.

Of course, state-of-the-art bathrooms featuring marble and gold-plated faucets were not in everybody's reach in the 1990s. This brings us to the important question raised by Mary Cavender: Whose everyday are we interested in? American social history in general, and everyday history in particular, has tended to have an implicit agenda of focusing on ordinary people, as distinct from elites. While the social historians of the 1970s were interested in class, that focus has become much less popular in recent years. The experience of particular groups and classes (other than the always popular women) has been largely ignored in favor of a more expansively conceived "Soviet citizen," whose attitudes and worldview have been investigated by Stephen Kotkin, Jochen Hellbeck, and others.[31] This has its benefits, but we should be careful about its homogenizing implications. Even the 1936 Soviet Constitution recognized the existence of two nonantagonistic classes (working class and collectivized peasantry) plus a white-collar "stratum" (*prosloika*) in Soviet society, implying that at the very least we would expect to find separate byts for workers, *kolkhozniks*, and white-collar employees. In fact, scholars have agreed on the existence of a hierarchy of groups with different duties and entitlements, comparable (I have suggested) to the old imperial estates (*sosloviia*).[32] "Youth," though not a social category but an age cohort, was often distinguished in Soviet social analyses (including those of NKVD *svodki*) and has also been a popular topic for historians in the West.[33] It seems self-evident that the generalizations about everyday life that fit the case of middle-aged working parents are not going to apply perfectly to their teenage or twenty-something children.

I would go further than Cavender and suggest that the everyday approach can profitably be applied not only to elites but even to high politics. That is what I am trying to do in my current book on the political and personal dynamics of the Politburo over thirty years, which is conceived as an everyday-life approach to Stalin's inner circle—the rules of the political game, dealing with the boss, competing and coexisting with others in the circle, survival strategies, privileges, obligations and expectations, patterns of sociability and friendship, working hours, and so on.[34] The premise is that byt at the very top (eight to twelve people at any given time) had its own rules and conventions different not just from those of ordinary people but also from those of middle-level Communist functionaries and professional elites.[35] Stalin might be the maker of those rules, but he too had to take account of them, unless and until he decided to change them. His associates, "working toward Stalin" although they undoubtedly were, had additional personal and institutional agendas of their own that, like the rules, evolved over time. High politics is not only a sequence of events but a milieu and a set of habits that affect the way events play out.

In the Politburo, as in the communal apartment, everyday interactions had their dialectics: mutual dependence, on the one hand, and individual interests and preferences, on the other. When dealing with the longue durée, it is important to be alert for such dialectical oppositions. Take the well-known phenomenon of Soviet obedience and conformity, generally seen as a product of (justified) fear of the consequences of disobedience. It is perfectly true that Soviet citizens tended to behave in this way—except on the occasions when they didn't, as, for example, when ordinary citizens got drunk and made obscene gestures to portraits of the leaders.[36] Stalin's inner circle, similarly, generally did their best to fulfill and anticipate Stalin's desires. But sometimes they didn't, as, for example, when Molotov and Mikoyan fell into disgrace with Stalin toward the end of Stalin's life and were meant to be banned from evening movies at the Kremlin but for a time, with the connivance of their Politburo colleagues, showed up anyway.[37] At the level of ordinary people's everyday, the post-Soviet rhetorical emphasis on self-sufficiency that Shevchenko notes might well be seen to exist in dialectical relationship to the attitudes of dependency (*izhdivencheskie nastroeniia*) so often deplored by state authorities in the Soviet period.[38]

If the burden of the argument in this section has been to encourage attention to the way everyday patterns change over time, this is not to deny that certain patterns persist, among them, citizens' hope or expectation that the state will provide. It was my own experience of the peculiarities of Soviet everyday life in the late 1960s that sent me back to the 1930s to find its roots. The postwar "sovietization" of Eastern Europe included not only an export of institutions but also, involuntarily, an export of the behaviors that certain institutions appear to generate, such as *blat* (the informal exchange of favors) and other second economy activities, or bureaucratic *perestrakhovka* ("overinsurance" to minimize risk). Even China under Mao displayed some everyday behaviors that Soviet historians find familiar, unwilling though Sinologists may be to accept any link.[39]

TRANSNATIONAL PERSPECTIVES

Transnational perspectives, such as those discussed by Choi Chatterjee and Elizabeth McGuire in this volume, are something of a novelty in everyday studies. But if we stop to think about the development of anthropology, it's clear that a certain kind of transnational perspective—that of the anthropologist, coming from one culture and observing another—has always been built into scholarly studies of the everyday. Indeed, participant observation by an outsider was traditionally the basic method of anthropological fieldwork. In the Soviet Union, where for many decades anthropological work by foreigners was difficult if not impossible, all resident foreigners became amateur observers of the Soviet everyday, even as they participated in their own distinctive everyday, shaped by the special rules that the state imposed for the marked category of foreigners.

With respect to Russia, travelers' accounts have long been a staple of the popular literature on the country, going back to the seventeenth century; and scholars have made extensive use of these sources. The tradition continued through the twentieth century. In the 1930s foreigners with progressive views flocked to the Soviet Union to observe "the socialist experiment" firsthand, and many—like Sidney and Beatrice Webb, Lion Feuchtwanger, and André Gide—wrote books about it. In the late Soviet period, it was all but obligatory for Moscow-based foreign correspondents to write a book about their experiences, usually focused on their contacts with dissidents. These two examples remind us that foreigners come with their own interpretive baggage as observers of everyday life, whether it is the belief that a new socialist world was in the making in the 1930s or, fifty years later, an equally idealistic commitment to the emergence of "civil society." Few supporters of the "building socialism" story were left by the time of the Soviet Union's collapse, and it may well be that in another thirty years the 1990s story about the building of democracy will seem equally implausible. But that doesn't negate the value of these accounts for future scholars trying to reconstruct patterns of everyday life.

The transnational/foreign visitors' perspective has its own advantages as well as pitfalls. Whatever the outsiders' expectations and biases, they are usually open to being surprised. They have the potential to defamiliarize the Russian everyday simply because what they see and experience is, to them, unfamiliar. They register anomalies—on the one hand, things that don't fit the picture of the way locals talk about their lives; on the other, things that don't jibe with whatever standard story (socialism in the making, revolution betrayed, totalitarianism, etc.) they heard in their home countries before they went there. Those anomalies linger in memory and sometimes result in new interpretations, as I think was the case with the "revisionist" challenge to the premises of traditional Sovietology, particularly the totalitarian model, back in the 1970s. My generation of American and European exchange students of the 1960s—the first beneficiaries of organized country-to-country scholarly exchanges with the Soviet Union—was astonished to discover the importance of those "interstices" of Soviet life noticed by Fred Starr (another member of the cohort): those everyday practices like close, mutually supportive friendship groups and use of networks of connections and personal ties that flourished in the space between the formal structures we had read about. We were struck by the coexistence in Soviet discourse of two starkly contrasting versions of the Soviet world: how it was supposed to be (*v printsipe*), and how it actually was (*v praktike*).[40] This wasn't what the totalitarian model or modernization theory had led us to expect; and much of what happened in Soviet studies for the next couple of decades involved the working out of anomalies observed firsthand.

In our scholarly writing, we often draw on our own firsthand observations without actually referencing ourselves as source. I will break this habit to comment on Susan Reid's question about whether the Soviet apartment was a site for presentation of self in the sense posited by Erving Goffman with implicit reference to twentieth-century Western settings. While one senses that Reid remains unsure about the answer to the larger question about the apartment, her answer on the narrower question of display cabinets is a qualified "yes." This interests me because, as a foreign exchange student in Moscow in the 1960s, I was strongly impressed by the contrary, namely, the near absence of Goffmanesque presentation of self in the Soviet apartment (with the possible exception of the display cabinets). It seemed to me that the comparative uniformity of Soviet furnishing, the lack of choices, *removed* interior design from the sphere in which the self and its individual, discerning taste must be presented, and thus, from my perspective, simplified life. I had the same reaction to the offering of food and drink to guests, whether formally invited or just happening to be there. From my youth in Australia, I remembered much agonizing about menus, appropriate wines, and Elizabeth David recipes if guests were coming to dinner. But in the Soviet Union, it seemed, you bought whatever you could find in the store (say, *polufabrikaty* rissoles), and threw in vodka if you were a drinker or wanted to make it an occasion. For most people, it seemed, food was not a sphere in which one had to show taste and individuality, any more than apartment furnishings were. It was not that Soviet people lacked their own conventions and pressures about presentation of self, but rather that the sites of such presentation were different and, perhaps, fewer. As a Soviet citizen, you presented yourself to the world, sometimes in a quite performative sense, and you also made some consumer choices and wished you could make more; but the two activities were not as tightly linked as in the world I had come from.

Foreign observers are not the only source of transnational perspectives. The everyday interactions between people of different ethnicities within the Soviet Union offer a very fruitful field for research that is only beginning to be explored.[41] The possibilities for research on the impact of the breakup of the Soviet Union on these relations are equally rich, especially in connection with complex personal and familial links that were changed or severed as a result, as Benjamin Sutcliffe's essay on Ulitskaia's novel reminds us. Marriage is a great creator of interethnic links, hence of transnational perspectives. In the immediate postwar period, there was an attempt to forbid all marriages to foreigners, and the Soviet state continued to make difficulties about marriages of Americans and Europeans to Soviet citizens for several decades. By the late Soviet period, however, marriages to foreigners, especially from the Third World, seem to have been on the increase, forging lasting connections and creating transnational households.[42] McGuire's work has made us aware of the networks of Soviet-educated persons in China, which presumably have their counterparts—often Lumumba University alumni—in India, Africa, and the Middle East.[43]

The Soviet Union was (by most people's definition) an empire, and empires create complex webs of transnational connections, many of which survive in memory even after the empire's demise. Just as everyday echoes of the lost Austro-Hungarian Empire continued to resonate throughout the interwar period, so the echoes of the Soviet Empire remain with us in the twenty-first century. This is partly a matter of the export of metropolitan culture: everyday cultural practices (how to eat, drink, dress, receive guests, and bring up your children) traveled outward into the empire along with Pushkin and the Red Army choir, making *kul'turnost'* an imperial value.[44] But there is also reverse transmission (periphery to metropolis) to be considered, as Erik Scott's insights on Georgian cuisine remind us.[45] The transmission patterns between the Soviet Union and Eastern Europe in the postwar period are particularly interesting because—untypically for empires—each party believed itself to be the culturally superior one.[46]

In the old days of the French and British empires, travelers in Africa or Asia could always tell, by a multitude of everyday indicators, whether they were in a French or British imperial possession or sphere of influence. Even after decolonization, many signs of the former power were still there. It was the same with the Soviet imperial presence, not just in the Soviet republics but also in Soviet-bloc countries in Eastern Europe. Throughout the Soviet bloc, people had to know at least some Russian (however much they resented it); and the similarity of institutions produced similarities in everyday habits (which is not to deny the persistence of striking differences, for example, in the Polish attachment to the church). Soviet-style kul'turnost' was not without influence in Eastern Europe, although it was also mocked, but even more noticeable were the second economy behaviors related to state control of distribution and chronic shortages, which appear to have been similar not only in the Soviet Union and Eastern Europe but also in China.

CONCLUSION

The days when the Soviet cultural empire stretched into Asia and halfway across Europe are gone, and so—at least in its pure form—are the patterns and possibilities of everyday life that came with membership in that sphere. What remains is the memory, but that too is a powerful form of virtual presence. Memory may be nostalgic, an attempt to recover a lost world, as in *Good Bye Lenin!* and *Staraia kvartira*. It may be negative, focusing on recollections of frustration about shortages and invasion of privacy and contempt for the meagerness and constrictedness of Soviet life. Or it may be both at once, as in Svetlana Boym's *Common Places*. But anthropologists looking at societies and cultures anywhere in the former Soviet bloc would be at a loss to understand their present without reference to the past that they have escaped (or, from another perspective, lost). It is not surprising that the current cohort of anthropologists working on the region is more historically conscious than their predecessors, or, for that matter, that historians have become more anthropological. Everyday habits generally change incrementally. Sudden changes are rare, occurring mainly in the aftermath of defeat in war or, as in the truly exceptional case of the Soviet Union and Eastern European "people's democracies," catastrophic regime collapse. What follows such events is not only an abrupt reconfiguration of political, ideological, and economic structures but a traumatic reorganization of byt to which nobody can be indifferent. Historians have often privileged other aspects of life, but it is the everyday we all live in. Elusive though it may be, we cannot afford to leave it outside our field of vision.

NOTES

1. Serguei Oushakine in this volume, summarizing the message of Vitalii Manskii's 1999 documentary *Chastnye khroniki. Monolog* (Private chronicles: Monologue).

2. The notion of "interstices" is borrowed from S. Frederick Starr, "Leningrad, 1966–67: Irrelevant Insights in an Era of Relevance," in *Adventures in Russian Historical Research: Reminiscences of American Scholars from the Cold War to the Present*, ed. Samuel H. Baron and Cathy A. Frierson (Armonk, N.Y.: M. E. Sharpe, 2003).

3. See Regina Garnier, *Subjectivities: A History of Self-Representation in Britain, 1832–1920* (New York: Oxford University Press, 1991).

4. For me, nothing equals Andrei Platonov's *Vprok* (a work greatly disliked by Stalin, and for good reason) at conveying the specific mix of utopianism and impracticality characteristic of the first phase of the Soviet collectivization drive, but I found it impossible to capture this in a quotation when I was writing *Stalin's Peasants*.

5. Vera S. Dunham, *In Stalin's Time* (Durham, N.C.: Duke University Press, 1990). Although Dunham characterized this fiction as "middlebrow," she was actually using the whole range of contemporary-themed prose published in Soviet journals and in book form in the 1940s and 1950s as her source base.

6. Frances Spufford, *Red Plenty* (London: Faber and Faber, 2010).

7. Alexei Yurchak, *Everything Was Forever, Until It Was No More: The Last Soviet Generation* (Princeton, N.J.: Princeton University Press, 2006); Sergei I. Zhuk, *Rock and Roll in the Rocket City: The West, Identity and Ideology in Soviet Dnepropetrovsk, 1960–1985* (Washington,

D.C.: Woodrow Wilson Center Press; Baltimore, Md.: Johns Hopkins University Press, 2010).

8. Nataliia Lebina, *Entsiklopediia banal'nostei: Sovetskaia povsednevnost', kontury, simvoly, znaki* (St. Petersburg: Dmitrii Bulanin, 2006).

9. Petr Vail' and Aleksandr Genis, *60-e: Mir sovetskogo cheloveka* (Ann Arbor, Mich.: Ardis, 1988).

10. Svetlana Boym, *Common Places: Mythologies of Everyday Life in Russia* (Cambridge, Mass.: Harvard University Press, 1994); Rachel Polonsky, *Molotov's Magic Lantern: A Journey in Russian History* (London: Faber and Faber, 2010).

11. Elif Batuman, *The Possessed: Adventures with Russian Books and the People Who Read Them* (New York: Farrar, Straus and Giroux, 2010).

12. In addition to *Common Places*, Svetlana Boym has also written a comparative study of nostalgia, less directly drawing on personal experience: *The Future of Nostalgia* (New York: Basic Books, 2001).

13. Daphne Berdahl, "'(N)Ostalgie' for the Present: Memory, Longing, and East German Things," *Ethnos* 64, no. 2 (1999).

14. I have drawn on the Wikipedia entry for Marjorie Quennell, http://en.wikipedia .org/wiki/Marjorie_Quennell, accessed July 9, 2012.

15. See Ransel's chapter in this volume, "The Scholarship of Everyday Life."

16. Stephen Lovell, *Summerfolk: A History of the Dacha, 1710–2000* (Ithaca, N.Y.: Cornell University Press, 2003).

17. Sheila Fitzpatrick, *Stalin's Peasants: Resistance and Survival in the Russian Village after Collectivization* (New York: Oxford University Press, 1996); Fitzpatrick, *Everyday Stalinism: Ordinary Life in Extraordinary Times* (Oxford: Berg, 2002).

18. See Caroline Humphrey, *The Unmaking of Soviet Life: Everyday Economies after Socialism* (Ithaca, N.Y.: Cornell University Press, 2002); Olga Shevchenko, *Crisis and the Everyday in Post-Socialist Moscow* (Bloomington: Indiana University Press, 2009).

19. See Catherine Merridale, *Ivan's War: Life and Death in the Red Army, 1939–1945* (New York: Metropolitan Books, 2006) on the everyday life of soldiers during the Second World War. The social-psychological approach was first put forward in E. Iu. Zubkova, *Obshchestvo i reform, 1945–1964* (Moscow: Rossiia molodaia, 1993).

20. Fitzpatrick, *Everyday Stalinism*, chap. 8; Robert W. Thurston, *Life and Terror in Stalin's Russia, 1934–1941* (New Haven, Conn.: Yale University Press, 1996); Orlando Figes, *The Whisperers: Private Life in Stalin's Russia* (New York: Metropolitan Books, 2007).

21. Ilia Utekhin, *Ocherki kommunal'nogo byta* (Moscow: OGI, 2001); Paula Messana, *Kommunalka: Une histoire de l'Union sovietique a travers les appartements communautaires* (1995); Julia Obertreis, *Tränen des Sozialismus: Wohnen in Leningrad zwischen Alltag und Utopie 1917–1937* (Cologne: Böhlau, 2004); Steven E. Harris, "Moving to the Separate Apartment: Building, Distributing, Furnishing and Living in Urban Housing in Soviet Russia, 1950s–1960s" (PhD diss., University of Chicago, 2003).

22. David L. Ransel, *Village Mothers: Three Generations of Change in Russia and Tataria* (Bloomington: Indiana University Press, 2000); Mie Nakachi, "Replacing the Dead: the Politics of Reproduction in the Postwar Soviet Union, 1944–1955" (PhD diss., University of Chicago, 2008).

23. Brian Lapierre, *Hooligans in Khrushchev's Russia: Defining, Policing and Producing Deviance during the Thaw* (Madison: University of Wisconsin Press, 2012).

24. Natal'ia Baranskaia, "Nedelia kak nedelia, povest'," *Novyi mir*, no. 11 (1969): 23–55.

25. I offer an overview in Sheila Fitzpatrick, "Things under Socialism: The Soviet Experience," in *The Oxford Handbook of the History of Consumption,* ed. Frank Trentmann (Oxford: Oxford University Press, 2012).

26. On cars, see Lewis H. Siegelbaum, *Cars for Comrades: The Life of the Soviet Automobile* (Ithaca, N.Y.: Cornell University Press, 2008); on television, see Kristin Roth-Ey, *Moscow Prime-Time* (Ithaca, N.Y.: Cornell University Press, 2011); and for oral histories, see M. Vitukhnovskaia, ed., *Na korme vremeni: Interv'iu s leningradtsami 1930'kh godov* (SPB, 2000).

27. Penelope Lively, *A House Unlocked* (London: Viking, 2001); Edmund de Waal, *The Hare with Amber Eyes: A Hidden Inheritance* (New York: Farrar, Straus and Giroux, 2010).

28. Charles Hachten, "Separate yet Governed: The Representation of Soviet Property Relations in Civil Law and Public Discourse," in *Borders of Socialism: Private Spheres of Soviet Russia,* ed. Lewis H. Siegelbaum (New York: Palgrave Macmillan, 2006), 70–73.

29. Sheila Fitzpatrick, "Life and Times," in *In the Shadow of Revolution: Life Stories of Russian Women from 1917 to the Second World War,* ed. Sheila Fitzpatrick and Yuri Slezkine (Princeton, N.J.: Princeton University Press, 2000).

30. See Krisztina Fehervary, "American Kitchens, Luxury Bathrooms, and the Search for a 'Normal' Life in Postsocialist Hungary," *Ethnos* 67, no. 3 (2002).

31. Stephen Kotkin, *Magnetic Mountain: Stalinism as a Civilization* (Berkeley: University of California Press, 1995); Jochen Hellbeck, *Revolution on My Mind: Writing a Diary under Stalin* (Cambridge, Mass.: Harvard University Press, 2006).

32. See Sheila Fitzpatrick, "Ascribing Class: The Construction of Social Identity in Soviet Russia," *Journal of Modern History* 65, no. 4 (1993); and the reworked, slightly expanded version in Fitzpatrick, *Tear Off the Masks: Identity and Imposture in Twentieth-Century Russia* (Princeton, NJ: Princeton University Press, 2005).

33. See, for example, Juliane Fürst, *Stalin's Last Generation: Soviet Post-war Youth and the Emergence of Mature Socialism* (Oxford: Oxford University Press, 2010); Anne E. Gorsuch, *Youth in Revolutionary Russia: Enthusiasts, Bohemians, and Delinquents* (Bloomington: Indiana University Press, 2000); B. A. Grushin, *Ispoved' pokoleniia* (Moscow: Molodaia gvardiia, 1962); Corinna Kuhr-Korolev, Stefan Plaggenborg, and Monica Wellmann, eds., *Sowjetjugend 1917–1941: Generation zwischen Revolution und Resignation* (Essen: Klartext, 2001).

34. Sheila Fitzpatrick, "Politics as Practice: Thoughts on a New Soviet Political History," *Kritika: Explorations in Russian and Soviet History* 5, no. 1 (Winter 2004): 27–54. "Politburo" here is shorthand for the inner circle of Soviet leaders under Stalin, with which it roughly but not exactly coincided at any given moment; the time span is from the late 1920s to the ousting of the "antiparty group" in 1957. The book, under contract with Princeton University Press, has the working title *Playing on Stalin's Team: The Years of Living Dangerously in Soviet Politics.*

35. As analyzed in Mervyn Matthews, *Privilege in the Soviet Union: Elite Life-Styles under Communism* (London: George Allen & Unwin, 1978); or my own *Everyday Stalinism,* chap. 4.

36. For examples from the Khrushchev and Brezhnev periods, see Vladimir A. Kozlov, Sheila Fitzpatrick, and Sergei V. Mironenko, eds., *Sedition: Everyday Resistance under Khrushchev and Brezhnev* (New Haven, Conn.: Yale University Press, 2011).

37. Strobe Talbott, ed., *Khrushchev Remembers* (Boston: Little, Brown, 1970), 309–10.

38. See Fitzpatrick, *Stalin's Peasants,* chap. 5.

39. For a comparative look at such behaviors, see Alena Ledeneva, "Blat and Guanxi: A Comparative Analysis of Informal Practices in Russia and China," *Comparative Studies in*

Society and History 50, no. 1 (2008); and S. A. Smith, "Talking Toads and Chinless Ghosts: The Politics of 'Superstitious' Rumors in the People's Republic of China, 1961–1965," *American Historical Review*, April 2006, 405–27.

40. For a range of American students' reactions, see Baron and Frierson, *Adventures in Russian Historical Research*; Loren R. Graham, *Moscow Stories* (Bloomington: Indiana University Press, 2006). Michael Frayn's novella *The Russian Interpreter* (London: Viking Press, 1966), by an alumnus of the British student exchange, is perhaps the most eloquent (and very funny) evocation of 1960s Moscow for a foreigner. See also Sheila Fitzpatrick, *A Spy in the Archives* (Melbourne: Melbourne University Press; London: I. B. Tauris, 2013) on the experience of being a foreign student in Moscow in the 1960s.

41. See, for example, Michaela Pohl, "The Virgin Lands between Memory and Forgetting: People and Transformation in the Soviet Union, 1954–60" (PhD diss., Indiana University, Bloomington, 1999); Erik R. Scott, "'Familiar Strangers': The Georgian Diaspora in the Soviet Union" (PhD diss., University of California at Berkeley, 2011); Michael Westren, "Nations in Exile: The Punished People in Soviet Kazakhstan, 1941–1961" (PhD diss., University of Chicago, 2012); as well as Benjamin Sutcliffe's chapter in this volume.

42. See Ellen Barry, "Russians and Syrians, Allied by History and Related by Marriage," *New York Times*, July 1, 2012. Also note Owen Matthews, *Stalin's Children: Three Generations of Love and War* (London: Bloomsbury, 2008), on the long-prevented marriage of two very different people, a Welsh academic and a Russian *intelligentka*, in the context of the 1960s and from the perspective of their son.

43. Elizabeth McGuire, "The Sino-Soviet Romance: How Chinese Communists Fell in Love with Russia, Russians, and the Russian Revolution" (PhD diss., University of California at Berkeley, 2010); Julie Hessler, "Death of an African Student in Moscow: Race, Politics and the Cold War," *Cahiers du monde russe* 47, no. 1 (2006).

44. Kiril Tomoff, "A Pivotal Turn: Prague Spring 1948 and the Construction of a Cultural Sphere," *Slavonica* 10, no. 2 (2004); and his manuscript in progress, "Soviet Imperial Circuits: Music and Transnational Cultural Connection in the Soviet Cultural Empire, 1945–1958."

45. Erik R. Scott, "Edible Ethnicity: How Georgian Cuisine Conquered the Soviet Table," *Kritika: Explorations in Russian and Eurasian History* 13, no. 4 (2012): 831–58.

46. For pioneering work on material culture taking Eastern Europe *and* the Soviet Union as its field, see Susan E. Reid and David Crowley, eds., *Style and Socialism: Modernity and Material Culture in Post-war Eastern Europe* (Oxford: Berg, 2000); David Crowley and Susan Reid, eds., *Socialist Spaces: Sites of Everyday Life in the Eastern Bloc* (Oxford: Berg, 2002). On cultural interrelations between the Soviet Union and Poland, see Patryk Babiracki, "Staging the Empire: Soviet-Polish Initiatives in Propaganda, Science, and the Arts, 1945–1953" (PhD diss., Johns Hopkins University, 2008); between the Soviet Union and Czechoslovakia, Rachel Leah Applebaum, "Friendship of the Peoples: Soviet-Czechoslovak Cultural and Interpersonal Contacts, 1945–1969" (PhD diss., University of Chicago, 2012).

BIBLIOGRAPHY

Andrusz, Gregory. *Housing and Urban Development in the USSR.* Albany: State University of New York Press, 1984.

Ashwin, Sarah. *Gender, State, and Society in Soviet and Post-Soviet Russia.* London: Routledge, 2000.

Attwood, Lynne. *Creating the New Soviet Woman: Women's Magazines as Engineers of Female Identity, 1922–1953.* New York: St. Martin's Press, 1999.

———. "Housing in the Khrushchev Era." In *Women in the Khrushchev Era,* edited by Melanie Ilic, Susan E. Reid, and Lynne Attwood, 180–81. Basingstoke: Palgrave Press, 2004.

———. *The New Soviet Man and Woman: Sex Role Socialization in the USSR.* Bloomington: Indiana University Press, 1990.

Balina, Marina, and Evgeny Dobrenko, eds. *Petrified Utopia: Happiness Soviet Style.* London: Anthem Press, 2009.

Balzer, Marjorie. *The Tenacity of Ethnicity: A Siberian Saga in Global Perspective.* Princeton, N.J.: Princeton University Press, 1999.

Baranskaia, Natal'ia. *Den' pominoveniia: Roman, povest'.* Moscow: Sovetskii pisatel', 1989.

Barker, Adele, ed. *Consuming Russia: Popular Culture, Sex, and Society since Gorbachev.* Durham, N.C.: Duke University Press, 1999.

Barker, Adele, and Jehanne Gheith, eds. *A History of Women's Writing in Russia.* Cambridge: Cambridge University Press, 2002.

Barthes, Roland. *Writing Degree Zero.* Translated by Annette Lavers and Colin Smith. New York: Hill and Wang, 1968.

Beumers, Birgit, ed. *The Cinema of Russia and the Former Soviet Union.* London: Wallflower Press, 2007.

Bolton, Jonathan H. "Writing in a Polluted Semiosphere: Everyday Life in Lotman, Foucault, and de Certeau." In *Lotman and Cultural Studies: Encounters and Extensions,* edited by Andreas Schönle, 320–44. Madison: University of Wisconsin Press, 2006.

Bourdieu, Pierre. *Outline of a Theory of Practice.* Translated by Richard Nice. Cambridge: Cambridge University Press, 1977.

———. *Practical Reason: On the Theory of Action.* Translated by Randal Johnson et al. Stanford, Calif.: Stanford University Press, 1998.

Boym, Svetlana. *Common Places: Mythologies of Every Day Life in Russia.* Cambridge, Mass.: Harvard University Press, 1994.

Brumfield, William, and Blair Ruble, eds. *Russian Housing in the Modern Age: Design and Social History.* New York: Woodrow Wilson Center Press and Cambridge University Press, 1993.

Buchli, Victor. *An Archeology of Socialism.* Oxford: Berg, 1999.

———. "Khrushchev, Modernism, and the Fight against *Petit-bourgeois* Consciousness in the Soviet Home." *Journal of Design History* 10, no. 2 (1997): 161–76.

Buckley, Mary, ed. *Perestroika and Soviet Women.* Cambridge: Cambridge University Press, 1992.

———. "Soviet Interpretations of the Woman Question." In *Soviet Sisterhood: British Feminists on Women in the USSR,* edited by Barbara Holland. Bloomington: Indiana University Press, 1985.

Burawoy, Michael, and Katherine Verdery, eds. *Uncertain Transition: Ethnographies of Change in the Postsocialist World.* Lanham, Md.: Rowman and Littlefield, 1999.

Burbank, Jane, and David L. Ransel, eds. *Imperial Russia: New Histories for the Empire.* Bloomington: Indiana University Press, 1998.

Cavender, Mary. *Nests of the Gentry: Family, Estate and Local Loyalties in Provincial Russia.* Newark: University of Delaware Press, 2007.

Certeau, Michel de. *The Practice of Everyday Life.* Translated by Steven Rendall. Berkeley: University of California Press, 1984.

Chatterjee, Choi, and Karen Petrone. "Models of Self and Subjectivity: The Soviet Case in Historical Perspective." *Slavic Review,* no. 4 (Winter 2008): 967–86.

Clark, Katerina. *The Soviet Novel: History as Ritual.* 3rd ed. Bloomington: Indiana University Press, 2000.

Cohen, Stephen. *Rethinking the Soviet Experience: Politics and History since 1917.* New York: Oxford University Press, 1985.

Cohn, Edward D. "Sex and the Married Communist: Family Troubles, Marital Infidelity, and Party Discipline in the Postwar USSR, 1945–1964." *Russian Review* 68 (July 2009).

Crowley, David, and Susan E. Reid, eds. *Socialist Spaces: Sites of Everyday Life in the Eastern Bloc.* Oxford: Oxford University Press, 2002.

De George, Richard T. *Soviet Ethics and Morality.* Ann Arbor: University of Michigan Press, 1969.

Di Maio, Alfred John, Jr. *Soviet Urban Housing.* New York: Praeger, 1974.

Dobson, Miriam. *Khrushchev's Cold Summer: Gulag Returnees, Crime, and the Fate of Reform after Stalin.* Ithaca, N.Y.: Cornell University Press, 2009.

Dunham, Vera. *In Stalin's Time.* Durham, N.C.: Duke University Press, 1990.

Eliot, T. S. *The Complete Poems and Plays 1909–1950.* New York: Harcourt Brace Jovanovich, 1971.

Evtuhov, Catherine. *Portrait of a Russian Province: Economy, Society, and Civilization in Nineteenth-Century Nizhnii Novgorod.* Pittsburgh: University of Pittsburgh Press, 2011.

Field, Deborah A. "Irreconcilable Differences: Divorce and Conceptions of Private Life in the Khrushchev Era." *Russian Review* 57 (October 1998): 599–613.

———. *Private Life and Communist Morality in Khrushchev's Russia.* New York: Peter Lang, 2007.

Field, Mark G., and Judyth L. Twigg, eds. *Russia's Torn Safety Nets: Health and Social Welfare during the Transition*. New York: St. Martin's Press, 2000.

Fitzpatrick, Sheila, ed. *Cultural Revolution in Russia, 1928–1931*. Bloomington: Indiana University Press, 1978.

———. *Everyday Stalinism: Ordinary Life in Extraordinary Times*. Oxford: Berg, 2002.

———. *Stalin's Peasants: Resistance and Survival in the Russian Village after Collectivization*. Oxford: Oxford University Press, 1994.

———. *Tear Off the Masks: Identity and Imposture in Twentieth-Century Russia*. Princeton, N.J.: Princeton University Press, 2005.

Fitzpatrick, Sheila, and Yuri Slezkine, eds. *In the Shadow of Revolution: Life Stories of Russian Women from 1917 to the Second World War*. Princeton, N.J.: Princeton University Press, 2000.

Friedgut, Theodore. *Political Participation in the USSR*. Princeton, N.J.: Princeton University Press, 1979.

Geyer, Michael, and Sheila Fitzpatrick, eds. *Beyond Totalitarianism: Stalinism and Nazism Compared*. Cambridge: Cambridge University Press, 2009.

Ghodsee, Kristin. *Lost in Transition: Ethnographies of Everyday Life after Communism*. Durham, N.C.: Duke University Press, 2011.

Goffman, Erving. *The Presentation of Self in Everyday Life*. Edinburgh: Edinburgh University, 1956.

Goldman, Wendy. *Women, the State and Revolution: Soviet Family Policy and Social Life, 1917–1936*. Cambridge: Cambridge University Press, 1993.

Goscilo, Helena. *Dehexing Sex: Russian Womanhood during and after Glasnost*. Ann Arbor: University of Michigan Press, 1996.

———, ed. *Fruits of Her Plume: Essays on Contemporary Russian Woman's Culture*. Armonk, N.Y.: M. E. Sharpe, 1993.

Goscilo, Helena, and Yana Hashamova, eds. *Cinepaternity: Fathers and Sons in Soviet and Post-Soviet Film*. Bloomington: Indiana University Press, 2010.

Goscilo, Helena, and Andrea Lanoux, eds. *Gender and National Identity in Twentieth-Century Russian Culture*. DeKalb: Northern Illinois University Press, 2006.

Grant, Bruce. *In the Soviet House of Culture: A Century of Perestroikas*. Princeton, N.J.: Princeton University Press, 1995.

Gronow, Jukka. *Caviar with Champagne: Common Luxury and the Ideals of Good Life in Stalinist Russia*. New York: Berg, 2003.

Halfin, Igal. *From Darkness to Light: Class Consciousness and Salvation in Revolutionary Russia*. Pittsburgh: University of Pittsburgh Press, 2000.

———. *Terror in My Soul: Communist Autobiographies on Trial*. Cambridge, Mass.: Harvard University Press, 2003.

Harris, Steven E. *Communism on Tomorrow Street: Mass Housing and Everyday Life after Stalin*. Washington, D.C.: Woodrow Wilson Center Press; Baltimore, Md.: Johns Hopkins University Press, 2013.

———. "'I Know All the Secrets of My Neighbors': The Quest for Privacy in the Era of the Separate Apartment." In *Borders of Socialism: Private Spheres of Soviet Russia*, edited by Lewis Siegelbaum. New York: Palgrave Macmillan, 2006.

———. "Moving to the Separate Apartment: Building, Distributing, Furnishing, and Living Urban Housing in Soviet Russia, 1950s–1960s." PhD dissertation, University of Chicago, 2003.

Haxthausen, Baron August von. *The Russian Empire: Its People, Institutions, and Resources.* Translated by Robert Faire. London: Frank Cass & Co., 1968.

Heldt, Barbara. *Terrible Perfection: Women and Russian Literature.* Bloomington: Indiana University Press, 1987.

Hellbeck, Jochen. *Revolution on My Mind: Writing a Diary under Stalin.* Cambridge, Mass.: Harvard University Press, 2006.

Hirsch, Francine. *Empire of Nations: Ethnographic Knowledge and the Making of the Soviet Union.* Ithaca, N.Y.: Cornell University Press, 2005.

Hoch, Stephen. *Serfdom and Social Control in Russia.* Chicago: University of Chicago Press, 1986.

Höjdestrand, Tova. *Needed by Nobody: Homelessness and Humanness in Post-Socialist Russia.* Ithaca, N.Y.: Cornell University Press, 2009.

Holland, Barbara, ed. *Soviet Sisterhood: British Feminists on Women in the USSR.* Bloomington: Indiana University Press, 1985.

Humphrey, Caroline. *Karl Marx Collective: Economy, Society and Religion in a Siberian Collective Farm.* Cambridge: Cambridge University Press, 1983.

———. *The Unmaking of Soviet Life: Everyday Economies after Socialism.* Ithaca, N.Y.: Cornell University Press, 2002.

Hutchings, Stephen. *Russian Modernism: The Transfiguration of the Everyday.* Cambridge: Cambridge University Press, 1997.

Ilič, Melanie, Susan E. Reid, and Lynne Attwood, eds. *Women in the Khrushchev Era.* Basingstoke: Palgrave Press, 2004.

Jones, Jeffrey W. *Everyday Life and the "Reconstruction" of Soviet Russia during and after the Great Patriotic War, 1943–1948.* Bloomington: Slavica Publishers, 2006.

Jones, Polly, ed. *The Dilemmas of De-Stalinization: Negotiating Cultural and Social Change in the Khrushchev Era.* London: Routledge, 2006.

Juviler, Peter. "Communist Morality and Soviet Youth." *Problems of Communism* 10, no. 3 (1961): 16–24.

———. "Marriage and Divorce." *Survey* 48 (1963): 104–17.

Kamenskii, Aleksandr. *Povsednevnost' russkikh gorodskikh obyvatelei. Istoricheskie anekdoty iz provintsial'noi zhizni XVIII veka.* Moscow: Izd. RGGU, 2006.

Kelly, Catriona. *Children's World: Growing Up in Russia, 1890–1991.* New Haven, Conn.: Yale University Press, 2007.

———. *A History of Russian Women's Writing, 1820–1992.* Oxford: Clarendon Press, 1994.

———. "Ordinary Life in Extraordinary Times: Chronicles of the Quotidian in Russia and the Soviet Union." *Kritika: Explorations in Russian and Eurasian History* 3, no. 4 (Fall 2002): 631–51.

———. *Refining Russia: Advice Literature, Polite Culture, and Gender from Catherine to Yeltsin.* Oxford: Oxford University Press, 2001.

Kharkhordin, Oleg. *The Collective and the Individual in Russia: A Study of Practices.* Berkeley: University of California Press, 1999.

Kiaer, Christina, and Eric Naiman, eds. *Everyday Life in Early Soviet Russia: Taking the Revolution Inside.* Bloomington: Indiana University Press, 2005.

Kon, Igor, and James Riordan, eds. *Sex and Russian Society.* Bloomington: Indiana University Press, 1993.

Kotkin, Stephen. *Magnetic Mountain: Stalinism as a Civilization.* Berkeley: University of California Press, 1995.

Lapidus, Gail Warshofsky. *Women in Soviet Society: Equality, Development, and Social Change.* Berkeley: University of California Press, 1978.

———. *Women, Work, and Family in the Soviet Union.* Armonk, N.Y.: M. E. Sharpe, 1982.

Lebina, Nataliia. *Entsiklopediia banal'nostei: Sovetskaia povsednevnost', kontury, simvoly, znaki.* St. Petersburg: Dmitrii Bulanin, 2006.

Lefebvre, Henri. *The Critique of Everyday Life, Vol. 1, Introduction.* 1947; London: Verso, 1991.

———. *The Critique of Everyday Life, Vol. 2, Foundations for a Sociology of the Everyday.* 1961; London: Verso, 2002.

———. *Everyday Life in the Modern World.* Translated by Sacha Rabinowitz. New York: Harper & Row, 1971.

Levi, Giovanni. "On Microhistory." In *New Perspectives on Historical Writing,* edited by Peter Burke, 93–113. University Park: Pennsylvania State University Press, 1991.

Liljeström, Marianne, Eila Mäntysaari, and Arja Rosenholm, eds. *Gender Restructuring in Russian Studies.* Slavica Tamperensia 2. Tampere, Finland: University of Tampere, 1993.

Lotman, Yuri M. *Universe of the Mind: A Semiotic Theory of Culture.* Translated by Ann Shukman. Bloomington: Indiana University Press, 1990.

Lovell, Stephen. *Summerfolk: A History of the Dacha, 1710–2000.* Ithaca, N.Y.: Cornell University Press, 2003.

Lüdtke, Alf, ed. *The History of Everyday Life: Reconstructing Historical Experiences and the Ways of Life.* Princeton, N.J.: Princeton University Press, 1995.

Manning, Roberta. *The Crisis of the Old Order in Russia: Gentry and Government.* Princeton, N.J.: Princeton University Press, 1982.

Marker, Gary, Joan Neuberger, Marshall Poe, and Susan Rupp, eds. *Everyday Life in Russian History: Quotidian Studies in Honor of Daniel Kaiser.* Bloomington: Slavica Publishers, 2010.

Marrese, Michelle. *A Woman's Kingdom: Noblewomen and the Control of Property in Russia, 1700–1861.* Ithaca, N.Y.: Cornell University Press, 2002.

Marsh, Rosalind, ed. *Women in Russia and Ukraine.* Cambridge: Cambridge University Press, 1996.

Matthews, Mervyn. *Privilege in the Soviet Union: Elite Life-Styles under Communism.* London: George Allen & Unwin, 1978.

Matza, Tomas. "Moscow's Echo: Technologies of the Self, Publics, and Politics on the Russian Talk Show." *Cultural Anthropology* 24, no. 3 (2009): 489–522.

Mayakovsky, Vladimir. *Bedbug and Selected Poetry.* Bloomington: Indiana University Press, 1975.

Merridale, Catherine. *Night of Stone: Death and Memory in Twentieth-Century Russia.* New York: Viking Press, 2000.

Nakhimovsky, Alexander, and Alice Nakhimovsky, eds. *The Semiotics of Russian Cultural History: Essays by Iurii M. Lotman, Lidiia Ia. Ginsburg, Boris A. Uspenskii.* Ithaca, N.Y.: Cornell University Press, 1985.

Narskii, Igor. *Fotokartochka na pamiat': Semeinye istorii, fotograficheskie poslaniia i sovetskoe detsvo (avtobio-istorio-graficheskii roman).* Cheliabinsk: Entsiklopediia, 2008.

Newlin, Thomas. *The Voice in the Garden: Andrei Bolotov and the Anxieties of Russian Pastoral, 1738–1833.* Evanston, Ill.: Northwestern University Press, 2001.

Oushakine, Serguei. *The Patriotism of Despair: Nation, War and Loss in Russia.* Ithaca, N.Y.: Cornell University Press, 2009.

Patico, Jennifer. *Consumption and Social Change in a Post-Soviet Middle Class.* Washington, D.C.: Woodrow Wilson Center Press and Stanford University Press, 2008.

Paxson, Margaret. *Solovyovo: The Story of Memory in a Russian Village.* Washington, D.C.: Woodrow Wilson Center Press; Bloomington: Indiana University Press, 2005.

Phillips, Sarah D. *Disability and Mobile Citizenship in Postsocialist Ukraine.* Bloomington: Indiana University Press, 2011.

Polonsky, Rachel. *Molotov's Magic Lantern: A Journey in Russian History.* London: Faber and Faber, 2010.

Pomerantsev, Vladimir. "Ob iskrennosti v literature." *Novyi mir,* no. 12 (1953): 218–45.

Pushkareva, Natalia. "'Istoriia povsednevnosti' i 'istoriia chastnoi zhizni': Soderzhanie i sootnoshenie poniatii." *Sotsial'naia istoriia* 8 (2004): 93–112.

———. "Istoriia povsednevnosti: Predmet i metody." *Sotsial'naia istoriia* 11 (2011): 9–54.

Raleigh, Donald J. *Russia's Sputnik Generation: Soviet Baby Boomers Talk about Their Lives.* Bloomington: Indiana University Press, 2006.

———. *Soviet Baby Boomers: An Oral History of Russia's Cold War Generation.* Oxford: Oxford University Press, 2011.

Randolph, John. *The House in the Garden: The Bakunin Family and the Romance of Russian Idealism.* Ithaca, N.Y.: Cornell University Press, 2007.

Ransel, David. *Mothers of Misery: Child Abandonment in Russia.* Princeton, N.J.: Princeton University Press, 1988.

———. *A Russian Merchant's Tale: The Life and Adventures of Ivan Alekseevich Tolchënov, Based on His Diary.* Bloomington: Indiana University Press, 2008.

———. "A Single Research Community: Not Yet." *Slavic Review* 60, no. 3 (Autumn 2001): 550–57.

———. *Village Life in Late Tsarist Russia.* Bloomington: Indiana University Press, 1993.

———. *Village Mothers: Three Generations of Change in Russia and Tataria.* Bloomington: Indiana University Press, 2000.

Reid, Susan. "The Khrushchev Kitchen: Domesticating the Scientific-Technological Revolution." *Journal of Contemporary History* 40, no. 2 (2005): 289–316.

Reid, Susan E., and David Crowley, eds. *Style and Socialism: Modernity and Material Culture in Post-War Eastern Europe.* Oxford: Berg, 2002.

Ries, Nancy. *Russian Talk: Culture and Conversation during Perestroika.* Ithaca, N.Y.: Cornell University Press, 1997.

Rivkin-Fish, Michele. "Tracing Landscapes of the Past in Class Subjectivity: Practices of Memory and Distinction in Marketizing Russia." *American Ethnologist* 36, no. 1 (2006): 79–95.

———. *Women's Health in Post-Soviet Russia: The Politics of Intervention.* Bloomington: Indiana University Press, 2005.

Roberts, John. *Philosophizing the Everyday: Revolutionary Praxis and the Fate of Cultural Theory.* London: Pluto Press, 2006.

Rogers, Douglas. *The Old Faith and the Russian Land: A Historical Ethnography of Ethics in the Urals.* Ithaca, N.Y.: Cornell University Press, 2009.

Rogger, Hans. *National Consciousness in Eighteenth-Century Russia.* Cambridge, Mass.: Harvard University Press, 1960.

Roosevelt, Priscilla. *Life on the Russian Country Estate.* New Haven, Conn.: Yale University Press, 1995.

Sahadeo, Jeff, and Russell Zanca. *Everyday Life in Central Asia: Past and Present.* Bloomington: Indiana University Press, 2007.

Sanborn, Joshua. *Drafting the Russian Nation: Military Conscription, Total War, and Mass Politics, 1905–1925.* DeKalb: Northern Illinois University Press, 2003.

Schönle, Andreas. *The Ruler in the Garden: Politics and Landscape Design in Imperial Russia.* Bern: Peter Lang, 2007.

Scott, James. *Domination and the Arts of Resistance: Hidden Transcripts.* New Haven, Conn.: Yale University Press, 1990.

———. *Weapons of the Weak: Everyday Forms of Peasant Resistance.* New Haven, Conn.: Yale University Press, 1985.

Sergeev, Andreev. *Stamp Album: A Collection of People, Things, Relationships and Words.* Moscow: Glas Publishers, 2002.

Shevchenko, Olga. *Crisis and the Everyday in Postsocialist Moscow.* Bloomington: Indiana University Press, 2009.

Shlapentokh, Vladimir. *Love, Marriage, and Friendship in the Soviet Union: Ideals and Practices.* New York: Praeger, 1984.

———. *Public and Private Life of the Soviet People: Changing Values in Post-Stalin Russia.* New York: Oxford University Press, 1989.

Siegelbaum, Lewis H., ed. *Borders of Socialism: Private Spheres of Soviet Russia.* New York: Palgrave, 2006.

———. *Cars for Comrades: The Life of the Soviet Automobile.* Ithaca, N.Y.: Cornell University Press, 2008.

Smith, Douglas. *The Pearl: A True Tale of Forbidden Love in Catherine the Great's Russia.* New Haven, Conn.: Yale University Press, 2008.

Smith, Mark. *Property of Communists: The Urban Housing Program from Stalin to Khrushchev.* DeKalb: Northern Illinois University Press, 2010.

Sosnovy, Timothy. "Housing in the Workers' State." *Problems of Communism* 5, no. 6 (November–December 1956): 31–39.

Stites, Richard. *Revolutionary Dreams: Utopian Vision and Experimental Life in the Russian Revolution.* New York: Oxford University Press, 1989.

Sutcliffe, Benjamin. *The Prose of Life: Russian Women Writers from Khrushchev to Putin.* Madison: University of Wisconsin Press, 2009.

Thompson, Terry L., and Richard Sheldon, eds. *Soviet Society and Culture: Essays in Honor of Vera S. Dunham.* Boulder: Westview Press, 1988.

Utekhin, Il'ia. *Ocherki kommunal'nogo byta.* Moscow: OGI, 2001.

Utekhin, Ilya, Alice Nakhimovsky, Slava Paperno, and Nancy Ries. *Communal Living in Russia: A Virtual Museum of Soviet Everyday Life.* http://kommunalka.colgate.edu/index.cfm.

Varese, Frederico. *The Russian Mafia: Private Protection in a New Market Economy.* Oxford: Oxford University Press, 2001.

Verdery, Katherine. *What Was Socialism, and What Comes Next?* Ithaca, N.Y.: Cornell University Press, 1996.

Yurchak, Alexei. *Everything Was Forever, Until It Was No More: The Last Soviet Generation.* Princeton, N.J.: Princeton University Press, 2006.

———. "Russian Neoliberal: The Entrepreneurial Ethic and the Spirit of 'True Careerism.'" *Russian Review* 62 (January 2003): 72–90.

Zorin, Andrei. "In Search of a New Identity: Visions of the Past and Present in Post-Communist Russia." In *Myth and Memory in the Construction of Community: Historical Patterns in Europe and Beyond,* edited by Bo Stråth. New York: Peter Lang, 2000.

Zubkova, Elena. *Russia after the War: Hopes, Illusions, and Disappointments, 1945–1957.* Armonk, N.Y.: M. E. Sharpe, 1998.

CONTRIBUTORS

Mary Cavender is author of *Nests of the Gentry: Family, Estate and Local Loyalties in Provincial Russia*. She is currently researching hunting in the imperial period, with a focus on etiquette, the experience of nature, and comparative studies of European elites. She teaches modern European and Russian history at The Ohio State University.

Choi Chatterjee is Professor of History at California State University, Los Angeles. She is the author of *Celebrating Women: Gender, Festival Culture and Bolshevik Ideology, 1910–1939* (2002), and coauthor of *The Twentieth Century: A Retrospective* (2002). Beth Holmgren and Choi recently published an edited volume that seeks to recast Russian-American relations in a post–Cold War framework entitled *Americans Experience Russia: Encountering the Enigma, 1917 to the Present* (2012). She is currently working on a history of American Communist women and their formative experiences in the Soviet Union.

Deborah A. Field is Associate Professor in the Department of History and Art History at Adrian College. She is author of *Private Life and Communist Morality in Khrushchev's Russia* (2007), as well as numerous articles. She is currently working on a post–Cold War textbook on Russian history in the twentieth century with Choi Chatterjee and Lisa Kirschenbaum (forthcoming, 2014).

Sheila Fitzpatrick is Honorary Professor at the University of Sydney and Professor Emerita at the University of Chicago. Her books include *Everyday Stalinism* (2000), *Tear Off the Masks* (2005), and *My Father's Daughter: Memoirs of an Australian Childhood* (2010). She is currently writing a memoir of Moscow in the 1960s (*A Spy in the Archives*) and a study of Stalin and his team. Her next research project is on displaced persons after the Second World War.

Steven E. Harris is Associate Professor in the Department of History and American Studies at the University of Mary Washington. He is a modern Russian historian with research interests in Soviet mass housing and urbanization, and transnational cultural contacts during the Cold War. His book *Communism on Tomorrow Street: Mass Housing and Everyday Life after Stalin* was published in the spring of 2013 by the Woodrow Wilson Center Press and the Johns Hopkins University Press.

Elizabeth McGuire is a postdoctoral fellow at the Harvard Academy for International and Area Studies. Her book manuscript is titled *The Sino-Soviet Romance: Chinese Communists in Love with the Russian Revolution.* Her second project is titled *Communist Neverland: The Russian International Children's Home and the Global Family It Created.*

Serguei Oushakine, Associate Professor of Slavic Languages and Anthropology at Princeton, has conducted fieldwork in Siberia, as well as in Belarus and Kyrgyzstan. His research is concerned with transitional processes and situations: from the formation of newly independent national cultures after the collapse of the Soviet Union to posttraumatic identities and hybrid cultural forms. His first book, *The Patriotism of Despair: Loss, Nation, and War in Russia* (2009), focused on the communities of loss and exchanges of sacrifices in provincial post-Communist Russia. His current project explores Eurasian postcoloniality as a means of affective reformatting of the past and as a form of retroactive victimhood. Oushakine's Russian-language publications include edited volumes on trauma, family, gender, and masculinity. He serves as Director of the Program in Russian and Eurasian Studies at Princeton.

Karen Petrone is Professor of History and Chair of the History Department at the University of Kentucky and a specialist in Russian and Soviet cultural and gender history. She is author *of Life Has Become More Joyous, Comrades: Celebrations in the Time of Stalin* (2000) and *The Great War in Russian Memory* (2011), a *Choice* Outstanding Academic Title for 2012. She is editor (with Valerie Kivelson, Michael S. Flier, and Nancy Shields Kollmann) of *The New Muscovite Cultural History: A Collection in Honor of Daniel B. Rowland* (2009) and editor (with Jie-Hyun Lim) of *Gender Politics and Mass Dictatorship: Global Perspectives* (2011).

Peter C. Pozefsky is Professor of History at the College of Wooster in Ohio. He is author of *The Nihilist Imagination* (2003), an examination of the close relationship between Russian radicals and literature in the late nineteenth century. He is currently studying representations of Stalin and Stalinism in contemporary Russian cinema.

Natalia Pushkareva is Professor and Senior Research Fellow at the Institute of Ethnology and Anthropology at the Russian Academy of Sciences as well as the Head of the Women's and Gender Studies Department. Dr. Pushkareva has published widely: her publications include nine monographs and nineteen volumes of collected essays, among them *Women in Medieval Rus* (1989), *Women in Russia and in Europe at the Dawn of the Modern Age (1996)*, *Women in Russian History from the 10th to the 20th Century (1997)*, *"There are our sins . . .": Sexual Culture in Russia from the 10th to the 19th Century* (1999), and *Gender Theory and Historical Sciences* (2008). She is also editor of the yearbook *Sotsial'naia istoriia* (Social history) and serves as the president of the Russian Association for Research in Women's History.

David L. Ransel is Robert F. Byrnes Professor of History at Indiana University and the author of more than seventy articles and several books on the history of Russia, most recently, *A Russian Merchant's Tale: The Life and Adventures of Ivan Alekseevich Tolchënov, Based on His Diary* (Indiana University Press, 2009). He is currently at work on two projects. The first is an oral history study of civic identity and social attachments of the two most recent generations of Russian workers in the industrial suburbs of Moscow. The second examines the emergence of civil society activism in current conflicts over preservation of Russian national historical sites and protected ecological zones.

Susan E. Reid is Professor of Russian Visual Culture in the Department of Russian and Slavonic Studies, University of Sheffield. She has published widely on painting, visual and material culture, gender, and consumption in the Soviet Union, especially in the 1950s and 1960s. She is also editor (with David Crowley) of *Pleasures in Socialism: Leisure and Luxury in the Eastern Bloc* (2010). She is currently completing a book on everyday aesthetics, socialist modernity, and consumption in the Khrushchev-era standard apartment, provisionally entitled *Khrushchev Modern: Making Oneself at Home in the Soviet 1960s*.

Douglas Rogers is Associate Professor of Anthropology at Yale University. He is author of *The Old Faith and the Russian Land: A Historical Ethnography of Ethics in the Urals* (2009) and a number of articles on political, economic, and religious transformations after the end of the Soviet Union. He is completing a book-length study of the oil industry in the Perm Region entitled *Oil Culture: Producing the New Russia*.

Olga Shevchenko is Associate Professor of Sociology at Williams College, where she teaches courses on socialism and postsocialism, culture, consumption, images, and identity. She is the author of *Crisis and the Everyday in Postsocialist Moscow* (2009) and a range of articles and book chapters on contemporary Russian popular culture, everyday political discourse, memory, and nostalgia. Her ongoing projects are an edited volume on the intersections of memory and photography and a collaborative ethnographic study that looks at Soviet-era family photographs and generational memories of socialism in Russia.

Elizabeth Skomp is Associate Professor of Russian at Sewanee: The University of the South. She is the author (with Benjamin Sutcliffe) of *Liudmila Ulitskaia's Art of Tolerance* and has published several articles on women's prose and post-Soviet literature. She is presently completing a manuscript entitled *Reconceiving Motherhood: Representations of Maternity in Russian Literature and Culture since Brezhnev.*

Benjamin Sutcliffe is Associate Professor of Russian at Miami University. He is author of *The Prose of Life: Russian Women Writers from Khrushchev to Putin* (University of Wisconsin Press, 2009) and, with Elizabeth Skomp, the first monograph on contemporary Russian author Liudmila Ulitskaia. His articles have appeared in the *Russian Review,* the *Slavic and East European Journal,* and other venues.

Ilya Utekhin teaches anthropology at the European University at St. Petersburg as well as at the St. Petersburg State University. He also works in visual anthropology as a photographer and as a documentary filmmaker. He is the author of *Essays on Communal Living* (2001), a study on communal housing in post-Soviet Russia. He is the creator, along with Alice Nakhimovsky, Slava Paperno, and Nancy Ries, of *Communal Living in Russia: A Virtual Museum of Soviet Everyday Life* (http://kommunalka .colgate.edu/). His research interests include the anthropology of technology, cognitive science, human-computer interaction, interactive design, anthropological studies of disability, ethnomethodology, and conversation analysis.